MW00534610

FFICER WOUNDED I

HUGE HIGHWAY FUND DIVIDED

Little Rock Planter Is First to Abandon

OFFICERS **ID**

Figures in Georgia

Release Denied Floyd Hamilton

Judge Refuses Application For Freedom on Two Charges

DALLAS, May 17, (AP).—Judge Noland G. Williams decided after a habeas corpus hearing Wednesday that Smoot Schmid, sheriff, had a legal right to hold Floyd Hamilton, brother of Raymond Hamilton, on warrants from Houston county, where he has been charged with being an accessory to murder and aiding a prisoner to escape.

Floyd Hamilton sought his release through the proceedings on the ground that Schmid was illegally restraining him of his ... since an indictment ... him with robbery of ... rand Prairie State bank ... een dismissed.

Houston county warrants ... outgrowth of Floyd's participation in the prison ... at the Eastham prison ... nuary 16, in which Raymond four other convicts ... Major Crowson, a...

BANDITS MA ESCAPE IN C

H. D. Humphrey Shot Times Through Body Friday by Men Sou Fayetteville Robbery

MECHANIC IS INJ

Webber Wilson Cut In By Flying Glass as Collide Before Affray

Ed Crowder Slain In Fight at Prison

JUDGES TO GET

ED CROWDER

CONVICT FROM DALLAS STABS HIM TO DEATH

Houstonian Cut 15 Times With Home-Made Dirk in Dim Light of Farm Barracks.

Special to The Chronicle.
Eastham Prison Farm, Weldon ...

Barrow Gang Robbed Three Oil Stations Here, Knierim Bank

Directed Robbery of Stations ... Knierim

H. D. Darby and Sophia Stone Kidnaped and Taken to Magnolia, Ark.

5:30 P. M. H. D. Darby telephone the sheriff from Magnolia, Ark., statin that both he and Miss Stone were uni jured. Kidnappers had forced them of the car at that place.

Deputy Is Kill As Bandit Trail Into West Dall

Officers in Ambush for Odell Chandler, Who Escaped After Recent Grapevine Bank Job

Makes Good Boast

When Got Away Posing as Posseman, Bragged Would Kill if Caught

Death Is Imminen For John K. Stre Noted Texas T

MOTHER PLEADS FOR HAMILTON

Mrs. Steve Davis Visited Governor Allred Tuesday and Asked That He Spare the Life of Her Son.

New Barrow Hunt in Polk

Gunman Seen in City, Officers Told.

Polk county depu

You've read the story of Jesse James
of how he lived and died.
If you're still in need;
of something to read,
here's the story of Bonnie and Clyde.

BONNIE PARKER, 1934

ON THE TRAIL OF
BONNIE & CLYDE
THEN AND NOW

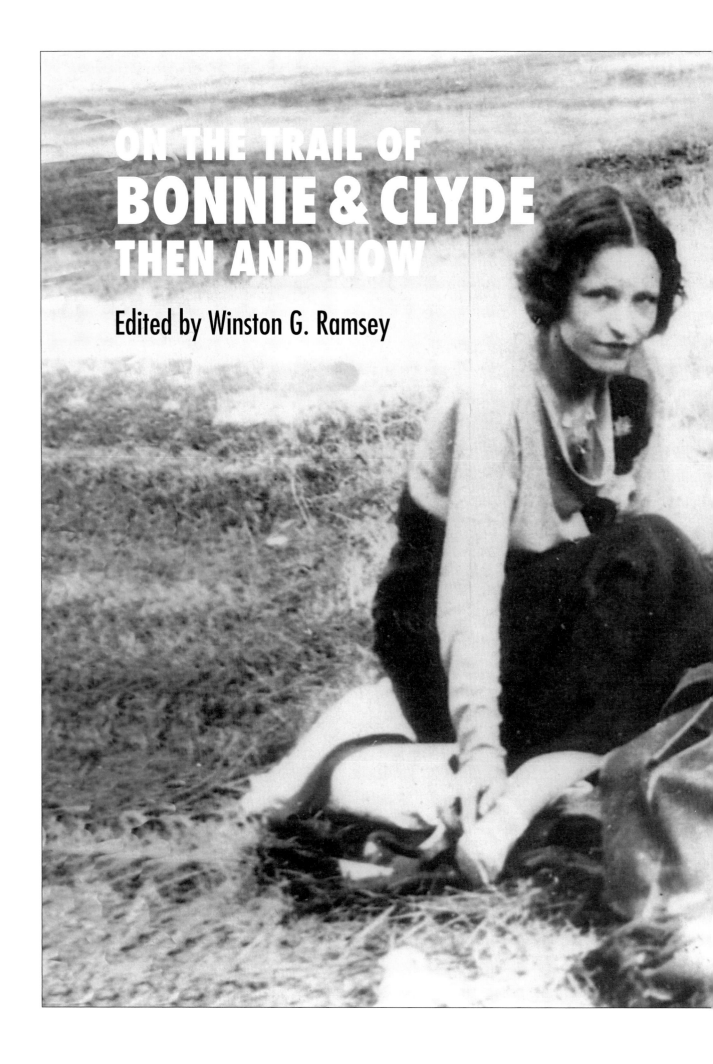

ON THE TRAIL OF
BONNIE & CLYDE
THEN AND NOW

Edited by Winston G. Ramsey

Credits

ISBN: 1 870067 51 7
© After the Battle 2003
Designed by Winston G. Ramsey,
Editor-in-Chief After the Battle.

PUBLISHERS
Battle of Britain International Ltd
Church House, Church Street,
London E15 3JA England

PRINTERS
Printed and bound in Spain by Bookprint
on behalf of Compass Press.

FRONT COVER
Bonnie Parker and Clyde Barrow,
April 1933. Reproduced from a painting by
AlekSandra d'Allure.

REAR COVER
Bonnie in her casket at the McKamy-
Campbell Funeral Home (Dr Allen B.
Campbell). Her grave is now in Crown Hill
Cemetery, Dallas.

FRONT AND REAR ENDPAPERS
Press reports of the period.

FRONTISPIECE
Browning Automatic Rifles, stolen from the
National Guard, were vital additions to
Clyde's armoury as they enabled him to
outshoot the opposition on several
occasions. In this picture he appears to be
loading a magazine — each took 20 rounds
of military .30-06 ammunition.

EXTRACTS
The source of all extracts is quoted where
known, and the Editor formally apologises
for any errors or omissions while gratefully
acknowledging permission received.

*Fugitives — The Story of Clyde Barrow and
Bonnie Parker* by Mrs Emma Parker and
Nell Barrow Cowan, first published in
1934 by the Ranger Press Inc, extracted by
kind permission of Joe Bauske.
The Roaring Twenties reproduced with
acknowledgement to Professor J. K.
Galbraith of Harvard University.
The Strange History of Bonnie and Clyde by
John Treherne, published in 1984 by
Jonathan Cape, used by permission of the
Random House Group Ltd.
Bonnie and Clyde — A 21st Century Update
by James R. Knight and Jonathan Davis,
published in 2003 by Eakin Press, Austin,
Texas.

PHOTOGRAPHS
For photo sources, see pages 296-297.

Acknowledgements

Although I have always had an interest in the life and times of Bonnie and Clyde, being based in the East End of London, some 5,000 miles from the scene of the action, has made on-the-spot research somewhat difficult. So this book could never have been produced without the help of friends and colleagues on the other side of the Atlantic. Foremost amongst many who gave me their time and drove many miles to photograph the scenes of crime are Marty Black and Jim Knight.

Marty's interest was first aroused by a road sign on the outskirts of Stuart, Iowa, advertising its connection with the outlaws. As he passed this way fairly regularly when visiting his in-laws, I persuaded Marty to stop on one trip to take photos, and this led to his excellent detective work on the nearby Dexfield Park gun-battle. Marty explored the location on four occasions to make sure he had covered all the ground, and he interviewed the surviving witnesses, being fortunate to speak with Bob Weesner before he died. Marty also covered Grapevine, Kansas City, Platte City, Wellington and Erick, and also accompanied me on my visit to Texas and Louisiana in May 2003.

Jim Knight, with his own book *Bonnie and Clyde A — 21st Century Update* already on the stocks, was most generous with his time and expertise, and he visited all the sites in his neck of the woods, notably Alma, Fayetteville and Fort Smith, Commerce, Joplin, Lucerne, Middletown, Oronogo, Poteau, Reeds Spring and Springfield. Jonathan Davis, his co-author, also spent a day guiding us around the relevant Dallas locations.

I am also indebted to so many others who assisted: Pat Delaney who flew to Okabena and Wharton for me; Mary Arthur and Dave Chael in Enid, Oklahoma; Timothy R. Brookes in East Liverpool, Ohio; Kenneth Crabtree in Miami, Oklahoma; Cleo Davis in Hillsboro, Texas; Robert Droz, Maps from History; Terry Eckert in Las Vegas; Gail Fuhrr in Marshall, Texas; Jane Garrison at the FBI; Jay Glass; Bob Goeken and Pat Holst in Everly, Iowa; Dave Hale, Washington, D.C.; Ronald Haraldson and Erik and Mariellen Mosbo in Rembrandt, Iowa; Carol, Helen and Lenard Hardy; Jed Howard and Valerie Cranston in Carlsbad, New Mexico; Jim Hounschell and Cheryl Cobb of the Missouri State Highway Patrol; Renee Hylton and Ralph Wilcox of the National Guard Bureau; Martin Jones, Lawrence, Kansas; Kevin Knoot, State Historical Society of Iowa; Cindy McMullen, Lufkin, Texas; Jeanne Christie Mithen in Topeka, Kansas; Bruce Moore, Huntsville, Texas; Roger Natte, Fort Dodge and Knieram in Iowa; Diane Pepper, Platte City, Missouri; Charles Powers, Grand Prairie, Texas; Jeane Pruett, Ranger, Texas; Karin Ramsay (no relation) who visited Celina, Denton, Paradise, Pilot Point and Ponder; Colin Rogers, historian of the Pre '50s Classic American Auto Club; Chuck Schauer and John Binder in Chicago; Tony Scott, Yorkville, Illinois; Earleene Spaulding, Baxter Springs, Kansas; Christina Stopka and Judy Shofner at the Texas Rangers Hall of Fame and Museum in Waco, Texas; Amie Treuer in Dallas Public Library; Gwen Walker, Stringtown, Oklahoma; and especially Rick Williams for allowing me to include his unpublished research on Middletown, Ohio.

Finally, I am very grateful to the Bonnie and Clyde historians who generously shared information and/or provided photographs: Frank Ballinger and his web site (http://texashideout. tripod.com); Joe Bauske of the Ranger Press Inc; Dr Allen Campbell; 'Boots' Hinton and Ken Holmes of Southwestern Historical Publications; Sandy Jones of the John Dillinger Historical Society; Bill Kingman; Professor E. R. Milner; John Neal Phillips and Phillip Steele.

WINSTON G. RAMSEY, SEPTEMBER 2003

Contents

Clyde Chestnut Barrow — born March 24, 1909, died May 23, 1934. Clyde, the fifth child of seven born to Henry and Cumie Barrow, came into the world near Teleco, Texas, and left it aged 25 near Gibsland, Louisiana, shot to death in a police ambush. Like many tenant farmers unable to make ends meet, Henry had moved his family to the shanty-town beside the railroad tracks in West Dallas where he scratched a living selling scrap metal or anything else that might make some money. Life was hard and jobs were scarce so when the horse that drew his cart was killed in a road accident, Henry decided to go into the garage business instead. He moved the small wood-frame building which was their home to Eagle Ford Road where the front part was converted into a service station which opened in 1932. In this picture, printed from negatives captured by police in Joplin, Missouri, in April 1933, Clyde sits on the bumper of a 1932 Ford convertible stolen from Robert F. Rosborough in Marshall, Texas, the previous month. He is armed with both a sawn-off shotgun and a Krag-Jorgensen, the Norwegian-designed .30-40 calibre rifle adopted by the US military in 1894.

Introduction

In the days when fuel was 12 cents a gallon, this was the Barrow's combined home and garage at 1620 Eagle Ford Road. Besides gas, they also sold groceries, sodas and snacks.

'Twelve murders in two years! That is the record of the vicious pack led by the slight, dapper Clyde Barrow and his cigar-smoking woman companion Bonnie Parker. In two years the acts of this pair and their various associates have surpassed by far the crimes of Oklahoma's notorious "Pretty Boy" Floyd.

'The criminal records of the Barrow brothers, Clyde Chestnut and Marvin Ivan, known as "Buck", started with petty thefts.

'Barrow never remained near the scene of one of his crimes. Driving at seventy or eighty miles an hour in stolen cars, always prepared to shoot with machine guns, pistols and shotguns, Clyde Barrow became one of the most dangerous criminals in the history of the South-West.

'Whole communities were terrorized by this murderer. State and county officers in Iowa, Missouri, Kansas, Arkansas, Oklahoma and Texas attempted to capture Clyde Barrow by shooting it out with him. Again and again the officers were met with deadly charges of buckshot from sawed-off shotguns or riddled with machine gun bullets from the weapons of the desperado and his woman companion who killed without mercy, frequently ambushing their attempted captors.

'So Clyde Barrow became the Middle West's Public Enemy No. 1. The United States Government, recognizing Barrow's menace, joined hands with the various States in what has been called America's mightiest manhunt.'

So wrote the Press on May 24, 1934 — the day after Bonnie Parker and Clyde Barrow had been shot to death by lawmen in Gibsland, Louisiana.

America in the 1920s and 1930s faced a crime wave of unprecedented proportions. The temperance movement against the evils of drink had led to attempts at prohibition in the 1850s but it was not until the First World War that it gained strength. While Britain just restricted licencing hours, other nations brought in outright bans: Canada in 1917, Norway in 1919 and the United States in 1920. The forbidding of the sale of alcoholic drink was manna from heaven for the underworld and organised crime lost no time in satisfying the demand. This in turn fuelled vicious

The old Star Service Station still stands although the road has since changed its name to Singleton and the numbering to 1221. Clyde's father sold the property in 1940 for around $800 to Mr and Mrs S. E. Willis. They said that 'the place was in awful shape — nothing but a two-room shack with an outhouse. We rebuilt it and raised all our children there.' The Willis's continued to operate the garage until 1959 when they sold to Mr. W. M. Thomas, who in turn, sold to the ADA Investment Corporation in 1973 for a reported sum of $44,000.

Jim Knight, author of *Bonnie and Clyde — A 21st Century Update*, comments that 'through their publicity they became known as bank robbers, but the fact is that bank robbery was actually a somewhat rare event in their career. For every bank robbery, there were scores of grocery store, service station, or small time payroll heists. In this they were distinctly different from most of the other big-time names — 'Pretty Boy' Floyd, Dillinger, the Barkers etc. Bonnie and Clyde had much more in common with the hundreds of petty thieves who roamed the country during the Great Depression than with the big city operators.' *Above:* A typical filling station in Texas in the 1930s and one more than likely robbed at one time or another by Bonnie and Clyde.

gang warfare, culminating in the notorious St Valentine's Day Massacre in Chicago in February 1929.

Later that year, in October, came the stock market crash in New York which brought on a worldwide economic crisis and a massive era of depression and unemployment. It was this event, rather than prohibition, that led to Clyde Barrow's gang — and other well-known individuals like 'Baby Face' Nelson, 'Pretty Boy' Floyd, John Dillinger and 'Ma' Barker — into robbery and murder on a grand scale.

The killing ground for Clyde Barrow and his attractive girlfriend Bonnie Parker was the central states of the Midwest from Texas in the south through Oklahoma, Arkansas, Missouri to Iowa in the north. In those days, communications between the hundreds of small communities was by overhead telephone and telegraph wires — easily cut to isolate whole towns after a particular robbery. Police two-way radios were a thing of the future and, although lawmen were now mounted in automobiles rather then on horseback, catching lawbreakers was still akin to the days of the old Wild West.

Firearms had won — or tamed — America so it was second nature for criminals to go about their business armed to the teeth. Yet to increase his firepower and out-gun the lawmen Clyde Barrow went one better . . . he robbed National Guard armouries of their military weaponry, his favourite tool of trade being the Browning Automatic Rifle developed as a light machine gun in 1918. Using military .30-06 calibre 150-grain full-jacketed ammunition with a velocity of nearly 3,000 feet per second, on full auto the 20-shot magazine could be emptied in 2½ seconds. Some 52,000 BARs had been produced by the end of the war so there were plenty for Clyde and his gang and any they lost were easily replaced by robbing another armoury.

He developed a cut-down version with the barrel reduced in length to that of the gas-operated recoil piston with a shortened stock. (W. D. Jones describes how Clyde then had three magazines welded together to create what he called his 'scatter-gun' but it is doubtful if the internal spring could be so adapted to feed 60-odd cartridges smoothly to the breach.)

The other asset Clyde used to good effect was his remarkable driving skills. Bearing in mind that in the 1930s only main roads would have a tarmac surface — blacktop as it is called in the US — he could still motor hundreds of miles on gravel-surfaced side roads at top speed at night without rest.

And in those days the police had no right of hot pursuit — once across the state line he was as free as if he were in another country. Transportation of stolen vehicles was a federal offence, and although the Bureau of Investigation (the US-wide enforcement agency which later became the FBI) issued wanted posters, and listed major criminals as Public Enemies, it was left to local police to apprehend most lawbreakers.

When the eight-cylinder Fords appeared in the spring of 1932, this gave Clyde another edge over the slower police vehicles and wherever possible thereafter he always stole a V-8. There is even a letter purported to have been sent by Clyde to Henry Ford in April 1934 — just a month before he died — extolling the merits of the new engine. If it *was* written by Clyde it is an ad man's dream: 'For sustained speed and freedom from trouble, the Ford has got every other car skinned . . . what a fine car you got in the V-8'.

Bonnie and Clyde historian Jim Knight explains that 'what set Bonnie and Clyde apart from the many, many, almost anonymous outlaws was the fact that they became famous, and they became famous partly because of the "Star Crossed Lovers" angle. It was certainly not unusual for an outlaw or gangster to carry along a "moll" but none of them ever attained the stature of Bonnie Parker with the Press.

'Other reasons why they became famous, even though most of their jobs were piddling affairs, include the fact that Clyde seemed to attract gun-fire. Whether he was just plain trigger-happy or simply unlucky, he was involved in a lot of killings — mainly of police officers — and that sort of thing always attracts a lot of news coverage.

'Finally, Bonnie and Clyde became famous in spite of their predominately small-time operations because nobody could catch them. Clyde's one overriding talent was his ability to escape, regardless of the odds. He and Bonnie simply survived long enough to become household names in the American Southwest of the early 1930s.'

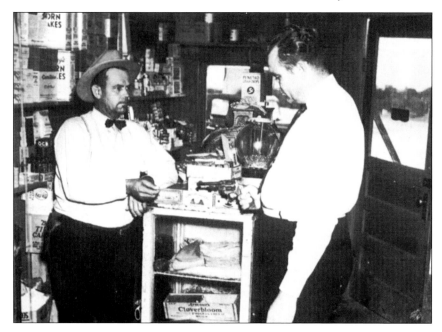

A typical Barrow gang hold-up of a small store re-enacted by police officers.

Another shot from the same captured film. Bonnie Parker was born a year after Clyde — on October 1, 1910 — in Rowena, Texas, some 250 miles south-west of Dallas. Bonnie's father Charles was a bricklayer but he died when she was four so his widow, Emma, took Bonnie, together with her brother and sister, to live with her mother who lived in Eagle Ford Road. This part of Dallas was known locally as 'Cement City' because of the nearby Portland Cement Works. This move was some eight years before the Barrows arrived on the scene. In September 1926 when she was not quite 16, Bonnie wed Roy Thornton but the union was not destined to last. Thornton would absent himself for weeks at a time so Bonnie supported herself working as a waitress at Hargreaves Cafe on Swiss Avenue. By January 1929 the marriage was over; soon afterwards she got a new job at Marco's near the court house on Dallas's Main Street but the cafe closed later that year when the stock market crashed. Just after the New Year, during a visit to see her elder brother, Hubert (nicknamed 'Buster'), Bonnie met the man who was to change her life and lead to her early death. Clyde was then on the run for the robbery at Denton and was arrested at Bonnie's mother's house in February.

William Daniel 'W. D.' Jones with Robert Rosborough's 1932 Ford Convertible. The Model T which had been Ford's mainstay for over 15 years was discontinued in May 1927 to be followed by the Model A although this was not available for another seven months. However by 1931 the popularity of the Model A was fading and Ford, knocked into second place in the sales league table by Chrysler, desperately needed something new to beat the competition. That 'something' was the V-8 engine — an eight-cylinder power plant which came to epitomise American vehicles — then as now. The Model 18 released on March 31, 1932 was an instant success, and over one million V-8s had been sold by the end of the year. *Autocar* road-tested the convertible cabriolet in August and reported that the 65 bhp engine gave 'a tremendous reserve of power . . . acceleration is devoid of hesitation, the car veritably shoots forward the instant the throttle is depressed. It is a car which gets along at a remarkably high speed without effort . . . even 65 or 70 can be maintained. It can be taken round curves fast . . . an exceptional car to handle.' No wonder Clyde latched onto the V-8-powered Fords in their various guises for his ideal getaway car.

Clyde Barrow was aided and abetted by a number of partners in crime — friends, family and associates who came and went during his five-year career of robbery and murder.

First there were his two brothers, Marvin, nicknamed 'Buck' and six years his senior, and his younger brother who appears to have simply been known by the initials 'L.C.'

Buck was born March 14, 1903, in Jones Prairie, Texas, and it is debatable as to who led who astray but Clyde and Buck clashed with the law just before Christmas 1926 when they were caught stealing turkeys from a neighbour. Clyde got off but Buck spent a week in jail. Then, in October 1929, during the robbery in Denton, Texas, Buck was apprehended and sentenced to a five-year term. He escaped from the Texas State Penitentiary at Huntsville in March 1930 but was persuaded by his new wife Blanche to return to finish his sentence. He was released on a conditional parole in March 1933. Four months later he was dead having suffered fatal wounds in gun-battles in Missouri and Iowa.

L. C., Clyde's younger brother by four years having been born on August 13, 1913, is believed to have accompanied Bonnie and Clyde on a number of occasions although his participation in their crimes has not been proven. After their deaths, he was arrested on a robbery charge in Dallas on October 27, 1934 for which he received a prison term of five years. He was released in 1938 but was returned to jail in 1942 for violating his parole. Aged 66, he died on September 3, 1979.

In 1999, Robert Rosborough described how his automobile came to be stolen from the side of his parents' house *(above)* at 200 Rosborough Street in Marshall, a town 140 miles east of Dallas. 'I was about to leave on a dinner date with Marie, my soon-to-be wife. I was shocked when I walked out and saw my 1932 Ford was gone. I had a bad habit of leaving the keys in the car but I wasn't even out of it 15 minutes before it was gone. I thought someone was playing a prank on me, but since I didn't have a car, I had to cancel my date. A few days later, Police Chief Clarence Ezell burst into my insurance office waving a telegraph at me. He joked, "We've got you now!" The telegraph was sent from Joplin. Bonnie and Clyde had shot three police officers and drove off in the Ford. The other officers wrote down the license plate and traced it back to me. They knew my car was stolen and they knew I wasn't involved with the Barrow Gang. I sold the car not knowing how famous Bonnie and Clyde really were. Had I known then what I know now, I would have sold it for much more. There's no telling what that car would have sold for!' (See also pages 97-99.)

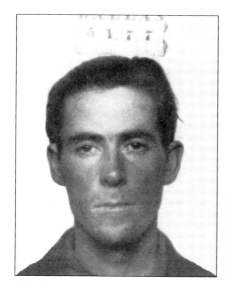

Left: **Marvin Ivan Barrow (1903-1933) married Blanche Caldwell (1911-1988)** *(right).* **A trained beautician, Blanche met Buck in late 1929 or early in 1930. Married in July 1931, they had but a** few months together before they were separated for over a year while Buck finished his prison sentence. Four months after he was released, he was dead.

The other family member who must be considered part of Clyde's gang was Blanche Caldwell, a farmer's daughter from Oklahoma. She married Buck on July 3, 1931 in the full knowledge that he was an escaped convict, having been on the run since he escaped from Huntsville in March the previous year. Blanche persuaded Buck to surrender himself which he did two days after Christmas in 1931.

Although not a gun-wielding accomplice, Blanche was nevertheless present during a number of robberies carried out by Buck during the time that Clyde was in prison. She lost the sight in one eye as a result of the shoot-out at Platte City in July 1933 and was captured six days later when Buck was fatally wounded at Platte City. Blanche was sentenced to ten years but served her time as a model prisoner so was released early in March 1939. She died in Dallas on December 24, 1988 aged 77.

William Daniel Jones (1916-1974). An early member of the gang, after his arrest on November 16, 1933 he gave an 18-page statement to the Assistant District Attorney for the State of Texas detailing his six-month stint with Bonnie and Clyde, claiming that he had known Clyde in all for about 11 years.

Non-family members of the gang came and went, joining Bonnie and Clyde at different times and places. The main dramatis personae were William Daniel Jones, usually nicknamed 'W. D.' or sometimes 'Dub' or 'Deacon'; Henry Methvin; the Hamilton brothers Floyd and Raymond; Joe Palmer; Ralph Fults and Ted Rogers.

The leading member of the gang was William Daniel Jones who spent six months on the run with Bonnie and Clyde. He joined them on Christmas Eve 1932 and was implicated in five of their murders. He escaped with Bonnie and Clyde from the Dexfield Park fire-fight in July 1933 but left the gang permanently the following month.

Two months later he was arrested by Dallas police, giving them a long statement concerning his period of service with the gang. He was sentenced 15 years for his participation in the killing of Sheriff Malcolm Davis in January 1933, and two years for harbouring Bonnie and Clyde at a subsequent trial in 1935.

W. D.'s role with the gang was epitomised as 'C. W. Moss' in the 1967 film *Bonnie and Clyde* although the movie character was really an amalgamation of Raymond Hamilton, Jones and Henry Methvin. Released from prison by 1950, following the death of his wife Jones became an addict, serving time in a rehabilitation centre. On August 20, 1974 he met a violent end when he was shot dead in Houston after an argument.

They say that there is honour amongst thieves but Henry Methvin has gone down in the history books as the betrayer of Bonnie and Clyde which directly led to their deaths at the hands of Texas and Louisiana lawmen in May 1934.

Having been sprung from Huntsville Prison on January 16, 1934, Methvin participated in several robberies with Clyde and the killing of the Highway Patrol Officers Wheeler and Murphy at Grapevine, Texas, on Easter Sunday. He was also involved in the murder of Constable Campbell at Commerce, Oklahoma, five days later.

After double-crossing Bonnie and Clyde in May 1934 by informing the authorities of their imminent arrival in Bienville parish in Louisiana, the local sheriff turned a blind eye to Methvin's past crimes as a reward for his assistance in setting up the ambush. However the Oklahoma police were not so favourably inclined towards him and used a clever ruse that a collector in that state wanted to purchase one of the guns he had used when with Bonnie and Clyde. This led Methvin to visit Shreveport, whereupon he was promptly arrested for the murder of Constable Campbell.

He was sentenced to death but, because of his co-operation in the apprehension of Bonnie and Clyde, on appeal this was commuted to life imprisonment. He was never indicted for the Grapevine murders and was paroled in March 1942. In April 1948, he was killed when he was hit by a train at Sulphur, Louisiana, in what may have been suicide.

Henry Methvin (1911-1948) — the gang's 'Judas Iscariot'. Methvin rode with Bonnie and Clyde from January to May 1934. Given a full pardon for his co-operation with the authorities in setting the fatal trap near his father's farm at Gibsland, Louisiana, although guilty of murder, he was even spared the electric chair.

Raymond Hamilton was Clyde's main partner-in-crime from early 1932. He was falsely identified as the killer of John Bucher in Hillsboro, Texas, in April 1932 and, after a series of robberies, was apprehended in December in Bay City, Michigan. Returned to Dallas to face a capital charge, Clyde broke him out of Eastham in January 1934 and he remained at large until captured at Howe, Texas, in April. He escaped from death row at Huntsville in July and was only recaptured in April 1935. He was executed the following month.

His brother Floyd's role with the gang was more of a quartermaster, providing logistical support. In 1935 he received a prison term of two years for harbouring Bonnie and Clyde. For this and other robberies he served more than 20 years behind bars — the last 18 on America's top security prison island, Alcatraz. He was released on parole in 1958 and died in July 1984.

Joe Palmer fired the fatal bullet which killed Major Crowson during the breakout from Eastham Prison Farm in January 1934. Although ill health caused the gang to later leave him behind in Joplin, Missouri, Palmer rejoined Bonnie and Clyde when Ray Hamilton left with Mary O'Dare but departed again after Grapevine. He was caught in June 1934, convicted of the killing of Major Crowson, and sentenced to death. He escaped from Huntsville with Hamilton but was recaptured in August and executed on May 10, 1935 a few minutes before Hamilton in the same electric chair.

Ralph Fults first met Clyde in 1930 when they were both serving time at Huntsville. After their release, Fults joined the duo for the robbery at Mabank, Texas, on April 18, 1932 when he and Bonnie were captured, spending the night together in the Kemp lock-up. Fults spent the next three years in jail, being released in January 1935. He soon teamed up with Raymond Hamilton for a series of robberies but both were

Partners in crime: the Hamilton brothers Raymond (1913-1935) *(left)* and Floyd (1908-1984). Of the two, Ray was undoubtedly the more notorious. He had first linked up with Clyde Barrow in March 1932 but Ray already had a criminal record for stealing cars. Then on April 30 came the robbery in Hillsboro (see page 53) which resulted in the death of John Bucher. Ray split with Clyde in September and carried out several bank robberies before he was caught at a roller rink in Michigan in December. On the 15th he was transferred to Dallas where his mug shot was taken the following day.

apprehended in April that year and Fults was returned to prison. He was released in January 1944 and died in 1993.

Ted Rogers was another small-time member of the gang. He was with Clyde on the raid on the gun shop in Celina, Texas, in April 1932, and that same month most probably fired the

Ray's elder brother, Floyd, was never a formal member of the Barrow gang. This mugshot was taken when he was first arrested in April 1934 for a robbery with Ray. When released, subsequent crimes led to a sentence of 20 years being imposed in 1938. Floyd made a name for himself in 1943 when he escaped from the workshop on Alcatraz with three other prisoners. One man was shot and killed; the other two captured at the water's edge while Floyd hid in a cave for two days. Finally, tired and cold, he returned to the prison to give himself up — the only man known to have escaped *into* Alcatraz!

fatal shot which killed John Bucher in the jewellery store in Hillsboro, Texas, although Raymond Hamilton was indicted for the murder. He was arrested on an unrelated charge the following month and met up with Ralph Fults in jail. Committed to Huntsville, two years later Rogers was stabbed to death by another prisoner.

Joe Palmer (1904-1935) received his come-uppance for the murder of Major Joseph Crowson, a guard at the Texas State Penitentiary at Huntsville, when he was executed at the same prison the following year.

Ralph Fults (1911-1993) pictured aged 19 in Huntsville Prison in Texas. He spent less than a month with the Barrows in the spring of 1932, his recollections being written up by John Neal Phillips in *Running with Bonnie and Clyde*.

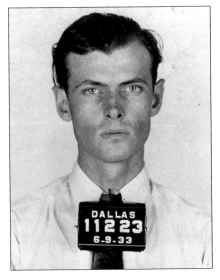

Ted Rogers appearance was very much like Raymond Hamilton, who had been mistaken for Rogers in the Hillsboro killing. Rogers later admitted to other prisoners at Huntsville that in fact he was the one that had killed John Bucher.

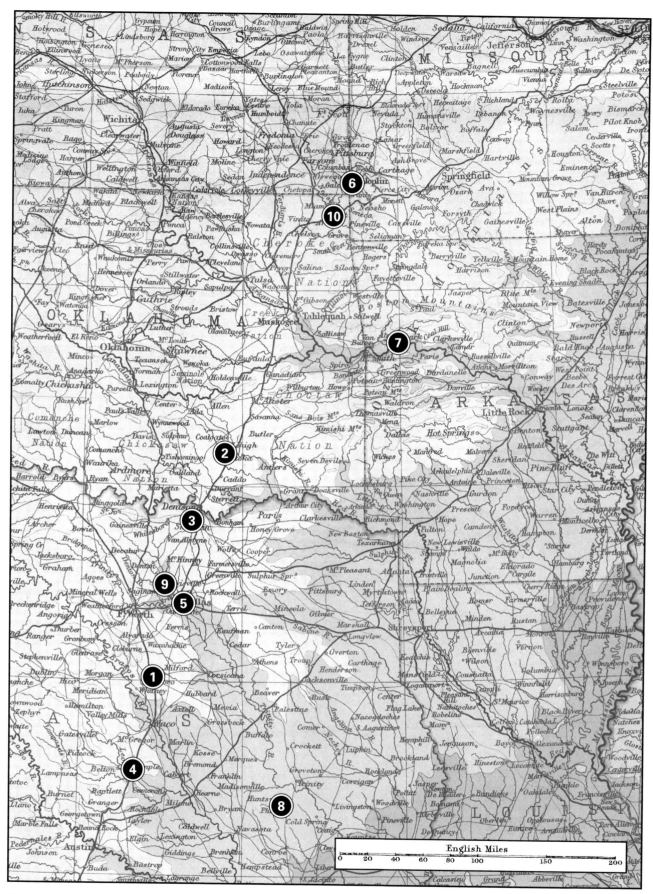

The Barrow gang ranged across 500,000 square miles of central America. Filling stations and stores were robbed; banks were held up; and lawmen were killed in a two-year crime spree which included at least 13 murders: [1] Hillsboro, Texas. [2] Stringtown, Oklahoma. [3] Sherman, Texas. [4] Temple, Texas. [5] Dallas, Texas. [6] Double killing at Joplin, Missouri. [7] Alma, Arkansas. [8] Huntsville, Texas. [9] Double killing at Grapevine, Texas. [10] Commerce, Oklahoma. Clyde Barrow is believed to have personally been responsible for seven of the murders, three are attributed to W. D. Jones, one was certainly carried out by Buck Barrow and one by Ted Rogers by his own admission. But first let us look at what was happening in the wider world . . . in 'dry' America!

November 1918 saw the end of the First World War which America had joined in April 1917. The United States' attitude to the war in Europe had gone through several phases: from traditional isolationism in 1914; the desire to maintain neutral status come what may; and a refusal to take extreme measures against Germany even after American lives were lost in U-Boat attacks. The presidential election in 1916 was fought against a background of efforts to keep America out of the war but when unrestricted U-Boat warfare began in February 1917 America broke off diplomatic relations with Germany, declaring war two months later.

By 1918 the United States had increased its army from 200,000 to 3½ million of which 2 million had been sent to the Western Front. Over 50,000 American servicemen lost their lives in France, the majority in the last six months before the Armistice. Demobilisation was rapid — perhaps too rapid — its speed sowing the seeds of the post-war depression which gripped the country in 1921. It was in that year that one of the last US soldiers left France. Here the body of the Unknown Soldier is brought ashore from the cruiser USS *Olympia* at the Washington Navy Yard for burial at Arlington National Cemetery.

The Roaring Twenties

The decade of the Twenties, or more precisely the eight years between the post-war depression of 1920-21 and the stock market crash in October of 1929, were prosperous ones in the United States. During that period the total output of the economy increased by more than 50 per cent. The preceding decades had brought the automobile; now came many more and also roads on which they could be driven with reasonable reliability and comfort. There was much building. The downtown sections of many of the mid-continent cities date from these years. It was then, more likely than not, that what is still the leading hotel, the tallest office building, and the biggest department store went up. Radio arrived, as of course did gin and jazz.

These years were also remarkable in another respect, for as time passed it became increasingly evident that the prosperity could not last. Contained within it were the seeds of its own destruction. The country was heading into the gravest kind of trouble but almost no steps were taken during these years to arrest the tendencies which were leading to disaster.

It was the stalemate of trench warfare which had cost so many lives that led directly to the creation of the weapon that has been described as 'the gun that made the Twenties roar' — the Thompson sub-machine gun. Colonel John Thompson believed that what the army needed was a powerful hand-held offensive weapon — a 'trench broom' he called it — which could be fired from the hip as the infantrymen went over the top protected by his own firepower to sweep down the enemy trenches.

Although Thompson initiated his idea in September 1917, giving the task of designing the weapon to Oscar V. Payne with Theodore H. Eickhoff as chief engineer, it was developed too late to be of use in the war. Nevertheless, as some $500,000 had been invested, Brigadier General Thompson (as he now was) put his mind to what other uses his 'trench broom' might have, and he saw it as an ideal police weapon to counter the increasing crime wave by motorised criminals. Contracts were placed by Thompson's company, the Auto-Ordnance Corporation, with Colt for manufacture of the gun — much to the annoyance of John Browning, the gifted inventor of the Browning Automatic Rifle — the preferred weapon of Clyde Barrow — as Colt was also contracted to make the BAR. Auto-Ordnance also promoted the Thompson gun for the protection of large estates and commercial operations for although existing legislation in some cities, including New York and Chicago, restricted the sale of concealable handguns to civilians, the 'Tommy Gun' as a military weapon was not so controlled!

At least four things were seriously wrong, and they worsened as the decade passed.

First, income in these prosperous years was being distributed with marked inequality. Although output per worker rose steadily during the period, wages were fairly stable, as also were prices. As a result, business profits increased rapidly and so did incomes of the wealthy and the well-to-do. This meant that the economy was heavily and increasingly dependent on the luxury consumption of the well-to-do and on their willingness to reinvest what they did not or could not spend on themselves. Anything that shocked the confidence of the rich either in their personal or in their business future would have a bad effect on total spending and hence on the behaviour of the economy.

The Thompson Submachine Gun
The Most Effective Portable Fire Arm In Existence

THE ideal weapon for the protection of large estates, ranches, plantations, etc. A combination machine gun and semi-automatic shoulder rifle in the form of a pistol. A compact, tremendously powerful, yet simply operated machine gun weighing only *seven* pounds and having only *thirty* parts. Full automatic, fired from the hip, 1,500 shots per minute. Semi-automatic, fitted with a stock and fired from the shoulder, 50 shots per minute. Magazines hold 50 and 100 cartridges.

THE Thompson Submachine Gun incorporates the simplicity and infallibility of a hand loaded weapon with the effectiveness of a machine gun. It is simple, safe, sturdy, and sure in action. In addition to its increasingly wide use for protection purposes by banks, industrial plants, railroads, mines, ranches, plantations, etc., it has been adopted by leading Police and Constabulary Forces throughout the world and is unsurpassed for military purposes.

Information and prices promptly supplied on request

AUTO-ORDNANCE CORPORATION
302 Broadway *Cable address: Autordco* New York City

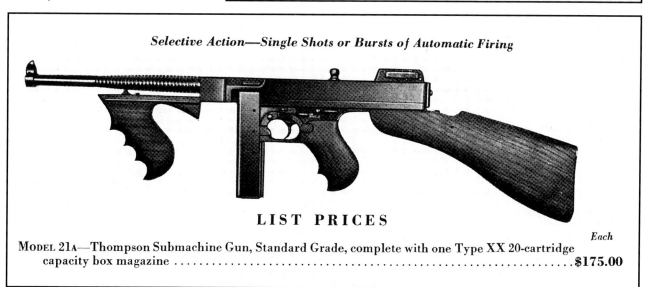

Selective Action—Single Shots or Bursts of Automatic Firing

LIST PRICES

Each

MODEL 21A—Thompson Submachine Gun, Standard Grade, complete with one Type XX 20-cartridge capacity box magazine **$175.00**

The first supplies of what was officially termed the 'Thompson Submachine Gun Model 1921' were delivered in March that year, one of the first customers being the Irish Republican Army which ordered 500. Although US customs intercepted the IRA's main shipment, some guns got through and were first used in an attack on a British troop train at Drumcondra on June 16.

American criminals fighting in the prohibition gang wars were rather slow off the mark in seeing the potential of the revolutionary new weapon and it was not until September 1925 that the first Tommy gun was used in a shooting in Chicago. Fortunately for the intended victim, he dropped to the ground just in time and the burst went over his head. Al Capone ordered three Thompsons in February 1926 and it is said that he carried out the first operation with the new weapon personally in a hit against the Cook County Assistant State's Attorney William McSwiggin on April 27. He was machine-gunned as he emerged

from the Pony Inn at 5613 West Roosevelt Road with a boyhood friend, Tom Duffy. A bootlegger Jimmy Doherty, who was coming out at the same time was literally cut in two by the blast of fire so it was never proven whether McSwiggin was the real target or whether he had merely been caught in the cross-fire of a gangland killing. In any case, no one was ever brought to justice for the murders — the first in America by the Thompson. This is the Pony Inn today — now renamed Sarno's Restaurant — with all traces of the machine gun ambush obliterated by the new brickwork.

Secondly, during the First World War the United States ceased to be the world's greatest debtor country and because its greatest creditor. A debtor country could export a greater value of goods than it imported and use the difference for interest and debt payment. This was what America did before the war. But a creditor must import a greater value than it exports if those who owe it money are to have the

wherewithal to pay interest and principal. Otherwise the creditor must either forgive the debts or make new loans in order to pay off the old ones.

During the Twenties the balance was maintained by making new foreign loans. Their promotion was profitable to domestic investment houses. And when the supply of honest and competent foreign borrowers ran out, dishonest, incompetent, or fanciful borrowers

were invited to borrow and, on occasion, bribed to do so.

Obviously, once investors awoke to the character of these loans or there was any other shock to confidence, they would no longer be made. There would be nothing with which to pay the old loans. Given this arithmetic, there would be either a sharp reduction in exports or a wholesale default on the outstanding loans.

Capone soon received a taste of his own medicine. His headquarters was located in the Hawthorne Hotel in Cicero, the borough just west of downtown Chicago. Shortly after 1 p.m. on Monday, September 20, a convoy of six automobiles drove slowly down 22nd Street led by a car masquerading as a police vehicle. Capone was seated in the hotel restaurant having just finished lunch when the sound of the bell on the police car brought him to his feet. As the cavalcade pulled up at the kerbside, suddenly from the window of every vehicle came deadly

streams of lead — a thousand rounds were said to have been fired in all — as gunmen raked the building. As a finale, a man in overalls calmly stepped forward and emptied his Thompson down the hallway of the hotel. These Hollywood film stills, although not strictly accurate in detail, nevertheless gives a good impression of the day the 'Chicago Pianos' played their deadly tune in Cicero. Capone survived the fusillade unscathed as he hit the floor under a table as soon as he heard the first shots.

This is where the attack — mounted by the North Side gang led by George 'Bugs' Moran — actually took place. Capone's complex occupied the 4800 block of 22nd Street (later simply called Cermak as American usage normally drops the word 'Road' or 'Street'). In the foreground the Anton Hotel with the Hawthorne and its smoke shop and restaurant beyond.

The third weakness of the economy was large-scale corporate thimble-rigging. By far the most common was the organization of corporations to hold stock in yet other corporations which in turn held stock in yet other corporations. In the case of the railroads and the utilities, the purpose of this pyramid of holding companies was to obtain control of a very large number of operating companies with a very small investment in the ultimate holding company. By the end of the Twenties, holding-company structures six or eight tiers high were commonplace.

Former Chicago area police officer Chuck Schauer with Marty Black and gangland historian John Binder who guided us on our Chicago tour . . . plus a gangster's moll!

Finally, and most evident of all, there was the stock-market boom. Month after month and year after year the great 'bull' market of the Twenties roared on. Sometimes there were setbacks, but more often there were fantastic forward surges. The summer of 1929 was the most frantic summer in American financial history. By its end stock prices had nearly quadrupled as compared with four years earlier. Transactions on the New York Stock

Seventy-five years later Marty does his bit for history! The lone gunman who stepped forward to rake the hotel lobby is believed to have been Peter Gusenberg.

The crime wave which had been fuelled by Prohibition had left more than 700 dead in Chicago alone, but it was the horrific massacre on St Valentine's Day in 1929 which shocked the world and finally brought about Capone's downfall. The man himself had a perfect alibi for Thursday, February 14 as he was entertaining guests at his Florida retreat but it was clear that the hit was against Moran personally as the S.M.C. Cartage Company office on North Clark Street *(above)* was one of his trucking depots.

The garage was demolished in 1967, the bricks being sold off as souvenirs. Our comparison was taken from the steps of the rooming house across the street which was believed to have been used as a look-out.

The official police report describing what took place is succinct and to the point: 'At 10:05 a.m. Feb. 14, 1929, a Cadillac auto drove up to the garage at 2122 N. Clark St., and five men got out, two of which were dressed in the uniforms of police officers. They went into the garage and lined the men they found there, up against the wall and shot and killed them, after which they got in their car and made their escape. The following are the men that were killed: Dr. Reinhardt H. Schwimmer, Parkway Hotel [an optometrist]; Albert R. Weinshank, 6320 Kenmore Ave. [a cleaner]; Adam Heyer, 2024 Farragut Ave. [an accountant]; John May, 1249 W. Madison St. [mechanic]; James Clark, 6036 Gunnison Ave. [a German whose real name was Albert Kachellek]; Frank Gusenberg, Morrison Hotel; Peter Gusenberg, 434 Roscoe St. At 12:30 P.M. Feb. 14, 1929, Sergt. E. Yates and Officer N. Olson made five photos and one plan of the above.' The dead are from L-R: Peter Gusenberg, Weinshank, Clark, Heyer, May and Schwimmer. Although hit seven times by .45 slugs, Frank Gusenberg was still alive when police arrived and was rushed to the Alexian Brothers Hospital where he died at 1.30 p.m.

The dead are removed from the rear entrance of the building to be taken to the Braithwaite Morgue at 2129 Lincoln Avenue. Seventy .45 cartridge cases were found on the floor of the garage and two fired 12 gauge shotgun shells. There were also a number of spent bullets which had struck the wall. A poor Alsatian dog tied up to one of the trucks was going beserk when police arrived.

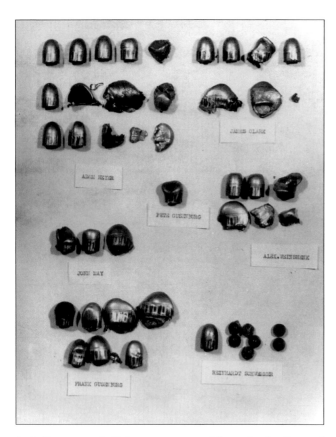

Left: Numerous bullets were removed from the bodies and although forensic science was then still in its infancy, police mounted an extensive operation to try to account for the whereabouts of every Thompson which had been sold by Auto-Ordnance to private individuals. (The overall record for Tommy gun bullet wounds was that of Joe Aiello who was hit 59 times on October 23, 1930.)

Chuck Schauer shows off one of the 1921 Thompsons still held in the Chicago Police Department armoury. Some of the weapons in the cabinet have the horizontal foregrip which identifies them as the US Navy Model. The Cutts compensator on the end of the muzzle was an optional extra available from 1926 to cut down both recoil and the tendency of the barrel to climb during full automatic fire.

By the end of the decade, the Thompson had become synonymous with the American gangster. Dubbed 'the Chicago piano', the 'chopper' or the 'typewriter', as William J. Helmer describes it in his history of *The Gun That Made the Twenties Roar* 'along with jazz, flappers, bathtub gin, speakeasies, one-way rides and bullet-proof limousines, the Tommy gun became a familiar symbol of America's "roaring" twenties'. And as one legend was born, so another died . . .

On January 13, 1929, Wyatt Earp, famed gunfighter and Western marshal, died peacefully at his home in Los Angeles. Back in October 1881 he had survived the shoot-out with the Clanton-McLowery gang at the OK Corral in Tombstone, Arizona — now his ashes lie in the Hills of Eternity Memorial Park at Colma, California. His original headstone was stolen in 1957 and for many years his grave was marked only by a simple plaque. Now this imposing headstone marks Wyatt's last resting place.

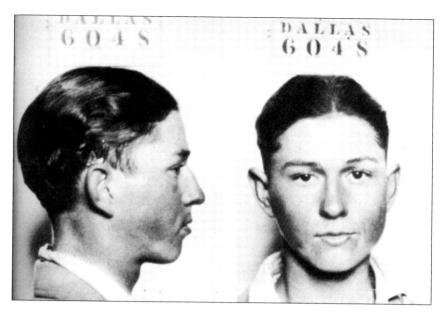

Meanwhile, down Texas way, Clyde Barrow had already had his first brush with the law. In December 1926 he hired a car to visit his girlfriend's relatives but he didn't tell the rental company that he planned to take it to Broaddus, some 200 miles south-east of Dallas. When he failed to return it on time, the vehicle was reported as stolen and the local sheriff came looking for him. Instead of explaining the situation, Clyde just abandoned the car and hitch-hiked back to Dallas where he was soon arrested. Although in the end the rental company did not press charges, Clyde was still finger-printed and photographed. Each police department assigned prisoners a reference number: thus to Dallas police Clyde became No. 6048 but, for example, he was No. 765 to police in Ohio (see page 37).

Exchange ran to five million or more shares a day. Few, it seemed, held shares for their income. What counted was the increase in capital values.

The boom was inherently self-liqui-dating. It could last only so long as new people, or at least new money, swarmed into the market in pursuit of the capital gains. This new demand bid up the stocks and made the capital gains. Once the supply of new customers began to falter, the market would cease to rise. Once the market stopped rising, some, and perhaps a good many, would start to cash in. If you are concerned with capital gains, you must get them while the getting is good. But the getting may start the market down, and this will one day be the signal for much more selling. Thus it was certain that the market would one day go down, and far more rapidly than it went up. Down it went with a thunderous crash in October 1929. In a series of terrible days, of which Thursday, October 24 and Tues-day, October 29 were the most terrify-ing, billions in values were lost, and thousands of speculators — they had been called investors — were utterly and totally ruined.

J. K. Galbraith, Professor of Economics, Harvard University, 1969

Then, as the decade came to a close, came an almighty crash. No sooner had Charles E. Mitchell, chairman of New York's National City Bank, confi-dently announced at the beginning of October that 'the markets generally, are now in a healthy condition', than panic on Wall Street led to the loss of millions . . . the great American slump had begun.

A spectacular crash on the stock mar-ket yesterday ruined tens of thousands of small speculators and involved a depreciation of security values variously estimated at from £2,000,000,000 to £3,000,000,000.

It was 'Black Saturday' for Wall Street, and today groups of financiers met to consider the situation, which affects every part of the country.

The handwriting on the wall indicates that the 'bull' movement of the last five years has definitely given way to a liquidation market, and that there is no certainty that the shares dumped upon the market yesterday will be snapped up, as hoped by investment trusts and other large financial buyers.

The strength of the wave of selling which engulfed the market is shown by the fact that during the first half-hour trading was at the rate of more than 8,500,000 shares for the customary full five-hour day. The tape machine was overburdened, and it was not until an hour and twenty-five minutes after the twelve o'clock closing gong had sounded that the final prices were known even to traders.

The frantic selling rush was chiefly in small lots by frightened or over-extended speculators from every part of the country.

The immediate fate of the market depends upon conferences over the weekend regarding proposals for organ-ised support to check the decline.

Among the factors which contributed to yesterday's selling were sensational operations by Mr. Jesse Livermore. Mr. Livermore is known to Wall Street as 'the best man on Stock Market tape speculation the world has ever known'. He is a clever 'bear' willing to stake his last cent on his own judgement, but can-not be held to be entirely responsible for what occured, though the circum-stances were exceptionally favourable for such a plunging speculator.

As a boy Mr. Livermore was a tape-machine board marker in a Boston brokerage house, and developed such skill that he acquired the name of 'the boy plunger'. He has made millions, lost them, and recovered. It was not, how-ever, until the last two or three weeks that Wall Street began to associate his name with every decline.

Mr. Arthur Cutten, the most promi-nent of 'bulls', with whom Mr. Liver-more has waged a titanic struggle on the Stock Market, is in many respects very different. He is calm and slow of speech, while Mr. Livermore is quick, nervous, and excitable.

There is no personal battle between the two men, but they represent the direct pull and haul against each other of a wide variety of economic factors, all of them powerful.

The Daily Telegraph, October 21, 1929

No sooner had Clyde been let off the hook for the hire-car business than he got involved with brother Buck in making a few dollars by selling stolen turkeys for Christmas. Although they got arrested by police and charged, they were subsequently released with a warning. During this period, the brothers were regularly involved in petty crime but the first recorded robbery which resulted in a custodial sentence took place in November 1929. Clyde was then 20 and Buck 26. On Friday, November 29, taking along an accomplice Sidney Moore, they set out from Dallas in a stolen Buick heading in the direction of Wichita Falls, 150 miles to the north-west, not far from the Oklahoma border.

At Henrietta they stole a Ford and then burgled an empty house in which they found some jewellery. On the way back to Dallas they reached Denton in the early hours of Saturday morning. Driving down West Oak Street, they spotted the Motor Mark Garage at No. 311. There was no one around so, forcing the back door, they bodily removed the office safe which they put in the car. However, just as they were about to drive off, they were spotted by a patrol car. Clyde put his foot down but lost control turning into Piner Street. The police opened fire and brought down Buck but Clyde managed to escape. Moore raised his hands and the pair were taken into custody.

November 29, 1929 – Denton, Texas

One man was shot through both legs, another was arrested and a third man escaped, following the theft of a safe from the Motor Mark garage here at an early hour Saturday morning. The man who was shot gave his name as Buck Barrow of Dallas, and he and another man arrested giving his name as S. A. Moore of Dallas, face charges of burglary and theft over the value of $50.

The three men were surprised by Night Officers Clint Starr and I. E. Jones after the garage had been broken into. The safe taken from the building had been placed in a small automobile to which the officers gave chase on West Oak Street. As the automobile rounded the corner at Piner Street it struck a curb and was wrecked. The three men ran and were fired on by Starr. Barrow dropped and a second man halted. The third made good his escape.

The men were lodged in the city jail and officers said the men tossed a quantity of jewelry from the jail windows. It was recovered.

County Attorney Earl Street said the car in which the men were riding had been stolen in Henrietta.

A. Smith, owner of the garage, said the safe contained $30.40.

Entrance to the building was gained by prying the office door open with a pinch bar.

Record Chronicle, November 30, 1929

Left: **Karin Ramsay took the comparison of the Motor Mark Garage for us in December 2002. 'My first disappointment was to discover that a typically daring location of a Bonnie and Clyde robbery, only two blocks west of the court-house, was now a parking lot for Verizon where even the curbing has changed so that numbering is difficult to determine. I stopped a postman to help me confirm my deduction as there is no "311" and the closest to that is "309" which is the back door of the**

Verizon building which sits behind the parking lot, a building which actually fronts onto the street to the south of West Oak. The parking lot obviously belongs to Verizon because the sign at the curb says "Verizon PARKING ONLY — NO THRU TRAFFIC". But Clyde would certainly have ignored that sign!'
Right: **'Piner is a side street about 70 yards further down West Oak Street (in front of the bank sign). Here the car crashed leading to the capture of Buck Barrow and Sidney Moore.'**

Convicted of burglary, Buck was sentenced to a five-year term in the State Penitentiary at Huntsville. The 'Walls Unit', as it is often called, was the first to be established in the Texas prison system and dates from 1848 although this picture was taken circa 1935. [1] South Building which incorporated 'Old Seven Row' — the original Death Row — where Raymond Hamilton and Joe Palmer met their deaths on May 10, 1935 while seated in the 'Old Sparky' electric chair (see page 12). [2] Hospital Building where Buck was treated for his Denton gunshot wounds. [3] East Building. [4] West Building. [5] Administration. [6] Education, canteen and library. [7] Prison director's residence. [8] Various workshops for convicts. [9] Prison rodeo ground.

The Walls Unit as it appears today. The facade was changed in 1942. In the left background is the old prison rodeo arena where events were held until 1986 since when it has been used as a car park. [1] The new Death House. The electric chair was moved here in the 1950s but execution now takes place by lethal injection. (Old Sparky is now displayed in the Texas Prison Museum — see page 282.) [2] The 'Seven Row' in the old South Building is now sealed from entry from there and is now only reached from the second floor of the hospital [3]. [4] Chapel built in the early 1950s. Buck was working as a trustee in the prison's farm kitchen when he escaped on March 8, 1930. Bruce Moore took the comparison for us in April 2003.

While Buck was cooling his heels inside, an event occurred in the life of his brother which would change the course of history: Clyde Barrow met Bonnie Parker. Strictly speaking we should be introducing her with her married name of Bonnie Thornton but by now her marriage to Roy Glenn Thornton (above left) was virtually over. She had not seen her husband at all during 1928 and when he did show up in January 1929 Bonnie told him they were finished. A short time afterwards Roy was sentenced to five years for a robbery at Red Oak, a town 15 miles south of Dallas. Above right: This is how a documentary of the period depicted the meeting of Clyde with Bonnie as she left the cafe where she was working as a waitress. Bonnie certainly did work in several cafes in Dallas but had been out of work since Marco's closed with the stock market crash in November 1929. The 1934 documentary recreated the scene outside Baltimore's Dairy Lunch located at 1106 Main Street. Right: Today the whole of the 1100 block is a car park.

However the truth of that first meeting is somewhat different as Bonnie's mother explains. 'I had never heard Clyde Barrow's name and didn't dream that such a boy existed till January 1930. Bonnie, still out of work after the closing of Marco's Cafe, had gone to stay with a girlfriend in West Dallas. This girl had broken her arm and Bonnie went to help with the work. Clyde's folks lived near, and here it was Clyde came and met my daughter. It all came about so simply, as such momentous and life-changing things often do. Clyde dropped by this girl's house, Bonnie was there, and they met. That was the beginning. Bonnie Parker met Clyde Barrow in the kitchen of a simple home in West Dallas, and at the time she met him, she did not know that he had ever had any trouble with the law.' Yet no sooner had they met — and fallen in love at first sight — they were parted when, early the following month, police mounted an early morning raid on Mrs Parker's house. Clyde was discovered still asleep on the couch and promptly arrested. Left: That house stood here in Cockrell Street, on the site of which the Dallas police have just inaugurated their new headquarters. Quite ironic when one bears in mind that this is where Bonnie and Clyde's love affair first blossomed!

March 11, 1930 – McLennan County Jail, Waco, Texas

Clyde was first sent to Denton to answer for the Motor Mart robbery but, with insufficient evidence to convict him, he was transferred to Waco where other charges were outstanding. *Above:* McLennan County Jail lay just behind the court-house on Washington Avenue. It can be seen in the left background on the corner of 6th Street and it was here on Sunday, March 2, that Clyde was put in a first floor cell. He appeared before the resident JP, Aubrey A. Morris, the following morning and charged with five counts of car theft, the burglary of the Green store at the junction of 19th Street and Reuter Avenue, and for receiving and concealing stolen property. On Tuesday, Clyde and his partner Bill Turner were indicted by the Grand Jury convened under the notorious 'hanging judge' Richard Munroe. Two days later the pair confessed to their crimes and pleaded guilty. Both defendants assured Judge Munroe that they were remorseful and contrite over their criminal activities and, accordingly, lenient sentences were handed down: 25 four-year concurrent terms for Turner and seven concurrent two-year terms for Clyde, i.e. providing he behaved himself he would only serve 24 months.

The old jail was replaced by a new building in 1952 combined with an annexe to the main court-house. *Below:* Clyde's name appears second on the census of the jail population. (Frank Hardy heads the list — see page 78.)

Name..Barrow, Clyde...........................	Leave This Space Blank
Alias.Clyde Barrow, Elvin Williams, Eldin	F.P.C...13 29 W MO 9
....Williams, Jack Hale, Roy Bailey.......	26 U 00 9
No...1768....Color....W......Sex..Male	Ref.........

RIGHT HAND

1. Thumb	2. Index Finger	3. Middle Finger	4. Ring Finger	5. Little Finger

LEFT HAND

6. Thumb	7. Index Finger	8. Middle Finger	9. Ring Finger	10. Little Finger

Officer's Signature

Date ....

Prisoner's Signature

X *Clyde Barrow*

FOUR FINGERS TAKEN SIMULTANEOUSLY

FOUR FINGERS TAKEN SIMULTANEOUSLY

Left Hand	L. Thumb	R. Thumb	Right Hand

Another location expunged from the map of Waco is 1015 South 5th Street (right) where Nell, Clyde's elder sister, was staying. When his mother travelled to Waco on the interurban line from Dallas to see her son, Bonnie, now madly in love, tagged along. They would undoubtedly have met Nell here although they were put up by Bonnie's cousin Mary during their brief stay in the city. After the Monday court hearing, Bonnie penned a note to Clyde: 'Hello Sugar, Just a line tonight, as I'm so lonesome. Just think, honey, today is the first time I have seen you in two weeks, and just a very few minutes today. But it sure was sweet just to get to see you. Those laws are all so nice, sugar. They aren't like those Denton laws. Your mother is spending the night with me tonight. I wanted her to stay so she could see you again tomorrow. Dearest, I'm going to get me a job and stay up here; I couldn't make it in Dallas anymore without you. Sugar, how I wish you were out of all this awful trouble. I don't see how I can get along if you go away.'

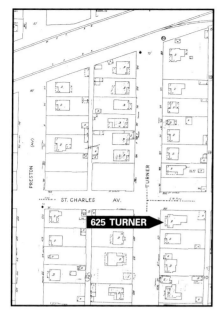

Bonnie continued: 'You didn't act like you were very glad to see me today. What's wrong? Don't you love me any more? I know how you feel, honey. I guess you are awfully worried. Listen dear, I won't write much today because I'll see you tomorrow, we hope, and for a long old time. And honey, just remember I love you more than anything on earth, and be real, real sweet and think of me, down here thinking of you. Your lonesome baby, Bonnie. P.S. Don't worry, darling, because I'm going to do everything possible and if you do have to go down, I'll be good while you're gone, and be waiting — waiting — waiting — for you. I love you.' That offer to do anything for the man with whom she was now crazily in love was to lead Bonnie into committing her first criminal act although nothing was

known about it until after her death in 1934 when Mary explained what happened in the book *Fugitives*. 'One of the boys in jail with Clyde was named William Turner. He had a gun concealed in his house out in East Waco but he didn't dare ask his sister or mother to bring it to him, fearing they might get caught in the attempt and be implicated. He didn't hesitate to use Bonnie for the purpose, if she was game. [But] with the man she loved behind bars, Bonnie was game for anything.' By coincidence, Turner lived at No. 625 Turner, a turning off East Waco Drive. *Above:* Unfortunately all the properties north of St Charles Avenue have been demolished with the expansion of State Highway 84, including the historic house on the south-eastern corner where Bonnie found the pistol.

Although Turner had provided Bonnie with a sketch showing where to find the house key and where the gun and ammunition were hidden, the place had to be ransacked before the weapon was found in the window seat. Mary described how she was shivering with fright when Bonnie told her she was going to stage a jail break. According to Mary, Bonnie 'put on two belts, one under her dress to hold her slip tight to her body, and another on top. She slipped the gun between her breasts in the pocket the two belts made'. But therein lies an enigma which has never been satisfactorily explained. The Texas Rangers Hall of Fame and Museum in Waco exhibit this Smith & Wesson Model 10 *(left)* captioned: 'When Clyde was in the McLennan County Jail in March 1930 Bonnie visited him several times. Officers searched her and confiscated this Smith & Wesson on one visit', noting that the pistol was a gift to the museum from

Dr Neill Simpson. The press reports confirm that the prisoners certainly had a gun to hold up the jailer but, if it was the Turner revolver that was confiscated, how did they obtain a second weapon? Surely Bonnie would have been rigorously searched on subsequent visits having already been caught trying to smuggle a pistol into the jail? *Right:* A second query is raised by this 1903 Colt Auto which US Marshal Clint Peoples claims is the one which Bonnie slipped to Clyde. It was once on loan to the Texas Rangers but had been withdrawn from display when we visited the museum in May 2003. Nevertheless, a photo of the automatic has appeared in many books and articles on Bonnie and Clyde but how could the actual pistol used in the successful escape subsequently have come into Peoples's possession, especially when Clyde carried it to Middletown and disposed of it there as we shall see in the next chapter?

N. OF CLOSE
MAY 1433

THE WACO TIMES-HERALD

WACO, TEXAS, WEDNESDAY, MARCH 12, 1930—16 PAGES

NUMBER 53

TRIO LEAVES TRAIL OF STOLEN CARS

SMUGGLED PISTOL AIDS SUCCESSFUL BREAK FOR YOUNG THUG TRIO

FUGITIVES IN JAIL DELIVERY HEADING WEST

Sheriff's Office Here Gets Telephone Call From Brownwood Stating Trio Believed Seen There

THEFT OF MANY CARS REPORTED

Turner and His Pals Abandon First Car Here With in Few Blocks After Escape From Jail

(Left) Night Jailer Stanford, answering Willie Turner's (2) request for a bottle of milk, finds himself looking into a gun in the hands of Emory Abernathy (1). Turner, Abernathy and a third thug, Schoolboy Barrow, then locked Stanford in the cell and—

(Right) Going down one flight of stairs Turner and Barrow (2) and (3) seized Turnkey Jones while Abernathy (1) held the gun on him. Jones tried to hide the jail keys between his trousers, but the crooks found them, unlocked the outer jail door and escaped.

GUNSHOT INTO BREAST FATAL FOR WACO MAN

Dave Scott Dies In Hospital After Being Found at His Home With Pistol Near His Body

WACO SLEUTHS ENJOY RADIO CONCERT, THEN ARREST A PERFORMER

LEE WHATLEY TAKES STAND AT HIS TRIAL

State Closes Its Case Wednesday Morning in Slaying of Sam Kus, Restaurant Operator

Left is Clyde "Schoolboy" Barrow, and right, Willie Turner, two of England's hopefuls who escaped from McLennan county jail last night. Abernathy had not been in custody long enough to have his face mugged.

New Developments In Jail Break Case

DEEP RUTS OF

COURT DENIES FLAGS FLY AS

On Wednesday March 12, the break-out was headline news. The captions to the two pictures recreating the escape read as follows: *Left:* 'Night Jailer Stanford answering Willie Turner's [2] request for a bottle of milk, finds himself looking into a gun in the hands of Emory Abernathy [1]. Turner, Abernathy and a third thug, "Schoolboy" Barrow, then locked Stanford in the cell.' *Right:* 'Going down one flight of stairs, Turner and Barrow [2] and [3] seized Turnkey Jones while Abernathy [1] held the gun on him. Jones tried to hide the jail keys between his trousers, but the crooks found them, unlocked the outer jail door and escaped.'

The county jail break Tuesday night which resulted in escape of three men, William Turner, Elmer (*sic*) Abernathy and Clyde Barrow, brought new developments Wednesday morning which may add new zest to the capture of the fugitives whose whereabouts are not known at this time by Sheriff Leslie Stegall.

Judge Richard L. Munroe announced Wednesday he would set aside provisions that sentences of Turner and Barrow would run concurrently, and possibly sentence both men to serve their terms consecutively. Turner, upon a strong recommendation of the Fifty-fourth district jury was sentenced to four years in each of 25 cases, the sentences to run concurrently. If Judge Munroe sentences him to a consecutive sentence he will have to serve 163 years, since he has been convicted on a federal charge which brought him a three-year sentence. Turner was sentenced Tuesday morning by Judge Munroe.

Barrow, upon the jury's recommendation, was sentenced to serve two years in each of

The turnkey, S. Huse Jones, ran to the public entrance and spotted them running north on 6th Street. *Left:* Although this is the new court-cum-jail building, the route is the same, your editor following in the trio's footsteps 73 years later. *Right:* Proceeding north on 6th just crossing Columbus where several pistol shots were exchanged between Jones and Abernathy.

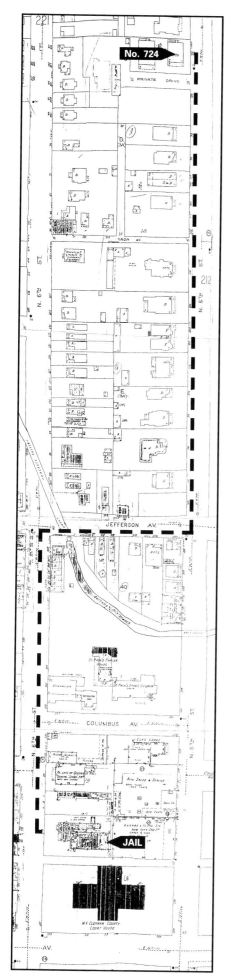

Approaching the junction with Jefferson.

Having turned right, it is almost certain that the three escapees would have crossed the road diagonally to reach North 5th Street.

Left: Today North 5th is one way . . . but that would hardly have bothered Clyde!
Right: And so up the road for a couple of hundred yards to where Mr Byrd's car was parked outside No. 724.

Sadly, all the houses in the 700 block at the top of the street have gone but the tell-tale steps from the sidewalk pinpoint where they once stood.

seven cases, the sentences to run concurrently. Both men were charged with burglary and theft. Abernathy had not been tried in the district court here. He is charged with 10 cases of burglary and theft.

The entire state of Texas has been covered by Sheriff Stegall in trailing the three men by telegrams, he said Wednesday. A phone call from the sheriff at Meridian early Wednesday morning brought the information that three men passed through there in a Ford sedan but reports of their passing were not received in time for the sheriff to stop them.

About 7:30 p.m. Tuesday, Night Jailer J. P. Stanford, unarmed, went to the second floor of the jail where the three were confined, to carry Turner a bottle of milk. When he opened the door of the cage he was stopped by Turner, then Abernathy poked a gun into his ribs and ordered Stanford to 'stick em up.' Stanford was locked in a cell after he was robbed of his keys. Huse Jones, on duty at the turnkey's desk downstairs, was then held up and keys to the final jail door taken from him.

After driving up 5th for about ten blocks, they reached Brook Avenue where they cut through to North 7th *(above)*. **Here they switched cars for one belonging to Dr William L. Souther before high-tailing it out of town.**

Several shots were fired by Jones at the three men as they ran up Sixth Street. Investigation conducted showed they took a car parked in the 700 block on North Fifth Street belonging to a man named Byrd. When they reached 2000 North Seventh Street, they appropriated the Ford coupe of Dr. W. L. Souther, which he had just purchased. No abandoned autos had been reported to county officers although they may be found today and a string of stolen cars reported by individuals, Sheriff Stegalls said.

The auto stolen from the J. M. Byrd house, 724 North Fifth Street at 7:45 p.m. Wednesday, and believed to have been taken by the three prisoners, Emery (*sic*) Abernathy, William Turner and Clyde Barrow who made their escape from the county jail 15 minutes earlier, was found by Waco police officers in front of the Dr. W. L. Souther home, 2005 North Seventh Street, where another car was stolen.

Dr. Souther reported to officers at 7:30 o'clock this morning that a car which he had borrowed was taken from in front of his house last night at about 8 o'clock. He did not report it because he thought the owner of the car had come after it he said.

When his own car broke down earlier in the day he had borrowed this car he stated. The Byrd car was delivered to its owners by Officers Wiley Stem and J. R. Doty.

Failure of the police to hear of the second stolen car, resulted in a 12-hour start of prisoners ahead of officers who broadcast over the state license number of the stolen Byrd car.

The Waco Times-Herald, March 12, 1930

Left: **At last we found a building which still stands — the doctor's house No. 2005. (Perhaps a word of explanation will be helpful here for our British readers to explain the American system of numbering their houses. Each block, i.e. the built-up area between two streets, is allocated 100 numbers, even though each block may not contain that many houses. Navigation is made easy by each road sign announcing the block number. Thus Dr Souther's house lies 20 blocks from where North 5th Street begins at the Missouri-Kansas-Texas Railroad. South of the tracks the roads have the prefix 'South'. Each town in the States broadly follows the same pattern. As in Britain, odd numbers are on one side of the street and even numbers on the other.**

As soon as Clyde and his two fellow prisoners had cleared Waco, they headed north. The car they had taken from outside Dr Souther's house was dumped along the way — possibly in Oklahoma — and at least two other vehicles stolen and abandoned as the trio moved through Missouri, Illinois, Indiana to Ohio. There they surfaced on the afternoon of Monday, March 17 in Middletown having covered well over 1,000 miles in the last six days. They were first spotted acting suspiciously outside Gough Lamb Cleaners on Charles Street and it was Frank South, standing on the extreme left of this line up of 1929 Dodge delivery vans, who noted down the number on the licence plate and passed the information on to his friend Bernard Krebs who worked at the Baltimore & Ohio Railroad depot in West Middletown.

March 17-18, 1930 — Middletown, Ohio

Two of the trio of alleged gangsters who are believed by police to have participated in a series of robberies here Monday night were captured this morning following a thrilling chase from the B. & O. Depot in West Middletown to Auburn Street and Crescent Boulevard, Lakeside, during which several shots were fired by police.

The two who were captured are registered at police headquarters as William Turner, 21, of Waco, Texas, and Emory Abernathy, 24 of Hillsboro, Texas. Police have a description of the third member of the trio and are continuing the search for him.

Turner was captured by Police Officer Harry Richardson in an alley near Auburn Street and Crescent Boulevard where he had run after the trio had abandoned their auto at Auburn Street and Henry Avenue and left afoot. Turner stopped and surrendered to Officer Richardson after the officer fired one shot during the pursuit.

Abernathy was arrested by Officer Tom Carmody and Constable Lummie Bailey about an hour later in the east end near the Big Four railroad crossing where he was trying to 'bum' a ride out of town.

This afternoon, Police Officers Tom Carmody and Charles Porter, and W. J. Sortman, sergeant of B. & O. railroad police and J. A. Wheeler B. & O. lieutenant, captured the third member of the gang in Avalon after a brief chase during which several shots were fired.

He is registered at police headquarters as Robert Thorn, age 17, of Indianapolis. According to police he has admitted participating in a series of robberies in Cincinnati and cities of the Miami Valley. The youth is said to have had a gun, which he threw in the canal when the officers captured him.

Police also say they received a wire from Waco, Texas, confirming the story of the jail break of Turner and Abernathy.

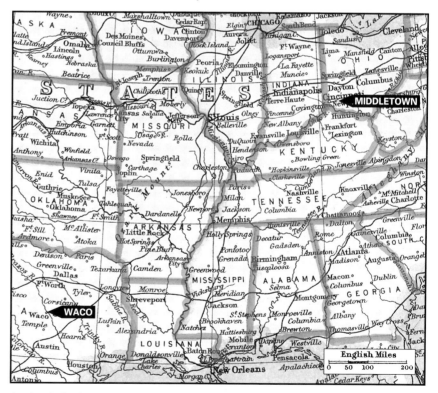

As the theft of automobiles is going to feature regularly throughout our story, it will probably be helpful to explain American terminology of the period. A 'sedan', what would be termed a saloon in Britain, had four doors while a 'coach' was a two-door sedan. (Ford called its sedans by the proprietary names Tudors and Fordors.) A 'coupe' had two-doors with wind-up windows, while a 'roadster' — what we would now call a convertible — had removable semi-transparent side screens made of isinglass. Sport coupes had rumble seats (dickey seats) unlike business coupes which did not have these folding seats at the rear.

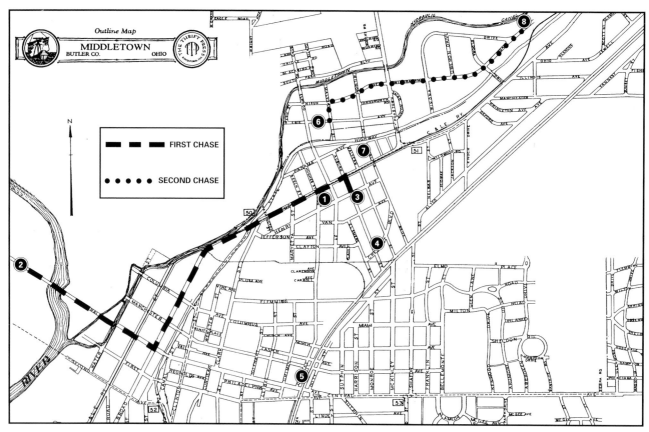

The abortive Middletown affair of March 1930 — which led to Clyde and his companions being labelled in the newspapers 'the Baby Dumbbell Bandits' and to the capture of all three men — has been researched in detail by Rick Williams. Rick has made an exhaustive study of the events, sorted fact from fiction, and has traced the route taken in precise detail. In March 2003, he was joined by Jim Knight and together, 73 years later almost to the day, they retraced Clyde Barrow's tyre tracks around the city. Rick describes what happened and Jim took the pictures.

[1] Is the location of Gough Lamb Cleaners on Charles Street. [2] The approximate area of West Middletown and the train depot where the first chase began. [3] The car chase ends here at the intersection of Auburn and Henry; trio flees on foot. [4] The alley where William Turner was captured. [5] The Big Four rail station where Abernathy was captured. [6] The home of Orville Baird where Clyde stole the car and began the second car chase. [7] This is Catalpa and the dry canal bed where the Middletown police cruiser was parked when Clyde was spotted on the far side. [8] The spot where Clyde surrendered.

Rick continues the story: 'Tuesday morning, March 18, found police responding to several reports of break-ins around the city. This is the dry cleaners building today with the same smoke-stack. The original building stood where the lettering ends. The right-hand section was added in the mid-1930s. From here, Henry Avenue is to the right and Tytus Avenue to the left. Middletown police officers Harry Richardson and George Woody were dispatched to the B & O rail office after being notified of an overnight burglary. While taking the report, B & O clerk Bernard Krebs provided the officers with descriptions of Barrow and his companions, and their license number; Indiana tag #163-439. Richardson and Woody finished taking the statement from Krebs and walked outside to their patrol car. It was now after 8 a.m. As they discussed the particulars of the crime, both officers observed a car coming down the West Middletown hill heading slowly towards town. It was a Ford coupe with three men inside. It bore an Indiana license plate, tag #163-439.'

32

Rick: 'Looking west along Route 122 in West Middletown. This is the curve that Barrow rounded when he suddenly saw the police car parked at the B & O depot. The railroad tracks are to our rear. This is where the first car chase began.'

Officers Richardson and George Woody were investigating the robbery at the B. & O. ticket office in West Middletown where $57.97 had been taken from a safe Monday night. Bernard J. Krebs, ticket agent, gave the officers a license number of an auto in which three men had stopped at the depot Monday afternoon for a train schedule. As the officers left the ticket office they noticed a coupe containing three men coming down the West Middletown hill. Checking the license number of the oncoming car, they found it to be the one they were seeking. They immediately took chase and the bandit auto gained speed rapidly.

'All that is left of the depot is the red-brick building on the left. At one time the white building in the center was thought to have been part of the original depot but research showed it was built in 1950. This is where the police car was parked when Clyde had taken the wrong road and had mistakenly returned to Middletown. He saw the police vehicle at the same moment that officers Richardson and Woody spotted them.

'Barrow accelerated and headed across the Great Miami River bridge into Middletown itself', says Rick. 'Looking back, the three fugitives couldn't miss the police car pulling out of the depot in pursuit. Unfortunately the bridge they used to cross the river has gone — replaced by the new one on the right. West Middletown is behind where Jim and I are standing.'

'After crossing the bridge, Barrow sped the Ford into town and took the first left (at the first tall building) onto Main Street. Richardson and Woody saw the turn and stayed with them. Quickly taking the right-angle where Main Street changes to Tytus Avenue, Barrow continued speeding north-east. The chase had now covered about two miles, leaving the downtown area behind them as they entered the quiet residential neighborhood of Lakeside'.

Traveling west on Central Avenue the bandit car swerved sharply north off Main Street and on to Tytus Avenue. The police car drew close to the fleeing bandits as they cleared Auburn Street. When ordered to stop, the driver turned sharply into Auburn Street

'After just over a mile on Tytus, Richardson and Woody had closed the distance and now made a move to halt the fleeing car. Richardson pulled alongside the Ford while Woody ordered Barrow to stop the car. Barrow responded by sharply taking the next right onto Auburn Street (on the right just past the bench seat). Reacting swiftly, Richardson skidded the patrol car onto Auburn, staying right behind Barrow. Officer Woody leaned out his side and fired a shot at the swerving auto. Most of the houses and buildings in these pictures are the same ones that existed back in the 1930s', says Rick.

whereupon Officer Woody fired. The police car again drew close to the fleeing trio as they neared Henry Street. Police again fired and the driver swerved the car to the curb, stopped and the three fled afoot, each running in opposite directions.

'Richardson again closed the distance as Woody fired once more into the back of the coupe. Perhaps the close pursuit or the gun-fire became too much for him, because Barrow abruptly slammed on the brakes and the car skidded up onto the curb at the intersection of Auburn Street and Henry Avenue. Abandoning their stolen car, the three men fled on foot, each man going in a different direction. I am standing on the corner by the kerb which was struck by the car. This spot is one block east of the previous photo. Abernathy ran south on Henry (to the right); Turner continued east on Auburn (to the left) and Clyde Barrow fled north on Henry (behind photographer). The house is the original one which stood there in March 1930 — it was built in 1924'.

Officer Richardson set off in foot pursuit of William Turner who ran south on Auburn. After almost two blocks, Turner cut east into an alley near Auburn and Crescent. Richardson fired a shot and ordered Turner to halt. Dashing into the alley, Richardson found Turner standing there with his hands in the air. Offering no physical resistance, Turner was taken into custody and walked back to the patrol car.' Rick explains that 'in this picture *(left)* we are looking east on Auburn in the direction where Turner was pursued by foot. The dead end of Auburn can just be seen in the distance about two and a half blocks distant' *Right:* 'This is the alley where Turner surrendered. From here Auburn and Henry are two blocks to the left.'

Officer Woody fired at one of the fleeing men. The bullet went wild and the man escaped in a nearby alley. After capturing Turner, Officer Richardson notified police headquarters and several other police officers were dispatched to the scene and a diligent search started.

After some questioning at police head-quarters police say Turner stated he was sent to a Texas prison for 99 years following con-viction of a murder committed during a store hold up in Waco a short time ago. He is also said to have admitted to police he has been arrested on robbery charges before.

Abernathy, police say confessed to escap-ing from a prison at Waco with Turner and another man last week after knocking down a guard. He is said to have told police he and Turner boarded a freight train for Wichita Falls, Texas, where they stole the automobile which they were driving this morning. Aber-nathy, police say, states he and Turner first drove to Joplin, Missouri, where they picked up a third party but would not state whether or not he is the same man who was in the car this morning. He is also said to have told police he had 17 years' time yet to serve on a highway robbery charge in Texas.

Rick: 'Abernathy escaped this way — south on Henry. It is believed he ran two blocks ahead, then turned left onto Charles Street. The dry cleaners they burglarized is right on Charles, less than one block away.'

'Barrow ran north on Henry, taking a quick left into the alley (between the small brick shed and garage on the left) to dodge a third shot fired by Woody. Probably following procedure to back up his partner, Woody did not pursue so Barrow escaped.'

'Richardson and Woody called for assistance and a search of the area was begun for the two remaining suspects. Turner was taken to headquarters but refused to answer questions. About an hour later Middletown police officer Thomas Carmody and Constable Lummie Bailey spotted Abernathy at what is now Middletown's historic rail station *(right)*. He was trying to hitch a ride out of town when Carmody and Bailey cautiously approached him with guns drawn. Abernathy offered no resistance but the officers were justified in regarding him with caution. A quick pat-down search revealed he was carrying a loaded pistol. He was transported to city jail to join Turner in being vigorously questioned. By the afternoon Turner and Abernathy had admitted their true identities to Chief of Police Otto Kolodzik. All this time Clyde Barrow was still at large . . . but where was he?'

'Despite remaining within a few blocks of the abandoned car, thus far Barrow had managed to elude the search. Years later Clyde told his sister Marie that he had hidden under a house in the neighbourhood. Meanwhile officers Carmody and Porter were sitting in their patrol car keeping watch at the end of Catalpa Drive where it dead-ended into the south bank of the recently drained Miami-Erie Canal. In the back seat were B & O Railroad detectives J. A. Wheeler and W. J. Sortman. Just after one o'clock, Carmody spotted Barrow on foot on the other side of the deep canal ditch. Jumping down into the dry canal bed, Carmody ordered Porter to take the cruiser up to the Germantown Road bridge and cross it to the north side, hopefully cutting off Barrow's escape in that direction. Carmody crossed the canal ditch and clambered up the other side. Believe it or not', says Rick, 'Verity Parkway running left to right in this picture has now replaced the canal! This had been dug in 1825 but in September 1929 had been drained and was waiting to be filled in. The field on the opposite side where Clyde was spotted is where the restaurants now stand.'

'Seeing Carmody coming after him, Barrow bolted north through a field, emerging onto Erie Avenue where he ran east. Carmody might have felt confident when he saw Barrow heading almost directly where he had ordered Porter to go in the patrol car. Now becoming desperate, Barrow unexpectedly dashed into the yard of Orville Baird at #2103 *(above)* and leaped into the car parked in front of the house. He started it in seconds and quickly drove off, still heading east on Erie. Carmody wasn't the kind of man to give up his quarry that easily. Firing his revolver at Barrow, he continued to chase him on foot.'

'Porter's patrol car now appeared at the far end of Erie, effectively cutting off Barrow's escape route. Clyde saw the police car and quickly took a side street north for one block, then turned right onto what is now Wilbraham Road, once more heading east. Porter saw Carmody still doggedly pursuing Barrow on foot. He pulled alongside Carmody, slowing just enough to allow him to jump on the running board. Turning onto Wilbraham, they saw Barrow crossing Germantown Road. As the cruiser raced down Wilbraham the local lawmen knew something that Barrow did not: the road was a dead-end, bordered by heavy woods and a swift-moving industrial waterway known as the Hydraulic Canal. This time, there would be no place to run. Jim Knight (arrowed) is standing on the sidewalk at the point where the road ended in 1930.'

'The chase ended here. As both cars sped through the last few hundred yards of the street, Barrow realised he was on a dead-end road. Taking a bold gamble, he veered the car left onto a lawn and drove between #2945 and #2949 Wilbraham *(above)* which were then the last houses on the street. Roaring into the backyard and seeing the canal ahead, Barrow slammed on the brakes and sprang from the car. Clutching the pistol that Bonnie had smuggled to him in Waco, he ran to the canal bank, desperately looking for a way out. From opposite sides of the houses, the four-man posse emerged with guns drawn and ordered Barrow to surrender. This was a critical moment for the fledgling criminal. He knew he was trapped, but he was armed. It took Barrow only a split second to decide on a course of action. For the last time in his life when faced with this kind of situation, Barrow threw the pistol into the deep and murky canal, raised his hands and surrendered'.

Searching their automobile police found burglary tools, including equipment with which to break open a safe, three suitcases full of clothing, several cans of beans and a quantity of cigars and cigarettes. The car bore an Indiana license number 163-439. A pair of Oklahoma license plates were found in the rumble seat of the coupe.

Police state they firmly believe the three were responsible for the three gasoline station and ticket office robberies Monday night, hinging their belief on the report that the same car was seen at the B. & O. ticket office Monday afternoon and parked near the Canal late in the afternoon and early in the evening.

Krebs told police the third member of the trio, who is short and dark was the one who came into the ticket office and asked for the information pertaining to a train schedule.

The Middletown Journal, March 18, 1930

In closing, Rick says that when Clyde was taken to police headquarters, at first he claimed to be Robert Thorn, 17, of Indianapolis. 'He insisted he was a hitchhiker in the car when first chased by police that morning but Chief Kolodzik had already been in contact with Waco authorities and put the pressure on Barrow. As his story quickly crumbled, he admitted his true identity and to being the third Waco escapee. He did however lie about his age, as he had done in Texas, hoping for leniency. Middletown police filed charges of burglary against all three for all the reported break-ins the previous night although prosecution was deferred to the more serious charges awaiting them in Texas. The Waco authorities arrived on Friday (March 21), headed by McLennan County Sheriff, Leslie Stegall, who took custody of the three men, and all were back in Texas the following day.'

Having carried out more car thefts and committed armed robbery all within a week of escaping from prison, the judge in Waco now ruled that instead of serving his seven two-year sentences concurrently, Clyde would now spend the full 14 years in the State Pen. He was transferred to Huntsville (see page 23) on April 21. This unretouched mugshot has been copied from the last original print in Clyde's official file held by the Texas Department of Criminal Justice Classification and Record Division. In September 1930, Clyde was shipped out from the 'Walls' to continue his sentence working on the prison farms located a few miles to the north of Huntsville near Weldon: Eastham Camp 1 and Eastham Camp 2. And it was at the former camp that some say that Clyde killed for the first time in October 1931. *Below:* The 'Old Camp' was built in 1917 and had a reputation for brutality and prisoners were routinely whipped or beaten. High-riders on horseback would trample any would-be escapees and the only certain way of getting transferred was self-mutilation.

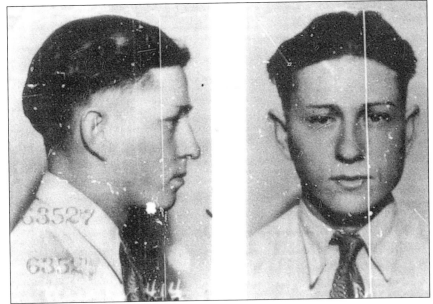

October 29, 1931 – Eastham Camp 1, Weldon, Texas

Rude dirks fashioned from old files, flashed at the fist fight at the Eastham Prison Farm, Weldon, last night, and took the life of Ed Crowder, 30-year old desperado from Houston. Crowder died from 15 stab wounds in the chest and back.

Aubrey Scalley, 30, under 50-year sentence from Dallas County for highway robbery, is being held under guard in the barracks here in connection with the stabbing.

Captain B. B. Monzingo in charge of the farm, said the fight came without warning about 11 o'clock last night.

Crowder and Scalley occupied adjoining bunks in the barracks here. For some reason — I have not found out — they got to quarrelling. Other prisoners told me they suddenly drew home-made knives and went at each other. The men locked in a death grapple in the dim light — a few lights were left burning all night in the barracks as a protection against breaks under the cover of night. They swayed back and forth trying to get their arms loose for a murderous thrust.

Other convicts scattered from the two men. It is sort of an unwritten law among convicts that when two men have a grudge to settle they let them fight it out.

Finally the men broke apart, knives flashed and Crowder sank to the floor with 15 wounds in his body. Scalley received a few minor wounds. By that time guards had arrived on the scene. They took Crowder to the hospital, and he died there a few minutes afterward. Scalley's wounds were treated and he was placed under guard.

Scalley and Crowder were about the same size and weight and worked together cleaning up the barracks, seeing that the water barrels were filled and other tasks about the buildings.

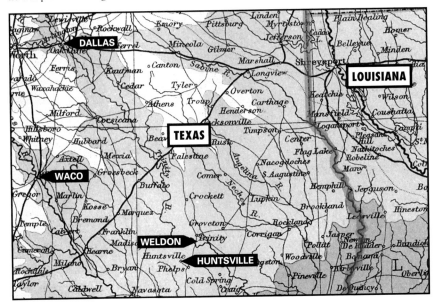

As these were work camps, prisoners were not held in separate cells but slept together in large dormitories. Violence became a way of life — both from the guards and other prisoners — and Clyde was picked on by 'Big Ed' Crowder. According to one account, Clyde was 'bought' for three packets of cigarettes and the brutality he suffered changed him 'from a schoolboy to a rattlesnake'. Clyde's sister says (in *Fugitives — the Story of Clyde Barrow and Bonnie Parker* to which she contributed with Bonnie's mother) that 'he saw a "lifer" knife a young boy to death before his eyes one night' and that 'the incident ate into Clyde's mind'. However, Ralph Fults (see page 12), was one of the inmates at the time, later becoming a member of Clyde's gang for a short while, and his biographer John Neal Phillips says that 'the family never knew the full story'. He says in *Running with Bonnie and Clyde* that 'Clyde found a short length of pipe and concealed it in the leg of his trousers. As soon as he stepped in from the fields, Clyde baited the hook by walking toward the toilets after the other prisoners had finished there.'

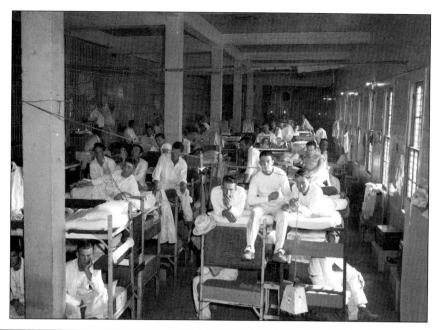

It is believed they got in a quarrel over their duties that smouldered during the day an burst into a mortal combat just before midnight.

'Seizing any opportunity to catch a victim alone, "Big Ed" closed in while Clyde was pretending to urinate. With Aubrey [*another prisoner serving a life term*] looking on, Barrow suddenly spun around to face Ed, who stood near a large concrete column [*the last one in the picture at the top of the page. Ed.*], smiling at the small convict. Without a word, Clyde lunged forward, weapon in hand. "Big Ed" never felt a thing. He crumpled to the concrete floor in a bloody heap, a piece of his skull torn away. Aubrey quickly pulled his knife, cut himself on the abdomen, and sank the blade deep into the man's ribs. By the time the guard on duty was able to pick his way through the gathering crowd, Barrow had returned to his bunk. The guard took one look at Aubrey, then examined "Big Ed" lying face up near the commodes. He merely shook his head and turned away. The incident was never investigated. Everyone knew of Ed's belligerent nature, and his passing was not mourned. The massive head wound went unnoticed. No one cared.'

An entry on Houston police records to the effect that Ed Crowder was reported 'stabbed to death in a fight with Aubrey Scalley at prison farm,' had 'closed the books' Friday.

Crowder's body is being held here while a sister in Houston gets in touch with other relatives in Oklahoma.
The Houston Chronicle, October 30, 1931

The camp was closed in the 1950s and gutted for storage. The comparison *(centre)* was taken for us by Bruce Moore who also matched up the interior shot of the old dormitory *(above)*, now sub-divided, where Crowder is said to have been killed.

As 1931 drew to a close, two of the major players in America's gangland were taken out of circulation. On October 24 Chicago's Public Enemy No. 1, Al Capone, until then regarded as impregnably entrenched in his underworld of bootlegging, prostitution, corruption and murder, was in the end found guilty of simple income tax evasion. Although he was cleared of 18 of the 23 counts against him, he was sentenced to ten years to be served in a federal penitentiary for three felonious violations of the income tax law plus an additional year in the county gaol for two convictions of not filling in tax returns. He was also fined $50,000 and had to pay prosecution costs of over $7,600. 'The pronouncement of the sentence yesterday morning was dramatic,' wrote one reporter present in court. 'Judge Wilkerson's words, sharply clipped and incisive, rang clear in the hushed court — a small chamber crowded with two hundred persons. After curtly dismissing all the legal arguments offered by defending counsel, Judge Wilkerson ordered the defendant to the bar. Ponderous of body, neatly dressed in a heather-coloured suit and wearing a white silk handkerchief in the breast pocket, Capone stepped slowly forward, his jet-black and piercing eyes fixed on the grim-faced judge and his hands clasped behind his back. As the judge pronounced the maximum sentence for each conviction, Capone's eyes hardened and his fingers locked and unlocked. The final pronouncement hit Capone like a slap in the face. Flushed and angry, his round, usually placid face contorted into lines of sullen hatred, he turned, to be confronted by a marshal and two deputies who led him away.' To ensure that the fines were paid, the government put attachments on Capone's palatial Florida house, his business properties, including gambling dens and vice houses, and even his personal wardrobe! Judge Wilkerson refused bail and, as he was being led away, he was served with a demand for unpaid taxes of $137,324. Capone began to serve his time in Atlanta, the toughest of the federal prisons, but in August 1934 he was transferred to the new top security prison, Alcatraz (see page 201). Capone was released with remission in November 1939, spending his last years in Florida. Although he always feared being cut down in the street from a machine gun hit, in the end he died of a heart attack on January 25, 1947.

Gangland America

Two months after Capone was sent down, America's second best-known criminal was shot dead in a cheap boarding house in Albany, New York. Jack 'Legs' Diamond had got his nickname as a 'lad with legs' during his criminal beginnings as a petty thief before the First World War. By the time the war was over, Diamond had seen the inside of two prisons, first as a burglar and then as an army deserter. He joined Jacob 'Little Augie' Orgen and Arnold 'Mr Big' Rothstein as their top enforcer and was so efficient at dealing with the opposition, that he was eventually put in charge of some of their rackets. Backed with a loan of $200,000, he was even sent to Europe to purchase drugs but was refused entry to Britain, and when he arrived on the Continent, Belgian police merely escorted him on to Germany. Having attracted much press coverage, he was forced to return to the States empty-handed. By 1924 he had his own Hotsy Totsy Club on Broadway where he was fawned over by the society women of the period. As his biographer Dr Gary Levine wrote (in 1979): 'The public avidly followed his

wild parties, his arrests, his battles with rivals, and his love affairs'. He also bore a charmed life, achieving yet another sobriquet: 'the clay pigeon of the underworld' when he survived several attempts on his life. He was critically wounded when Little Augie was murdered in October 1927; shot five times three years later when gangsters sought repayment of money Diamond owed their boss, and survived a shotgun blast in April 1931. When he emerged from hospital he proudly declared: 'I made it again. Nobody can kill Legs Diamond. I am going to settle a few scores just as soon as I get my strength back. Just you wait and see.' However, within days he was indicted on prohibition charges although he reputedly bought his acquittal by bribery. In December he was again on trial, this time for kidnapping a 17-year-old truck driver who he tortured to reveal his supplier, but again he was found not guilty. After celebrating his freedom he returned to his room, worse the wear from drink, and collapsed on his bed. Within the hour he was dead, shot three times in the head as he slept.

As far as the Barrow family were concerned, 1931 ended badly for them with both Marvin and Clyde in prison. *Above:* Buck had married Blanche in July (see page 11) while still an escaped convict and her father did his utmost to persuade his new son-in-law to return to prison to finish his sentence. Blanche *(right)* and his mother Cumie added their pleas and finally, at the end of the year, he agreed, providing he could spend Christmas at home. So on December 27 the family drove him back to Huntsville, where he knocked on the front door, much to the surprise of the warden, W. W. Waid. In fact, the warden was so impressed at Buck's voluntary surrender that he admitted him without increasing his sentence for having escaped.

Clyde, on the other hand, had been behind bars since the Middletown robbery in March 1930. His mother never ceased in her efforts to get the sentence amended from the judge's ruling that the various terms would be consecutive. If she could get this changed to concurrent, it would mean that Clyde would only serve two years instead of 14. Clyde was well aware of his mother's campaign on his behalf as he revealed in a letter to Bonnie just before Christmas 1930: 'Sugar, mother just about got my time cut to two years and I have been down here eight months already. If she does get it cut it won't take long for me to shake it off.' However, as Nell, Clyde's sister, explained, 'for many months it looked as if she would not be successful. Just before Clyde was released, in a moment of despondency, despair, and utter hopelessness with life, he had asked a brother convict to chop off his two toes with an axe so that he would be taken within the Walls and released from drudgery in the fields. This revolting incident had just occurred when Clyde's pardon was obtained on February 2, 1932. He came home to us on crutches.' Thus, as one brother entered prison, the other was released. 'My sister and I took him downtown and bought him a complete outfit, except shirt and gloves. Clyde insisted on a silk shirt and kid gloves and he walked us all over town until we found them. Back home that night, my sister and I had a serious talk. There was a new air about him — a funny sort of something that I could not quite put my finger on — but Clyde had changed.' In her efforts to get Clyde on the straight and narrow, Nell got him a job on a construction site in Worcester, Massachusetts, well away from the bad influences in Texas, but within two weeks he had quit. He returned to Dallas on March 17, much to Nell's anger that he had not stuck it out. 'I'll tell you this Clyde Barrow', she swore, 'you better not get involved ever again with that bunch you ran with before you went to the pen or you will end up dead for sure.' 'Don't worry sis,' replied Clyde, 'I've learned my lesson.' The background in all three photos looks similar and we know the one of Clyde *(left)* was taken pre-Joplin as another frame in the series (see page 112) was published on April 15. So the pictures of Buck must be dated between March 22, when he was released from Huntsville, and April 13, when the film was captured in Joplin.

In the folklore of the United States, if the six-gun tamed the West and the railroad opened up the continent, then the automobile conquered America. Distances in the States are vast so the motor car was — and still is — an essential part of the American way of life. Consequently, oil production — particularly in Texas — was booming. Henry Barrow saw the trend and, after he had the family home *(right)* moved from its original location near the Texas and Pacific railroad tracks to a new site on Eagle Ford Road, he laid plans to add a canopy and petrol pumps *(below left)*. As the map shows, the road was the main drag west out of the centre of Dallas so it was an ideal spot for a gas station which Henry believed would give him and Cumie a steady income in their old age. The work was nearly finished when Clyde returned home in March 1932.

PALESTINE. Another area of development in the Anderson county oil field was reached when gasoline from the new refinery located four miles north-east of Neches was turned into the pipe lines of the Humble Oil and Refining company and carried to loading stations in both Neches and Jacksonville.

This refinery, although not completed in all its detail, is doing business. The deliveries to the loading stations are for railroad shipments to points more than 50 miles distant from the plant. Big tanker trucks will furnish delivery to all points within a radius of 50 miles of the new plant.

The Humble Oil and Refining company, owner and developer of the local oil field, has completed a number of stations in Jacksonville and other East Texas towns and is building three stations in Palestine.

SAN ANTONIO. Two offsets to the company's R. C. Appling No. 1, new Guadalupe county gusher, have been announced by the Magnolia Petroleum company. South offset to the well, production of which was estimated at the rate of 6,400 barrels daily after it came in last week, will be on the L. V. Echols tract. A south-west offset will be on another tract.

GONZALES. Operations in Gonzales county are beginning to take on considerable proportions, as shown by the extensive leasing in nearly all parts of the county.

BRENHAM. Oil development will start in the near future in the Niederauer block, about two miles north of Brenham. A derrick has been erected on the T. S. Estes place, machinery has arrived and drilling will start by November 1.

Several thousands of acres have been leased for oil purposes, and geologists who have made surveys are hopeful that some good producers will be brought in.

MIDLAND. High points of field activity in the West Texas Permian basin during the past week comes from an extension affected in the Fisher county area, a well of unusual performance in Upton county, and the Pecos county area.

Houston Post-Dispatch, October 27, 1929

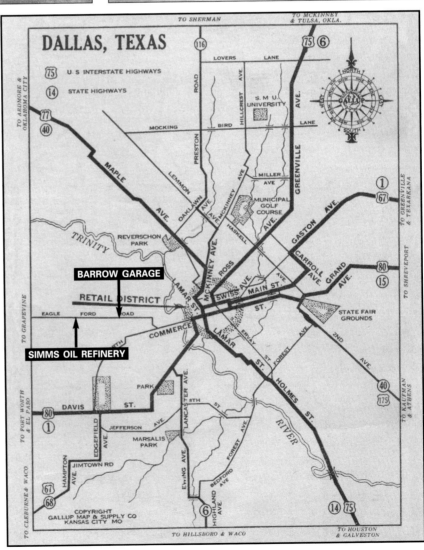

42

March 25, 1932 — Dallas, Texas

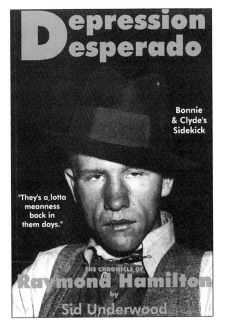

Whatever declarations of reform Clyde may have given to the judge in Waco, or sister Nellie in Dallas, it was all insincere for no sooner had he returned home than he was planning a robbery — right on his own doorstep! As oil was the 'in' thing, what better than to break in to the offices of an oil company, and one lay conveniently a few blocks further down the Eagle Ford Road at No. 2435. *Above:* Backing on to the railway line, this is the site the Simms Oil Refinery occupied in the 1930s. Clyde's companions on this raid were two ex-cons — both of whom have since left their indelible mark on criminal history. *Left:* The career of Raymond Hamilton — at one time billed in Texas as Public Enemy No. 1 — was documented by Sid Underwood in 1995. *Right:* The following year John Neal Phillips published his research into the life and times of Ralph Fults. *Below:* Two more Bonnie and Clyde desperados of the 21st century, James R. Knight (right) and Jonathan Davis, released their excellent update at Gibsland in May 2003 and guided your editor around the Dallas locations . . . which included re-creating the break-in to the Simms compound!

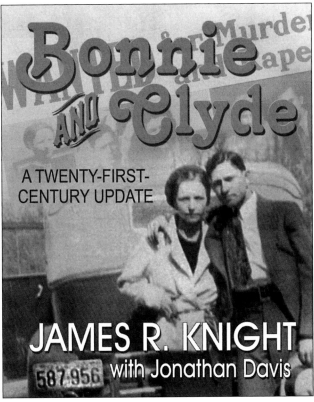

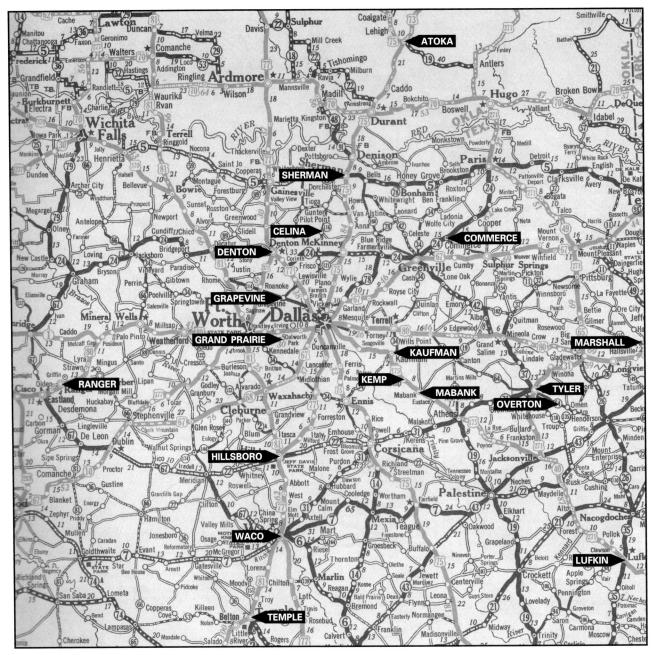

April 18, 1932 – Mabank, Texas

WELCOME TO
MABANK, TEXAS
EST.1900

The Simms robbery was a fiasco. After cutting through the perimeter fence at the back near the railway tracks, taking four employees hostage and bashing open the safe with a club hammer and cold chisel, it was found to be empty. Ralph Fults was legally free on a pardon but Hamilton was an escapee from McKinney jail, having cut the bars of his cell with hacksaw blades supplied by Fults. The whole purpose of the Simms operation was to raise sufficient funds to provide weapons and recruit manpower to mount a raid on Eastham Farm prison camp to free as many of the inmates as possible. Life at the place had been a living hell and Clyde and Fults wanted retribution. Apart from undertaking sorties with Fults to sound out possible accomplices, Clyde took Bonnie to the prison to act as a go-between to pass on a message about the impending operation and on April 17 she mingled with the visitors posing as the cousin of one of Clyde's friends — a further step on her part along the road to a life of crime. We have highlighted Mabank *(left)*, and other towns relevant to the Bonnie and Clyde story, on this road map of 1933.

A man and a woman, two of three alleged store burglars, were in the Kaufman county jail here Wednesday following a gun-battle with officers at 7 o'clock Tuesday evening in the mud bottoms of Cedar Creek, west of Mabank. The man, resisting arrest by allegedly firing, was wounded in his left arm when a deputy returned the fire. The third member of the trio escaped by running, after all the others had failed in an all-day attempt to escape with allegedly . . . looted goods.

The following day Clyde and Fults set out to steal a couple of cars to be used in the getaway and Bonnie, now committed, went with them. When she left home she told her mother that she had got a job with a company in Houston demonstrating cosmetic products. Reaching Tyler, they stole a Buick and a Chrysler before heading back to Dallas. On the way down they had stopped in Mabank where Fults purchased some ammunition at Bock's gun shop on East Market Street *(above)*.

The trio used their feet, two mules, two automobiles and pistols in an effort to escape.

David Drennan, Mabank chief of police,

said he surprised the two men and a woman early Tuesday attempting to burglarize the H. Bock store at Mabank. They ran to an automobile parked nearby and drove west.

Fults' post-war recollection was that the store was located in nearby Kaufman but his memory was at fault as all the press reports prove otherwise. Bock's gun shop was here at No. 121 — now The Dance Connection. Fults told Clyde that the store was well supplied and he proposed that they call back after hours that night and relieve Mr Bock of some of his stock.

Cruising into town at midnight, they drove up to the rear of the building (indicated *above* by Marty Black) but the suspicions of the town's police chief Dave Drennan had already been aroused. As they were working on the padlock on the door, Drennan approached, pistol in hand. Clyde opened fire and the police officer fired back before raising the alarm. Meanwhile Bonnie was crouching on the floor of the car. With the town about to wake up there was no option but to beat a hasty retreat.

Their car stalled in the mud of Cedar Creek bottom west of Mabank. The trio immediately appropriated two mules, one of them known for its pitching, and rode the stolen animals five miles to Kemp. When they reached Kemp they exchanged the mules for an automobile without the consent of either of the owners. They started back toward Mabank again, being forced to abandon their automobile when they struck the Cedar Creek bottom mud.

Then they fled on foot, but officers, trailing them throughout the day, drew closer. Finally, Drennan and his deputy spied them about 7 p.m. Officers said the two men began to shoot and the deputy returned the fire. One of the men was wounded in the arm and captured. The other ran.

The wounded man and the young woman, who said they were from Dallas but did not give their names, were taken to Kaufman, the county seat. Officers believed they were close on the trail of the third member of the party in the Cedar Creek bottom.

Questioned about their feat of staying on the pitching mule for five miles, the alleged burglars said they had ridden in a rodeo at Tulsa.

The automobile first abandoned was registered in Tyler. Officers believed it was stolen.

The Kaufman Daily Herald, April 20, 1932

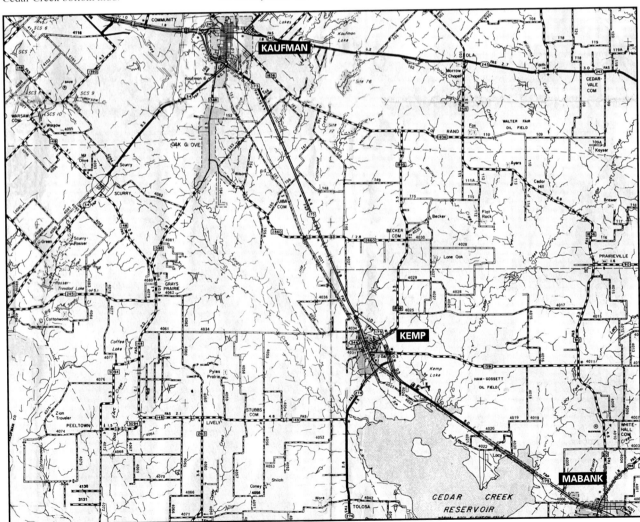

Bonnie Thornton, 23, whose home was said to be in Dallas, and Ralph Fults, who told Kaufman county officials his home was at McKinney, two of a trio of alleged Mabank burglars, today were pondering over their unsuccessful attempt to escape officers after a pursuit that covered much of the south part of the county, as charges of burglary and two charges of theft were drawn against them.

The two must face trial here on charges of burglarizing the H. Bock store at Mabank, alleged theft of two mules and charges of automobile theft.

Fults, who first said Tulsa, Oklahoma was his home, was suffering from a wounded left arm, sustained when members of the trio fired after Chief of Police David Drennan of Mabank, Deputy Marshal Jeff Pledger and Ollie Alexander closed in upon them following an all-day pursuit. The officers returned fire. Fults and the young woman surrendered after being shot but the third member of the trio escaped and had not been apprehended late this afternoon.

According to a report from Athens today, the trio were believed implicated in the theft of a third automobile in connection with the burglary at Mabank. The bandits abandoned their first car, a 1931 Chevrolet sedan, at a point a mile beyond Eustace.

The Kaufman Daily Herald, April 21, 1932

The two cars raced north towards Kemp — a route impossible today as the road dead ends where it meets the new bypass (which are called beltline roads in the US).

A few hundred yards further on they hit Cedar Creek. Today the highway crosses the marshland on an embankment *(above)* **but in the 1930s this could well have been the course of the old road** *(below)*. **And it was here that the affair degenerated into a Keystone Cops saga. The cars bogged down and as Police Chief Drennan and Officer Ballard, who had given chase, approached, the trio mounted two mules and splashed through the mud five miles north to Kemp. There a second automobile was stolen but, instead of continuing north, they drove back south again towards Mabank! This car when it reached Cedar Creek also mired at which point they continued their flight on foot. As the officers closed in, a gun-battle ensued in which Fults was wounded and Bonnie captured. Clyde managed to elude his pursuers, steal another vehicle in Kemp, and eventually make his way back to Dallas.**

The officers reported that they relieved Fults (who later identified himself as Jack Sherman from Tulsa) of an automatic pistol but the mud-splattered girl carried no weapons. She claimed that she had played no part in the fight and didn't know what she had done during it. They were both taken to Kemp — this is the main street today *(above)* where most of the shops are closed — and both put in the calaboose which lies at the western end of 11th Street *(right)* on open ground behind the town hall (called a city hall in the US). Reportedly, the tiny lock-up — whose usual occupants would be local rowdies or drunks — was surrounded on this occasion by 30 armed men and was visited by many curious townspeople. At 4ft 10ins, Bonnie would barely have been able to look out of the two small barred windows unlike our 5ft 2½in 21st century 'moll'.

The Kemp calaboose has to be the most unique building still standing from the whole Bonnie and Clyde era, knowing that she spent the night locked up here with Fults. And the interior is completely free of graffiti and rubbish — unbelievable in this day and age after some 70 years! 'I remember my momma going down there to look at Bonnie', recalls Abbie Lou Williams, 'and Bonnie got so mad she spit in my mother's eye. That really tickled my father as no one ever had the nerve to stand up to my mother before!'

Left: The next morning, April 20, they were taken to Kaufman and lodged in the city jail, an imposing building constructed in 1884 facing Washington Street. *Right:* The ornate building was torn down in 1953, all that is left being this single block of stone. Yet the inscription which accompanies it is the most damning indictment of what is now euphemistically called

'progress' that we have ever come across . . . anywhere in the world during over 30 years of producing *After the Battle*: 'Let these fragmented remains of the historic old courthouse which once stood on this spot remind us of the loss of our heritage due to apathy and misguidance so that we may zealously regard and preserve that which remains.'

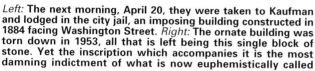

Name	Bonnie Parker			Leave This Space Blank
Alias				F.P.C.
No.	Color W	Sex F		Ref.

RIGHT HAND

1. Thumb	2. Index Finger	3. Middle Finger	4. Ring Finger	5. Little Finger

LEFT HAND

6. Thumb	7. Index Finger	8. Middle Finger	9. Ring Finger	10. Little Finger

Officer's Signature	Prisoner's Signature
Date	X *Bonnie Parker*

Four Fingers Taken Simultaneously			Four Fingers Taken Simultaneously	
Left Hand	L. Thumb	R. Thumb	Right Hand	

We discovered Bonnie's prints in the files of the Missouri State Highway Patrol. Although the only place she was ever imprisoned was Kaufman, 500 miles away, it would appear that they were requested by Ed Portley, the Chief of Detectives in Joplin, following the fracas there the following year. She languished in Kaufman for two months and, when she appeared before the Grand Jury, she claimed that she had been kidnapped and did not know who the two men were. These were early days in the Bonnie and Clyde story and their names were yet to be linked by police. Fults offered to plead guilty to armed robbery and another theft if the woman was set free; he received a sentence of 15 years while Bonnie regained her freedom on June 17.

49

Suicide Sal . . . by Bonnie Parker

We each of us have a good "alibi"
For being down here in the "joint;"
But few of them really are justified
If you get right down to the point.

You've heard of a woman's glory
Being spent on a "downright cur,"
Still you can't always judge the story
As true, being told by her.

As long as I've stayed on this "island,"
And heard "confidence tales" from each "gal,"
Only one seemed interesting and truthful —
The story of "Suicide Sal".

Now "Sal" was a gal of rare beauty,
Though her features were coarse and tough;
She never once faltered from duty
To play on the "up and up".

"Sal" told me this tale on the evening
Before she was turned out "free",
And I'll do my best to relate it
Just as she told it to me:

I was born on a ranch in Wyoming;
Not treated like Helen of Troy;
I was taught that "rods were rulers"
And "ranked" as a greasy cowboy.

Then I left my old home for the city
To play in its mad dizzy whirl,
Not knowing how little of pity
It holds for a country girl.

There I fell for "the line" of a "henchman",
A "professional killer" from "Chi";
I couldn't help loving him madly;
For him even now I would die.

One year we were desperately happy;
Our "ill-gotten gains" we spent free;
I was taught the ways of the "underworld";
Jack was just like a "god" to me.

I got on the "F.B.A." payroll
To get the "inside lay" of the "job";
The bank was "turning big money"!
It looked like a "cinch" for the "mob".

Eighty grand without even a "rumble" —
Jack was last with the "loot" in the door,
When the "teller" dead-aimed a revolver
From where they forced him to lie on the floor.

I knew I had only a moment —
He would surely get Jack as he ran;
So I "staged" a "big fade out" beside him
And knocked the forty-five out of his hand.

They "rapped me down big" at the station,
And informed me that I'd get the blame
For the "dramatic stunt" pulled on the "teller"
Looked to them too much like a "game".

The "police" called it a "frame-up",
Said it was an "inside job",
But I steadily denied any knowledge
Or dealings with "underworld mobs".

The "gang" hired a couple of lawyers,
The best "fixers" in any man's town,
But it takes more than lawyers and money
When Uncle Sam starts "shaking you down".

I was charged as a "scion of gangland"
And tried for my wages of sin;
The "dirty dozen" found me guilty —
From five to fifty years in the pen.

I took the "rap" like good people,
And never one "squawk" did I make,
Jack "dropped himself" on the promise
That we make a "sensational break".

Well, to shorten a sad lengthy story,
Five years have gone over my head
Without even so much as a letter —
At first I thought he was dead.

But not long ago I discovered
From a gal in the joint named Lyle,
That Jack and his "moll" had "got over"
And were living in true "gangster style".

If he had returned to me sometime,
Though he hadn't a cent to give
I'd forget all the hell that he's caused me,
And love him as long as I live.

But there's no chance of his ever coming,
For he and his moll have no fears
But that I will die in this prison,
Or "flatten" this fifty years.

Tomorrow I'll be on the "outside"
And I'll "drop myself" on it today:
I'll "bump 'em" if they give me the "hotsquat"
On this island out here in the bay . . .

The iron doors swung wide next morning
For a gruesome woman of waste,
Who at last had a chance to "fix it",
Murder showed in her cynical face.

Not long ago I read in the paper
That a gal on the East Side got "hot",
And when the smoke finally retreated,
Two of gangdom were found "on the spot".

It related the colorful story
Of a "jilted gangster gal".
Two days later, a "sub-gun" ended
The story of "Suicide Sal".

'Only a mother can appreciate my feelings when I walked into that Kaufman jail and saw Bonnie behind the bars', wrote Mrs Parker. 'Death would have been much easier. It was while she was waiting for the Grand Jury to meet that she wrote her *Suicide Sal* poem. Bonnie was 'Sal' and Clyde the perfidious 'Jack' who threw Sal down. It is clear from the numerous quotations used that Bonnie was learning the jargon of gangdom and striving desperately to fit into it and become part of it.

To my inner consciousness there seemed to be a strange and terrifying change taking place in the mind of my child!' Although this is the final published version of the poem which was begun in Kaufman jail, it is believed that Bonnie polished it over the next year, viz, the reference to — 'the island out here in the bay' — Alcatraz — which she would not have known about in 1932. *Suicide Sal* first became public knowledge when a copy was found in the Joplin apartment in April 1933.

April 20, 1932 – Celina, Texas

Three unmasked men robbed two stores in Celina Monday night, knocked the night watchman on the head with a revolver, locked up the Mayor and two companions in a box car on the Frisco Railroad, robbed them of $16 in all, stole the keys out of Deputy Sheriff 'Dutch' Stelzer's automobile, to cut off pursuit, and headed south shortly after 12 a.m.

Although none of the men have been identified by anyone with whom they came in contact, the Collin County Sheriff's department is on the trail of a suspect.

The men first walked up to Nightwatchman Floyd Perkins, asking him the address of a certain party there. When he gave them the desired information, one of the men knocked him in the head with a six-shooter and left him.

A little farther down the street they met Mayor Francis and two companions, the only persons on the streets at that time, shortly after 12 o'clock. They took him and his companions to a box car on the Frisco Railroad tracks, robbed him of $14, one of his companions of $1.50 and the other of 50c, locked them in the car and continued on their foray.

Next, they entered a drug store, gaining entrance through the back door. However, they evidently desired nothing there, everything being left as usual, according to the proprietors.

From the drug store, they journeyed next to a hardware store on the public square, gaining entrance as in the first operation through the back door. They took two shotguns from the shelves and apparently took some shotgun shells also. Shells were strewed all over the floor.

Still desperate to get his hands on some weapons, two days after the abortive attempt to steal guns in Mabank, as Bonnie was pining for him in Kaufman jail, Clyde appeared with three associates in Celina — a small town some 30-40 miles north of Dallas (see map page 44). *Top:* **This picture, taken for us in May 2003 by Karin Ramsay, shows the Celina Drug Store (just behind the STOP sign), which was broken into by mistake. By coincidence, a local gun shop is now on the right indicated by a sign: 'Longhorn Gun & Tackle — Celina Gun Club'.** *Above:* **Karin explains that 'the railroad tracks are barely 20-30 yards away from the hardware store which was subsequently robbed of the shotguns. This is where Celina's Mayor, F. M. Francis, and friends were locked inside a box car.'**

The bold intruders then 'swiped' the keys out of Deputy Sheriff 'Dutch' Stelzer's car, cutting off pursuit, and headed south in their own car.

In conversation with these editors Thursday morning, Deputy Sheriff Claude West said that although the Sheriff's department has no definite knowledge concerning these bold bandits, Sheriff Ed Blakeman and his force are on the trail of a suspect whom they think will lead materially toward solving this unprecedented West Collin raid.

McKinney Courier Gazette, April 21, 1932

Karin found the hardware store closed and boarded up for rent.

A rear upstairs entrance is visible behind the fence.

With so many petty crimes being committed during the Depression years, identification of the perpetrators was as difficult for the police then as it is for them today. This hold-up in Lufkin is a good example: was Clyde involved or not? It has the hallmarks of his modus operandi but on the face of it there was little to link it to him. Yet over the next two years, many crimes would be attributed to the 'Barrow gang' — rightly or wrongly — because they were convenient scapegoats, both for the police, the press, and even for other criminals anxious to offload their own evil deeds. The murder which follows is a good example.

April 25, 1932 – Lufkin, Texas

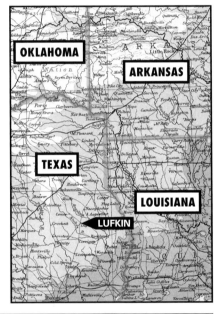

Two service station operators on South First Street were held up at the point of six-shooters last night near 12 o'clock and robbed by two well-dressed but unmasked men, the cash register of the two places being relieved of something like $10 each.

The hijackers stopped first at the Magnolia station on South First and Burke Avenue, following the operator, Kenneth Bevins, into the office after he had filled up the tank of the Chrysler car of the two strangers with gas where a pistol was shoved into his face with the request to 'put 'em up' when the young man had registered up the sale and was securing change.

After rifling the register, the hijackers made Bevins get into the car, where he was kept quiet under threat of immediate death. They then drove off and stopped at the Gulf service station on South First, just beyond the residence of E. J. Conn where young Miller in charge of that station, was held up and his register rifled. He, too, was forced into the car under threat of death if he made an outcry.

The two young men were then rapidly driven something like four miles out of town to the south and made to get out of the car with the hijackers making a turn around and returning to this city. The Chrysler car was found on South Raguet this morning and the assumption is that the robbers had another car located somewhere in the city, which they evidently entered and left Lufkin in.

The two men were utter strangers to the service station boys, with their coolness and determination in issuing orders and the fact that they were well-dressed being impressed upon those compelled to obey their orders.

A description has been given to the city and county officers, and every effort is being made for their apprehension, with the change of cars being in favour of their making a complete getaway.

Lufkin Daily News, April 26, 1932

Unfortunately, as we have found at many other locations, very few buildings from the 1930s survive today in the States. So many were built of timber and, when the wood rotted, they were just pulled down. And also no one thought that they would have had any historical significance 70 years later. When we contacted Lufkin, Cindy McMullen in the Kurth Memorial Library replied that 'there are no longer any garages located in the downtown area'. *Top:* 'This is First Street today and *(left)* the location of the Magnolia station at the junction with Burke Avenue.' *Right:* 'The Gulf garage was here on a site now occupied by several retail businesses.' Both Clyde and Ray Hamilton were later identified as the robbers by their fingerprints.

52

April 30, 1932 — Hillsboro, Texas

John N. Bucher aged 61, was instantly killed at midnight Saturday night by two unidentified bandits. Mr. Bucher, who is one of the pioneer garagemen and expert jewelers, lived in an apartment with his family immediately above the garage, filling station and jewelry store he operated. A few minutes before midnight he was called by name from outside the filling station, and upon

Hillsboro in Hill County lies 50 miles south of Dallas (see map page 44) and it was here in the early part of the century that John Bucher *(below)* **set up shop. (Of German extraction, although his name omits the 'sch' it is still pronounced Boosher.)** *Above:* **His main store was on the town square but the scene today** *(right)* **is poor by comparison with the excitement of yesteryear. Mr Bucher sits at the wheel of the Rambler on the right.**

Although all American vehicles are now left-hand drive, this was not always the case — look at the Ramblers! Prior to the introduction of the LHD Model T Ford in 1908, early automobiles duplicated the seating arrangement of horse-drawn transport where the driver sat on the right.

John Bucher combined his training as an optician with dealing in precious metal and gems — hence the large safe which stood inside the shop — a tempting target.

By April 1932, John Bucher had branched out to cash in on the motoring era and had moved from the centre of town [1] to new premises [2] on the road to Fort Worth where he had the facility to dispense fuel. *Left:* Although the road has now been superceded by Highway 77, the old Fort Worth road is still labelled as such on the map. *Right:* And its gravel surface remains! This is exactly how it must have looked in the 1930s when Clyde and two accomplices drove under this railway bridge on Saturday, April 30 on a mission which was to have far-reaching repercussions.

answering, he was informed by the person calling that they wanted to buy some guitar strings, and Mr. Bucher went downstairs and turned on the lights in the store and let the prospective customers into the place.

The case containing the guitar strings is at the back of the store. The customer followed Mr. Bucher to the show case and after getting the strings for him, they went back to the front of the store. As they went to the front another man entered the store. The purchaser of the strings tendered a $10 bill to pay for the strings, and Mr. Bucher, not having the change, called his wife to come down stairs and open the safe for him so he could get change.

Mrs. Bucher came down and opened the safe and as she opened the door of the safe and turned around the bandit shot Mr. Bucher one time, the bullet passing through his heart and out of his back, killing him instantly. As Mr. Bucher fell a pistol he had in his belt fell to the floor and was picked up by Mrs. Bucher, but the bandits forced her to place the gun on the counter and

remain still. One of the bandits then stepped over the body to the safe and secured between $15 and $40 in cash and about $2,500 worth of diamond rings. After rifling the safe, the bandits went out by the front door and seemingly vanished. It was not known whether they came to the place by automobile or left that way and no car was heard come or to leave.

Immediately after the bandits left, Mrs. Bucher notified the sheriff's department by telephone, from the apartment above the shop and the officers were on the scene of the murder in just a few minutes. At an early hour Sunday morning the murderer was still at large.

Mr. Bucher had been in the jewelry and automobile business in Hillsboro for the past 30 or 35 years. He was an excellent mechanic, and in the days before the advent of the automobile, conducted a bicycle rent and repair shop in connection with his jewelry business, and when the automobile appeared, he was one of the very first owners in Hillsboro of the new vehicle.

Mr. Bucher is survived by his wife, two daughters and two sons of Hillsboro who lived with him in their apartment above the filling station, and one son of Dallas.

He had many friends in this city and elsewhere that mourn his death. Throughout Sunday many people viewed the body at the Marshall & Marshall funeral home.

Declining to divulge what clues he and his force did have in the John Bucher murder case, Sheriff Jim Freeland stated Monday morning that the chances of solving the case and arresting the murderers looked brighter today, and it was his belief that the pair would be placed under arrest within the next few days. He did not predict an immediate arrest.

Following the tragedy Saturday at midnight, every officer in surrounding towns was notified by telephone of the murder and asked to look out for the pair. Sheriff Freeland and members of his force toured the countryside during the early hours of the morning and after a short rest the entire force again resumed their tour.

Clyde had been pally with Mr Bucher's son and was known by sight to the family so, when the idea surfaced to rob the safe, he volunteered to act as driver and wait outside in the car. With Clyde were Ted Rogers and an associate of Ralph Fults known just as 'Johnny'. Earlier that Saturday they first decided to 'case the joint' to check that the safe was still there so Johnny was sent inside on the pretext of purchasing a knife. Here, in the company of the local historian Cleo Davis, who personally knew the Bucher's son Oscar (since deceased), we arrive to case the joint in May 2003.

Clyde's plan was to return late that night and get Mr Bucher to open up with the excuse that they needed some strings for a guitar. They assumed that any loose cash would be locked in the safe so, by proffering a large bill in payment, they hoped this would make Mr Bucher unlock it.

Two men, said to be well-known police characters, were arrested in Fort Worth by the police department of that city on the belief that they might have been the men wanted. Members of the sheriff's department went to Fort Worth and brought the pair to Hillsboro Sunday afternoon, but on being taken before Mrs. Bucher she failed to identify the men and according to Sheriff Freeland, it is his positive belief that the men are not the two sought. They were being held in the county jail here, awaiting Bosque county officers. Burglary charges are said to have been filed against the pair in that county.

All Sunday and Monday morning, the sheriff's office has been crowded by residents of all sections of the county who have come in to hear about the developments in the case.

Hillsboro Evening Mirror, May 1, 1932

Cleo Davis discusses the changes made to the building with George May who lives there with his brother's family. In 1932 the house was split-level but since then it has been completely re-modelled. At the time of the robbery, the doorway lay between the two front windows and one went down steps into the shop. Inside there was another set of stairs leading up to the living quarters. After her husband was killed, Mrs Bucher raised the floor level and removed the upper area.

Back on that fateful Saturday evening, while Clyde waited outside with engine running, the other two awoke Mr Bucher and persuaded him to open up, saying they wanted a guitar string. It only cost 25 cents so when he was offered a $10 note, John Bucher called up to his wife to come and open the safe. As soon as she had done so Ted Rogers produced a pistol but, reaching inside the safe, Mr Bucher pulled out his own gun. At this point, Rogers fired, the bullet hitting Mr Bucher in the chest. While Johnny restrained Mrs Bucher, the contents of the safe were scooped up and the gang departed. *Above;* Not much chance of a robbery today with around 30 dogs roaming the place!

On Monday afternoon John Bucher was laid to rest in Ridge Park Cemetery ([3] on the map on page 54).

Funeral services for John N. Bucher, who died at his home in the northern city limits of Hillsboro, shortly after midnight Sunday morning as the result of gunshot wounds, were held at the First Baptist church Monday afternoon at 3 o'clock with Revs. Alvin Swindell and Melvin R. Cox officiating. Interment was in the Ridge Park Cemetery under the direction of Marshall & Marshall.

A large crowd of sorrowing friends attended the funeral and the floral offerings were very beautiful.

Sheriff J. W. Freeland announced Tuesday that Governor Ross Sterling has issued a proclamation offering a reward of $250 for the arrest of parties guilty of killing John N. Bucher, Hillsboro jeweler, Saturday night.

Hillsboro Evening Mirror, May 3, 1932

Sheriff Jim Freeland informed a *Mirror* reporter Friday morning that he had secured some valuable information, that he believes will help him and his force to bring the murderers of John Bucher to justice. The past two days members of the sheriff's department have visited adjoining counties seeking additional information on the case.

There have been no more arrests in the case. Thursday afternoon, Sheriff John Lewis of Bosque county en route to Meridian from Waco with two prisoners stopped in Hillsboro to have Mrs. Bucher view them but she failed to identify the pair and Sheriff Lewis carried them on to Bosque county.

Hillsboro Evening Mirror, May 6, 1932

Cleo points out his grave in the family plot to Texas lawman and Bonnie and Clyde aficionado, Ken Holmes.

In the John Bucher murder case two rumors that floated over Hillsboro Saturday afternoon were blown sky high later in the evening when Sheriff Jim Freeland, Deputy Sheriffs Bob Wilkinson and Kelly Rush and Mrs. John Bucher returned from Dallas after viewing Fred Mace, wounded in a gun-battle with Dallas police officers shortly before midnight Friday evening.

During the day Saturday, it was positively reported through rumors that the wounded man had been identified as one of the murderers. The Hillsboro officers and the widow of the slain man viewed the wounded man

and two other suspects, but none of the three were the men wanted as they were larger than the murderers.

It is known that the Hillsboro officers are seeking two men, that are believed to have police records, and since the murder have not been seen by officers in any section of the state.

The second rumor about two men being arrested in Kansas while trying to dispose of the Bucher diamonds was something that the local officers had not heard about and they denied that any such thing had happened.

The Hillsboro Evening Mirror, May 9, 1932

Raymond Hamilton, 19-year-old west Dallas desperado whose name has been blazoned across newspaper front pages almost daily for the last several months, faced two juries Wednesday within twelve hours before Judge Noland G. Williams in criminal district court No. 2. To both indictments of robbery Hamilton pleaded not guilty. He was sentenced to thirty years in one case and twenty-five years in the second.

The first jury began studying the Cedar Hill State Bank robbery case at 4 p.m. and returned its verdict at 5.30. The second jury began hearing testimony at 6.45 p.m. and at 8.45 p.m. went to its quarters to consider a verdict.

District Attorney Robert L. Hurt announced Wednesday night he would not try Hamilton on the indictment alleging he robbed the Cedar Hill bank again on November 25, but Hamilton will be tried Monday at Hillsboro on a charge of murdering J. N. Bucher, filling station operator, last April.

The Hillsboro Mirror, February 1, 1933

A special venire of 100 men was drawn Monday for the Raymond Hamilton murder case scheduled for trial in district court Monday morning March 13. The defendant is charged with the murder of John Bucher, Hillsboro businessman.

The case was called at the last term of district court, but was passed on the motion of the defense. The date of March 13 was set for the trial at the time case was passed.

The Hillsboro Mirror, March 8, 1933

Sheriff Jim Freeland issued this appeal in Monday's local paper. Later it was followed up by the distribution of the wanted poster *(below)* naming a Frank Clause and Clyde Barrow. These mug shots had been sent down from Dallas to be shown to Mrs Bucher but no wonder she was confused as there is not much facial difference between them. Being guilty of murder, even if only an accessory, put Clyde in a totally different category; now he was running from the law big time and the name 'Clyde Barrow' took on a whole new meaning. Although Ted Rogers was arrested on an unrelated charge a few weeks later, he was never connected with the Bucher murder — instead Raymond Hamilton, with whom he bore a very similar resemblance (see page 12), was implicated as the second man. Although Raymond was in Michigan at the time, his name was now firmly in the frame as John Bucher's murderer. He was arrested in December and, after facing an identity parade in Dallas for robberies at Grand Prairie and the Dallas Neuhoff Packing Company (see page 59), he was sent down to Hillsboro. After two attempts at identifying Hamilton, Mrs Bucher finally agreed that he was the man who had killed her husband. Returned to Dallas to face the armed robbery charges, in January 1933 he was found guilty and sentenced to 55 years. Now he was due to face the murder rap in Hillsboro.

$250.00 REWARD

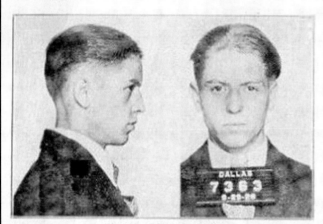

FRANK ALBERT CLAUSE

Frank Albert Clause—Description as follows: Age 21 to 22, weight 123 to 125, height 5 ft. 9½ inches, hair blond eyes hazel, complexion light, build slender. Tatoo, left arm. Heart-Love, right arm. Kewpie.

F. P. Class

32	0	18
4	1 M	

CLYDE CHAMPION BARROW

Clyde Champion Barrow—Description as follows: Age 22 to 23, height 5 ft. 6 inches, weight 135 pounds, eyes brown, hair dark and wavy, complexion, medium fair, build medium, said to walk with a limp, brown mole point of right shoulder. Tattoo, Heart-Dagger, Letters E. B. W. left front arm, Shield and Letters, U. S. N. and Girls Head right arm.

F. P. Class

29	MO	9
26	U	00	6

I hold Felony Warrants for the Parties whose Photographs appear above—

These parties are wanted for the brutal murder of J. N. Bucher on night of April 30th, 1932, and the robbery of his place. Articles taken were as follows: $35.00 to $40.00 in money taken, 71-100 carat ladies' ring in white mounting, three 51-100 carat ladies' ring in white mounting, five 33-100 carat ladies' rings in white mounting, one 51-100 carat ladies' ring in white mounting, five ladies' rings in white mounting, ranging from 25 to 15 points, one old model 45 caliber Colts pistol, blue barrel.

Our information is that these parties range from Fort Worth, Dallas, Waco, San Antonio, Houston, into the oil fields of East Texas. We hope to see these parties arrested in the near future, and receive the $250.00 reward offered by the Governor of Texas for the parties who committed this crime. Take no chances on them as they are desperate men. Barrow is out of Penitentiary on furlough at present.

J. W. FREELAND, Sheriff Hill County, Hillsboro, Tex.

The 'interurban' at Grand Prairie (see map page 44) was an electrically powered street tramline running between Dallas and Fort Worth. Up to 1934 the North Texas Traction Company serviced the transportation needs of the area and a similar service ran south to Waco. However, the advent of buses finally killed off the line after having run for 30 years. *Right:* This picture taken in 1911 shows the office which stood between Center and Southwest 2nd Streets.

July 29, 1932 — Grand Prairie, Texas

Last Friday, when all was quiet around the interurban station, two boys entered the lobby and leisurely sauntered to the ticket window. Almost instantly Agent Speer was invited to look down a gun barrel, the second fellow making his way around the cage, placing another gun near his head while he nervously ransacked the cash drawer. Completing the job as they thought they backed out and made their getaway in a practically new Chevy.

The alarm was given but the burglars got away, driving at high speed down the Belt Line Road toward Cedar Hill. Pursuing parties found an abandoned Chevy out near the cemetery but the men had gone.

Checking the losses at the station, Mr. Speer said they got away with $12.75 in cash, but left him $10.50 in another part of the drawer.

The abandoned car proved to be that of Mrs Buddy Swadley, which she left parked at the school building, where she is teaching a summer class. When she closed her class and started home she missed the car. The men took her car, staged the hijacking and drove to their own car parked near the cemetery.

The Grand Prairie Texan, August 5, 1932

For three months it appears that Clyde and Ray — now also a marked man — kept their heads down, the next robbery accredited to them not taking place until July 29 when they stole a pittance from the Grand Prairie interurban office. After the service was discontinued, the track was lifted and a second carriageway added to Jefferson Street. Today there is no trace of either the line or the office building.

The two bandits had stolen a car belonging to a teacher at the Alternative High School three blocks away. *Left:* This is where it stood on College Street. *Right:* Travelling south via Center Street, when they reached the cemetery at Southwest 3rd they dumped Mrs Swadley's Chevrolet and made good their escape. This was Clyde's first identifiable robbery since Bonnie had been released and when she returned to Dallas she declared that she was finished with him. 'I'm through', she told her mother, 'I'm never going to have anything more to do with him'. Famous last words! Bonnie was besotted with Clyde and no sooner was she back in Dallas then they ran off together — with Ray in tow — to Wichita Falls on the Texas-Oklahoma border. They only returned at the end of the month for the interurban job. Next on the list was the Neuhoff Packing Company.

From the Neuhoff Packing Company . . . to the American Airlines Center. This is where the next hold-up took place on Alamo Street on Monday, August 1. Clyde was not yet ready to use Bonnie as their driver but he told her to listen to the radio to find out if they had been successful. Instead, he and Ray took along Ross Dyer to act as wheelman. The involvement of Clyde in this particular robbery was not known until Hamilton's trial in January 1933.

August 1, 1932 – Dallas, Texas

Although he was twice tried Wednesday in two robbery cases and given sentences totalling fifty-five years in prison, and District Attorney Bob Hurt has elected not to try him again at this time on a third robbery indictment, Raymond Hamilton, debonair West Dallas gunman, Thursday was not through with his courtroom worries.

He has admitted he fears worst of all the 'murder rap' at Hillsboro where he will be taken Monday for trial on an indictment alleging he shot and killed J. N. Bucher, filling station operator, last April 30, during a hold-up.

Hamilton's two trials Wednesday, one for the robbery of the Cedar Hill State bank last October 8, when $1,401 was taken by a lone gunman, and the hold-up of the Neuhoff Packing Company last August 1, when approximately $400 was taken by two bandits were peculiar in that the defendant entered pleas of not guilty in each case, at the same time offering no testimony whatever in his defense.

After the Cedar Hill bank robbery case went to the jury, Judge Williams himself questioned prospective jurors and trial was begun shortly in the Neuhoff robbery case. Hamilton also entered a plea of not guilty in this case.

Henry Neuhoff, president of the firm, positively identified Hamilton as one of the two hold-up men. Asked who the other man was Neuhoff replied, 'He was Clyde Barrow.' This was the first time Barrow's name had been brought into the trials. Another witness to identify Hamilton in the Neuhoff robbery was Miss Elsie Weischlager, former bookkeeper for the company. She, too, said the other man was Barrow. Joe Neuhoff, secretary-treasurer of the company, also identified Hamilton.

All three witnesses told about the same story of how Hamilton and Barrow came into the company offices during the afternoon while Miss Weischlager was placing money in the company's pay envelopes. One of the men kept the trio covered while the other scooped up all the money. They ripped the two telephones from the wall before departing. They backed out of the offices, jumping off a loading dock to a waiting automobile in which a third man was believed to be waiting.

Dallas Times Daily Herald, January 26, 1933

Gentlemen gangsters! In sharp suits with fedoras at a rakish angle, Clyde and Ray look much older than their years, even though this snapshot is believed to have been taken early in 1934 during the brief period when Hamilton rejoined Clyde. Ray was then 20 and Clyde 24.

August 5, 1932 – Stringtown, Oklahoma

For the first time in more than twenty years an Atoka County officer has fallen victim to the gun of a desperado when Undersheriff E. C. Moore was shot and instantly killed by bandits at a dance at Stringtown about 11 o'clock last Friday night and Sheriff C. G. Maxwell was wounded so desperately that his recovery is still doubtful.

It has now been definitely established that there were at least three or four of the outlaws in the party, which had stolen an automobile at Corsicana, Texas, on Friday morning and had driven as far as Stringtown where they stopped at the dance.

Sheriff Maxwell and his Undersheriff Moore had gone to the dance to keep order. They noticed suspicious actions of the quartet and approached them as two of the men climbed into a car and one of them started to tilt a bottle of whisky.

'You four can consider yourself under arrest,' Sheriff Maxwell said as he and Moore walked up to the car. Neither had his gun out.

The desperadoes without a word opened fire and Moore fell with a mortal wound. He never drew his weapon. Sheriff Maxwell crumpled with pistol wounds in his chest, side, arm, wrist and leg, but he drew his gun and emptied it as the killer car sped away.

The slayers went only a short distance when they overturned the machine, a car with a Texas license. They commandeered one belonging to Cleve Brady (sic) of Stringtown and fled eastward.

The Brady car served them until they reached a point some fifteen miles east of Stringtown, near the home of John Redden, when a wheel came off. They secured another car at Mr. Redden's, telling him that their car had been wrecked down the road a distance and they wanted to take an injured person to a doctor. After getting in the Redden car they ordered Mr. Redden's son, who was driving it, to head east, continuing in that direction until the vicinity of Clayton had been reached, where they took the car belonging to Frank Smith of Seminole, in which they continued the journey back to Texas.

On August 5, Bonnie wanted to spend some time with her mother in Dallas so Clyde, Ray and Ross decided to have an evening out. Piling into a car that they had stolen in Corsicana, they headed for the Oklahoma border, 70 miles to the north. Distances meant nothing to Clyde so after crossing the Red River which forms the state line, they continued driving up what was then known as the Jefferson Highway. Five miles north of Atoka they came on a dance in full swing out in the open air at Stringtown. It was a lovely evening so the boys decided to pull over and have some fun — as any young males might do out on a Friday night. *Top:* **This is where it was held although the building was not standing at the time.** *Right:* **Duke Ellis, then 17, was playing in the band that night and clearly remembers their car pulling off the road and parking behind the dance platform which lay between him and the new building. When the shooting started, Duke ducked down behind the rock structure which then surrounded the well on which he is standing but it was not big enough so he ran to take better cover in an old garage.**

Sheriff Charles Maxwell with his deputy Eugene Moore must have suspected that the whisky-drinking Texans were likely to cause trouble but as they approached the car (note that there were only three occupants, not four as reported in the press), they were met with a fusillade from the pistols of Clyde and Ray Hamilton. *Left:* 'Gene', as Moore was known to his fellow officers, was killed instantly. *Right:* He fell just to the right of the telegraph pole. Sheriff Maxwell was hit several times but managed to draw his gun and empty it as Clyde pulled away. Several other lawmen present also fired at the car. The plan *(below)* was prepared for us by staff of the Atoka County Historical Society.

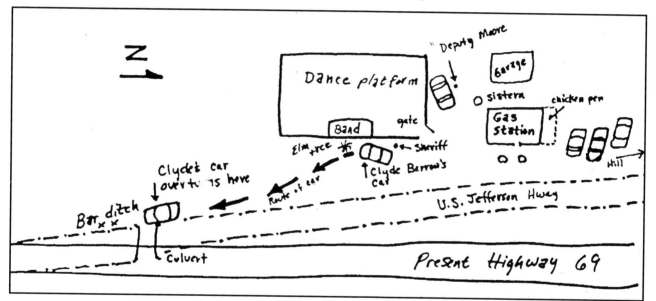

The Smith car was recovered on Sunday at Grandview, near Dallas, Texas, and was brought back here and delivered to its owner.

The possies of local officers and citizens chased the desperadoes all night and the greater portion of the next day. The bloodhounds were brought from McAlester as it was thought they might take to the hills on foot but the dogs were useless as matters worked out.

The entire force of the State Bureau of Identification, with the exception of one man, came down from Oklahoma City immediately after being notified to assist in the chase. Those from the state were: C. A. Burns, chief, O. P. Ray, former sheriff of Atoka county and assistant chief, C. M. Reber and DeArthur Wilson. Sheriffs and deputies from Coalgate, Antlers, Durant and McAlester also lent their assistance.

As Clyde gunned the car, in his haste it overturned in this culvert. The three outlaws climbed out and split up. Clyde and Ray heading across the railroad tracks on the far side of the road and into Stringtown.

That evening Robert Cates was out dating a young lady, Miss Betty Sue Scott. When he took her back home, they discovered that the Barrow gang had attempted to steal the car belonging to her father, Robert Scott (who incidentally, was Eugene Moore's father-in-law). When Mr Scott's car would not start they proceeded to the home of Walter Thacker. This is the 'Blue House' from where Clyde and Ray relieved him of his car.

The Thacker family were out visiting that evening and were sitting on the porch of brother Bill's 'Green House' *(above)* when they saw their stolen motor drive by. According to Duke, someone immediately jumped up and shouted: 'Hey, there goes our car!' (Note that the press report on page 60 is incorrect — there was no one by the name of 'Cleve Brady', known to be living in Stringtown at the time.)

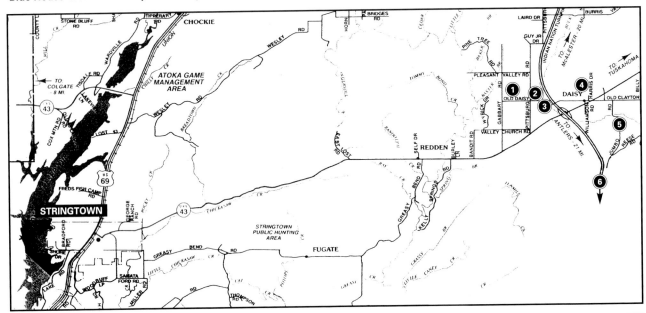

Travelling east on Highway 43, the Thacker's car got them as far as Daisy Road [1] where they ran out of gas. *Left:* It is still a dirt road today. *Right:* Clyde and Raymond then walked to this crossroads where the home of John Redden stood [2]. It was now midnight but they still awoke the family, giving the excuse that they had a woman in labour in the car further down the road and needed to get her to a doctor urgently.

Mr Redden offered his stepson Haskell Owens and his stripped down mail truck to take the woman to the doctor. Mrs Redden later stated that when the truck pulled out and turned the wrong direction from where the invented pregnant woman was supposed to be, she yelled out to her son. One of the men shouted back that they decided to go and get a doctor and bring him back.

Now this is a real bonus as it is not often we have been able to find an original bridge, crossed by Clyde Barrow, still in situ'.

After kidnapping Haskell Owens and exappropriating his vehicle they crossed Buck Creek [3] on the map.

Left: The pick-up was not very comfortable to travel on the back roads so Clyde stopped outside this store in Daisy [4] where they asked Guy Kellogg if he knew of a suitable vehicle. *Right:* Kellogg was not very helpful so, before turning right onto Jumbo

Road [5], Clyde and Ray argued as to whether they should go back and kill him. *Below:* In the event they decided not to waste time but to carry on but when they reached Cole Creek [6] the pick-up lost a wheel attempting to ford the stream.

Above: **From Cole Creek, Clyde and Ray, still holding Haskell captive, walked to Ed McDonald's house. The McDonalds had just won a new Ford car at the McAlester Trade Days a couple of weeks earlier and it was now standing outside.** **The outlaws shouted from the yard that they were 'Pretty Boy' Floyd and to throw out the car keys or have their roof shot off whereupon the McDonalds threw out the keys. (The house has been remodelled since the 1930s.)**

Above: **This is Needmore Corner near the McDonald house, named after a store which used to stand on this spot. Here Jumbo Road met the main highway *(below)* to Clayton, a journey of some 25 miles over the Jack Fork mountains.** **En route they ran out of gas but when another vehicle was seen approaching, they sent Haskell to shelter behind a tree 'because there might be trouble'. They quickly commandeered the car and promptly disappeared into the night.**

So what happened to Ross Dyer, reported in the press under his alias of Everett Milligan? When Clyde overturned the car trying to escape from the dance, Dyer simply walked to the nearest bus stop which stood outside this gas station and caught the next bus back to Texas . . . only to get caught as soon as he got there by the law!

Duke Ellis explores the site of the old gas station in April 2003. Ross Dyer was sent back to Atoka on August 12 and charged with murder, as were Clyde Barrow and Raymond Hamilton in their absence. However it appears that Dyer was never brought to trial, which led the Barrow family to believe that he shopped Clyde in exchange for his freedom.

Positive identification of the two who escaped was furnished Sunday by Constable H. Hunt of Grandview, Texas. One of them is Clyde Barrow, wanted for murder of J. Bucher, a merchant of Hill county, Texas, and Raymond Hamilton, pal of Barrow and wanted for hijacking and other crimes.

The third man was arrested at McKinney, Texas, and was identified as Everett Milligan of Dallas. County Attorney J. B. Maxey and special officer L. C. Harris went to McKinney and brought Milligan back to Atoka for questioning. He was later taken to the penitentiary at McAlester for safe keeping. He took a late bus out of Stringtown after the murder and was arrested by officers at McKinney upon information furnished from Atoka.

Another man, who possibly may have been the fourth of the criminal band and giving his name as James Acker of Winsboro, Texas, was found by a tourist car dangerously wounded near the Red River bridge south of Durant and taken to the Denison hospital. It has later been established that he has a criminal record in Texas and was removed from the Denison hospital to the jail at Sherman. According to his story he had been shot by a man who picked him up and robbed him of $7.00. However, there is a well-grounded suspicion that he is the fourth man of the murder party.

The Indian Citizen-Democrat, August 11, 1932

On Sunday, August 7, the funeral service was held for Eugene Moore who had been serving as Undersheriff of Atoka County for just over a year. He had married a Stringtown girl, Minnie Scott, in 1923 and they had three children: Charline aged eight, Billy June, six, and little Dwight Russell eight months.

After the service conducted by the Reverend H. O. Morris, Moore was taken to Calera, his boyhood home in Bryan county backing onto Texas, where he was laid to rest. Sheriff Maxwell eventually recovered from his wounds and died in June 1953 aged 73.

At Hillsboro, Clyde was an accessory to murder but his involvement in the Stringtown killing (usually described in press reports as taking place at Atoka, the nearest large town) well and truly destined him for the electric chair if caught. Now that he and Ray were clearly identified as the killers, the heat was really on and Clyde knew that he could never again openly visit his family on Eagle Ford Road. Any future meetings would have to be at a secret rendezvous . . . but meanwhile they had to lie low. It is believed that it was Bonnie who suggested they go to New Mexico to visit her aunt and uncle, Mr and Mrs Melvin Stamp, who lived at 522 North 6th Street *(above)* in Carlsbad.

August 13-14, 1932 – Carlsbad, New Mexico

Exhausted but otherwise uninjured, Deputy Sheriff Joe Johns early today was put out the car, in which he had been a hostage for nearly 24 hours, near San Antonio. The two men and a woman, who kidnapped Johns when he went to investigate a report that they acted suspiciously and had a number of guns, fled in the V-8 Ford coupe in which they left here.

Johns was the object of one of the greatest man hunts ever staged in the Southwest in which, it is estimated, nearly 300 men participated. The search had centered around the country south-west of here and it was believed that the trio would flee with Johns to the Mexican border.

Johns was called to the Stamp home near the canal west of the city early Sunday when Mrs. Stamp became suspicious of the two men who arrived last week with a niece of hers whom she had not seen or heard of for many years. The niece introduced one of the men, James White, 20 or 22, as her husband. The other man gave his name as Jack Smith, 19.

The men had a large sum of money with them and also several diamonds. Mrs. Stamp told sheriff's officials. Stamp, however, denied today that he or his wife had called officers.

Stamp stated that Johns had been looking the car over for several minutes when the two men came out of the house and ordered the officer to stick his hands up. Johns backed off, but seeing that the men meant business, did as ordered.

The men drove off after putting the ignition on Johns' car, and on another car nearby, out of commission. They fired one or two shots into the ground, Stamp said.

Officers here stated that the car in which the trio fled with Johns was registered at Rusk, Cherokee county, Texas.

White was described as being light complexioned with keen brown eyes. He was about 5 foot 2 inches tall and weighed about 130 pounds. Smith was about 5 foot 6 inches tall and would weigh 135 pounds. He was of a reddish complexion with sandy hair and blue eyes. The woman was very slender, about five feet, one inch, and would not weigh more than 85 or 90 pounds it was said.

The Daily Current-Argus, August 15, 1932

When Bonnie arrived unannounced, she introduced Clyde as her husband 'Jim', and Ray as his friend 'Jack'. Aunt Millie had no idea of the trouble they were in but her suspicions were soon aroused when her niece asked her to wash some blood-stained clothing. At the time, Mr and Mrs Stamp had let five acres of their land to Bill Cobb *(left)* on which he was growing cantaloupes (small melons). 'I was irrigating my patch when I first saw them', recounted Bill in 1997. 'At first I thought they were just schoolkids visiting but they were out by my can-taloupes practicing shooting. I was upset when they started shooting at them and was headed down there to jump them out when the motor died on my irrigation pump. By the time I got it fixed they had stopped shooting.' Some time later Mrs Stamp asked Bill to come up to the house *(right)* and look at something she had found under the mattress. 'There were solid packs of money — the most money I ever seen', he recalled. She also showed him the bloodstained clothes and then asked Bill if he would help her with a pretense so that she could call the law. Mrs Stamp told Bill to go back to watering his patch and she would come down as if to help him. She would then slip off to a neighbour's house to phone Deputy Sheriff Joe Johns.

Joe Johns had been sheriff of Eddy county from 1927-30 but now that he had served his time he was carrying on in the role of deputy. On receiving the call, he drove out to the Stamp's farm in his old Studebaker. Bill, who was watching events from behind his own car, remembers seeing Johns take the keys out of the car that was standing in the yard and throw them towards the fence. Then he saw the two men come out of the house. 'They shot at old Joe but he ran over by the chicken house.'

Police of three states searched Monday for two west Dallas men as Dallas detectives added the kidnapping of a Carlsbad (New Mexico) deputy sheriff to the growing list of crimes including murder and hijacking, which the officers say they have checked up against the men sought.

Dallas detectives were in communication with New Mexico authorities after the search for Deputy Sheriff Joe Johns ended in the morning when the deputy walked into the sheriff's office at San Antonio and told of being kidnapped by two men and an 18-year-old girl. Reports Sunday night said the decapitated body of Johns had been found ninety miles north-east of El Paso. The description of the girl fitted that of a Dallas girl who detectives said has been identified as a frequent companion of the two west Dallas men.

Detectives and deputy sheriffs who have sought the two men for several months redoubled their efforts with the hope that the two men would come to Dallas from San Antonio, where the abducted deputy was released.

New Mexico police joined Texas and Oklahoma police departments in the search for the men after being given information by Dallas police regarding their identity.

The two men are sought also in connection with the slaying of a deputy recently at Atoka, Oklahoma, for murder and robbery of a merchant at Hillsboro, for the robbery of Neuhoff Packing Company on Alamo and for numerous other crimes.

The Hillsboro Mirror, August 17, 1932

Mrs Stamp then came out of her back door only to fall to ground. Fearing that she had been hit, Bill ran over thinking the worst but when he reached her he found that she had just fainted.

'I threw some water over her face I got from the ditch.' This is the Stamp house as it appears today, photographed for us by Valerie Cranston.

While I was investigating the car west of Carlsbad of the two men and the woman who stuck me up, and after I had ordered them to get dressed and come to town with me, the two men suddenly appeared behind me and ordered me to stick up my hands. I started to reach for my gun but a warning shot from a shotgun fired into the ground made me change my mind and I put my hands up. The girl called 'Bonnie' then appeared and our wild drive started.

That feeling of thinking that you are near death is hard to describe. I wasn't nervous but kind of half resigned to it, but with the determination that I would take every chance offered to battle them should the time actually come for the end.

I don't think that I was as nervous as was Barrow who drove all the way. When he threatened to kill me once I told him that I guessed it was his business.

For the first time in my life I worked against the law as I routed the bandits around towns where I was afraid we would run into danger which might result in my being murdered.

I routed them around Odessa and after leaving there we all felt, I think, that most of the danger lay behind us, at least in-so-far as a shooting fray with the law was concerned. However, there remained the danger of an auto wreck as we weaved in and out among traffic and along slippery, muddy roads at 60 and more miles per hour.

After hitting a mud hole at one place which so covered the windshield with mud that the driver couldn't see through, he leaned out the door and drove at 70 to 80 miles an hour. How he drove like he did without wrecking the car I can't imagine. They did take off one or two bumpers as they sped past cars along the road.

On the whole they treated me pretty good although they kept a gun on me most of the time. Toward the last they did get a little careless but they never did give me a slight chance to get away without being practically certain of getting killed.

Occasionally they threatened me but as they let me go about 15 miles out of San Antonio. At 5:35 o'clock Monday morning the leader of the trio, whose name Dallas authorities say is Clyde Champion Barrow, shook hands with me. 'You shore have caused us a lot of trouble sheriff,' he said. I told him that he had caused me just a little trouble, too, and not a little worry. 'You haven't been bothered much,' he said as he drove off.

They asked me if I had enough money to get home on and as I happened to have some with me I told them yes. They never offered to rob me excepting that they took my gun. One of them looked at it as if he meant to give it back to me and then said, 'No sheriff, this is a pretty good gun, I guess I'll have to keep it.' They told me that if I didn't have enough money they would get it and I was afraid that they planned to high-jack somebody.

They made me promise that I wouldn't start any place for an hour and I took out my watch and waited quite a while. I heard a car coming and I thought that it might be them so I went off in the brush. After a while I decided to come out whether or not I met them.

I was a pretty tough looking customer when I approached a house as I had been wading through more than a mile of sticky mud and was haggard. At two different places when I asked if I might use a phone they wouldn't let me. One place they told me they didn't have a phone and when I told them I saw the line and told my story and offered to lay my bill-fold down and go off a ways until they could satisfy themselves as to who I was, they told me to go away, that they didn't want to bother with me.

Soon I came to a big house and saw some Mexicans nearby. I talked to them in Spanish and told them about my experiences and they told me to go up to the house and waved to a chauffeur. I handed him my bill-fold and asked him to go in the house and show it to the owner and call for the sheriff to come after me.

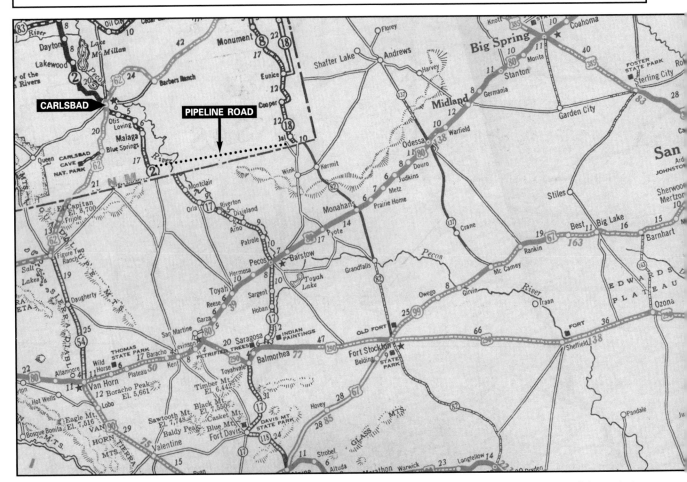

Unfortunately Deputy Johns could not recall the precise route after leaving New Mexico but this is the road map of the period.

The owner, C. J. Webster, a big oil man, came to the door and told me to come in. He told me to use the phone and when I finished sent me out on a big veranda where I had the first food since leaving Carlsbad. Neither the bandits nor myself had eaten a bite. Then Webster sent me into the sheriff's office in a big limousine.

Once when the bandits stopped the two men went to sleep and the girl, Bonnie Parker, asked me how I liked being a thief. I told her I never had had much experience — that this was the first experience I had ever had. 'You've had just 24 hours of it now,' she said, 'and we get 365 days of it every year.'

The men woke up then and said that they had tried to quit but couldn't. They said that the law wouldn't let them and told me that they had quit but that before they could get rested up after coming to New Mexico, I had gotten after them and started them again.

Of course I agree that they couldn't quit but the law isn't what keeps them from quitting. 'If we ever get caught, it's the electric chair for us,' one of them told me. That is the only implication they ever made to having killed anyone which Texas authorities claim they have done.

Shortly after leaving Carlsbad Sunday morning they wanted to come back and kill Mrs. Stamp. She had gone down on her knees and begged them not to hurt me when they left her home. They told her to shut up but they did say they wouldn't hurt me.

When they suggested going back and killing Mrs. Stamp I said, 'Oh, don't do that fellows.' They didn't say anything but kept right on driving.

They dropped me and the fellow called Raymond Hamilton by Dallas officers, but who gave his name here as Jack Smith, out of the car just before we got to Delaware and the others went on to get gas, returning in a very short time.

They put me back in the middle with Barrow, or White as he called himself here, driving, Hamilton on the outside and

Former sheriff Joe Johns (centre) flanked by Charles Wilson and Ray Zumwalt at the inauguration of Joe Johns Park in 1963.

the girl on his lap — just as we rode throughout the day and night and sped east along the pipeline road.

We turned south just before reaching Jal and missed Wink, going through Kermit and Monyhans but cutting around through Crane to miss Odessa. Then we wound around through the country on to San Antonio.

Once Hamilton and the girl dropped off to sleep and Barrow woke them up. 'Here,' he said, 'you wake up and tend to your business or we'll put the sheriff out.'

I didn't question them much but did a lot of listening. Once they talked in a slang or language that wasn't familiar to me. Another time, sometime late at night, they drove up before an old abandoned place and slowed up. 'Here's the place,' Barrow said. What he meant I never did know and they drove off.

SHERIFF JOE JOHNS, AUGUST 17, 1932

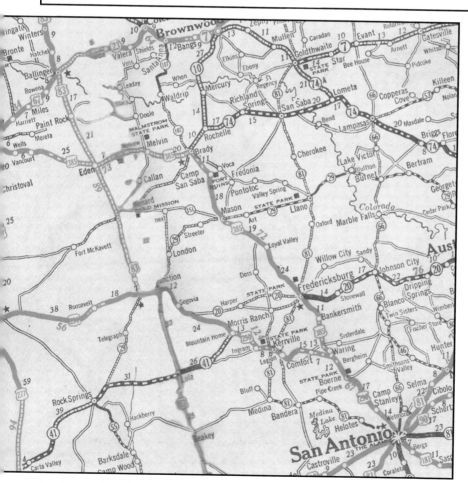

The distance from Carlsbad to San Antonio must have been in excess of 500 miles.

We asked local historian Jed Howard to comment on the route taken by Clyde. Jed writes: 'Our US Highway #285 [2/17 on the old map] runs south-east from Carlsbad to Pecos, Texas, and it was this particular road that Bonnie and Clyde took. (At the time there were still no paved roads in this corner of the state, so all of that fast driving was done on poorly graded dirt roads.) You will recall that they drove to Orla, Texas, where they got gas, but that is not really a town. It was simply a cattle loading pen on the railroad in the middle of nowhere that by 1930 had gained a single small filling station and nothing else. Orla is little more than that today and it isn't even named on many modern road maps. After getting gas they back-tracked to the state line to pick up their other rider, and then turned east, taking a privately developed road that had just recently been built across that area. In the late 1920s, a 1,000 mile natural gas pipeline had been constructed from the Texas oil fields to California. The company that built it (El Paso Natural Gas Co.) also developed a service road that ran beside the pipeline — a road that had its own bridge across the Pecos River. There is a small tributary to the Pecos River called Delaware Creek that joins the Pecos from the west very near that state line. The pipeline and its service road closely followed the creek to dip around the Guadalupe mountains to the west, and so the group was able to turn east on this pipeline road right at the Delaware, cross the Pecos, and avoid both towns and police for many miles. Pipeline Road still exists, as does the pipeline, and is used quite a bit by ranchers and hunters, but it has never been put on the road maps since it is, I think, still dirt, and since it was never a part of the public road system.'

With four people cramped in the coupe, no doubt Ray Hamilton and Bonnie were pleased when Clyde stopped outside San Antonio just after 5.30 a.m. on Monday morning (August 15) to let out Sheriff Johns. After the long 500-mile drive, the sheriff was dog-tired and had to rest before starting back to New Mexico. No doubt Clyde also needed a break as it was six hours before they were spotted 100 miles to the east — a distance that he would normally cover in a couple of hours. They needed another vehicle as two cars were always a good insurance against break-downs or the frequent blow-outs caused by high speed driving over poorly maintained back roads. It was shortly after noon that the Ford coupe appeared in the town of Victoria from where the road would lead straight to Houston via the bridge acrosss the Colorado River at Wharton.

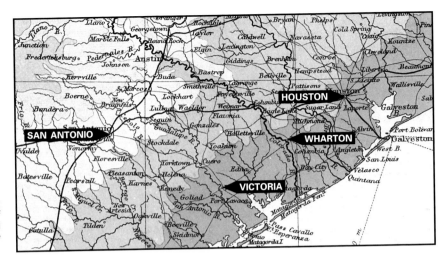

August 15, 1932 — Victoria/Wharton, Texas

Turning off Rio Grande Street, travelling south down Glass Street and left onto Stayton, the Ford coupe drove up and parked here (left) outside No. 205 West Stayton Street. A driveway (right) led to a four-car garage belonging to the Tracy

Apartments which faced North Glass Street around the corner. Although most of the other houses in the neighbourhood date from the 1930s, unfortunately the original building and garage were razed 20-30 years ago.

The garages were set well back from the street. Assuming that Clyde stayed behind the wheel of the coupe, it was Ray Hamilton who got out and walked towards a new 1932 Ford V-8 sedan belonging to Mr C. H. Hawkins, an agent with the local

Sinclair Oil Company. Mrs Hawkins had been out in the car and had just returned and driven up to her garage. She then went to her apartment from where both she and her husband witnessed the theft of their car.

A neighbour who also witnessed the cars driving away gave chase as they turned onto Rio Grande *(right)* **heading for Houston but he claimed later that engine trouble stopped him from overtaking the cars 'and giving the occupants a good whipping'. After he found out who he had been chasing, his complexion is reported to have significantly paled!**

While police of three states searched for two men wanted for questioning in connection with the kidnapping of a Carlsbad, New Mexico, Deputy Sheriff and recent murders and robberies in Texas and Oklahoma, three persons, two believed to be the hunted suspects, engaged two peace officers of Wharton in a gun-battle near Wharton, and escaped toward Houston late Monday.

Dallas deputy sheriffs who received a report of the shooting early at night were given the license number of a coupe abandoned by the men and said it was the same number as that of the coupe used by two men and a girl in the kidnapping of the Carlsbad deputy.

The Wharton police tried to stop two automobiles in which three men were travelling as they were driving from Victoria toward Houston. One policeman hid by the roadside and signalled the other officer with a flashlight to block a bridge to stop the cars. The signal was intercepted by the drivers of the two automobiles and the cars were turned around and headed back toward Victoria. The men fired at the officer by the roadside and he returned the fire.

The police found one of the cars, an eight-cylinder coupe, abandoned a few miles down the highway. The other automobile was an eight-cylinder sedan reported to have been stolen earlier in the day at Victoria.

Local deputy sheriffs were of the opinion that the occupants of the two automobiles were the suspects they seek and that they may have been two men and a girl instead of three men as reported. Since the kidnapped Carlsbad deputy was released near San Antonio, deputies believed the kidnappers may have started back to Dallas by way of Houston.

Pat Delaney flew down to Wharton in April 2003. He found that although the original bridge still stands, a second carriageway has now been built to the east of it, somewhat masking the view.

This is the original bridge at Wharton — a triple girder structure — as seen in the 1930s from the north side of the river.

Victoria police were immediately notified of the direction taken by the two Fords and an immediate telephone call was placed to lawmen in Wharton, 60 miles down the road, as there was an excellent chance of apprehending the cars as they crossed the Colorado bridge. Pat drew this rough sketch on site to give us a better idea of the layout. The second bridge now enables traffic to travel one way yet the configuration of the roadway with the bend towards Victoria is the same as in 1932. Only the railroad tracks have disappeared although the railway bridge over the river and overpass on the road remain.

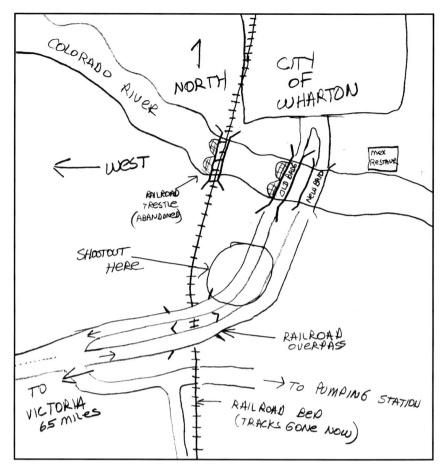

Dallas detectives were in communication with New Mexico authorities after the search for Deputy Sheriff Joe Johns ended in the morning when the deputy walked into the Sheriff's office at San Antonio and told of being kidnapped by two men and an 18-year-old girl. Reports Sunday night said the decapitated body of Johns had been found ninety miles north-east of El Paso. The description of the girl fitted that of a Dallas girl who detectives said has been identified as a frequent companion of the two West Dallas men.

New Mexico police joined Texas and Oklahoma peace officers in the search for the men after being given information by Dallas police regarding their identity.

The two men are sought also in connection with the slaying of a deputy recently at Atoka, Oklahoma; for murder and robbery of a merchant at Hillsboro; for the robbery of Neuhoff Packing Company on Alamo and for numerous other crimes.

The Dallas Morning News, August 16, 1932

Local historian Sidney Weisiger describes what happened: 'Deputy Seibrecht and City Marshal Pitman received word that a stolen 1932 Ford sedan bearing Texas license plate K 71-310 was headed toward Wharton. The two officers drove across the bridge on Highway 12 (this is called No. 59 today). Seibrecht got out of the car at the curve west of the railroad overpass while Marshal Pitman drove back east to the approach of the bridge. This was their plan of action. Deputy Seibrecht was to stay down in the highway ditch and watch for the stolen sedan. If he saw the car pass he would stand up and signal to Pitman who would then park his car across the bridge on the eastern side *(above)*, thus blocking traffic.'

'Seibrecht had not been at his station long in the ditch *(right)* when he noticed two cars, a coupe and sedan, head out on the side road *(below)* toward the pumping plant. The two cars stopped after going a short distance and the occupants seemed to be holding a consultation. The two automobiles then turned around and headed toward Wharton. The cars were not going fast and when they passed Seibrecht he saw the sedan was the one stolen from Victoria so he gave Pitman the signal and the Marshal started to drive his car onto the bridge to set up a road-block. However, Clyde was too smart to drive blindly into a trap and was probably going slowly enough to spot the man in the ditch.'

'The car turned around and came back west in his direction. The deputy pulled his gun and stepped onto the road to halt the cars. When within a few feet of him the man in the coupe fired point-blank through the windshield, spraying Seibrecht with shattered glass. Two shots were fired. As the sedan, which was behind the coupe, passed, the driver ducked down and the officer had to shoot through the door of the car and he thought he may have wounded the man. Seibrecht then had presence of mind enough to jump into the ditch to keep from being run down by the sedan. Marshal Pitman came over as soon as he was able but heavy traffic prevented the officers overtaking the fugitives. The coupe with the shattered windshield bearing Cherokee County plates was found abandoned a few miles from the shoot-out and the sedan stolen from Victoria was recovered in Carthage, Missouri, the following month.'

The scene of the shoot-out today. The law having missed a golden opportunity to capture the three outlaws, they lived to fight . . . and kill . . . another day. Fingerprints found in the abandoned coupe identified the trio as Clyde Barrow, Bonnie Parker and Raymond Hamilton. However it appears that Ray, travelling in the rearmost car, had either been unnerved by the incident or had enough excitement for a while as he parted company with Bonnie and Clyde and went to see his father in Bay City, Michigan. After further bank robberies in October and November, Ray was finally caught while roller skating with an associate, Gene O'Dare, on December 6. Apart from being indicted with offences of armed robbery, for which he was sentenced in January 1933 to a total of 55 years imprisonment, in March he was convicted of the murder of John Bucher (see page 57). Ray and Clyde would not meet up again until January 1934).

73

Main Street in Sherman, Texas in 1932 . . . or is it? Although it purports to give us a flavour of the time, it is in fact the parade held there on July 4, 1976 to mark the 200th anniversary of the forming of the United States.

Back in the 1930s, staff photographers were the exception, rather than the rule, on many of the smaller town newspapers — hence there is a distinct lack of contemporary photographs from the Bonnie and Clyde era.

October 11, 1932 – Sherman, Texas

Peace officers in North Texas and Southern Oklahoma were searching Wednesday for a young bandit who fatally shot Howard Hall in the robbery of a Little's suburban grocery store early Tuesday night of about $60. The bandit escaped with two confederates after firing four shots at Mr. Hall, one of them after Mr. Hall had fallen to the sidewalk at the side of the store.

A futile protest of Mr. Hall's 'you can't do that' aroused the ire of the bandit, between 20 and 25 years old, and Mr. Hall was shot down when he resisted curses and kicks and beatings from the bandit.

Mr Hall was 57 years old and was employed in the meat market of the Little store. With Homer Glaze, he was preparing to close the store at 6:30 p.m. when the bandit entered. They were alone in the store at this time.

The bandit posed as a customer and as Mr. Glaze opened the cash register to make change for a $1 bill tendered in payment, the bandit flashed a gun and rifled the till.

Angered by a remark from Mr. Hall at this point, the bandit threatened both employees and began pushing them toward the door, abusing and cursing Mr. Hall on the way.

Just as he reached the door he struck Mr. Hall on the head and knocked his glasses into the street. As he drew back to strike again Mr. Hall grabbed at his arm and the bandit opened fire.

The two men were standing in the doorway when the shooting began, according to witnesses of the event. The bandit fired four times and three of the shots took effect in Mr. Hall's chest. One shot was fired after Mr. Hall fell to the walk.

The bandit turned and attempted to fire at Mr. Glaze who was standing just inside the store but the gun snapped. He then started

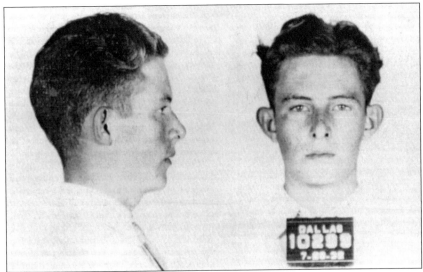

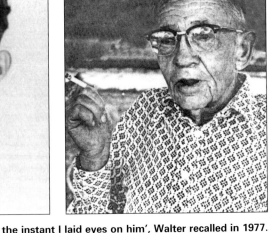

In July 1932, Clyde's younger brother, who was known simply by the initials L.C., was arrested by Dallas police on suspicion of car theft. This is his mugshot taken on the 28th. He was transferred to Sherman (see map page 44) to await trial. Walter Enloe (right) was helping the chief jailer, Mr R. V. Graham feed the prisoners in Grayson County Jail ([1] on plan opposite) at midday on Tuesday, October 11 when Clyde Barrow walked in. 'I knew it was him the instant I laid eyes on him', Walter recalled in 1977. 'Mr Graham knew it too. Clyde said he wanted to visit but we told him that nobody could visit while we were feeding the prisoners. We told him that he could come back later. When he left, he didn't just turn around and walk out — he backed out with his hands in both pockets of his overcoat.' Walter felt sure that he had a gun under his coat but, he says, 'he didn't come back'.

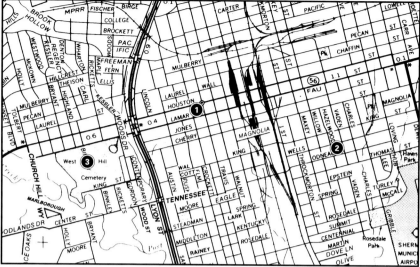

That same evening, just as Howard Hall was shutting up his grocery shop *(left)*, a customer entered. Homer Glaze, the assistant described what happened next: 'The man first called for a half-a-dozen eggs and then walked up to the meat counter and asked for a dime's worth of lunch meat. Taking these, he handed me a dollar bill. I stepped back to the cash register to make change and just as I opened the till he whipped out a black .45 and covered me with the announcement that he was holding the place up. Keeping me covered with the gun, he rifled the cash register of about $60 in bills.'

afoot down Wells Street and was seen to turn off on Hazelwood.

An ambulance was called and Mr. Hall taken to St. Vincent's Sanitarium across the street from the store. He died about an hour later from three wounds in the chest. Attendants said he was in a dying condition when he was brought in, although conscious for some time.

The bandit doing the shooting was described to police by Glaze as being about 20 or 25 years of age, small and of a light complexion. This description was phoned to every police department and was also broadcast over radio stations in Dallas.

Sherman Daily Democrat, October 12, 1932

In 1932 this was the location of Little's grocery store [2]. It was located at the corner of Vaden Street, which runs north and south and Wells Avenue which runs east and west, and was long and narrow with the short end facing Vaden (in the foreground). A long counter ran down the right-hand side facing a second door opening to Wells (where the car is parked). At the rear, and at right-angles to the main counter, was a short counter for serving meat, separated by a glass front. When the photo *(top left)* was taken in 1969, the old store was still standing — then named Beck's Grocery — but the building was on its last legs and was demolished. Homer continues his account: 'At this point Mr. Hall advanced around the south end of the meat counter and said: "Young man you can't do that." With an oath the bandit replied that he would show Mr. Hall whether he could nor not. He then backed me out around the end of the counter toward the center of the store, and called Mr. Hall over to us. Threatening us both with his gun, he began pushing us toward the Wells Avenue door, all the time abusing Mr Hall. Cursing, slapping and kicking Mr. Hall all the way, he shoved us to the door where he struck Mr. Hall such a severe blow on the head that his glasses went flying into the street. As he drew back to strike again Mr. Hall grabbed at his arm and the bandit opened fire.'

'Four shots were fired', continued Homer, 'three of them struck Mr. Hall and he fell out the door and onto the sidewalk. I was still inside the building and ran to Mr. Hall as he fell. The bandit who was outside now too, turned and attempted to fire at me but his gun snapped.' Mrs. L. G. Butler, the wife of another clerk in the store, also witnessed the shooting. She had driven up and parked her car on Wells and was just about to enter the store when she saw the bandit backing the two men towards the door. She retreated to the southwest corner of the store where she saw the shooting. She said the gunman fired three times at Mr. Hall before he fell and once as he lay dying on the sidewalk. *Above:* The site of the shop is now a small fenced garden in surburban Sherman. *Right:* Here, on this very spot, a man was murdered . . . for $60.

Left: After the shooting, the gunman ran from the store (where the car is parked in the distance), along Wells Avenue (now signed Wells Street) to the corner with Hazelwood Street.

Right: Turning right, he ran to where another man was standing beside a large black sedan. Two boys then saw both men get in and drive off.

Funeral rites for Howard Hall, 57-year-old grocery store employee who was shot to death Tuesday night by a bandit robbing the store, were held at the residence, 1027 East Lamar Street, Wednesday afternoon.

Dr. George Guthrell, pastor of the Christian church of Tyler, conducted the services, and paid tribute to Mr. Hall's courage and upright Christian life. Friends were present from Dallas and McKinney, and there was a large floral offering. Mr. Hall was born in McKinney and resided there before moving to Sherman 25 years ago.

Interment was in West Hill Cemetery, under the direction of Dannel-Scott funeral home.

Sherman Daily Democrat, October 13, 1932

Howard Hall's grave — with that of his wife Emma who died in 1970 — lies in West Hill Cemetery ([3] on the plan on page 75).

With only a few meagre clues to guide them, local peace officers widened the search for the bandit who fatally shot Howard Hall in the robbery of Little's grocery store Tuesday night by sending to officers throughout Texas and adjoining states, photos and detailed descriptions of the young man identified by witnesses to the shooting as Mr. Hall's assailant.

The hijacker and his two confederates are believed to have left Sherman travelling in a Buick sedan with a Kansas licence. A negro who lives near here on the Bells highway told officers he was stopped about three miles out on the highway Tuesday night by three men who borrowed his automobile pump. He said he offered them the use of his tire patch to fix their flat but they did not take time to repair the tire, merely pumping it up and leaving again at a rapid rate. The negro identified the photo of the man believed to have shot Mr. Hall as one of the three who used his pump.

While pumping up the tire one of the men tore a letter into bits and scattered it by the roadside. O. J. Neathery, Deputy Sheriff, recovered the letter and officers hope from it to gain the identity of the young bandit's two confederates.

Sheriff's officers in Denton told officers here they believe the trio passed through there Tuesday night after the robbery. Local officers hold to the view that the bandits started in one direction, cut back, and circled the town to travel in another.

The bandit whose photo has been positively identified by Homer Glaze, employee in Little's store who witnessed the shooting, as the man who killed Mr. Hall is wanted in half a dozen cities in Texas and Oklahoma for robbery or murder. He has been sought in connection with two killings, one in Hillsboro and another in Atoka, Oklahoma.

The bandits are believed by officers to have been in this vicinity for several days before the robbery. Highway officers told Sheriff Frank Reece they saw three men, one of them the man whose photo sheriff has, parked beside the highway near Bonham one day last week.

Sherman Daily Democrat, October 13, 1932

In the Name and by the Authority of the State of Texas:

THE GRAND JURY for the County of Grayson, State of Texas, duly elected, tried and empaneled, sworn and charged, at a term of the District Court of and for the _____Fifty-Ninth_____ Judicial District of Texas, in and for the said County, begun and held at the Court House thereof on the _____First_____ Monday in _____December_____ 1932____, to inquire of and true presentment make of all offenses committed within said County of Grayson, upon their oaths in said District Court of Grayson County presents that in said County of Grayson and State of Texas, on or about the_____11th_____ day of_____October_____ A. D. 1932____ . one _____Clyde Champion Barrow_____ _____ did then and there unlawfully **and voluntarily and with malice aforethought kill Howard Hall by shooting him with a gun,**

One could say that the jury is still out on who actually fired the fatal shots. Was it Ray Hamilton . . . linked in the press reports with the Hillsboro killing back in April . . . or was it Clyde as per the indictment issued by the District Court of Grayson County? As far as the Barrow and Parker families were concerned, when they saw Clyde and Bonnie on Halloween at the end of October, Clyde replied: 'We've been in Kansas for the past three weeks so we couldn't have done that. They just hung it on us for luck. But what's the difference now? They've got to hang it on somebody.'

Nell Barrow explains in *Fugitives* that during the month of November they committed several robberies in Missouri 'for police were looking for them in Texas and Oklahoma and didn't think they would go so far north'. This is the first reliable admission we have of Bonnie being directly involved in a hold-up.

November 30, 1932 – Oronogo, Missouri

Three bandits using what was described as a sub-machine gun held up the Farmers & Miners Bank at Oronogo at 11:30 o'clock today and escaped with less than $500 after a gun-battle with R. A. Norton, cashier and also with two garage men who exchanged shots with the bandits as they fled.

Fortunately, none of the group of Oronogo citizens was wounded by the machine-gun-fire of the bandits. Apparently the bandits also escaped the bullet-fire unscathed.

A Chevrolet sedan belonging to Hugo Weidler of Carthage and stolen from the front of the Weidler home on Lyon Street, between 7:45 and 8:30 o'clock this morning was used by the bandits in the bank robbery and abandoned a mile west of Oronogo where the bandits are believed to have entered a Ford V-8 black coupe and to have escaped to the westward. A woman driver was waiting in the Ford car, persons who had observed it, reported to officers. No later trace of the bandits was found by officers from Carthage and Joplin who answered the call and scoured the district.

The abandoned Weidler machine had one bullet hole through the left rear door. This bullet lodged in the door on the opposite side passing near the back of the front seat. The rear glass was broken out of the car but this was believed to have been broken by the bandit with the machine gun, in order to fire back down the street.

Instead of surrendering when he saw the bandits enter, one with the sub-machine gun and another with a revolver, Mr. Norton dropped down behind the window counter and opened fire through the desk partition. The bandit with the machine gun retaliated, the barrage of machine gun bullets cutting two holes through the partition the size of a half a dollar. Fortunately Mr. Norton was protected by a heavy steel plate, installed behind the partition for such emergencies. When his gun jammed, however, and upon urging by A. A. Farrar, Frisco train dispatcher at Joplin who was a customer in the bank, Norton surrendered and stood up with his hands above his head.

The bandits then smashed large glazed glass in a partition door next to the wall and both stepped in behind the counter. The machine gun operator approached Norton in a threatening manner and placed the gun in the cashier's ribs. Norton said later that as far as he recalled, the man with the machine gun said nothing but his companion urged: 'Leave him alone! Get the money and let's

get out of here.' They scooped up what cash was in sight and fled to the Weidler car, the driver of which had been honking the horn impatiently because of his observations of the alarm being spread up the street.

Jack Watson, a miner, working in a prospect derrick just across the street north from the bank, taking refuge behind some timbers, had been calling out an alarm 'They're robbing the bank!' The shots also had helped apprise citizens up the street of the robbery and a crowd of eight or ten had gathered at the Wetsel garage, a block and a half from the bank, by the time the bandit car started out.

Burley Wetsel proprietor of the garage, and Carl Capp, mechanic, had obtained high powered rifles from the garage and had started in the direction of the bank, when they saw the bandit car start out and head towards them. The garage men and several spectators who had gathered ducked behind the brick wall of a building across the alley east of the garage and waited for the bandit car to come by. As it did so they opened fire and the bandit with the machine gun retaliated, pouring eleven bullets into the fender, radiator and dash of a gasoline truck, the bullets missing Wetsel probably not more than a foot. On Wetsel's other side, two machine

Top: **This is the building that housed the Farmers & Miners Bank in Oronogo which was robbed by Clyde and two associates in November 1932. The town lies just north of Joplin, Missouri, just a few miles from the state line with Kansas. Clyde with Bonnie, Frank Hardy and Hollis Hale, two friends from Dallas, rented accommodation in a tourist camp a few miles away in Carthage before reconnoitering the area for a suitable bank to rob as the gang's finances were non-existent. The one in Oronogo was combined with the local post office and postmaster's residence, the bank occupying the low section of the building on the left, the entrance being the door just in front of the left-hand car. Bonnie checked the bank out and Clyde worked out an escape route to Kansas. By the last day of the month — Wednesday 30th — all was ready. However, with bank robberies becoming a fact of life during the Depression years, when the Barrow gang hit Oronogo they were in for a rude awakening!**

gun bullets went through a drain pipe on the building.

Wetsel and Capp emptied their high powered rifles at the speeding car as it went down the road.

No pursuit was organised immediately at Oronogo. Sheriff Harry Stephens was notified here and he and James Watson and Dempsey Southard, special Frisco officers, and Deputy Sheriffs James Leary and Glenn Stemmons went ot Oronogo armed with high powered rifles and shotguns but of course, the bandits had made good their escape.

The Ford car in which the bandits are believed to have escaped was reported to have had an Illinois license.

The bandits in the hurry to get away dropped a few one-dollar bills and some silver on the floor. There was blood on some of this money, this causing the conclusion that one of the bandits had probably cut his hand in stepping through the door from which they had smashed the glass.

Mr. Norton said he did not believe any of the bandits was 'Pretty Boy' Floyd, Oklahoma desperado who is much sought. He said he had studied pictures of Floyd and none of the bandits resembled him.

Mr. Norton said the bandits were from 20 to 25 years old. He did not observe the

This is the view, looking east, of downtown Oronogo today. The large building in the centre stands on the corner of what was the main street in 1933. That street ran at right angles to the larger road in the foreground, which, at the time, was a small side street. Burley Wetsel's garage stood approximately where the silver building in the foreground stands today.

bandits closely, as to their clothing he said, 'All were well dressed'.

The robbery today is believed to be the first bank robbery in Jasper county in which a sub-machine gun has been used. The bullets

appeared to be smaller in size than the standard .44 caliber which it is said is the caliber of the generally used sub-machine gun.

Carthage Evening Press, November 30, 1932

In the last day of November they decided to rob the Oronogo Bank. Clyde told me later they had sent Bonnie in to look things over several days before. Clyde still wasn't taking her with him on any of his actual hold-ups. This time he left her about five miles out of town to wait, and he and the boys went in to raid the bank. Their finances were in a bad way, Clyde said — down to about $2, I believe — and they figured that the Oronogo Bank would furnish them enough to get by on for the rest of the winter. They left Hollis in the car out in front, and Clyde and Frank Hardy went into the bank with drawn guns.

This affair didn't turn out as expected. Evidently bank officials hadn't been so dumb as the boys had figured, and had become suspicious of Bonnie's visit. Anyway, they were ready for them.

'Gosh, Sis, they began popping at us the minute we got inside the door,' Clyde told me afterwards. 'We'd have beat

it right then, if we hadn't needed money so bad. But as it was, I held them off and Frank made a dive for the cage and scooped what he could get his hands on. Then we left in a hurry, let me tell you!'

The paper stated that they got $115, but when the money was counted, Frank insisted he had only $80. This, they split three ways and went back to the tourist camp outside of Carthage.

Immediately upon their arrival both Frank and Hollis began to make excuses to get to town, saying they'd better go and buy some ammunition. They left and never did come back, and when Clyde read the papers, he found out he'd been double-crossed. The thief had stolen from the thief. He and Bonnie had about $25 for all their troubles.

FUGITIVES, NELL BARROW, 1934

This robbery is described by Clyde's sister in *Fugitives* so it is interesting to compare descriptions of what took place from both sides of the fence. At the same time, one must always remember that press reports, written to a deadline, are rarely accurate in every detail and this case is a good example. The notion that the

robbers were armed with a machine gun was changed the next day. In a follow-up story in the same paper on December 1, the headline now stated that the 'Oronogo Bank Robbers used sawed off shotguns. Belief that they had machine gun apparently exploded by more complete investigation today.'

The old bank building was pictured for us by Jim Knight in November 2002 — exactly 70 years after Clyde shot the place up. Subsequently the building has seen use as a cafe although

Jim explains that nothing remains inside remotely resembling a bank. In fact, he writes that the interior looks like someone's old tool shed!

Exit Raymond Elzie Hamilton . . . enter William Deacon Jones! He had been friends with Clyde since boyhood and Jones had badgered him to join his gang but Clyde told W. D. (as he was nicknamed) that he was too young and that he would only get into trouble. Although he looks much older in this picture which was taken in March 1933, Jones is said to have been just 16 years old (his date of birth has never been established with total accuracy). However, after Hamilton quit, Clyde was obviously in need of a reliable partner and just before Christmas 1932 they met up in Dallas as Jones explains: 'L. C. Barrow, Clyde's brother, who had been a friend of mine for some time, and myself were riding round Dallas in his Model A Ford Coupe with Maudine Brennan and another girl. We had half a gallon of whisky with us and were drinking it freely. We started riding around when it became dark and took the girls home about 8.30 and then went to a little stand on the right-hand side of Eagle Ford Road. Clyde and Bonnie passed by where we were. They were driving a Ford V-8 coupe, with two wheels on the running board with a khaki top. L. C. saw them and suggested that we follow them, which we did. They drove on down a side road to a gravel pit and we drove up behind them and parked there. We talked to them there and Clyde suggested to me that I go with them "down the road", as he put it, although he did not say where. I agreed to go with them and I got in the car. We started south of Dallas and drove to a point about three miles this side of Temple [see map page 44]. We went to a tourist camp a short way from Temple and rented a cabin. They slept on the bed and I had a pallet on the floor. We stayed there all day and the following night and early next morning about eight o'clock, we left and went into Temple.' Clyde's plan was to rob a store or hold-up a filling station but in the statement that Jones subsequently gave police in November 1933 (from which this quotation has been taken), in an attempt to exonerate himself he claimed that he chickened out of actually taking part in the robbery. However in an article published in 1968 he admitted that he had kept watch outside the store armed with a revolver, while Clyde went inside to 'get us some spending money'.

December 25, 1932 – Temple, Texas

Public indignation flared up yesterday as police of a dozen counties sought the two men who Christmas afternoon shot and fatally wounded Doyle Johnson, 27-year-old employee of the Strasburger stores.

Johnson was shot down in front of his home at 606 South 13th Street when he tried to prevent the theft of his small roadster.

He had jumped on the running board just as the car was started. Two shots were fired, from different pistols. The second struck Johnson in the neck and went through the spinal chord.

The pair drove off but abandoned the car several blocks away. They jumped out leaving the car doors open, and were picked up by a woman in a coupe.

Police notified officers in surrounding counties but an all-day search failed to find them or a trace of the coupe. A black coupe, similar in description to the one sought by police here, was seen to pass through Lampasas late Sunday night headed towards Lometa. The car, witnesses said, was travelling at a high rate of speed. Two men on the highway just out of Lampasas also saw the car, they reported.

The license number of the car was issued in Bastrop county. Sheriff John Bigham said. He called the sheriff of Bastrop county and traced the ownership of the car. The registration however, corresponded to a Chevrolet coach instead of a coupe. It is possible that the license plates were stolen from the coach and put on the coupe, police said.

Henry Krauser, father-in-law of Doyle Johnson, ran out into the street to stop the car thieves. He was followed by Clarence Krauser, of Taylor, brother-in-law, and by Mrs. Johnson.

The two men had been pushing the car from in front of the residence. When they saw the trio come from the house, they got into the car and started to drive off. Mr. Krauser shouted to them and Clarence Krauser came up to the side of the car and spoke to the men.

Both of the men jumped out and forced the Krausers and Mrs. Johnson to retreat at the point of a gun. Clarence Krauser stepped behind a tree near the sidewalk and Mrs. Johnson started back to the house as did Henry Krauser.

Clyde and W. D., on foot, came this way. This is the present day view looking down South 13th Street from West Avenue H

As they walked down 13th Street, a Model A Ford roadster stood parked outside No. 606, facing the wrong way down the road. Not having a Model A with us when we visited Temple in June 2003, we had to make do with a Buick . . .

where it lodged just under the skin. The bullet had struck the spinal chord and physicians said paralysis would have set in.

After Johnson fell from the side of the car the pair started the car and drove away.

Police working on the case telephoned all surrounding towns to keep watch for a Ford roadster with two men in it. Later they found the car abandoned near Avenue F and 17th Street.

A negro woman living near the place where the car was left told police she saw two men drive up in the roadster and jump out, leaving both doors open just as the car was when police found it. She said a woman driving a small car went on Avenue F, slowed down at that intersection and reached over and opened the door on the right side of the car and the two men jumped inside. She drove away to the south.

Questioned what kind of car it was, the negro woman said it was 'like that one' and pointed to a small black Chevrolet coupe. Police have only the description given by the negro woman to work with. Johnson was employed by Strasburger's market on South First Street. He was born July 22, 1905, in Johnson county and moved to Temple with his parents in 1918.

Temple Daily Telegram, December 27, 1932

The men shouted to Henry Krauser to stop where he was and just at that time Doyle Johnson, who has been awakened by his mother came running from the house.

The men had started for the car and by the time Johnson got to the car they were inside ready to drive off. He rushed up to the driver's side of the car and jumped on the running board.

The driver, a small man in a dark coat, took his revolver in his left hand and stuck it into Johnson's body. Evidently Johnson grabbed at the gun for when it went off the bullet struck the left front fender, pierced it and bounced off the brake box onto the ground where it was found. It was from a .38 caliber gun, police said.

The bullet which struck and fatally wounded Johnson was from a .41 or .45 caliber gun, probably shot from the gun of the driver's companion on the right side of the car.

The bullet struck Johnson on the side of the neck entering the right side of the neck about midway and ranging slightly downward. It went straight through to the left side

. . . but this is what it should look like!

81

Left: This is the view from the front room window of No. 606, now occupied by Samuel R. Jones who kindly allowed us to take these photos. *Right:* The Johnson family had just finished their Christmas dinner and Doyle who owned the car was having a nap.

His father-in-law Henry Krauser spotted two men about to steal the car and tore down these steps to remonstrate with them. He was followed by his brother Clarence and Doyle's mother. *Bottom:* This must be the tree behind which Clarence sheltered.

We saw a Model A Ford roadster parked on the street, and Clyde told me to get that car. I did, and about that time a woman came out of the house and started screaming. I got out and started to run, and Clyde told me to get back in the car and start it. The car was parked the wrong way so that the left side was next to the curb. Clyde was standing out in the street. I had gotten out on the curb side, but when Clyde told me that I got back in the car, and did not stop in it. I crawled on through the car and got out on the street where Clyde was.

While this was happening, an old man had come out of the house and started toward the car, but Clyde, standing in the street, had pulled his pistol by this time, and ordered him to stop and the old man stopped. Clyde got in the car, under the steering wheel, and was trying to start the car, and another and younger man came out of the house and came up to the car on the side where Clyde was sitting under the steering wheel. Clyde raised his pistol and fired at this man three times. I did not see the man fall as I started running. Clyde got the car started and drove on down and I jumped on the running board and got in the car and we jumped out of it and ran back and got in the car with Bonnie Parker.

W. D. JONES, NOVEMBER 1933

After he got the money we walked away towards Bonnie and before we got halfway back to the car, Clyde stopped alongside a Model A roadster that had the keys in it. I don't know if he'd seen something over his shoulder that spooked him or what. But he told me, 'Get in that car, boy, and start it.' I jumped to it. But it was a cold day and the car wouldn't start. Clyde got impatient. He told me to slip over and he'd do it. I scooted over. About then an old man and an old woman run over to the roadster and began yelling, 'That's my boy's car! Get out!' Then another woman run up and began making a big fuss.

All the time, Clyde was trying to get it started. He told them to stand back and they wouldn't get hurt. Then the guy who owned it run up. Clyde pointed his pistol and yelled: 'Get back, man, or I'll kill you!' That man was Doyle Johnson, I learned later. He came on up to the car and reached through the roadster's isinglass window curtains and got Clyde by the throat and tried to choke him.

Clyde hollered: 'Stop, man, or I'll kill you.' Johnson didn't move, and Clyde done what he had threatened. About then he got the car started and we whipped around the corner to where Bonnie was waiting. We piled into her car and lit a shuck out of town.

W. D. JONES, NOVEMBER 1968

Inevitably, in any crime, the witnesses describe the events differently but over the intervening years, W. D. materialy changed his version of what took place. Both he and Clyde fired, and it would appear that the fatal round came from the gun of the man in the passenger seat, i.e. Jones. The delay in starting the car was an important factor in what happened and the Model A was particularly awkward to get going at the best of times, let alone on a cold day. First you had to put both 'mule ears' up on the steering wheel (the left lever controlled the spark, the right one the fuel). You then turned the ignition key, pressed down on the clutch with the left foot, reached over and pulled out the choke, put your right heel round the accelerator, your right toe on the starter button, then pushed down the starter. Once the engine caught you had to release the choke, release the toe starter, pull the spark lever down part of the way, then nurse the engine for 30 seconds. And, after all that, it would die on you if you had forgotten to turn on the fuel valve under the dash!

Your Editor re-enacts the shooting. Doyle Johnson fell mortally wounded here [1]. Clyde and W. D. drove around the corner, turning left onto West Avenue F, to meet Bonnie on the corner of South 17th Street [2]. Here Doyle's car was abandoned as Bonnie picked them up and continued down South 17th to West Avenue H where she would have turned left towards the Waco road.

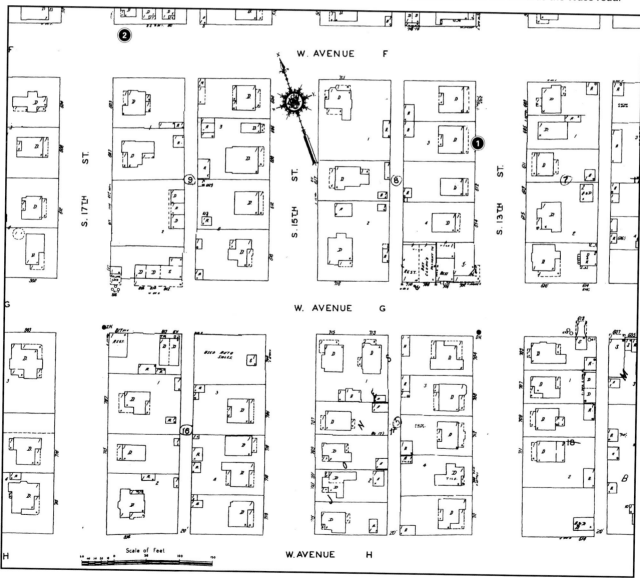

Above: This is West Avenue F having just turned the corner . . . although in his desperate attempt to escape, Clyde would hardly have bothered about the nicety of driving on the correct side of the road! *Right:* Bonnie picked them up on this corner where the road meets South 17th. Later she admitted that 'I was sure scared and I'd have driven away if Clyde hadn't been in a jam. As it was, I never heard so much screaming and hollering in my life, and it looked like the whole town was going to be right on us in a minute. I knew it wouldn't matter if W. D. got caught, for he hadn't done anything to get electrocuted for, so I didn't worry any about him. It was Clyde I was scared about. I shifted gears and came alongside the car and called to Clyde to let the thing go and come on, quick. It was just here that W. D. let him have it. The man who was holding Clyde sort of crumpled up, Clyde jerked loose and ran around and jumped on the running board. W. D. followed him, and I stepped on it.'

This is the road on which they would have left Temple for Waco. Today the main road through town — Highway 290 — leads directly onto the interstate but then it dog-legged along Nugent and turned north onto 15th *(above)*. It was near here that the old White City Tourist Court stood until it was pulled down in 1945, and locals still like to claim that this is where Bonnie and Clyde stayed although Jones says they were at 'a tourist camp on the main highway going south out of Temple'.

84

Doyle was buried in Hillcrest Cemetery on Tuesday, December 27, his grave in Section K being marked by this simple stone. Local people were incensed at the killing, their anger being particularly heightened because the murder had occurred on Christmas Day, and a reward fund was quickly opened for the 'arrest and conviction of the desperados'.

Doyle Johnson, 26, market man, died early today of a pistol wound in the neck received Christmas afternoon when two young men attempting to steal his automobile shot him from the running board and left his body in the street near his home.

Authorities believed the men planned to steal Johnson's automobile and abandon a stolen car in which they were travelling. It was said the two were not residents of Temple and there was no idea as to their identity. They abandoned Johnson's car within two blocks of his home, entered a machine driven by a woman and sped south.

Johnson's roadster had been parked in front of his house. As he and his wife and baby celebrated Christmas the wife noticed the young men wearing dark overcoats and light hats getting into the car. She told her husband. He reached the car just as they started it and as he remonstrated one drew a pistol and fired.

Dallas Evening Journal, December 26, 1932

Bonnie said that when Clyde reached the car 'he was breathing hard and as mad as I've ever seen him. "You dumb punk!" he said to W. D. "They didn't have any guns, either of them. We could have got away without killing him if you'd used your head. Now you've got a murder chalked up against you. I ought to kick your rear till you had to ride on your stomach a week. I told you you'd get into trouble if you came along, but, damn it, I didn't think you'd do it so sudden!"' In his statement to the police, Jones relates that before they got to the next tourist camp, Clyde made him hide in the rumble seat which he closed on top of him! He says that they hid out in East Texas, staying at tourist camps and avoiding towns . . . until Friday, January 6, 1933 when they returned to Dallas.

As 1932 came to an end, America was in the deepest depths of the Depression and figures printed in the *American Bankers' Association* Bulletin noted that bank robberies were at their highest having reached a peak of 631 (77 burglaries and 554 hold-ups) for the year. Small banks in small towns with few employees were easy prey to armed bandits and more than 80 per cent of the banks were robbed in towns of less than 10,000 people. City banks were not so vulnerable but were still attacked by professional bandits, heavily armed, and prepared to shoot it out for the chance of netting a large haul. By comparison, Bonnie and Clyde were extremely small fry and the crime in 1932 which captured the nation's attention was the kidnapping of the baby son of Colonel Charles A. Lindbergh. When Lindbergh flew from New York to Paris in May 1927 he became a worldwide hero: thus the kidnapping of his son for a $50,000 ransom horrified the world. The money in marked notes was handed over through an intermediary but Charles Junior was never seen again alive.

At 10.22 on Saturday night Captain Charles Lindbergh, the lone American aviator, arrived at Le Bourget aerodrome, Paris, after a record-breaking journey of 3,000 miles from New York, which was performed in 33½ hours.

The Paris airport has never in its history witnessed such scenes as those of Saturday night, when a crowd estimated at between 100,000 and 200,000 swept down the iron barriers and, despite the efforts of a force of five hundred troops and police, swarmed on to the landing-ground as soon as Lindbergh's machine was sighted.

Shortly after ten o'clock there arose a murmur of long suppressed excitement as the Ryan monoplane swung into the field of light created over the aerodrome by the searchlights and arc lamps. Twice the pilot made a circuit of the landing-ground, and then, having carefully chosen his point of descent, came down with a neatness and precision which astonished observers when it is revealed that Lindbergh could never look straight ahead, but only by means of a periscope arrangement.

'Hullo, boys, I'm here!' said Lindbergh as he thrust his head out of the cockpit, and then, as though he could not quite believe that he had succeeded, he said 'I'm Lindbergh. Where am I?'

The Daily Telegraph, May 23, 1927

Two months later, the badly decomposed body of a child was discovered by a truck driver just four miles from the Lindbergh home at Hopewell, New Jersey. Two years later one of the marked bills was handed over for payment of fuel at a gas station. The attendant noted the licence number of the vehicle and a German immigrant, Bruno Hauptmann (centre), arrested. Found guilty, he went to the electric chair in April 1936.

As the Depression worsened, unemployment increased according to the dictum: 'Last hired, first fired.' In 1932 there was no government insurance or intervention and the only assistance for the unemployed was provided piecemeal from hand-outs by states and charities. The interregnum between President Roosevelt's election in November and his inauguration in January 1933 saw the United States at its lowest ebb with Socialists and Communists vying to fill the vacuum. Poverty and hardship stretched from the industrial heartlands of the East to the agricultural communities of the Mid-West. Farmers, already struggling to survive in a climate of foreclosures, were then dealt a hammer blow when devastating dust storms raged across the Great Plains, coining a new phrase:

the 'Dust Bowl'. Texas was particularly hard hit in January 1933 when clouds of dust swamped the wheat fields. As credit ran out and properties and farms were repossessed by mortgage companies and banks, thousands were lured to the so-called 'Golden West' beyond the Rocky Mountains. Setting out in overloaded, rickety transport, they headed west on the migrant trail: the now legendary Route 66. *Above:* The last barrier to be negotiatied before entering California was the mighty Colorado River. The 'Old Trails Bridge', as it is now called, had been built in 1916 when it was then the longest triple-hinged arch bridge in the country. It was very narrow with a sharp 90-degree right-hand turn at the western end followed by a steep gradient up the cliff.

California at last! Along this narrow road came thousands of weary travellers seeking a better life in the promised land. The old bridge still stands although it has not been used for traffic since 1947. Travellers now speed by on the nearby interstate highway . . . yet what memories must this old abandoned roadway hold.

At the beginning of 1933, Clyde's former compatriot Raymond Hamilton *(left)* was cooling his heels in Hill County Jail. He had been arrested on December 6 and had been transferred from Dallas to Hillsboro just after Christmas for his impending trial for bank robbery at Cedar Hill and the murder of John Bucher (see page 57). Meanwhile, lawmen from Atoka were standing by to seek his extradition for the Stringtown killing (page 60). *Above left:* The county jail was constructed in 1893 and has now been preserved as a cell-block museum. *Above right:* When Ken Holmes was City Marshal of Meridian he often brought prisoners to the jail through this door.

The cells are constructed from riveted bands of steel rather than bars, the same being evident in the photo of the McLennan jail on page 28 from which Clyde escaped. In spite of this form of construction, it was still Clyde's intention to try to smuggle Hamilton some hacksaw blades hidden in a radio with the help of Ray's brother Floyd.

While Ray was languishing in Hillsboro, his partner in the Cedar Hill robbery, Les Stewart, and Odell Chambless, brother-in-law of his former partner Gene O'Dare, held up the Home Bank (above) in Grapevine (see map page 44) on December 29.

The take was nearly $3,000 but during their escape Les got caught. Odell carried on to Dallas where he went to stay with Ray's married sister, Lily McBride, who lived not far from the Barrow family at the Star Service Station.

January 6, 1933 – Dallas, Texas

Deputy Sheriff Malcolm Davis of Fort Worth was killed instantly Friday night by two charges of buckshot fired by one of two men whom Davis and a group of other officers attempted to arrest at 507 County Avenue, in West Dallas.

The officers were waiting at the house expecting Odell Chandler, sought for the December 29 bank robbery at Grapevine. Two men drove up just at midnight. Davis was one of the officers in the yard. He was fired on as one man waited in the automobile while his companion walked up to the porch.

The man who went in the porch fired through a window at Deputy Sheriff F. T. Bradberry who was sitting on a divan inside waiting.

The officers had sought Odell Chandler since his escape on December 29 after taking part in the $2,850 hold up of the Grapevine Home Bank. He got away by posing as a posseman.

Chandler boasted on the day of the robbery that he carried 'a jacket full of bullets and would use them' before being caught. He made this boast to two Grapevine community farmers. W. A. Shumaker and Jesse Trigg, while forcing them to drive him toward Dallas.

Chandler left their car in the outskirts of West Dallas that evening. Officers say he has been away from Dallas since then and that they had learned he intended to return Friday night.

The shooting occurred at the home of Mrs Lily McBride, who the officers say is a sister of Raymond Hamilton, charged in the Cedar Hill bank hold-up of November 25. Earlier in the night Les Stewart, arrested just after the Grapevine robbery, said he was with Hamilton in the Cedar Hill job.

Lillian lived down County Avenue (above) a turning off of Eagle Ford Road, but the street has since been renamed Winnetka (just as Eagle Ford is now Singleton). On the evening of Friday, January 6, Clyde called round to see Lillian to check if the hacksaw blades had been delivered to Ray. Lillian was out but her sister Maggie Fairris told him that the police had been round earlier in the day looking for Odell as a result of Les spilling the beans to the DA about their connection with the Hamiltons. Clyde told her that he would return at midnight, but she was to leave a red light on in the window if it was not safe to stop. W. D. Jones, Clyde's new partner, would be with him, while Bonnie would be on hand to drive the car if necessary. It was a shear coincidence that the lawmen returned around 11 p.m. to set a trap for Chambless (note the press spell his name incorrectly in this early report). As they were pursuing him for the Home Bank job, most of the officers were from Tarrant county in which Grapevine is situated: Assistant District Attorney W. T. Evans and Special Ranger J. F. Van Noy with Deputies Malcolm Davis and Dusty Rhodes from the Fort Worth office, and Deputy Sheriff Fred Bradberry to represent Dallas county.

January 1933. The Chief of Detectives in the Dallas County Sheriff's Department, Bill Decker, stands in for Clyde in this police re-enactment of the killing of Deputy Sheriff Malcolm Davis (above) outside No. 507 County Avenue. There are reports that W. D. fired pistol shots from the seat of the car although he denies that he was armed in his statement given to police in November after he was captured.

While Bradberry, Rhodes and Van Noy sat down in the front room to question Maggie Fairris, Evans and Davis took up station on the rear porch (opposite). Having put her children to bed, Maggie said the officers told her to turn off the lights but she asked permission to leave the children's night-light on . . . in reality the red warning light to keep Clyde away. Just after midnight the lawmen were alerted when a car came slowly down County Avenue. It passed No. 507 and turned the corner. Sheriff Bradberry insisted that the red light be turned off and when the car reappeared it pulled up at the kerb and a man in an overcoat got out. Bradberry told Maggie to open the door. As she did so, she shouted a warning: 'Don't shoot! Think of my babies!' at which Clyde pulled out his shotgun from under his coat and fired at the right-hand window where he suspected a shot to come. The officers inside hit the floor as those at the back came running and, as Davis rounded the corner, Clyde fired and the sheriff fell mortally wounded.

Mrs. McBride was absent. Mrs Maggie Fairris, 18, who the officers say also is a sister of Hamilton, was there when the shooting took place. Two small children also were in the house.

The officers were deployed in the small frame house so as to cover all entrances. They saw a small coupe pass several times before it halted. When it stopped they watched one man get out and walk up to the front porch. He carried a sawed-off shotgun.

Obeying instructions of officers, Mrs Fairris, who had been sitting by the radio all evening, arose and opened the front door.

Just after she opened the door shooting began. The man on the porch fired several shots through a large window by which Deputy Bradberry had sat all evening.

Officers in the front part of the house fell flat on the floor and began returning the fire. They were hampered some by the presence of Mrs. Fairris at the door, from which she dared not flee for fearing of running into a line of fire.

Deputy Davis and his partner, who had been guarding the rear door, left their post when the shooting started and going into the yard ran toward the front so they could help their comrades.

As they hove into view both the man on the porch and the man in the car began firing at them. Davis fell mortally wounded. The man on the porch dashed back to the machine. The motor in the car was running and they quickly disappeared.

Officers said they believe the two men in the coupe were Odell Chandler and Clyde Barrow, the latter long sought as the outlaw companion of Raymond Hamilton in a series of hold-ups and killings in Texas, Oklahoma and New Mexico.

Other officers with Davis, the 52-year-old deputy who was killed, included W. T. Evans, investigator for the District Attorney at Fort Worth, and Deputy Sheriff Dusty Rhodes or Fort Worth, Special Ranger J. F. Van Noy and Deputy Sheriff F. T. Bradberry of Dallas. Evans was working as the partner of Davis and was in the yard with him when he was killed.

Dallas Morning News, January 7, 1933

Left: May 2003. Jonathan Davis takes over as Clyde in our recreation with Jim Knight as the victim. Right: According to the press report, Clyde's first shotgun blast went through this window and it does look as if the sash has been replaced in the police photo (top).

Left: **The back porch where Davis and Evans took up station before running up the left-hand side of the house** *(right)* **towards the road.**

The night Malcolm Davis was killed we went to Clyde Barrow's mother's house. We just stayed there a few minutes and we then drove down Eagle Ford Road, headed toward town, and turned to the left on County Avenue, the street where Lillie McBride lives. We went north on County for one block, turned to the left and went west on this street for one block, then turned left off this street onto another street which runs on into Eagle Ford Road. We stopped at a house where Floyd, brother of Raymond Hamilton, lived at that time.

Bonnie Parker and I stayed in the car, and Clyde Barrow got out and went around behind the house. He just stayed a few minutes and came back and got in the car. He didn't say who he had talked to there. We then drove south to the corner of this street and turned left onto Eagle Ford Road, and headed back toward Dallas. We travelled one block toward town on Eagle Ford till we came again to County Avenue, and turned left. We went on past Lillie McBride's house, and past the first cross street beyond this, and then turned the car around and put the lights out.

We were still driving the same Ford V8 coupe with the khaki top and the two wheels on the running board, which we had left Dallas in just before Christmas Day, and Clyde was wearing his overcoat and had that 16-gauge shotgun under his coat, swinging from his arm or shoulder at this time. We also had a rifle in the car lying up on the back of the seat, and Clyde had a pistol, the same pistol he had used to shoot the man at Temple a few days before. I think it was a .45 caliber revolver. Bonnie Parker had a .41 caliber pistol. This was the one I had at Temple, and I did not have any pistol.

We pulled up and stopped in front of Lillie McBride's house and Clyde told me to get behind the wheel. He got out on the left-hand side of the car and went around the back of it, and I crawled over Bonnie and got under the wheel.

Clyde walked around behind the car and on up to the house. Bonnie and I were still sitting in the car. I didn't notice whether there was a light on in the house. Clyde had gotten up on the porch before the first shot was fired. Then I heard a shotgun fire. I hadn't heard a word spoken up to this time. This was a shot fired by Clyde. Just about the time the shot was fired I saw two men come around the corner of the house, on the side of the house nearest Eagle Ford Road. Then the shot rang out and Bonnie told me to start the motor. I saw one of those two men fall, and I began starting the motor. I was so excited. Bonnie fired her pistol twice or three times and Clyde fired again. I do not know where Clyde was standing when he fired the second time. He might have come back close to the car by the time he fired this shot.

Clyde told me to move over, out from under the steering wheel, and I did. Bonnie had moved close to the door of the car while she was firing, and I moved over against her, and Clyde started the car, driving off very fast. He drove on down County Avenue to Eagle Ford, turning to the right in a westerly direction. We had a siren on the car and he started it going full blast. We drove on up a block or two on Eagle Ford, before turning on lights. We drove on past Mr. Barrow's filling station, where we had stopped before the shooting. We drove on to the first boulevard, and turned to the right. I think this was Westmoreland Road. We turned north on it. It was pouring down rain at this time and it had been raining off and on all that night.

We crossed the river and turned to the left on Industrial Boulevard. We went on through the town of Irving and on toward Grapevine. I went to sleep and when I woke up Clyde told me we were in the edge of Oklahoma.

W. D. JONES, NOVEMBER 1933

Sheriff Davis was laid to rest just inside the entrance to the cemetery at Grapevine — a name which was to become **synonymous with the deaths of more lawmen at the hands of the gang a year hence (see page 218).**

January 26, 1933 – Springfield, Missouri

Two men and a woman, suspected as robbers of Oronogo, Ash Grove and Stockton banks who Thursday night kidnapped Thomas A. Persell, 26, Springfield motorcycle policeman, and released him several hours after on a lonely country road a few miles from Joplin, were being sought Friday by south-west Missouri peace officers.

Persell, who has established a fine record in his service with the motorcycle squad, was kidnapped at the point of a gun about 6 o'clock Thursday night as he halted a motor car near Benton Avenue and Pine Street.

He said he was taken on a ride of more than 100 miles and finally kicked out of the car near Joplin minus his revolver and a package of cigarettes.

Conversation of his abductors regarding towns which they avoided led the young officer to suspect them of the robberies.

His description of his captors, particularly the woman, who had flaming red hair, led police to believe that they might be the trio which held up the Sac River Valley bank at Stockton, November 14, and obtained $9,049. The robbers of the Stockton institution fled in a two-door Ford sedan with Oklahoma licenses, but abandoned it a short distance from the town and got into another new Ford driven by a red-haired woman, believed to have been a former resident of near Stockton.

The robbers who held up the Oronogo bank escaped under gun-fire, and conversation of his captors, who willingly talked of the gun-battle, indicating that they figured in it led Persell to suspect that they were the principals in the hold-up.

Several arrests, however, have been made in the Stockton robbery, Jimmy Grizzie, Cedar county farmer and Bob Brady, an ex-convict, being held at Liberal, Kansas, on a kidnapping charge, are being held as suspects.

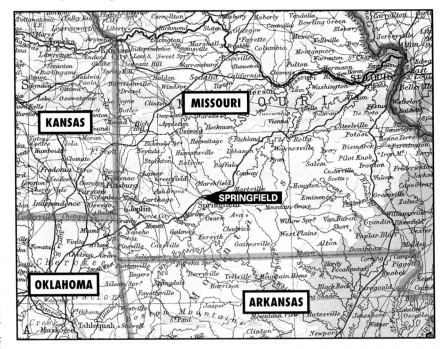

Springfield, Missouri, is perhaps better known as the location of the US Medical Prison . . . not because it was the city where Bonnie and Clyde kidnapped a police motorcyclist! Three weeks after the murder of Sheriff Davis, Clyde, Bonnie and W. D. Jones were cruising the streets of Springfield looking for a car to steal — or more particularly a Ford V-8. Clyde had immediately latched onto the eight-cylinder version when it appeared the previous year and they had already stolen a tan-coloured model earlier that afternoon: Thursday, January 26. However, Clyde felt that the colour might be too distinctive so he ditched the car although, unbeknown to him, the replacement had a dodgy generator. That afternoon, police motorcyclist Tom Persell was on patrol and, when he spotted them cruising, he had an intuition that the occupants were up to no good and were probably looking for a car to steal. *Top:* When they slowed to look over a likely vehicle parked here outside the Shrine Mosque ([1] on the map opposite) on St Louis Street, Persell decided to pull them over.

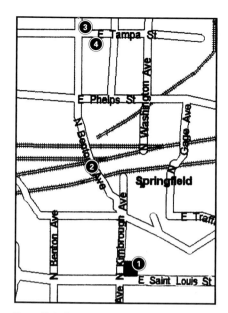

Persell followed as Clyde turned off of St Louis onto Kimbrough *(above)* before making a half-turn left to cross the railroad tracks on the Benton Avenue viaduct [2] — just as the white car is doing in Jim Knight's picture taken in April 2003.

A few minutes before 6 o'clock Thursday night, as I was cruising near the corner of Kimbrough Avenue and St. Louis Street, I noticed suspicious actions of three persons in a V-8 model Ford coach. A girl was riding in the front seat with two men and they looked as if they were trying to 'spot' a car.

They slowed down near a car with a Washington license which was parked in front of the Shrine Mosque but continued west on St Louis Street. A short time later I saw the machine turn east on Mitchell Street, in the rear of the mosque.

Becoming suspicious, I rode there and turned off my lights and a few minutes later they returned and went north over the Benton Avenue viaduct. I pulled up beside the machine and ordered the driver to stop but he declared that he didn't have any brakes.

At the end of the viaduct he turned east on Pine Street and stopped, and I noticed that the girl had gone into the back seat of the car. Her arm was laying on the back of the seat and she had something in her hand, but I didn't know until later that it was a .45 army automatic.

As I pulled up beside the machine, the driver stepped out with a sawed-off automatic shotgun in his hand and ordered me to hold up my hands and step into the car. He jerked my gun out of the holster and threw it to his companion in the front seat.

As I got in the front seat, the man with the gun swung around and shouted to a boy across the street: "Get the hell out of here," and as he got into the machine I thought I saw the boy run down an alley.

The driver was the only person who talked for a time, and he was quite profane. He asked me if I didn't know better than to stop a car with an out-of-state license and I told him that that was what I was getting paid for.

He then told me I would have to show him the way out of town and I told him to turn off Pine Street on Washington Avenue. We drove to Center Street and from there to National Avenue. We left National Avenue at Division Street and went to Glenstone. They appeared to be unacquainted with the streets.

We turned on highway 66, towards St. Louis, but the driver asked me if there wasn't a road to cut across and hit near Joplin and I told him there was. He then ordered the girl in the back seat to look at a map, meanwhile turning back to Glenstone.

We drove about a mile further and they ordered me to get in the rear seat when they covered me with a blanket. The girl held her pistol on me and we drove up to a filling station and the gasoline tank was filled.

After leaving the filling station they told me to climb over into the front seat again and I did breaking one of their suitcases in doing so. I also saw a veritable arsenal bigger than the one at the police station.

The car was well stocked with guns. They had a couple of sawed-off shotguns, a couple of rifles, I don't know how many pistols, and this Thompson sub-machine gun. They were damn proud of it — like kids with their first toy. Said they stole it up in Ohio somewhere.

THOMAS PERSELL, JANUARY 27, 1933

Jim: 'I took this shot from the north end of the viaduct looking south. Clyde would have been driving towards me.'

93

Jim: 'By the time they reached this spot, Clyde had been signalled by Persell *(left)* to pull over but he kept going, not wanting to be trapped on the bridge.' *Right:* 'The building on the right is the Pitts Church [3] which has stood on the corner of Benton and Pine Streets since 1911 although Pine has since been renamed Tampa — or more correctly East Tampa.'

The Bank of Ash Grove was robbed January 12, of $3,500 by two bandits. A companion remained in the car. Two suspects were picked up late Thursday at Pawhuska, Oklahoma, but no identification of the pair has been made.

Persell first saw the bandit car, a Ford coach of V-8 make, near the Shrine Mosque. Suspicious of the actions of the occupants, he followed the machine which went over the viaduct. He ordered the driver to stop and the machine drew to a halt at the end of the viaduct, a few feet east on Pine Street.

As Persell stopped by the machine, he said, the driver covered him with a sawed-off automatic shotgun and ordered him to get into the car. He crawled into the front seat, between two men. The girl rode in the rear seat holding a .45 army automatic on him at all times.

S. S. Perry, 24, of 630 Sutter Avenue, and James Patterson of 1143 North Fremont Avenue saw the kidnapping and ran to the W. W. McMasters grocery store at Benton and Pine. Mr. McMasters called police, and an immediate search of the surrounding territory was launched by Persell's fellow officers.

According to Perry's report to police, the gunman removed Persel's gun from the holster, forced Persell into the machine and ordered Perry back into the store. Patterson, who was walking on the north side of Pine Street, told a similar story.

The abductors ordered Persell to tell them the best way to get out of the city and he told them to go to Glenstone road. After leaving the city they started toward St. Louis on highway 66 but turned back and traversing highway 65, they turned off at Crystal Cave, going to Pleasant Hope.

Persell lost his bearings several times, he said, but he was positive they drove through Fair Play, Morrisville, Golden City and Greenfield. Before leaving Glenstone road, the motorcycle officer was put in the rear seat and the kidnappers halted at a filling station for gasoline. They also stopped at Golden City and a curious night watchman started to investigate the machine but changed his mind. Persell said the watchman flashed his torch.

The leader who drove the machine told the officer that he had had a lot of trouble at Ash Grove once. They talked of a gun-battle at Oronogo and one of the men told Persell that some monkey from the bank had fired on them once. The driver was the most voluble, but all repeatedly told the officer how lucky he was not to have been 'bumped off,' Persell said. They refused to return his revolver when they released him.

During the search Thursday night, Mr. Greenwade and a companion, A. Harmon, street car motorman, stumbled upon the trail of Persell and his abductors but did not know it until they heard the officer's story Friday.

Mr Greenwade decided when he heard the car went north on Washington Avenue that the kidnappers were hunting a country road. He followed their route to Crystal cave and then to Ebenezer. He found no trace of them and returned to Springfield by Grant Avenue road. Mr Greenwade said he expected to find his son-in-law tied to a tree or lying bound by the side of the road.

Mrs. Persell and Mrs. Stanley, his mother, were improving Friday from nervous shock, suffered when first reports of the abduction reached them. Mrs. Stanley went to police headquarters Thursday night, but was removed to her home by physician's order.

The Springfield Press, January 27, 1933

'Clyde eventually turned right on Pine and stopped opposite the church — about where the white car stands [4]. Persell parked his motorcycle and approached the car only to find himself looking down the barrel of a sawn-off shotgun! After the officer had been relieved of his pistol — a fine .44 Russian-calibre Smith & Wesson with stag-horn grips which he had on loan from a former officer (Tommy Fielder who had resigned to become a taxi driver) — Persell was ordered into the car.'

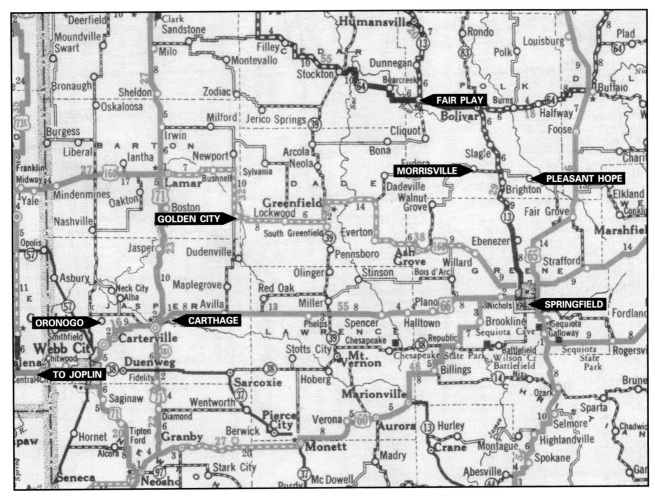

The crazy six-hour ride of Tom Persell — as depicted on a map of the period. The towns he remembered are marked. Driving in a large half-circle north and west, and stopping twice for gas, the car died just outside Oronogo. It was a town that Clyde was familiar with as they had robbed the Farmers & Miners Bank there the previous November (see page 78-79).

Normally Clyde would just have stolen another car but, for some reason, this time he chose to stick with the one they already had. So instead he decided to get a replacement battery as W. D. Jones explains. 'We drove about 150 miles before the car's battery run down and the car quit. The generator wasn't working right. We was just outside a little town so Clyde told me, "Boy, you're gonna have to go get a battery. Take him with you." And that's what we done. Me and that policeman went into town and took a battery out of a car and took turns carrying it back to where Clyde and Bonnie was waiting. You'd have thought we was working buddies. We had a pair of pliers and a wrench and that policeman worked right hard to get that battery in the car like Clyde wanted.' *Left:* From previous visits they knew that a Chrysler was usually parked outside this house belonging to Roy Ferguson but he had garaged the car the day before, so instead they pinched the battery out of Wayne Watson's car across the street. Driving on to Joplin, they released Tom Persell outside the city at Poundstone's Corner. As the officer got out of the car he asked Clyde if he could have his pistol back saying: 'You've got all the guns you need', but Clyde replied succinctly: 'We can use it'. *Right:* Three months later, with publication of the Joplin photos (see pages 108), Tom recognised Jones and his pistol with its tell-tale grips hanging on the front of the car! When Jones was later arrested, Tom Persell went to Dallas to ask him what happened to his pistol. W. D. told him that it was left behind at Dexfield Park. Persell discovered that it was now in the possession of a police officer in Des Moines but, because he could not supply the serial number, he never did get it back!

March 11 and 18, 1933 – Baxter Springs, Kansas

An unmasked bandit held up the Ray Kirkendoll grocery on West Twelfth Street, this city Saturday night obtaining $53.76 from the cash register and a small sum of money from Claude Parham, clerk at the store.

The robbery occurred at about 8:30 when Parham and Everett Stone were looking after the store. Mr. and Mrs. Roy Talbot and small daughter were in the store making a purchase, when the robber entered. The bandit produced two guns and ordered Parham to hold up his hands. He then ordered him to lower his hands, thinking perhaps that the clerk with his hands elevated might attract attention from passers-by. Parham was then ordered to get the money out of the register and place it in a sack, which he did.

After forcing the folks in the store to lie down the man made his getaway through the rear door, with a word of warning to them to remain where they were for a time.

Baxter Springs Citizen and Herald,
March 13, 1933.

The Ray Kirkendoll Grocery on West Twelfth Street, was the scene Saturday night of a return visit by the same bandit group that robbed the store just a week previous.

Saturday night, between 9:30 and 9:45, while Ray Kirkendoll, and his two sons, Ray, Jr., and Robert, Claude Parham and Everett Stone, employees, and John Hunt, a customer, were in the store, a smiling stranger entered the store, took two or three steps inside and ordered Kirkendoll to stick up his hands.

He was closely followed by a tall, slender man, who has been identified to have been the same man who held up the store a week previous. Both men carried guns and forced all the people in the store to hold up their hands.

Kirkendoll was ordered to empty the cash register, which he did, of approximately $25. John Hunt and the others were searched, and small sums of cash were taken. A watch was taken from Hunt as well as a small sum in change. Hunt was able to outwit the robber and saved his billfold, which contained some currency.

The lock to the rear door was secured by a padlock, and Ray Kirkendoll Jr., was made to get up from the floor and unlock it.

A Mrs. Banks, who lives about a block from the grocery, told the officers that the robbers parked their car about a block north of the store, and that while the robbery was in progress, one man remained at the wheel of the car. She said that she saw the men leave the store and run to the car, after which they drove north and left the city.

From the descriptions given by the victims, it was unquestionably the same group that paid the return visit to the store. It was also probable that these are the same men who robbed a grocery at Cardin a week ago and also Saturday night.

Chief of Police John Moyer and Night Marshal Harlin had been patrolling the city Saturday night, and Moyer had just left the Kirkendoll store a few minutes before the bandits entered.

Baxter Springs Citizen and Herald,
March 20, 1933

At the time, robbing small stores and stealing cars were commonplace and there is no real way of singling out all those in which the Barrow gang were involved. Baxter Springs — whose claim to fame is that it is the 'First Cow Town in Kansas' — is a good example. Roy Talbot, pictured *(left)* beside the rear door of Kirkendoll's store in 1973, was convinced that these robberies were carried out by Clyde Barrow — but were they? What *is* special about Baxter Springs is that the old store still survives, particularly when it closed for business in 1978! This is something pretty unique in the States where any old redundant building — especially a wooden one — has a job to survive a few years, let alone 70!

But there is certainly one petty crime which can be attributed to Clyde one hundred per cent . . . because he was pictured prominently with the stolen property! We refer of course to the theft of Robert Rosborough's Ford V-8 which we mentioned briefly on page 10. It is the very existence of the series of photographs of Clyde, Bonnie and W. D. Jones (see pages 108-113) which sets the Barrow gang apart from all the other Depression desperadoes. Without these pictures, all we would have would be mere mugshots in a police archive, but with these informal snapshots, Bonnie and Clyde become alive as individuals, posing as tough guys, fooling around, and as friends . . . and lovers. That is why the theft of the car is so important. It is difficult to pinpoint the exact date in 1933 when it was stolen, as its loss is not reported in the local paper but it has to be March. Robert, *(left)*, was then dating his wife-to-be, Marie Watson, *(right)*. Late that afternoon he called at his parent's home on Rosborough Street to freshen up. Bobbie, as he was called, had a penchant for always leaving his keys in the car and that day was no exception.

Robert Franklin Rosborough died at 7:35 Thursday, November 7, 2002, at Marshall Regional Hospital. He was 97 years of age.

Mr. Rosborough is a fourth generation son of Marshall. His paternal great grandfather, Wyatt Jones Rosborough (1833-1909), was the founder of Rosborough Springs. On his maternal side, he is a descendant of James Cutler Bonham, who fought for Texas independence in the Alamo.

'Bobbie' was born the son of James Craig Rosborough and Hazel Bonham Rosborough on Christmas Eve 1904 in Marshall. He attended Marshall public schools and graduated from Texas Agricultural and Mechanical College in 1926 with a degree in business administration. While in college, he was in the Cadet Corps and was a member of the Ross Volunteers and the Troop B Cavalry. After graduation, Mr. Rosborough sold insurance and established his own insurance agency, Rosborough & Byrne, in 1929 in Marshall. From 1942 to 1945 he served as a Captain in the United States Army Air Corps during World War II.

Mr. Rosborough was the retired owner and president of Marshall Oil Company and Rosborough Oil Company. He has served as a past director of the Marshall Federal Savings and Loan Association, the People's State Bank, and as past president of the Caddo Savings and Loan Association. He was president of the Harrison County Community Chest in 1958-1959.

He was a past president and the eldest living member of the Marshall Lakeside Country Club where he was a four-time winner of the Club Championship. He had three holes-in-one to his golf credit. He was the recipient of the Seventy-Five Year Freemasons Pin in 1996. He was an honorary member of the Marshall Rotary Club which he joined in 1934 and served as secretary from 1933 thru 1937. He was an active member of the Martex Syndicate.

Mr. Rosborough was a lifelong member of the First Methodist Church and has served numerous years as a steward in the church.

Marshall News Messenger, November 9, 2002

March 1933 — Marshall, Texas

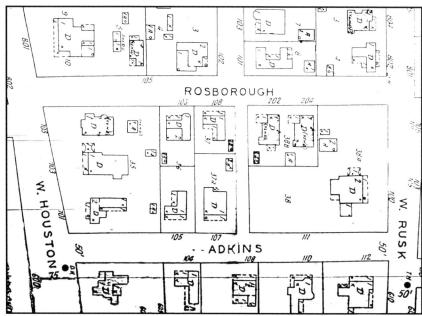

One of our greatest disappointments during the production of this book is just missing interviewing Mr Rosborough who still lived in Marshall (see map page 44), although not in the same house as in 1933. For his last months, he had been living in a residential home and we were trying to reach him by telephone at the very moment when he was taken into Marshall Regional Hospital. He died there on November 7, 2002. He was 97.

Fortunately we were able to talk to Bobbie's daughter Gail *(left)*. She told us that the road had been named after her grandfather — the first person who had built a house on the street — and that Robert's great grandfather founded Rosborough Springs, a town located a few miles south of Marshall. *Right:* This is the plan from 1932 on which his parents' — James and Hazel — house is marked No. 202 although its present street number is 200.

Left: **Bobbie Rosborough with Bess and Sport and the 1933 five-window coupe which replaced the 1932 Ford** *(above)* **stolen by Bonnie and Clyde.**

Robert F. Rosborough was one of the unlucky car owners who had to give up a Ford to Clyde Barrow. Rosborough's car was stolen outside his family home in Marshall more than 50 years ago. He had owned the car for only two months and had just parked it 15 minutes before he discovered it missing.

Rosborough said, 'I had just returned home on the afternoon of April 10, 1932 *[This date is completely wrong — even the year is incorrect — Ed].* I was preparing for a date when my mother asked if I would go get the milk bottles from the porch. I went outside and my car was gone.'

He said his first thought was that someone was playing a joke on him because he had left his keys in the car. Later he found out it wasn't a joke, but he had no idea the thieves would turn out to be criminal legends.

Rosborough said the car was a brand-new Ford V-8, and it was capable of speeds up to 60 miles per hour. 'That's why most desperadoes of those days stole Fords; for the speed,' he said.

Rosborough said he did not realize that Bonnie and Clyde were in fact the persons who had stolen his car until after the bloody incident that brought the duo notoriety in Joplin, Missouri.

Rosborough said after the Joplin ordeal, Marshall Police Chief Clarence Ezell came into his insurance office and laughingly said, 'We've got you!' Joplin authorities had traced the license plate from the first three numbers visible in the picture and had notified Ezell about the incident.

Within days of the Joplin films being found they were published in the *Marshall Messenger* but the pictures were cropped so tight that the tell-tale number plate was cut off. It would appear therefore that the *Messenger* slipped up badly in not making the connection in what would have been a marvellous front page scoop.

Only when the local police chief Clarence Ezell called on Bobbie at his office — which still operates under the name of Rosborough & Byrne in the original building on East Rusk — that he realised that his car was involved. It was returned to him in a filthy condition, littered with stale food and dirty underwear. It was only later that the infamous duo became household names . . . but by that time Bobbie had disposed of the car!

We visited the house from where the car was stolen — still as pristine today as the day it was built

Authorities later found the car abandoned outside a cafe in Vinita, Oklahoma. The car was returned to Rosborough thirty days later, on May 15, 1932 (*sic*).

When the car was back in Marshall, Rosborough said he found clothing believed to have belonged to Bonnie, a tripod and machine gun holes in the floor boards. The car had been driven 3,500 miles.

Rosborough traded the car in some time after it was returned to him. 'I wish now that I would have held on to it,' he said.

Marshall News Messenger, March 10, 1985

The present occupier, Mrs Ladonna Manning, was very interested to hear from Gail about what had happened at her house . . . and was amused to learn that another Ford had been stolen from the very spot where her Ford was parked!

Time and again I am told — by my own organization and by others — that I penalize myself by quality.

Friendly critics protest our putting into the Ford V-8 what they call "twenty-year steel." They say such quality is not necessary; the public does not expect it; and that the public does not know the difference anyway.

But I know the difference.

I know that the car a man sees is not the car he drives — he drives the car which the engineer sees. The car which is seen, comprises beauty of design, color and attractive accessories — all desirable, of course. The best evidence that we think so is that they are all found on the Ford V-8.

But these are not the car. The car proper, which is the basis of all the rest, is the type of engine and its reliability; *the structure of chassis and body, ruggedly durable; the long thought and experiment given to safety factors; the steady development of comfort, convenience and economy. These make the car.*

A car can be built that will last two or three years. But we have never built one. We want the basic material of our car to be as dependable the day it is discarded as the day it is bought. Ford cars built 15 years ago are still on the road. It costs more to build a durable car — but two items we do not skimp are cost and conscience. A great many things could "get by" — the public would never know the difference. But we would know.

HENRY FORD, DEARBORN, MAY 15, 1933

Yet Bobbie still had the car, albeit in miniature and the wrong colour! The Franklin Mint added the Ford to their list in

February 2000 but produced it in red with whitewalls instead of green (see press report page 114).

On March 22, 1933, Buck was paroled from Huntsville Prison. It had been some 14 months since he had seen his brother and he wanted to catch up with Clyde but Blanche was fearful as to what it might lead to. However Buck insisted so a few days after his release, in a newly-purchased Marmon sedan, and with Blanche's little dog Snowball, they set off north for a rendezvous near Fort Smith, Arkansas. Bonnie and Clyde with W. D. were then travelling in two Fords, one being the 1932 coupe which they had recently stolen from Bobbie Rosborough. On the way they stopped twice to take photographs of each other fooling around with their guns, the first time in open countryside, the second in a more rocky location. Meeting up, they decided to continue north and find a place where they could stay together and catch up on all the news. Passing through Fayette-ville — where Clyde most probably noted a possible robbery opportunity — they crossed the state line into Missouri and entered Joplin. It was Friday, March 31.

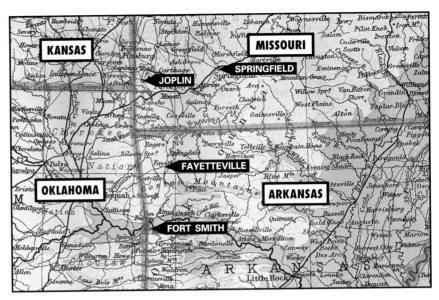

March 31-April 13, 1933 — Joplin, Missouri

A gun-battle with two desperados at a residence in Freeman Grove, in the south part of the city, last night had claimed the lives of two officers. J. W. (Wes) Harryman, 41-year-old Newton county constable, was killed instantly by buckshot from a sawed-off shotgun, used by one of the desperadoes. Harry McGinnis, 53, Joplin motor car detective, died at 11 o'clock last night in St. John's hospital as the result of shock and loss of blood from several wounds. His right arm had been shot away at the elbow: four buckshot struck him in the left side, and one slug struck his left cheek.

Three other officers who participated in the gun-battle escaped unscathed, although shots were fired at two of the officers.

The desperadoes, who have tentatively been identified as Ivy (Buck) Barrow, 27 years old, and his brother, Clyde Barrow, about 28, both of Dallas, Texas, known to Texas officers as 'bad men', shot their way to freedom, although one of them, believed to be Clyde Barrow, is believed to have been wounded.

Fleeing with the two men in a motor car were two women, one of whom, police apparently have established, is the wife of Ivy Barrow. Both young women are known to Dallas police.

The last trace of the car, as it sped southward out of Joplin at a high rate of speed, was west of Seneca, where it was reported seen by several persons.

On the way into town they stopped at a filling station where Blanche and Bonnie made enquiries about places to rent. As it happened, the owners of the garage, Mr and Mrs Ellis Smith, had a house available — No. 2314 *(above)* in Virginia Avenue — so the girls quickly put down a month's rent as a deposit.

However, the following day the two women came back and said that they had decided not to take the house so the Smiths returned the deposit and thought no more about it. No doubt what had happened in the interim was that Clyde had found a more suitable apartment for rent in the Freeman Grove area.

Not only was it built of stone rather than wood but it had garage space available. It was also more secluded yet the main road was only 100 yards away should a quick getaway be necessary. *Left:* No. 3347½ 34th Street, pictured by Blanche in 1933 and *(right)* by Jim Knight in November 2002.

Altogether, the gang had three vehicles, but only Buck's Marmon was legal, Clyde's two being stolen. For a lengthy stopover it was essential to get the Fords under cover but unfortunately only the left-hand garage nearest the front door was empty, the other one being used by the tenant of the main house next door, a salesman named Harold Hill. Buck quickly did a deal with him to take over his half of the garage which took care of the two stolen Fords. These were always reversed inside which after the event neighbours said did look unusual as most drivers avoided backing into exhaust fumes. *Above:* Behind the two houses there was an alleyway leading to the garage of the adjoining property which faced onto Oak Ridge Drive round the corner. *Right:* This double garage stood directly behind the apartment and could be overlooked from its windows so Buck rented that garage as well to get his own vehicle off the street.

Looking at the rear of the Barrow's apartment with the Marmon's garage on the right.

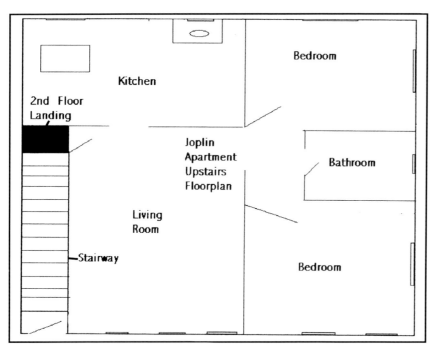

Kitchen

2nd Floor
Landing

Bedroom

Joplin
Apartment
Upstairs
Floorplan

Bathroom

Living
Room

—Stairway

Bedroom

Safely tucked away in their new home, with the curtains closed against prying eyes, the two brothers settled down to what they might have hoped would be an opportunity to relax. Buck did his best to persuade Clyde to relinquish his life of crime but, with more than one murder to his credit, Clyde knew that there was no turning back for if the law caught up with him he would inevitably face the electric chair. Cooped up all day, Bonnie and Blanche soon began to get on each other's nerves while W. D. must have felt the odd man out. To relieve the pressure it appears that during the 12 days that they spent in Joplin, they sallied out to rob at least one grocery store, the office of a tourist camp, and to relieve the owner of the Neosho Milling Company of the contents of their safe which included some diamonds. Neighbours had already began to be suspicious of the goings on in the apartment but it was the latter hold-up that was Bonnie and Clyde's undoing as the vehicle used matched the description of one of their cars. Although the Joplin city police were unaware of exactly who they were up against, thinking they might be bootleggers, State Trooper Kahler of the Missouri State Highway Patrol applied for a warrant to search the apartment.

Police, in a search of the house later, found a small-sized arsenal and five diamonds. The gems were identified as having been taken in a recent burglary of the Neosho Milling Company establishment.

Five officers went to the house about 4 o'clock yesterday afternoon, Harryman armed with a liquor search warrant. Members of Troop D of the state highway patrol previously had been 'tipped off' that two men suspected of having staged the Neosho robbery, as well as recent highway robberies in this vicinity, were at the residence.

In one car, driven by Detective Tom DeGraff, were Harryman and McGinnis, Harryman riding in the front seat with DeGraff and McGinnis riding in the rear seat. In the other car were Troopers G. B. Kahler and W. E. Grammer. Kahler being the driver.

The dwelling, which has a garage on the ground floor, is situated just in the rear of another residence at Thirty-fourth Street and Oak Ridge Drive. The officers drove west from Main Street to the residence, the highway patrol car leading . Kahler stopped his car just west of the house. DeGraff, seeing the garage partly open and one of the men at the door, drove directly up against the door, telling Harryman 'I'll just head right in.' As he applied the brakes to the police car, the man at the garage door attempted to close it.

'Get in there as quickly as you can before they close that door,' DeGraff shouted, and Harryman leaped from the police car towards the partly-open garage door. As he did so, one of the men inside fired point-blank with a sawed-off shotgun, and Harryman fell inside the garage with ten or more slugs through his right shoulder and chest, mortally wounded.

As McGinnis leaped from the rear seat of the police car, his revolver in his hand, the desperadoes fired a volley of shots at him and he fell to the ground, his right arm almost severed at the elbow: four slugs from the sawed-off shotgun through the lower part of his abdomen on the left side of his body, and a bullet wound on the left side of his face at his mouth. By that time, DeGraff had applied the brakes to his car. He leaped out, crouched by the side of the car and fired through panes of glass in the garage door. Then he ran around the car to the east side of the residence.

Kahler's version of the shooting was that when he stopped his car just west of the residence, Grammer jumped out of the car and darted toward the garage door. One of the bullets fired by the desperadoes passed through the open windows of the patrol car, barely missing Kahler's head. Grammer had started around the west side of the residence to find another entrance, and Kahler had just got out of the car, with his revolver in his hand, when one of the desperadoes walked out of the garage with the sawed-off shotgun. Kahler said he fired several shots at the man, who then retreated inside the garage.

With only one bullet remaining in his revolver, Kahler retreated a short distance to reload when the man with the sawed-off shotgun again came out of the garage. He fired one charge at Kahler, the shot crashing against the corner of an adjoining residence, near where Kahler stood. Kahler, attempting to avoid being struck, tripped and fell and

the desperado apparently thought he had wounded him. The second bandit joined him saying 'Where did that other fellow go?' As the man with the sawed-off shotgun turned to return to the garage, Kahler took good aim and fired his last bullet. The man fell, he said, and then staggered into the garage. Kahler expressed belief his bullet had hit the desperado in the back.

Kahler then retreated a short distance to reload, but was unable to reload fast enough to fire any more shots at the man before they made their escape.

Grammer, in going to the rear of the residence just after the two cars had stopped at the residence, saw DeGraff, who shouted to him, 'For God's sake run to that house and phone the station to send more men out here.' He ran to the adjoining house, in which Harold N. Hill resides, and telephoned police. He ran out of the house just as the desperadoes and the young women were speeding away.

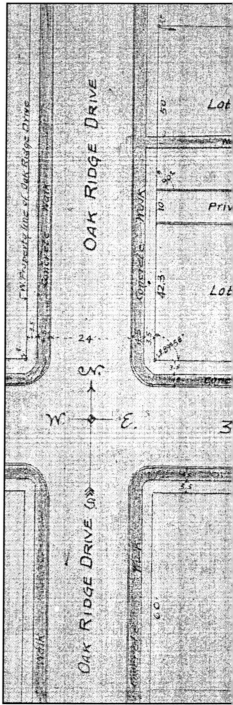

This scene-of-crime plan was prepared by the city engineer J. B. Hodgdon after the raid which took place on the afternoon of Thursday, April 13.

Jim Knight pictured the Barrow's view overlooking the road (34th Street) from the windows at the front of the apartment. *Left:* Looking down to where the police car drew up, temporarily blocking any escape. It was shunted diagonally across the road (see plan). *Right:* View from the side windows on the landing at the top of the stairs towards the spot where the state police car parked by the curb. The corner of the main house (No. 3347 Oak Ridge Drive) can just be seen on the right.

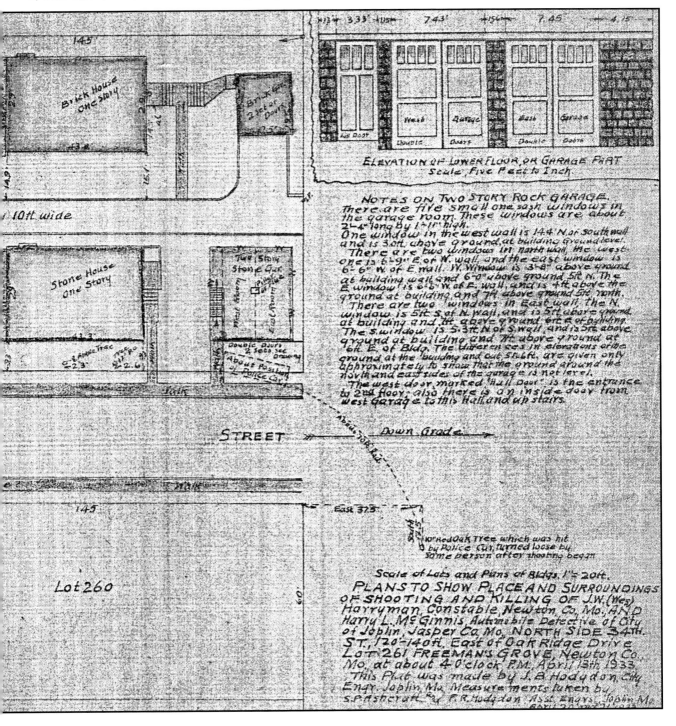

Looking down 34th Street from the corner of Oak Ridge Drive. In the foreground the main house which was owned by Paul Freeman in 1933. The Barrow's apartment block stands behind the pick-up truck, partially hidden by the trees. Note how 34th Street runs steeply downhill which enabled the police car to be pushed out of the way.

DeGraff said he ran to the Hill house to reload just as the desperadoes were running their car out of the garage. One of the men, he said, released the brake on the police car and it rolled down the tree-lined garage driveway across the street into a clump of small trees, as the desperadoes' car struck its bumper, DeGraff said one of the men stood menacing him with the sawed-off shotgun while the other man drove the car out of the garage.

One of the women, it was said, ran toward the police car as it rolled down the driveway, but was summoned back by one of the bandits. The woman and the man with the sawed-off shotgun then got into the car and sped east to Main Street, thence south on the Seneca road.

Papers found in the residence showed that Governor Miriam Ferguson of Texas had granted a full pardon to Ivy Barrow March 23, 1933, from a four-year sentence from Denton county, Texas, for burglary in 1929. A motor car certificate of title for a car purchased in Dallas, Texas, also bore the name Carl Beaty.

In a telephone conversation last night with Dallas police, Joplin officers learned that Clyde Barrow has been using the name of Jack or Carl Beaty, who resides at Dallas, which was the name found on a certificate of title to one of three motor cars used by the two men here. The Texas officers said both men were wanted at Abilene and Sherman, Texas, for highway robbery, and that it was reported Clyde Barrow had shot and killed four officers in various parts of the country.

The officers said they last heard of the Barrow brothers about six weeks ago in Michigan. Barrow's wife and the woman with Clyde Barrow are well known to Dallas police they said.

Captain L. E. Eslick, commander of Troop D of the state highway patrol, in a telephone conversation last night with Tulsa authorities, learned that Clyde Barrow is wanted for the killing of a sheriff in Atoka county, Oklahoma.

It also was learned last night that the woman with Clyde Barrow has been tentatively identified as Bonnie Parker.

Paul Freeman, owner of the Thirty-fourth Street residence, said two women and a man came to his home the first of this month to rent the house. He said she told him her husband's name was W. L. Callahan, that he was a civil engineer from Minnesota and that the woman with her was her sister. Police believe Callahan is Ivy Barrow.

Officers also expressed belief Ivy Barrow was the driver of the car in which the men and the women escaped, and that the man in the rear seat may have been Clyde Barrow.

In the residence, officers found an automatic rifle, four high-power rifles, a sawed-off shotgun and a revolver. A badge of the Police and Sheriffs' Association of North America, identical with one found at Tenth and Main Streets recently by a Joplin man, also was found in the house. Officers expressed belief the men used the badges in recent hold-ups, pretending they were officers.

The sawed-off shotgun which shot down the two officers was loaded with No. 1 buckshot, balls of lead almost as large as a small pea. Several shells, apparently hand-loaded with the buckshot, were found later inside the garage.

Among other things found in the house was a marriage certificate, showing Ivy Barrow, who gave his address as McCurtain, Okla., was married July 1, 1931 (sic), to Blanche Caldwell, also of McCurtain. Besides the five diamonds, which were found

The apartment has been owned since 1968 by DeWayne Tuttle who very kindly allowed Jim access to take his photos. A door at the bottom of the stairway leads into the garage. If only these steps could speak of the drama that Thursday long ago!

Of course both police and the press had difficulty in identifying who was who in the events which followed. Jim Knight has researched every aspect down to the last round fired and tells us that in fact by that Thursday Clyde already had it in mind to pack up and leave as he never liked staying in one place too long. The vehicle used in the Neosho robbery had already been replaced with another stolen Ford roadster belonging to Earl Stanton of Miami, Oklahoma, and was being road-tested by Clyde and W. D. on that very afternoon as it was running rough. They had only just backed into the garage to change one of the tyres when the police car pulled up in front. Reacting in a split second, Clyde blasted Constable Harryman with his shotgun as the policeman climbed out of the front passenger seat with his pistol drawn and then turned his gun on the Highway Patrol officer Harry McGinnis as he exited from the rear left-hand seat. Both officers had managed to

return the fire before they went down, hitting W. D. in the stomach. As Jones struggled up the stairs to get the girls and Buck who had been asleep, Clyde traded shots with the officers in the State Police car, one of whom had run down the alleyway to the rear of the building. Rejoining Clyde, the three of them first attempted to push the police car out of the way. Unable to release the handbrake they then opened the other garage door and piled into Rosborough's convertible. However, instead of getting in the car, Blanche had calmly walked off up the road calling for Snowball who had run off. McGinnis was lying in front of the garage so in a moment of compassion Buck dragged him out of the way as Clyde rammed the police car which rolled back across the road (see plan pages 102-103). We have included this picture, albeit of very poor quality, as it appears to be the only photograph taken the day after the double murder.

hidden in various parts of the house, officers also found a guitar, a number of letters and clothing. A money sack of the McDaniel National bank of Springfield was also found.

Ivy Barrow, according to prison records found among his effects, is 37 years old. 5 feet 4 inches tall and weighs 122 pounds. His complexion and eyes are brown and his occupation is that of a cook.

An investigation of the shooting was made late yesterday by J. D. Rice, Newton county prosecuting attorney, and Coroner J. A. Bigham of Newton county. Bigham said a coroners jury would view Harryman's body at 10 o'clock tomorrow morning at Main Street and County line. No time has been set for an inquest.

Dr. W. G. Hogan of Nock City, Jasper county coroner, said last night he will make arrangements this morning for an inquest in the death of McGinnis. The body of the city detective is at the Hurlbut Undertaking Company establishment.

McGinnis, who served as acting chief of detectives during the recent illness of Ed Portley, chief of detectives, had been an officer about eight years. He was born October 7, 1878, at Nevada, Missouri.

Turning left down the hill, they caught up with Blanche who was still calling for her dog before making a right onto Main Street two blocks further on, aiming for the Oklahoma state line ten miles away via the famous Route 66. *Above:* Jim took the picture looking east on 34th Street in 2002. *Below:* Comparison 69 years later.

Jim Knight photographed Detective Harry McGinnis's grave for us in Deepwood Cemetery in Nevada, a small town some 60 miles north of Joplin.

Surviving are his mother, Mrs W. J. Atchison, 407 South Cox avenue; two sisters, Mrs. M. F. Burson of Twin falls, Idaho, and Mrs D. A. Sullivan of Salt Lake City; two brothers, W. O. McGinnis, 618 Highland avenue, and M. L. McGinnis of Minneapolis, Minnisota, and ten nieces and nephews.

At the police station, an examination of revolvers carried by McGinnis and Harryman showed the Joplin detective fired three times and the constable fired once.

An examination of Harryman's body disclosed he had been shot ten times at the juncture of the right part of the neck and the right shoulder, the wounds occupying a space about four inches square. The carida artery and sub-clavian artery were severed. One slug passed through the body. Two slugs were removed and turned over to police.

Harryman was elected constable of Shoal Creek township, in Newton county, at the general election last November. Surviving are his widow, Mrs Atha Harryman; four daughters, Alga Harryman, Sadie Harryman, Grace Ollie Harryman and Sarah E. Harryman, all at home; two sons, Claude Harryman and John Wesley Harryman, at home; four sisters, Mrs. Gertrude Pery of Joplin, Mrs. Lula Bartlett and Mrs. Atha Shuck of Picher and Mrs. Sophia Bruce of Dallas, Texas, and two brothers, Buster Harryman of Dallas and Thornton Harryman of Picher. Funeral arrangements are incomplete.

Joplin Globe, April 14, 1933

Jim has even analysed the number of shots fired, revealing that the police officers were only able to get off 14 rounds (Harryman 1, McGinnis 3, DeGraff 4 and Kahler 6) which more or less matched those fired by the gang. Later, when recounting this episode to Clyde's sister, Bonnie claimed that she had grabbed a gun and fired from the windows 'but I know I didn't hit him, as he ran off down the street'. Yet Jones claimed that 'during the five big gun-battles I was in with them, she never fired a gun but she was a hell of a loader'. W. D. had been hit but he says that 'Clyde wrapped an elm branch with gauze and pushed it through the hole in my side and out my back so I knew the bullet had gone clean through me'. Clyde had also stopped a police bullet as Bonnie explains: 'Just as Clyde started to climb into the front seat, he looked down and saw blood streaming from his chest. I remember he stood there a second, gazing down, then whipped back his shirt and said: "Can you find it?" meaning the bullet. I probed the hole hastily with my finger tips, felt the flattened bullet, and with Clyde's help and a hairpin, pulled it out. It must have bounded back from the wall and struck him because it wasn't in deep.' *Left:* This door came from the top of the stairs in the apartment. DeWayne Tuttle, the present owner of the property, donated it to the Dorothea B. Hoover Museum in Schifferdecker Park, Joplin.

Newton county Constable John Harryman was buried in the family plot in the far corner of the Community Cemetery located on the outskirts of the little town of Saginaw, south of Joplin.

WANTED FOR MURDER
$600.00 REWARD
JOPLIN, MISSOURI

On April 13, 1933, these men shot and killed Detective Harry McGinnis and Constable J. W. Harryman at Joplin, Missouri, in suburban residence district.

Reward offered: $200.00 by the City of Joplin
$200.00 by the County of Jasper
$200.00 by the County of Newton
All rewards to be paid upon arrest and conviction

CLYDE CHAMPION BARROW

Age 23 years.
Height 5 ft. 7 in. BF.
Weight 125 pounds.
Hair Dark brown, wavy.
Eyes Hazel.
Complexion Light.
Occupation None
Home West Dallas, Texas.

This man is very dangerous; his record shows that he has killed at least three or four men before this and participated in several highway robberies.

FINGER PRINT CLASSIFICATION:
29 — MO 9
26 U 00 9

MELVIN IVAN BARROW

Age 31 years.
Height 5 ft. 5 in. BF.
Weight 110 pounds.
Hair Chestnut.
Eyes Maroon.
Complexion Ruddy.
Occupation Laborer.
Home Dallas, Texas.

This man was pardoned from the Texas Penitentiary on March 23, 1933, by Governor Ferguson.

FINGER PRINT CLASSIFICATION:
9 U 11 9
1 R 11 11

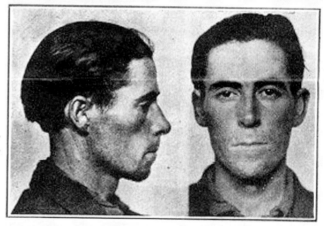

If more than one claimant for reward, parties offering reward will reserve right to apportion as they think proper.

These men made their getaway in a V-8 Ford Coach, Dark Green Color, 1932 model.

They were accompanied by two young women who lived with them in an apartment over the garage where the shooting occured.

The assistance and co-operation of all officers is requested in the apprehension of these men.

Notify Police Department, Joplin, Missouri

Thus, within three weeks of being released from Huntsville, Buck was again a wanted man, but whereas his earlier sentence had been for theft, now he was accused with Clyde of a capital offence. We now know that it was Clyde who fired the fatal shots which killed the officers but at the time the blame fell on 'Ivy' in both the press and police reports. Joplin police combined with the city counties of Jasper and Newton to put up a reward, $600 in 1933 probably being worth around $10,000 in today's money. The mug-shots were those already on file in Texas (see page 38) but in future there would be a whole new set of photos to use. Recovered in the apartment were two rolls of film which police rushed to the darkroom of the local newspaper for developing. Prints were made and three were reproduced in the Saturday edition of the *Joplin Globe*: 'Pictures of negatives found in the house and developed and enlarged by the art department of *The Globe* were identified yesterday by police as those of the Barrow brothers. The picture of one of the brothers was identified by DeGraff as the desperado with the sawed-off shotgun.' Police departments across the Midwest immediately requested copies of the photos to supplant the usual mug-shots used on wanted posters like those above. The fate of the original negatives has been an ongoing mystery ever since 1933. Although the Missouri State Highway Patrol took possession after the prints were made, the negatives now in their possession are copies made in 1963. Commander Jim Hounschell tells us that in the late 1980s he discovered that a local photographer, Karl Lee, had five of the negatives in his possession but he has since died. On the following pages we have brought together images from a variety of sources to recreate the original sequence of the captured film.

The film in the camera was developed and printed up in time for selected shots to appear in the press on Saturday. Since that day — April 15, 1933 — the names of Bonnie Parker and Clyde Barrow took on a whole new meaning.

Instead of being portrayed through bland police mug-shots, now a series of informal photographs gave a whole new insight into their persona and it is interesting to speculate whether they would have achieved the same legendary status if these pictures had never existed.

Joplin Globe

FULL ASSOCIATED PRESS REPORTS

JOPLIN, MISSOURI, SATURDAY MORNING, APRIL 15, 1933.—TWELVE PAGES.

Desperadoes Sought in Killing of Two Peace Officers

AIR FOR SUNDAY IS THE FORECAST

ARMER WEATHER ALSO REDICTED TO FOLLOW RAIN AND SNOW HERE.

ain and snow flurries continued night, as the temperature re-ned near the freezing mark. rmer weather was forecast for ay, but with possibility of rain ntinuing.

he federal forecast gave promise air weather Sunday. For south-. Kansas, which generally gov-. weather conditions for this ediate section, fair and warmer Sunday was predicted.

rospective relenting of the ther man by Easter Sunday ered thousands who plan vari-forms of entertainment and re-ous observances for that day. addition to sunrise services at ho and by various church ps in towns throughout the rict, egg hunts also are planned everal district towns and other ns of amusements also are on program.

xtensive preparations for ch services have been made. e mercury fell to the 33-degree k, one degree above freezing, re midnight last night. The ipitation during the day meas-.36 of an inch.

ainfall measurements in the dis-yesterday were as follows: ra, .15; Ozark Beach, .30; Boli-11; Caplinger Mills, .28; Green-.45; Osceola, .50; Beaver, .20, and Galena, Mo., .20.

urly temperatures were as fol-

Above are pictured the Barrow brothers—Buck and Clyde—Texas gunmen sought throughout the southwest as the slayers of J. W. (West) Harryman, 41 years old, a Newton county constable, and Harry Mc-Ginnis, Joplin city detective, who were killed late Thursday. In the upper left hand photograph the two brothers are shown posed together, with Clyde on the right. The picture in the upper right is of Buck Barrow sitting on the front bumper of a Ford V-8 motor car. The two guns he is holding and one leaning against the car are believed to be among those seized in the house from which the men fled. The motor car is believed the one in which they escaped. In the lower picture Buck Barrow is shown with his arm around a young woman, who has been identified as one of the two women who fled with the gunmen after the gun fight. Her name is not definitely known to authorities. The photographs are enlargings made by the art depart-ment of The Globe from small kodak negatives found among the effects of one of the women at the gunmen's hideout.

PART OF SHOALS PLAN IS OPPOSE

FERTILIZERS' INTEREST TAKE STAND AGAINST FED ERAL COMPETITION.

Washington, April 14.—(AP)—Fe-lizer and power interests foc joined in a reiterated demand th congress take out of the Roosev Tennessee valley plan all provisio implying possible government co petition with their industries.

Spokesmen for each told house military committee their dustries were expanded far beyo present consumption levels and th only with the aid of a subsidy fr the treasury could the governm compete at Muscle Shoals.

Alternative Is Suggested.
"Don't scrap a private industr urged Charles J. Brand, secret of the National Fertilizer Asso tion. "If you are going to put government into competition w us, buy existing plants."

W. L. Willkie, president of Commonwealth and Southern c poration, said six southern c panies of the group had outsta ing senior securities of $400,000, "I give as my deliberate ju ment that if this plan is carried the value of these securities ev tually will be destroyed." Will testified.

Tomorrow, the other side of power argument will be presen by Judson King, director of the tional Popular Government Lea Before nightfall Chairman McSw said be hoped to conclude heari on the administration's vast nessee basin project.

WORLD FLYING TROPHY TO AMELIA EARHA

Paris, April 14.—(AP)—Amelia E hart Putnam was awarded the Harmon international avia trophy today for her flight ac the Atlantic in May, 1932, the crossing ever accomplished b woman alone.

National awards for the Un States were: Aviators trophy, L Col. Roscoe Turner, who has considerable coast-to-coast flyin the United States, amateur tr

O FLIERS "BAIL OUT" WHEN PLANES COLLIDE

Jury Is Being Chosen to Pass On Mrs. Judd's Mental Status

The photographs were taken sometime between the theft in March of Bobbie Rosborough's Ford — for the technically-minded a 1932 Type B-400 five-passenger convertible sedan — and April 13 when the film was captured . . . and somewhere between Marshall, Texas, and Joplin, Missouri. *Above left:* Clyde at the wheel and Bonnie *(above right)* in the passenger seat. W. D. (seen *(right)* and *(below)* with Clyde) who took the photos tells us that 'Clyde really banked on them Fords. They was the fastest and the best and he knew how to drive them with one foot in the gas tank all the time.' Apart from W. D. Jones being mis-identified in the newspaper caption as Clyde's brother, the greatest repercussion was to befall Bonnie. W. D. explains: 'Bonnie smoked cigarettes *(below centre)* but that cigar bit folks like to tell about is phoney. I guess I got that started when I gave her my cigar to hold when I was making her picture *(below right)*. I made most of them pictures the laws picked up when we fled Joplin.'

Two different locations appear in the shots taken with Rosborough's Ford, the first being when the car is parked on a fairly open track bordered with an earth bank topped by brush. It would be nice to be able to include a comparison of the spot today but so many roads in the States have been completely altered in the past 70 years, it would be worse than looking for the proverbial needle in a haystack. The main clue is the picture of Clyde *(left)* which indicates that they have stopped just before a bend. No doubt Clyde has just carried out some target practice on the sign for W. D. tells us that 'Clyde liked to stay sharp and would sometimes hit the car brakes of a sudden, bounce out to the roadside and open up with that cut-off automatic rifle on a tree or a sign for practice'. *Right:* This frame was chosen by police to be used on wanted posters.

The car still bears Bobbie's number plate (called a 'tag' in America) and although tracing vehicles was not nearly as sophisticated as it is today, Clyde usually changed plates when crossing a state line as an out-of-state registration would be more likely to arouse suspicion. (The plates were removed at some stage as one of them was recovered from another car abandoned by the gang in June — see page 148.) They all took turns in posing by the car: Bonnie *(left)* and Jones *(right)*.

Left: W. D. Jones: 'Bonnie was always neat, even on the road. She kept on make-up and had her hair combed all the time. She wore long dresses and high heels and them little tams on her head. She was a tiny little thing. I reckon she never weighed more than 100 pounds, even after a big meal.

But them big meals was usually bologna-and-cheese sandwiches and buttermilk on the side of the road.' Right: Bonnie with Clyde. Although of poor quality, this the best frame showing the background — a hedge-lined dirt track — and also the last of the first series of pictures.

Another time . . . another place . . . but same car and same number plate and somewhere with a backdrop of a rocky outcrop and tall evergreens, possibly the Ozarks. Bonnie now wears a different dress and, although it is sunny, she must be chilly as she has donned a coat. Note the pistol in her belt which looks as if it is improvised from a man's necktie. Although the terrain is different, the fact that the plates have still not been switched would seem to indicate that this second series of pictures was taken not long after those on the first roll.

Bonnie was 22 and Clyde 24 when the pictures were taken but Jones looks far older then his 17 years.

It is a great pity that no one thought to ask W. D. where the pictures were taken but perhaps someone will still recognise the location.

'The meanest weapon in our arsenal,' explains Jones, 'was Clyde's automatic rifle we'd stolen from a National Guard armory. He had cut off part of the barrel and had got three ammo clips welded together so it would shoot 56 times without reloading. Clyde called it his scatter-gun. We had a couple of regular automatic rifles and some pistols. There was so many guns in the car it was hard not to show them when we got out at a filling station or tourist court.' *Left:* Although Clyde possessed at least one Browning Automatic Rifle (BAR) when these pictures were taken as 'an automatic rifle' was recovered by police from the apartment at Joplin, it is odd he did not display it here. *Above:* Now with some more weaponry to decorate the front of the car, W. D. prematurely releases the shutter on Clyde. Note the pump-action shotgun propped on the left of the radiator.

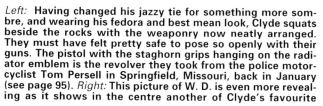

Left: Having changed his jazzy tie for something more sombre, and wearing his fedora and best mean look, Clyde squats beside the rocks with the weaponry now neatly arranged. They must have felt pretty safe to pose so openly with their guns. The pistol with the staghorn grips hanging on the radiator emblem is the revolver they took from the police motorcyclist Tom Persell in Springfield, Missouri, back in January (see page 95). *Right:* This picture of W. D. is even more revealing as it shows in the centre another of Clyde's favourite weapons. Jones explains: 'Clyde had that sawed-off 16-gauge automatic shotgun along with him all the time. It had a one-inch rubber band he'd cut out of a car-tire inner tube attached to the cut-off stock. He'd slip his arm through the band and when he put his coat on, you'd never know the gun was there. The rubber band would give when he snatched it up to fire. He kept his coat pocket cut out so he could hold the gun barrel next to his hip. It looked like he just had his hand in his pocket.'

NEWS AND LEADER

Largest Circulation Per Capita of Any City in the United States in the 50,000 to 75,000 Class

VOL. 5—NO. 46 — The *Springfield Leader*, Vol. LXVI—No. 11, Springfield Daily News, Vol. XLIII—No. 106. Member of The Associated Press   SPRINGFIELD, MISSOURI, SUNDAY MORNING, APRIL 16, 1933   Second Class Matter, Act of March 3, 1879.   ** PRICE 5 CENTS

COSTLY WINTER STORM BATTERS OZARKS!

Believe Joplin Killer Springfield Officer's Kidnaper

Religious Cult In Weird Rites

ROOSEVELT GIRDS FOR CONFERENCES WITH BIG POWERS

Officer Persell Identifies Murderer as His Abductor

Picks Clyde Barrow as One of His Kidnapers and Points Out Another Man and Woman As Likenesses of Others Who Made Him Captive

MILLIONS ROLL IN AS KEGS 'ROLL ON' BEER'S FIRST WEEK

SLAIN BY BANDITS

$5,000,000 FRUIT CROP NOT INJURED BY COLD WEATHER, BUREAU HEAD SAYS

Caption under masthead:
As soon as the Joplin pictures were circulated, Tom Persell in Springfield, immediately recognised Clyde Barrow as his abductor, although police were still unsure of the identity of the second man who appeared in the photographs.

Motorcycle Officer Tom Persell of the Springfield police force last night identified Clyde Barrow, Texas gunman sought for the murder of two peace officers Thursday at Joplin, as one of a trio of desperadoes who kidnapped him here the night of January 26.

Persell identified Barrow from photographs found in the gangster's hideout where J. W. Harryman, Newton county constable, and Harry McGinnis, Joplin detective, were murdered when they went to question the occupants. Pictures of a second man and a young woman, which likewise were found in the Joplin house, also were pointed out by Persell as likenesses of the other persons involved in his kidnapping.

Joplin officers were able to say definitely that one of the men pointed out by Persell was Clyde Barrow, wanted for numerous burglaries, robberies and fatal shootings.

They did not know definitely, however, whether the second man pointed out by Persell was Ivy 'Buck' Barrow, ex-convict brother of Clyde, or a third man reported to have associated with the Barrows in Joplin. If the picture proves to be of 'Buck,' then the Springfield motorcycle officer is mistaken in identifying him, as 'Buck' was pardoned from the Texas penitentiary only last March and was behind the bars at the time of the kidnapping.

The name of the woman whose picture was identified by Persell is not definitely known. She is believed, however, to be the 'Mrs. Callahan' — reputedly the wife of 'Buck' Barrow — who rented the bandits' house at Joplin from Paul Freeman.

The desperadoes and two women escaped in one of their three cars — a green Ford V-8 coach. Persell was kidnapped in a black Ford V-8 coach.

Left behind by the Joplin killers were a Marmon sedan and a third car. Seizure of the Marmon resulted in questioning at Dallas, Texas, of Carl Beaty, 31, who was cleared of any implication in the shooting. In a statement to Dallas police yesterday, Beaty said he had sold the car to 'Buck' Barrow on March 29, one week after Barrow had been released from the state penitentiary on a full pardon by Governor Miriam A. Ferguson.

Sunday News Leader, April 16, 1933

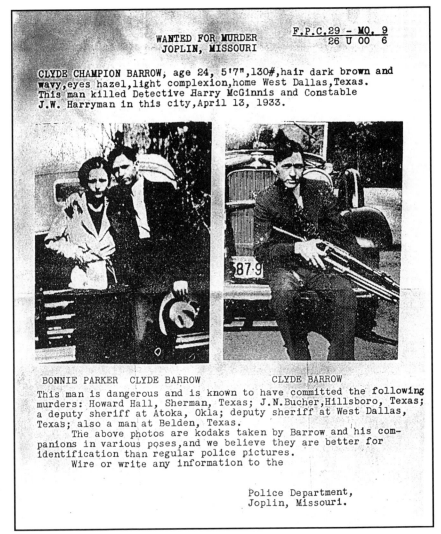

WANTED FOR MURDER
JOPLIN, MISSOURI

F.P.C. 29 - MO. 9
26 U 00   6

CLYDE CHAMPION BARROW, age 24, 5'7", 130#, hair dark brown and wavy, eyes hazel, light complexion, home West Dallas, Texas. This man killed Detective Harry McGinnis and Constable J.W. Harryman in this city, April 13, 1933.

BONNIE PARKER   CLYDE BARROW   CLYDE BARROW

This man is dangerous and is known to have committed the following murders: Howard Hall, Sherman, Texas; J.N. Bucher, Hillsboro, Texas; a deputy sheriff at Atoka, Okla; deputy sheriff at West Dallas, Texas; also a man at Belden, Texas.

The above photos are kodaks taken by Barrow and his companions in various poses, and we believe they are better for identification than regular police pictures.

Wire or write any information to the

Police Department,
Joplin, Missouri.

And as the police at Joplin commented on their own wanted poster, hastily rushed out with the new photos, 'we believe they are better for identification than regular police pictures'. (The reference to Belden probably refers to the murder of Doyle Johnson as there is a small town spelt Belton just outside Temple in Texas.)

114

April 27, 1933 – Ruston, Louisiana

The big man-hunt was on. Both my brothers were being tracked down like animals, and neither would be given the slightest chance, nor shown the least mercy when caught. Buck's chances of becoming a regular citizen were now gone forever. The chair was waiting for him, also. You can well imagine that ours was not a happy family during this period. We seldom spoke the names of the fugitives, and if someone mentioned them, another would hastily change the subject. Talking would do no good. We knew nothing about them except for a few hastily written words bidding us not to worry and not to believe all that we read in the papers.

They were constantly on the road during this time. Kansas, Louisiana, Missouri, Texas, Oklahoma, New Mexico, Iowa, and Illinois — there was never any telling where a letter would be postmarked. They avoided tourist camps and never slept in beds, living, eating, sleeping on the road, often going sixty miles an hour for hundreds of miles before stopping. They camped along little used country lanes in dense underbrush, sleeping always in relays so that someone would be on guard to call out and awaken them.

NELL BARROW, *FUGITIVES*, 1934

Clyde always aimed to put miles between crimes and by April 27 the action had moved to Louisiana. That Thursday morning they — Clyde, Buck, Bonnie and W. D. — were cruising the streets of Ruston. They needed money and the State Bank on North Trenton must have seemed an ideal choice. The old inscription is still visible on the end wall *(top)* and the old clock *(above)* but today the building is occupied by the National Independent Trust Company.

They also needed a second car and they spotted a Chevrolet further up North Trenton standing outside No. 400 *(above left)*. This was a boarding house run by Leonard and Lillian Brooks and two of their lodgers had just come home for lunch. Mr H. Dillard Darby had rushed back from his job as a mortician at the B. H. McClure Funeral Home, and Miss Sophia Stone, the home demonstration agent for Lincoln parish, was relaxing on the swing on the front porch. Suddenly a car stopped, a youth got out and jumped into Dillard's new Chevy. Having realised that he had carelessly left his keys in the ignition, Dillard reached the car with a bound, and even got his foot on the running board as it pulled away, but was forced to let go as it gathered speed. Dillard yelled to Sophia *(right)* to start her car so they could chase after the robber. Meanwhile Mr Brooks informed the sheriff what had happened and that the couple were headed north in pursuit on the Eldorado Highway. *Above right:* Sadly the old house has been demolished, the whole of the 400 block now being occupied by . . . a bank!

A 1933 model coach belonging to H. D. Darby, was stolen from in front of the L. K. Brooks residence during the noon hour today. Darby was just leaving the Brooks home after eating luncheon there when he saw a man get into his car and drive it off, his having left the keys in the ignition lock.

Darby was reported to have run towards his car and jumped on the running board in an effort to stop the thief but, seeing his efforts were futile, he jumped off the speeding car and immediately started in pursuit in a car driven by Miss Sophia Stone, home demonstration agent here.

Officers in Dubach were notified to be on the look-out and had the highway barricaded there. The bandit turned off toward Homer at Dubach and late reports of the chase stated that the bandit and the car were somewhere between Homer and Bernice as he had turned off on the Kimballtown-Lebon road.

Shortly after word of the theft was received by Sheriff Thigpen, deputies Clyde Frasier and Emmett Leggett were sent to join the chase. Mayor Charles Goyne and City Marshal W. D. Risinger also joined in the hunt.

Tearing up what is now Highway 167, a road-block had been set up 15 miles north of Ruston on this hill near Dubach. However, it would appear that the police vehicles had been pulled across the road just beyond the crossroads, giving an escape route down the Hico road (now the 151) to the left. Both the Chevy driver — W. D. Jones — and Dillard screamed round the corner — just as this truck is doing — taking the police by surprise.

Other automobiles from here also joined the hunt. Reports received from Dubach stated that the pursuers were close on the heels of the thief when the car came thru there and two cars from Dubach joined the chase.

No further information was received at press time today. Officials in all neighboring towns were communicated with by Sheriff Thigpen.

Ruston Daily Leader, April 27, 1933

H. D. Darby was reported to have been slugged and Miss Sophia Stone was kidnapped by two men and two women near the A. P. Foster store at Hico about 2 o'clock this afternoon.

Darby and Miss Stone were supposed to have abandoned the hunt for Darby's stolen car and had turned back when accosted by the two bandit pairs and forced to stop their car.

Darby was reported to have been slugged and thrown into the back of the bandit car. Miss Stone was believed to have been forced to abandon her car and enter the bandit car.

Keys to Miss Stone's car were reported to have been thrown away by the four bandits and it is believed that Darby and Miss Stone were taken somewhere into the swamps of Claiborne parish by the bandits.

No report of the condition of either Miss Stone or Darby could be obtained at press time.

Ruston Daily Leader, April 27, 1933

After a few more miles, Dillard realised he would never overtake the driver of his car so he pulled up and turned round to return to Ruston. Near Hico *(left)* **he was flagged down by a man who he thought was a friend of his, Warren Robinson. Unfortunately it was not — it was Clyde who had been following behind with Bonnie and Buck. Both Dillard and Sophia were held at the point of a gun and forced into the back seat of Clyde's car which Sophia later said contained 'enough guns and ammunition to start a small war'. The kidnapping was observed by a local farmer who promptly notified the sheriff's office.** *Right:* **Typical abandoned gas station at the Hico crossroads.**

Miss Sophia Stone and H. Darby drew the dragnet of evidence closer around the necks of Buck Champion Barrow and his brother Clyde Barrow today when they identified photos of Bonnie Parker alias Mrs Clyde Barrow and Blanche Caldwell, alias Mrs Buck Barrow, at the offices of A. J. Thigpen, sheriff.

Photographs of the two 'Gangster Molls' were sent to the sheriff and authorities at Joplin, Missouri, who were seeking the foursome who kidnapped Darby and Miss Stone Thursday afternoon and carried them into Arkansas as far as Magnolia.

Miss Stone and Darby positively identified the pictures of the two women as the companions of the Barrow brothers who took them for a 'ride' Thursday.

Bonnie Parker, alias Mrs Clyde Barrow, was identified as the woman member of the gang who pulled Miss Stone out of her car after Darby had been slugged by one of the Barrow brothers and jerked in the bandit car. Miss Stone said that Bonnie Parker cursed her and slugged her in the back of the neck with her pistol butt, shoving her into the bandit car also.

Miss Stone sustained no severe injuries

from the blow inflicted by Bonnie's gun as the weapon struck her on the back of the neck where a heavy braid of hair was entwined. Darby sustained no lasting injuries from his slug other than a large swollen and inflamed place on the right side of his neck.

Ruston Daily Leader, April 29, 1933

A car believed to be the one driven by the Barrow brothers and their two 'alias' wives, who kidnapped H. D. Darby and Miss Sophia Stone here last Thursday afternoon, was found abandoned and machine gun bullet riddled near Coleman, Texas, late today.

Sheriff A. J. Thigpen received word from Texas authorities that the car had been located near Coleman, Texas and rendered unusable by machine gun bullets which had riddled it beyond repair.

The sheriff stated his belief the bandits feared apprehension in their car which had been described to police officials of three states where they are wanted on charges varying from car theft and kidnapping to murder.

Ruston Daily Leader, May 1, 1933

Dillard would never speak about the kidnapping. Sophia died in January 2000 but fortunately Carolyn Carver was able to interview her in 1970. She said that Buck was sprawled half-drunk on the back seat and repeatedly he begged Clyde to stop the car, tie up the pair, and blow their brains out. They were constantly threatened with death and treated roughly. When they stopped in Bernice *(left)* to fill up, they were forced to the floor and warned that a 'blood bath' would ensue if they shouted out. It seems that lawmen in Bernice failed to recognise the outlaws and they proceeded north over the state line into Arkansas. Always driving on back-roads, at each crossroads Clyde would sound a siren on his car to try to make contact with W. D. but without success. As time passed, tensions eased and Sophia said that the gang 'got to liking them'. When they learned that Dillard was an undertaker, Bonnie replied: 'Well, when we get ours, you can fix us up real pretty' — a request which ironically was to come true! The couple were dropped off near Waldo (see map page 115) and given $5 to pay for a lift. Three days later, Dillard's stolen Chevy was found at McGehee, in eastern Arkansas . . . but Jones himself had disappeared.

May 12, 1933 — Lucerne, Indiana

The ordinarily quiet and peaceful village of Lucerne in the north-western part of Cass county was thrown into a state of wild excitement early today when bandits literally shot up the town in escaping after an unsuccessful attempt to rob the Lucerne State Bank.

More than two score shots fired by the bandits riddled the bank, crashed through the home of Mr. and Mrs. Court Miner and the Bell restaurant, whizzed by a score of citizens and wounded two slightly.

The tactics used by the thugs, two men and two women, resembled the wildest escapades of Chicago gangland and matched the tales of the wild and woolly West.

The wounded were Doris Miner, 22 years old, of Lucerne and Mrs. Ethel Jones, 22 years old, of Star City, who is in Lucerne visiting her parents, Mr. and Mrs. Ura Witters.

Les Bowlen, county councilman, and Homer Hunter, Logansport, who pursued the bandit car from Lucerne, traced the machine west of Winamac on road 14 where they lost the trail.

The bandit car ran into a herd of about twenty pigs and two sows on the flight northwest of Lucerne and killed two of the pigs. The bandit driver was an expert at the wheel or he would have been wrecked.

Miss Miner was dressing in the bedroom of her home across the street and west of the bank when two bullets sped through the weather boarding of the home, fragments hitting her on the left shoulder and left cheek, inflicting painful but not serious injuries.

Mrs Jones was standing in front of the Jesse Shects home, the first house west of the Miner residence, when a bullet grazed her right arm.

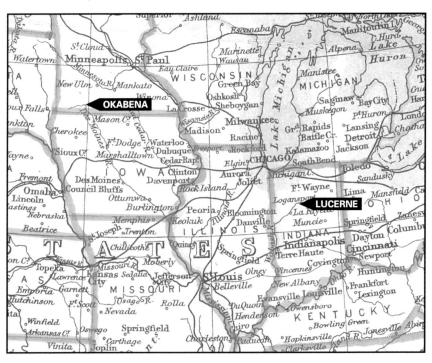

The next two bank robberies accredited to the Barrow gang were unbelievable in their ferocity, bearing in mind that both were committed in small isolated towns. And the modus operandi of both was the same: a break-in the previous night so that the staff were surprised by gun-wielding bandits already inside the bank when they opened up. The first hold-up took place on Friday, May 12, 1933 in Lucerne, Indiana — a state well removed from Bonnie and Clyde's normal stomping ground — the second robbery taking place a week later 500 miles away in Okabena, Minnesota.

The two bandits who raided the bank were concealed on the top of the vault when Cashier Everett Gregg opened the bank at 7:30 o'clock. A moment later, Lawson Selders, bookkeeper and assistant cashier, came in and the two of them commenced to get ready for the day's business.

Gregg and Selders had worked about a half hour putting the cash in drawers when Gregg stepped into the vault leaving Selders alone in the cage. Selders was working over an adding machine when he heard a noise above him and looked up.

A roughly-dressed young man, holding a pistol in each hand leaped up with a yell: 'Put em up.' Selders responded by lunging for the safety of the open vault. As he did so, a shot rang out. The bullet missed his head by inches.

Almost at that moment, Ed Frushour walked past the bank, heard the shot and looked in. The gunman beckoned him to enter and then shouted, 'Come in.' Frushour ducked away as three bullets crashed through the big plate glass window. A fourth hit near the top of the glass.

Gregg and Lawson, armed by this time and waiting for the bandits to appear in the cage, heard them leap down at the back of the vault. Then seven more shots fired by the bandits added to the din. The bullets crashed into the brick and cement reinforcement sheltering the vault.

The gunmen ran out of a back door. One of them turned and fired nine shots into the back wall and windows of the bank building before joining his companion in a Ford V-8 sedan in which the two women were seated.

The road in which the car was waiting when the men ran from the bank forms a loop south of the bank, coming back on the main street and State Road 16 at the Christian church, a block west of the bank.

As the car was speeding around the corner, Ura Witters, who had heard the shooting, attempted to wreck the vehicle by tossing a large chunk of wood into its path. The driver, a man, veered the car to the right and

Times change and the old State Bank is no more. It stood on the site just in front of the caravan and trailer.

into a soggy lawn but brought it safely back onto the nearby road and increased his speed.

At the Christian church the bandit car slowed up to permit a third fusillade of lead to be turned on the citizens who had rushed from their homes into the street to learn the cause of the firing and excitement.

It was here that Mrs. Jones and Mrs. Miner were wounded.

The bandit car headed west and vanished.

Les Powlen, driving a high-powered car, accompanied by Homer Hunter of Logansport, gave pursuit.

Standing in front of the Shects home when Mrs. Jones was injured were her husband, Myrle Jones; Mary Shects and George and Willard Witters. They crouched in terror as the hail of lead passed over their heads.

Mrs. Miner was out in the strawberry patch at the rear of her home when she heard the shots at the bank and the shots that hit

her home and injured her daughter. In all, four bullets struck the Miner house.

One of the bullets that was fired from in front of the Christian church passed through a telephone pole. A second was imbedded in the pole and two or three hit in the street. Another struck a cherry tree in the Miner yard.

Ruth Peckham, who lives on the main street about a block west of the Christian church, was an eyewitness to the shooting that took place just before the bandits drove from town.

Bert Hilkert, a rural mail carrier, drove by the bank just as Frushour was being shot at. The bullets missed his car by narrow margins. He kept on going until out of range.

J. A. Frushour, who runs a hardware store adjacent to the bank at the west, had just entered the back door of his place of business when he heard the shots and looked out in time to see the woman drive up in the car

JUST A FEW YEARS BACK

The accompanying picture recalls the morning of May 12, 1933, when bandits raided the Lucerne bank and literally shot up the town in making their getaway after the bold robbery attempt was thwarted by Cashier Everett Gregg and his assistant, Lawson Selders, photographed standing in front of the bank. Inset is a likeness of Miss Doris Miner, then 22 years old, wounded by one of the bullets fired by the bandits as they fled from town. She is now Mrs. Peter Handstra, wife of Rev. Handstra.

The attempted robbery and gun play resulted in the wildest scenes of disorder in the normally quiet and passive village and left an impression that will never be forgotten by those close to the bank when the firing started.

Unfortunately we have been unable to track down a photograph of the bank but this illustration *(left)* appeared in the local paper in September 1935. It is reproduced with its original caption. *Above:* A rear wall still stands.

119

and the gunmen retreat. He said he believed that had he been in the yard when the robbers came out of the bank that he would have been killed. He also said if he had had a gun he could have killed one of them.

That the bandits had been in Lucerne Thursday to look over the situation was testified by several persons including Mrs. Roscoe Hensell who said she saw the men twice the day before in the same car they used in making their escape. George Witters and Mrs. Elgie Hoover also said they saw the car and bandits Thursday.

The license number of the Ford was 625-096. It was issued at Greencastle, Indiana, to Carl Porter of Waveland.

How long the bandit car was in Lucerne Friday morning is a matter for conjecture but Ellsworth Hoover saw it parked in front of his home with the two women in it at 7 o'clock. Ura Witters verified this. At first the car was parked directly in front of the Hoover home. It was moved slowly until it was right along side the Witters home. The women drove from this point when they heard the shots. When Hoover went to work he spoke to them. At the sound of the third

The hardware store from where Ed Frushour saw the robbers emerge from the bank stood here.

The Miner house was struck several times although it has since been refaced.

shot, said Harry Thomas who lives near the bank, a big dark-colored sedan roared through Lucerne, going west. Others saw the vehicle too, but all agreed that it was going at such terrific speed they were unable to ascertain its make or even give a good description of it or the driver.

Those who saw the bandits leave town were alike in their stories that the women did a large part of the shooting and probably all of it during the parting fusillade.

Fourteen shells were picked up from the street in front of the Christian church. Five or six were found on the floor of the bank and DeWitt Stuart gathered up nine, one of which was unexploded on the premises in back of the bank.

Sheriff Stonebraker and Gols Thomason of the police department examined the shells and said they believed they were from high powered rifles and not from machine guns as Lucerne citizens believed because of the rapidity of the firing.

Sheriff Stonebraker called Karl Burkhardt, chief of the state criminal identification bureau at Indianapolis, and was advised a state investigator will be sent here. Burkhardt ventured the opinion that the bandits were the same gang who pulled a $40,000 hold-up at Terre Haute recently and said that the identity of the Terre Haute rob-

The getaway route. After shooting up the bank but getting no cash, the robbers piled into their car and drove down this street, away from the photographer. After one block they turned right down a short connecting street (where the log was thrown in their path) and then turned right again to come back to State Road 16, one block to the west of the bank.

This is where the short side road joins the main road again. They stopped at this corner next to the church, fired one last salvo in the general direction of the photographer, slightly wounding two women bystanders, turned left onto State Road 16 and fled west, pursued by two local men in a private car. There is nothing in the press report to identify the robbers other than the fact that two men and two women equate to Buck, Blanche and Bonnie and Clyde. So what other evidence is there to link them with this crime? In *Fugitives* — the account by Bonnie's mother and Clyde's sister published after their deaths — Nell says that they admitted to the robbery of the First State Bank at Okabena (see overleaf) although the description of the man throwing the log in front of the car fits perfectly the scenario in the Lucerne hold-up. The circumstances of both robberies are so very similar that it is more than possible that they carried out each of them.

bers was known but could not be located. Description of the bandits was meager. One of the women was said to have been blond about 20 years old and the other a brunette. The men were dressed roughly and little else could be said of them save that the one who ordered Selders to put his hands up was dark complexioned and appeared to have an unusually low hairline at the forehead.

The streets of Lucerne were crowded for hours after the shooting and hummed with the voices of everyone giving their versions of what had happened.

Cashier Gregg and Selders were probably as calm as anyone. Selders displayed unusual nerve in dodging away from under the menacing guns of the bandits and his action probably saved the bank from being looted.

Gregg said that had the men appeared in front of the vault they would have been at his mercy. He had a rifle. A repeating shotgun in the back of the bank was overlooked by the bandits. From appearances, they probably had so many guns on them they couldn't have toted another.

It was the first time that an attempt had been made to hold up the institution. The bank is capitalized at $25,000.

Pharos Tribune, May 12, 1933

They did hold up the First State Bank at Okabena, Minnesota, on May 16th (sic). That was the place where the whole town turned out to catch them — they committed the robbery in broad daylight — and Clyde was amused at Bonnie because she wouldn't shoot an old man who tried to wreck their car as they dashed down the square.

'Blanche refused to have anything to do with any robberies,' Clyde told us, 'so we had to leave her out of town waiting for us. The three of us went in and Bonnie stayed in the car in front of the bank. We locked the people in the vault and got away with $2,500, but everybody in town seemed to know about the hold-up before we did, and there was a regular reception committee waiting for us when we came out, everybody shooting right and left. I was driving with Bonnie beside me ready to hand me freshly loaded guns; Buck was in the back seat, and I couldn't depend on him to do any shooting, so when I saw this old man running out toward us carrying a great big log — he was on Bonnie's side of the car — I said, "Honey, shoot him before he wrecks us."

'Bonnie just sat there, and when I saw she wasn't going to do anything, I had to jerk the car away over to one side to keep from hitting him and the log, which he tried to throw under our front wheels. I almost turned the car over. "Why in the name of God didn't you shoot him?", I demanded. "It's a wonder we weren't all killed."

"Why honey, I wasn't going to kill that nice old man," Bonnie told me. "He was white-headed."

'Well I felt like I was white-headed too, before we got out of that town, and I told Bonnie that nice old man would have just loved to see us lying cold and dead, but she didn't seem to mind that part at all. I'm not trusting Bonnie to shoot any more than Buck after this.'

NELL BARROW, *FUGITIVES*, 1934

The church lies on the right with the bank just a block further down on the same side. As the getaway Ford left town Clyde drove through a herd of swine causing the sole casualties of the raid — two pigs!

The small town of Okabena (see map page 127) lies isolated amid the flat open countryside of south-west Minnesota, its location close to the state line being perfect for potential bank robbers seeking a quick getaway to a safe haven in Iowa.

May 19, 1933 – Okabena, Minnesota

Police of two states Saturday were seeking traces of two cursing bandits who Friday robbed the First State Bank of Okabena, Minnesota, and escaped with approximately $2,400 after mistreating a customer and threatening to shoot anyone who failed to obey their orders.

Okabena is a community of 300 inhabitants, about 185 miles south-west of Minneapolis in Jackson county. It is about 20 miles from the Iowa line toward which the bandits fled.

The bandits, flourishing their guns, rushed into the bank, one of them jumping over the railing and covering two employees, Sam Frederickson, cashier, and Ralph Jones, assistant cashier. Swearing, the other covered George E. Smith and W. J. Kelly, customers of the bank, and ordered them to hold up their hands.

When Smith, who is hard of hearing, was slow to obey orders, the bandit threatened to 'blow out his brains.' A moment later, when the four men were forced to lie on the floor, the bandit kicked Smith in the shoulder, as he failed to move quickly enough to satisfy him.

When Frederickson attempted to explain Smith was deaf, the bandits jammed their guns into his side and told him to 'shut up.'

The bandits then locked the four victims in the vault after looting the cash drawers and fled. Frederickson released himself through a second door and spread the alarm. Jones and a farmer, George Plasterer, jumped into a car and pursued the bandits, but after chasing them nearly three miles, lost track of them.

The Okabena Press, October 1931

The First State Bank on Main Street had already been targeted by two armed robbers in October 1931. In that case the bandits departed without firing a shot . . . in stark contrast to the day when the Barrow gang hit town!

Although the bank has been given a new facade, the tell-tale cornice on the roof can still be seen.

For the second time in less than two years the First State Bank of Okabena became the victim of the underworld when two desperate machine-gunners aided by two women, robbed the local bank and escaped with $1,419.03. Hiding in the bank during the night, the two men confronted R. M. Jones, assistant cashier, Friday morning, and forced him to open the vault and the safe inside.

Sometime during the night, believed to have been shortly after midnight, two men and two women, one conspicuously red-headed, broke into the bank through the south window in the directors' room. A bar was used to force the window, tearing out the screws which held the sash lock. After gaining entrance it was an easy matter to open the rear doors, put the screen back in place, and put the screws in the sash lock.

The robbers made their hiding place in the small room just in front of the safety deposit box vault. Here they greeted Mr. Jones when he was about to hang his hat in the morning.

During the night of May 18/19, 1933, the window into the manager's office at the rear of the building (above) **was forced and the back door opened** (below left). **The window has since been bricked up but its outline can still be discerned** (below right). **The addition to the left of the bank itself is where the Atz hardware store formerly stood.**

Leaving Buck and Clyde hiding in the bank ready for the manager to open up, Bonnie and Blanche drove out of town south-east in the direction of Lakefield to find a quiet spot to park up and wait for morning. This is the side road where Mr Hovenden spotted them and asked them if they were in trouble.

Leaving the men in the bank, each with a sub-machine gun, the two women drove about a half mile south-east of town on the diagonal road and parked there. The car was seen there as early as five o'clock a.m. D. B. Hovenden had even stopped to ask them whether they had car trouble when he drove to Okabena that morning, but they replied that the car was working all right. Shortly before eight o'clock the girls drove their car to the corner near the WNAX gas station where they stopped for further developments.

Mr. Jones and Mr. Frederickson came down town simultaneously a minute or two before eight but as Jones entered the bank, Frederickson first walked around to the rear where he stopped to talk with Aug Atz, then noticing nothing unusual came back again to the front and entered. Meanwhile, inside, the two men had ordered Mr. Jones to 'stick em up.' He backed up and tried to get Frederickson's attention, who stood in front of the back door. Suspicious of his movements, one of the raiders asked, 'Who is that guy?'

Nearer to the bank's opening time Bonnie drove the Ford closer and parked here beside the WNAX service station.

Mr. Jones said he didn't know the man, and consequently, when asked whether they had not come down together, he said they hadn't. The bandits didn't like the answer and threatened him if he were lying. Then with a machine gun pressed against him he

The interior of the bank — then and now — with the same door to the former director's office — now a store room.

was forced to open the vault which he did as the time lock had already opened.

When Frederickson came in he walked around and commenced opening windows. The surprise came to him when a man pressed the gun to his ribs with the order 'stick 'em up' and told to lay down on the floor behind the cage. When L. C. Pietz,

Poor Sam Frederickson, the cashier, now held-up for the second time in two years!

D. B. Hovenden, and Art Carlson and his two children were being admitted, he rolled over on the floor and set off the burglar alarm. By this time the safe had been opened. After scooping up all cash, the raiders ordered the cashier, his assistant, and

the customers and children into the basement. Without stopping to lock the basement door, which incidentally, had been locked the night before but was now open, they fled from the rear bank door where they were met by the two girls in a Ford V-8.

Pat Delaney visited Okabena for us in February 2003 to take the photographs and Dennis Hartman, the bank's president, kindly allowed him to picture the interior — the open plan arrangement now indicative of a cashless society.

Clyde and Buck made their exit from the rear door of the bank to where Bonnie had now moved the car. As they piled into the back seat, she turned immediately left down Main street — away from the photographer's position — towards the school at the far end of the street. As Bonnie accelerated away, the two men opened up with their BARs.

When Cleo Atz heard the burglar alarm which had been set off by Mr. Frederickson, she looked in a front window and there saw a man with a gun. She ran to tell her father and men at the implement store. Mr. Atz grabbed a .32 caliber revolver and hurried to the rear of his hardware store which adjoins the bank. He saw the men come out of the bank and just as they were climbing into the back seat he fired three shots at them believing he had wounded one. As the woman driver started a fast getaway, one of the men poked his machine gun through the rear car window, while the second woman handled one out of the side window, and riddled the back of the store. Only a small wrong guess on their part saved Mr. Atz's life.

As soon as they had been herded into the basement, Mr. Jones opened a window and crawled out. He ran across the street through the shower of bullets, and with Ted Milbrath's car was about to chase the bandits, but friends warned him that it would be plain suicide. Mr Frederickson ran back upstairs as soon as the men disappeared from the basement door, and called Heron Lake and Lakefield to watch for them.

Their route out of town took them past the hotel, down another block to the Stephenson corner, past the school house to the Mikelson corner, and then south out of Okabena.

Naturally, Pat examined the walls of the bank for any signs of the fusillade — could these be spang marks from long ago?

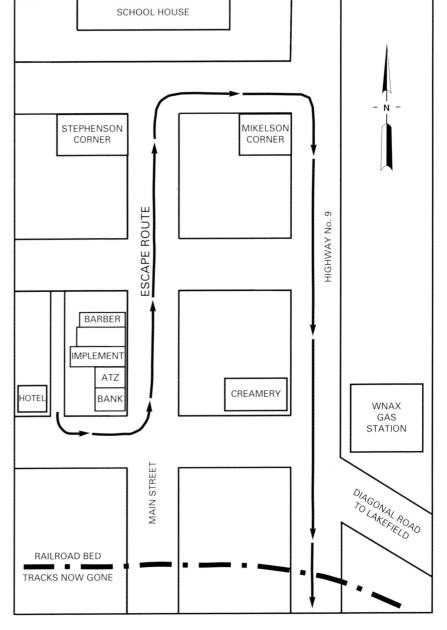

The implement shop *(left)* **still stands . . . but the barber shop** *(right)* **has gone — it stood behind the fencing on the right.**

Shooting almost continually on the way out of town, many lives were in serious danger and several buildings filled with bullet holes. The hardware store suffered the most, the hotel received several shots which went through upstairs rooms and the implement shop shows several scars. When in front of the school house a volley of shots was sent down Main Street, missing by inches many who had just come to town and others who had come out to see what was going on. Automobiles in the street were narrowly missed with bullets kicking up dust all along. One shot drilled the barber shop completely while another was lodged in the front door of the blacksmith shop. At the WNAX service station a bullet was sent into the car of Louis Kruse and the station was filled with a score of neat holes. At the same time a machine gun was sweeping the head of Main Street, drilling the bank, two windows in the hardware store, the implement shop; and the open space to the elevators, where slugs were also heard rattling on the sides, was thoroughly raked. Here again countless numbers narrowly escaped being hit.

Just across the tracks the raiders let loose at a hitch-hiker who flagged them for a ride, while a little farther they scared the horses of Morrison's incoming school bus. Farmers saw the car speeding south toward Iowa and it was traced as far as Iowa highway number nine.

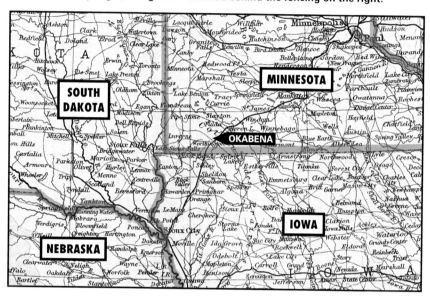

The two men were short, about five feet and five inches, and dark of complexion. The one had his hair combed back. Both were between the ages of 25 and 30 years.

The Okabena Press, May 25, 1933

After turning back south, and still with guns blazing, they raced hell for leather towards the Iowa state line some 20 miles away. It was a day that Okabenans would never forget . . . yet the sequel was still to come!

The local sheriff, Chris Magnussen and Bill Conley, the agent for the Minnesota criminal bureau, immediately mounted a manhunt and within ten days, police in Sioux City in neighbouring Iowa had made an arrest. But were Anthony DeStrain (above) and his common law wife known as 'Stormy' Cosier guilty? Both had criminal records and had been previously imprisoned for robbery and other crimes, and Tony DeStrain was on the current wanted list for a hold-up in Huron, South Dakota, on April 13. He was identified by eyewitnesses as being one of the Okabena robbers but DeStrain claimed he was in South Dakota at the time although he had no witnesses to back up his alibi.

Arrest of a man and a woman suspected of being members of the gang that raided the Okabena bank on May 19 was announced Wednesday by Melvin C. Passolt, superintendent of the state bureau of criminal apprehension.

Acting on information furnished by Superintendent Passolt, Sioux City police arrested Anthony Strain, about 27, and his wife Mildred, 23.

County Attorney B. E. Grottum secured extradition papers at St. Paul and forwarded them to Des Moines for the governor's signature.

Press report, June 1, 1933

Although the fact had been known that a man and a woman were arrested and identified as part of the quartet who robbed the First State Bank of $1,419.03 on May 19, the Press was refused permission to publish details last week by bank officials. The two held are Anthony DeStrain and Alice Morton, both being notorious characters with long criminal records.

Immediately upon arrest of the two at Sioux City, R. M. Jones, L. C. Pietz, D. B. Hovenden, Art Carlson, and Albert Sievert and Orlando Pietsch of Heron Lake left Monday afternoon and positively identified the couple as being connected with the robbery.

Tony DeStrain is also known as Tony Strain, age 27, and living in an apartment at 521 Jennings Street, where the couple were arrested Monday by Detectives Claude Bledsoe, Tom Farley, Everett Smith, and Tom Dempsey. The woman, Alice Morton, has a long list of aliases such as Alice Martin, Mildred Cosier, Flossie Haney, Mildred Dunn, and Mrs. Freddie Dunn. The arrests were kept a secret until identification was

made. In addition to Anthony and Alice, a brother of Tony's and a second woman whose name has not been disclosed are being sought, and warrants for their arrest have been issued.

The Okabena Press, June 8, 1933

With the arrest of Floyd Strain and companions following the robbery of the Okabena and Ihlen banks, many bank hold-ups are clearing up in Minnesota and other states. Floyd is a brother of Anthony Strain who is being held together with Alice Martin at Sioux City in connection with the local robbery and were arrested there May 29.

For more than a month police have been searching the Northwest for Floyd Strain when he suddenly popped up at Ihlen where he, with three other men, robbed the bank of $1,000. Then Saturday evening Sheriff Melvin Shells and deputies of Sioux Falls arrested him and three men and a woman at a hideout masked as a riding academy.

The Okabena Press, June 29, 1933

One of the most interesting court cases ever held at Jackson was held Monday and Tuesday, resulting in the conviction of Anthony and Mildred Strain, arrested for participation in the robbery of the First State Bank on May 19, 1933. The former was given a sentence not to exceed 80 years and the latter not to exceed 40 years.

As his alibi, Anthony Strain claimed to have been in Rapid City, South Dakota, bootlegging, but could not produce witnesses to prove the fact. Both Mr. and Mrs. Strain admitted their guilt in various robberies in which Tony served terms in two South Dakota penitentiaries and Mildred Strain served a term in the Sioux Falls penitentiary. They admitted their aliases and that they were man and wife under common law.

The Okabena Press, September 21, 1933

Memories of the Okabena bank robbery last May are brought back again by an Associated Press dispatch from Sioux Falls to the effect that another member of the Strain gang has been apprehended. Four members of this gang are responsible for the local robbery.

Jack Brune, arrested at Sioux Falls last week, was identified by the Canova, South Dakota, bank as one of the four men who robbed his bank last May. The Cottonwood county sheriff also took witnesses to Sioux Falls to view him as a Westbrook bank robbery suspect.

Tony Strain and Jesse Clemens, now in the Minnesota state prison for robbing the Okabena and Westbrook banks, were also connected with the Canova robbery.

The Okabena Press, February 8, 1934

Echo of the machine-gun robbery of the Okabena State Bank in 1933, for which Floyd M. Strain, 42, has been serving a 10 to 40-year term in the state prison since 1933, was heard by the state pardon board Monday and Tuesday of this week when release applications by 78 inmates of the state prison, men's and womens' reformatories, were considered.

Strain and his brother and sister-in-law were involved in the raid on the Okabena bank and all are still serving time. Strain asks his release now on the basis that he has helped invent a special device for twine baling machines at the prison. He claims he is the victim of wrong identification. Before he faced the Minnesota charge he served a two-year term in South Dakota for bank robbery and murder.

Press report, April 1946

The state pardon board, in special session last week, released the last of the Strain gang that held up and robbed the Okabena bank in 1933, shooting up the town as they made off with the loot in an automobile.

A short time ago the board released Floyd Strain under sentence up to 80 years. His release aroused much unfavorable sentiment especially in this part of the state, principally in Jackson county where the crime and trial took place.

Anthony Strain had served longer than Floyd whose trial for the robbery was delayed until he was released from the Sioux Falls penitentiary, where he was held on a murder charge.

The 'moll' of the gang, Mildred Strain, by common law marriage, was released from the women's penitentiary at Shakopee in 1943, after twice having escaped.

The Okabena Press, May 23, 1946

His brother Floyd was picked up in June and a fourth man some time later. In September 1933 he was sentenced to 80 years and at their trial for the crime, Tony DeStrain and his wife (above) 'suggested' that the law look into the Barrow gang, implying that the Barrows were responsible. Then the following year, in their series on Bonnie and Clyde published after their deaths, *True Detective* magazine claimed that 'bank employees identified pictures of the Barrow gang'. And when Nell, Clyde's sister, appeared in print in *Fugitives — The story of Clyde Barrow and Bonnie Parker* in 1934, she admitted that they *had* held up the First State Bank in Okabena although she got the date wrong and confused the details with the previous robbery at Lucerne, Indiana.

On May 17 Blanche suddenly appeared in Dallas on her own, having been sent on ahead to arrange a family get together. Both the Parker and Barrow parents had not seen their offspring since they left in March and Nell remembers how excited they were: 'We were all nervous, eager, and scared to death', she wrote in her book, 'I don't think there was ever a visit filled with so much happiness and sorrow. We had lived through a million hells since last we met, and we had no assurance that we should ever behold their faces again in this life.' Nell says that the meeting took place 'near Commerce, Texas, on a country road where there was a bridge over a ravine . . .

I remember that Clyde had to back his car off the bridge every time anybody came along.' We spent a considerable time investigating in Commerce (see map page 44) but the huge Delta county lake, constructed by the Corps of Engineers in the 1990s, has flooded the area north-east of the town. Allen L. Martin, former Commissioner for the area, told us that the water now covers Horton Bottom, which was the most likely place for the meeting, but locally people believe that they may have met on Dog Town Road *(above)*. It remains a quiet backwater, the tarmac eventually giving way to a simple track. Do the ghosts of Bonnie and Clyde haunt this spot, we wondered?

BONNIE PARKER Alias MRS. CLYDE BARROW

The mothers must have been extremely distraught when the Joplin photographs appeared in all the newspapers, and Mrs Parker particularly so because editors had chosen to focus on the most controversial shot of her daughter. Mud sticks, and this image of Bonnie as a gun-totin' tough — even though we now know the circumstances of the photo session — has lasted right up to the present day. Nell says that 'Bonnie and her mother walked down the road for a talk . . . Mrs Parker told me afterwards she had been trying to persuade Bonnie to come in and give up before it was too late.'

Mrs Parker said that Bonnie wouldn't hear of it. 'Clyde's name is up, Mama, ' she said. 'He'll be killed sooner or later, because he's never going to give up. I love him and I'm going to be with him till the end. When he dies I want to die anyway. Let's don't be sad. I'm in as big a spot as Clyde is. My name's up too. And though it may sound funny to you, I'm happy, just being with Clyde, no matter what comes.' *Above and below:* Commerce today — Clyde lives on!

June 10/11, 1933 – Wellington, Texas

Wellington, Texas, June 11. Two machine-gunning motorists today terrorised a farm family, kidnapped two officers and escaped with an injured woman companion after their automobile plunged over a road embankment.

Sheriff Dick Corey (*sic*) and City Marshal Paul Hardy, kidnapped in the sheriff's motor car, were driven to near Erick, Oklahoma, and left wired to a tree. They identified the gunmen as Clyde Barrow, Dallas (Texas) desperado, and Icy (*sic*) Barrow, his brother.

Steve (*sic*) Pritchard, a farmer, was threatened by two sub-machine guns when he went to the assistance of the motorists after the crash late last night.

At the insistence of the men, he bore the injured woman to his home to administer first aid, but pleaded that he be permitted to call a physician.

'We can't afford it,' said one of the men.

Pritchard's daughter-in-law, Mrs Jack Pritchard (*sic*), was shot in the hand when she knocked at the door of the house. The gunmen punctured the tyres of Pritchard's car with bullets.

While one of the men returned to the wrecked coupe to get a rifle, Lonzo Carter (*sic*), who lives with the Pritchards (*sic*), slipped away to the home of a neighbour and telephoned officers.

Both the terrorists were on guard when Sheriff Corey and Marshal Hardy arrived. They surprised the officers in the darkness, bound them with their own handcuffs and, taking the injured woman with them, made off in Corey's car.

The officers said they were tied up near Erick early today with barbed wire cut from a fence. They freed themselves thirty minutes later and notified officers at Sayre, Oklahoma, but the trail of the gunmen was lost on a highway leading toward Pampa, Texas.

The Barrow brothers are wanted for the slaying of two officers in a gunfight near Joplin, Missouri, recently.

New York Times, June 11, 1933

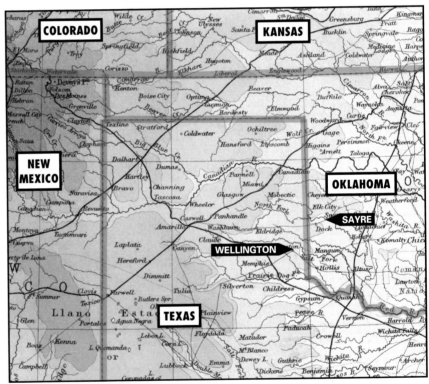

This terse report — although full of spelling mistakes — wired to New York from Wellington, Texas, on June 11, 1933, outlined one of the most dramatic events in the history of the Barrow gang. Shortly after 10 p.m. that Sunday night, Clyde, Bonnie and W. D. Jones were racing north along the newly-graded surface of Highway 4 to meet with Buck who would be waiting near Erick, just over the state line into Oklahoma. Some seven miles north of Wellington, and still 50 miles short of the rendezvous, the road crossed the Salt Fork branch of the Red River (which serves as much of the border between Texas and Oklahoma). However the last half-mile of the approach road was closed as a new bridge had yet to be built so a diversion sign had been set up 150 yards in front of the river directing traffic to use the old road and bridge. *Top:* This is where the detour sign stood — on the right-hand lane on what is now the four-lane Highway 83. The lattice-girder bridge is the one which was yet to be built, the left-hand more modern concrete structure more or less occupying the site of the old bridge.

Mr and Mrs Sam Pritchard lived in this house *(right)* a couple of hundred yards or so from the river and their son Jack and son-in-law Alonzo Cartwright were visiting and sitting on the front porch overlooking the road when they saw a speeding car miss the sign and smash through the barricade. At the last moment, the driver jammed on the brakes and tried to take avoiding action but it was too late. As the car hit the embankment which had been built up for the new bridge it took off in a cloud of dust, turning broadside in the air before crashing onto the dry river bed. *Top:* This is the same view of the road today with the overgrown drive to the house on the left and the bridge hidden by the bushes on the right. Marty Black, our intrepid Bonnie and Clyde investigator, undertook to visit Wellington for us and he travelled to this corner of Texas in April 2003.

We had been told that the Pritchard house was still intact, having stood for more than 70 years and into a new century, but before Marty arrived, the house had collapsed. The bridge can be seen in the background.

Jack and Alonzo rushed down the hill expecting to see the vehicle wrecked and the occupants dead. Instead they found the car — a 1933 five-window Ford coupe — still largely in one piece sitting upright but facing the way it had just come. They tried the doors but found them jammed. Suddenly a voice came from inside the car: 'Hey, can you give me a lift?' After working on the right-hand door for a few minutes they finally got it open and assisted the man out. He told them he didn't think he was hurt but that there were two more people inside. Both were unconscious and it was only with great difficulty that they were extricated. The woman's right leg was bruised and bleeding and had been burned with sulphuric acid from the battery, situated beneath the front floorboards, which had been smashed in the crash. The other passenger showed no visible injuries and his friend brought him round by shaking him. At this point Jack and Alonzo became somewhat alarmed as the men began passing out pistols, shotguns, rifles and ammunition and something which to the young farmers looked suspiciously like a machine gun. The slightly-built woman, wearing a plain gingham dress, was still unconscious so the taller of the two men ordered Jack Pritchard to carry her up to the house but, as soon as he had picked her up, she began struggling and kicking so violently that he nearly dropped her. Jack tried to quieten her by telling her he would go to fetch a doctor but this caused her to fly into a fresh frenzy of kicking, scratching and cursing. Meanwhile, the guns were being moved by the other two men. When the woman asked Jack if he knew who they were, she is reported to have told him: 'they're Clyde and Buck Barrow' but this may either be misreporting or because Bonnie did not want to reveal the identity of Jones.

This is where the rescue took place. Now it is nearer 15-20 feet to the river bed but it is believed to have been at least a 30-foot drop in 1933. Also the river has since been dammed upstream near Clarendon to create a reservoir so the actual flow is now considerably narrower and shallower than it was then. Water now only runs under the third pier of the bridge.

Met at the house by Mr. and Mrs. Pritchard, Bonnie was placed on the bed in the middle room. *Above:* This is the exterior window. *Below:* Marty then burrowed into the ruin to picture her room . . . and to save a piece of wallpaper as a souvenir! Present in the house apart from mum and dad were Jack's wife and their two young sons, Jack's younger brother Mitchell, and Alonzo's wife Gladys carrying her four-month-old baby John. The arrival of Clyde, W. D. and Bonnie turned the house into a bedlam as it was now dark with the only light coming from a single hurricane lamp. As the women were ordered to help Bonnie, the rest were threatened: 'Don't make any funny moves!' Clyde, limping, was pacing back and forth from the room to the porch and even Bonnie got up once and went to the front door, a puddle of blood trickling from her injured leg. She also had an ugly bruise to the left side of her face. Gladys managed to persuade her to lie down so that she could tend to the wounds. 'My mother and I bathed Bonnie', Gladys told Marty. 'She had dirt and sand on her face and in her hair and her leg was blistered pretty bad around the knee — it was the battery that burned her — the car didn't blaze up. All we had to treat her was some salve.' Meanwhile, Clyde and W. D., both armed with weapons recovered from the car, kept watch.

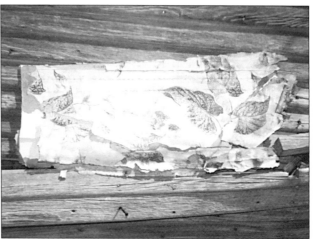

Although he was not well-versed in the notoriety of the Barrow gang, nevertheless Alonzo *(left)* was very anxious so he decided to try to slip away and get help. Biding his time, he waited until Clyde and 'Buck' were both in the room with Bonnie before tip-toeing out of the kitchen door to where his ancient Model T Ford was parked. Releasing the brakes, he gently pushed it down the track seen in the rather poor picture *(right)*. With one hand on the wheel, he continued to push while all the time expecting a shot in his back. Suddenly a voice rang out: 'Hey there! Where the hell ——?' and he heard footsteps running towards him. Clambering aboard, he let out the gears, the engine started, and he swung left onto the road towards Wellington, crouching low to try to escape the bullets he felt sure would follow . . . but nothing and he soon vanished from sight in the darkness. Driving as fast as the old car would go, after ten minutes there was a sudden loud report — a tyre had blown. With no spare, he was contemplating what to do next when he saw the lights of another car approaching. Fully expecting to see one of the outlaws at the wheel, he was relieved to see it was being driven by a neighbouring farmer so they both continued into town to the sheriff's office.

Sheriff George Corry and I had just put two drunks into cells and were preparing to leave the jail when a car made a hasty turn and wheeled to a quick stop in front of the building. As Alonzo Cartwright jumped from the automobile I recognised him, and noted that he appeared exceedingly nervous.

'What can we do for you?' I asked. He waited until he drew closer, then, in a low, excited voice, answered in broken sentences:

'There are two boys and a girl at our house. They ran their car off the dump of the new road and into the river. They are bad hurt. They had some guns in their car.'

At the mention of guns, Sheriff Corry interrupted, saying we had better go by the court-house and get some more ammunition and different types of guns. Perhaps to speed us to the relief of his loved ones, Cartwright said: 'They are all hurt pretty bad, especially the woman. You better hurry.'

I glanced at Corry. Although not long experienced as an officer he is a brave man and holds a fine record for service in the World War. 'Let's go,' he said.

Had we fully realised just what awaited us,

my story might have been a different one today, and perhaps we would have started upon our dangerous mission with heavier hearts than we had when we climbed into Corry's late model coach.

We stopped at a drug store and telephoned for an ambulance to follow us. Believing the trio to be seriously wounded, we did not get additional guns or ammunition. More than once within the next fifteen minutes we were to rue this lack of precaution.

We headed for the Pritchard home at high speed. As we flashed over the road we wondered who these strangers — two men and a wounded woman — might be to carry guns. For our informer, in his excitement, had forgotten the most important thing, and we did not know that we were racing into a death trap to be sprung by the most hardened, elusive and notorious criminals that ever roamed the roads of the Southwest.

We racked our brains for possible identity of the trio. No recent prison escapes answered the question. Bank robberies in this section are infrequent — and the immed-

iate country with its broad, open plains, affords poor territory as a hideout. Finally we decided a couple of boys and some girl must be on a drunk; probably some kids from a neighbouring town who carried a gun or two for a thrill. Somehow, the Barrow gang never crossed our minds. Operating over the entire Southwest, the gang turned up frequently in Texas with some hideous crime but heretofore had confined its activity to the eastern and central parts of the big state — I guess probably because all three — Clyde, Buck and Bonnie — were reared in Dallas, a distance of more than three hundred miles south-east of our little town.

We rose over the little incline which led down to the detour and noticed that someone had run the barricade.

'Wonder how those birds ever managed to miss the detour sign?' my companion asked, almost as if he were talking to himself.

'It beats me; they must have been drunk,' I answered. Just then we made the sharp right turn, through the gate and up the sandy road, down which Cartwright had rolled so dramatically in his ancient car a short time before.

Wellington City Marshal Paul Hardy *(left)* describes above the day when he and Sheriff George Corry faced death at the hands of Clyde Barrow. Even though this account was first published in 1937, by which time W. D. Jones' identity and membership with the gang was public knowledge since he gave his statement to Dallas police in November 1933 (see page 196), he is still mis-identified here by Marshal Hardy as Buck. *Right:* Seventy years on, Marty pictured the driveway from the point where it meets the highway. According to W. D.'s testimony, the car in which Corry and Hardy drove to the Pritchards was a Chevrolet.

The house in its abandoned state in the 1980s. The window to Bonnie's bedroom is on the left.

As we neared the house we noticed there was no light, and the low, mechanical sound of our exhaust was the only noise that disturbed the calm air of the brisk June night.

It was now extremely dark, and I remember that our headlights reflected brightly from the weather-beaten house. A frightened jack-rabbit darted into the road, loped several yards, then cut out of the road just in time to avert death by inches.

Wondering why the home had been plunged in darkness, we descended from the car, Corry taking the keys with him. We knew of course that we faced danger, but an officer often faces danger in his line of duty.

Silently, we made our way to the back door of the old house. It still appeared to be deserted. Suddenly we heard the mumbling of voices. Corry pushed the door open. I followed him inside.

A lamp, burning dimly, sat on a crude, home-made shelf, which shadowed its reflection. Our eyes focused upon the people in the adjoining room. They sat on the floor of that dim room, huddled together, motionless. We could barely see them by the dim, yellow glow of the smoking, kerosene lamp.

Quietly, we stepped across the floor into the middle room of the house. We saw the small woman lying on the bed. In that same glance I noticed that the sheets were stained with blood. Still, no one moved, or spoke.

'Where are the two boys?' I asked Mr. Pritchard.

'On the front porch,' he answered. He did not look directly at me and I thought his actions were a little peculiar. I opened the door and stepped out on the porch. Corry walked over to the woman.

'How are you feeling young lady?,' he asked. 'Are you badly hurt?'

She showed little concern but mumbled some sort of reply which I was unable to catch. He felt her pulse.

Finding no sign of the men on the porch I stuck my head back through the door and called: 'There isn't anyone out here.'

Corry went into the kitchen, got the lamp. He stepped out on the porch and standing beside me, held the lamp aloft in his left hand. Suddenly, something seemed to be telling me to turn around. I guess Corry felt the same impulse for he turned slowly at the same time. We looked into the vicious barrel of a sub-machine gun.

'Get 'em up, and get 'em up high!' came the order.

Behind the stock of that gun, the grim face of Clyde Barrow showed in the flickering rays of the kerosene lamp. Slowly we raised our hands. Before we got them up Buck Barrow (sic) stepped beside his brother, levelling a shotgun at my head. 'Keep 'em up,' Clyde growled. 'And no tricks.'

I heard the sound of running feet in the house. Bonnie Parker burst through the door. Her blazing eyes and her quick movements presented a striking contrast with the bleeding pitiful weakling we had seen on the bed two minutes before.

'Take their guns.' Clyde ordered. The petite Bonnie reached into my right trousers pocket and relieved me of my pistol. She took Corry's gun from his holster. Clyde took the lamp, which Corry still held aloft.

'You boys are just in time. We want to borrow your car.' Buck spoke with a hoarse accent, and a faint trace of a sneer appeared upon his face.

All the time I kept wondering why the ambulance had not arrived. I also wondered about young Cartwright. I knew that it was too much to hope that they would not get there. [*In fact Alonzo's car had broken down on the return trip and the ambulance had stopped to help a motorist with a flat tyre. Ed*]

Marty's comparison: 'Note that the trees to the left are exactly the same'.

Left: **This is the window through which Jones fired his shotgun at Gladys as it appeared in 1937.** *Right:* **Marty explains that 'this is the front corner of the house and the wall lying down contains the same window. At the time the windows had been opened or removed, and there were only fly screens covering the openings. The lawmen had already been captured and were in the front yard with the outlaws. Gladys was in the kitchen, seen in the shadows at the rear of the house (note the** stove), and was reaching up to lock the rear door, in a vain but understandable attempt to secure the home. W. D. was circling round the house (anti-clockwise) to ensure there weren't any more lawmen around, when he apparently saw movement in the darkened kitchen, and fired through one of the screens. Gladys was holding her young son on her hip and he suffered several small cuts on his head from the pieces flying off of the screen.'**

'Bang!' Suddenly a shot rang out through the still night. I jumped with such nervousness that Clyde jammed his gun into my ribs. We had just settled into the rear seat of the car. I turned sick. Perhaps young Cartwright slipping up on the house, had been seen, or maybe one of the family had made a false move. Worse still, what if Cartwright had told his story to some deputy who had come to assist us? Corry and I were in a precarious position. If someone rushed Buck, I knew that Clyde would not leave us alive: I knew that he would not let a posse overpower his brother without going to his assistance.

'Who was shot?' I kept asking myself the question until it went through my brain like the ticking of a clock.

Clyde had now stepped out of the car to go see what had happened but still carefully kept us all covered as he peered into the darkness.

Buck appeared around the corner, almost running. For the first time since our arrival he seemed to be nervous; Clyde was a little jumpy too.

'What's going on?' Clyde asked.

'Aw that dame reached for a gun and I gave her a shot in the hand,' Buck replied.

What really had happened was that Mrs Gladys Cartwright, frightened, had gone into the kitchen and reached up to latch the door at the top. Buck looking through the east kitchen window had seen her and, believing her to be reaching for a .22 rifle which was suspended over the door, had shot her hand with a sawed-off shotgun. Six slugs entered her hand, fourteen went through the door. The volley barely missed killing the woman and her four-month-old baby which she carried on her hip. The force of the blast did send bits of screen wire into the baby's scalp, but the injuries did not prove very serious.

'This is the back door in the kitchen,' writes Marty, 'now filled with debris. Gladys told me that her father kept a rifle mounted horizontally above that kitchen door, and perhaps W. D. was trying to prevent her from grabbing it, although I doubt this. The lawmen had earlier come in through the back door, grabbed the kerosene lamp from there and proceeded through the house, back to front, before exiting the front door where they were captured by the outlaws.'

Gladys was hit by six pellets on her right hand. This picture *(left)* shows her with her injuries in 1937. Gladys told Marty that all the pellets went right through except one which lodged just above her ring-finger knuckle, permanently destroying the ligaments or tendons, so that her ring-finger cannot bend. The other five went through her hand, below the knuckles and above the wrist. All those bones were broken, including the one below the thumb, except for the bone below the little finger. She said that was the only bone in her hand that wasn't broken. So where is the back door hit by the buckshot? At one time it was reported to be in the Panhandle Plains Historical Museum in Canyon but they no longer have any knowledge of its whereabouts. But don't worry, Marty found it *(above)* but we have withheld its location at the owner's request.

'Let's get out of here,' Buck growled. As he said this he noticed the other old car parked in the yard. Drawing a pistol he proceeded to shoot all four of the tires.

Corry and I were in the rear seat of the Sheriff's car. Clyde was under the wheel, and Bonnie sat next to him. Buck was on the right side, in front. He turned half around, covering us with the pistol Bonnie had taken from my pocket.

'Step on 'er,' Buck said. That was the only remark as Clyde Barrow deftly turned the car and, with the hands of a skilled driver, guided it over that sandy stretch of road leading to the highway. As we turned to enter the highway, my heart gained a beat. I saw a headlight far down the road.

'I wonder if that is the fool who went to town?' Clyde said, emphasizing the word 'fool' with an oath. He stopped, switched off the lights and waited.

'If it is, I'll kill him.' He made the statement calmly. I believed every word he said.

The car sped by us. We whipped into the highway and soon passed the other car. Satisfied it was not Cartwright, Clyde Barrow seemed to forget about the youth. Clyde halted my train of thought for a little 'back seat driving,' as he called it. I asked him how they came to miss the road.

'Aw, we're in a hurry.' He avoided the question, I guess because he was proud of his skill as a driver. 'We've got to make a meet north of here and we're plenty late now.'

After driving four or five miles we stopped. Bonnie transferred to the back seat beside me, and Corry was placed in front between the outlaw brothers.

'What town's north of here?' snapped Buck, who was far from talkative.

I told him Shamrock, Texas, and that it was about twenty miles from the river.

'That's plenty tough,' spoke Clyde. 'If it hadn't been for that jam back there we woulda met those guys two hours ago.' Buck merely grunted.

We were breezing along between fifty and sixty miles an hour, and Clyde seemed to know how to drive to avoid creating suspicion. When we met a car, he invariably pulled toward the centre of the road and crowded the approaching automobile almost into the ditch; this caused the approaching motorist to concentrate desperately upon his driving, and avoided any chance that Corry and I would be recognised.

'Did you coppers ever hear much about the two Barrow brothers?' asked Clyde, who was now very talkative. Something possessed me to string them along and, from what followed, I guess Corry felt the same way.

'No, I can't say that I have,' I answered, and then Corry said, 'We have no record of them in the office.'

They thought it was very funny, and all three laughed heartily. I then said that it seemed to me I had heard of Buck Barrow — that I thought he was in the pen — but that I couldn't remember having heard of Clyde. This resulted in another fit of laughter.

'Say, don't you mugs ever read the papers?' Bonnie asked.

We were getting close to Shamrock now, and Buck wanted to know if we were still on the right road. I assured him that we were.

'We gotta miss this Shamrock burg,' Clyde spoke up. He seemed to be taking charge a little more now.

'How do we turn to miss the main road?' he asked. I directed him to the first road this side of the town, but he didn't like the direction so he passed the road I gave him. He soon found himself tangled up in the south part of town with no outlet. He disregarded my directions entirely, and wandered about on side streets until he had cleared the town.

We drove west at high speed for about twenty minutes. Buck and Bonnie dug out a road map and asked me how far it was to Sayre, Oklahoma. I told them that Sayre was back the other way.

'The hell it is!' said Clyde.

I then told them that we were headed for Amarillo, Texas. 'Get this car turned around,' growled Buck and we were soon headed back toward Shamrock, driving at greater speed than ever. We drove around all towns. Buck said that he was taking no chances on anyone trying to head us off.

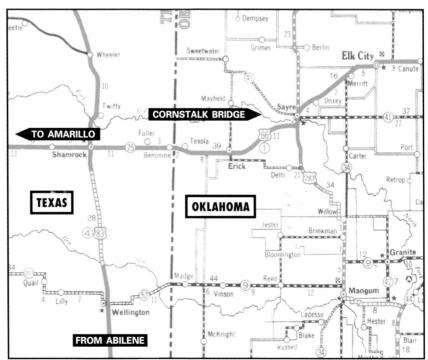

Having thoroughly investigated the Pritchard farm, Marty moved north-east into Oklahoma to look for the bridge over the North Fork of the Red River which was the meeting point for Clyde and Buck. Marty's' subsequent report to me, your Editor, was direct and to the point:' 'The "Cornstalk Bridge" where Bonnie and Clyde met Buck and Blanche — whew! You owe me BIG TIME for this one! Risking my life above and beyond the call of duty! Those directions we got were close but not quite close enough! I spent two afternoons hiking in wild boar and rattlesnake country (not to mention Water Moccasin snakes!) looking for the remains of that damn thing along the river bank, skinning my legs and arms in the thickets and brambles before I met a fellow who told me he had stumbled upon it while hunting a few years ago, and confirmed its identity with his "old timer" neighbors! Briefly, the river has narrowed considerably since 1933 (because of upstream damming) and it has meandered to the east. The original road *(left)* is now just a track. I parked my car a little ways back where the dirt road ends. Further on *(right)*, still heading due east, the track becomes weaker.'

Just east of Shamrock, Clyde stopped the car in front of a suburban filling station. It was closed. Clyde and Buck debated whether they should break into the station or not. While they were talking a car passed — it was going east and was moving slowly. The car went down the road several hundred yards then turned around and started back. Clyde grabbed the machine gun and jumped to the ground, sheltered by the car engine. He laid the barrel of the gun on the hood. His finger was on the trigger. The car approached us slowly — but it kept going.

'You don't know what you missed by not stopping,' said Clyde as he slid back under the steering wheel and started the motor of our car. We continued east for about six miles, where we stopped at another service station. Again the two men began debating as to whether they should break into the station.

'Why should we get 'hot' here just for a few gallons of gasoline?' asked Clyde.

'But we have to have gas,' countered Buck.

I asked them why they did not awaken the station man and buy the gasoline.

'I followed the vague (but adequate) directions I was given to head toward the NE, deeper into the scrub and groves of tamarack trees, as the man told me that the bridge was now in the woods and at least a quarter of a mile north of the northernmost area I had searched. Excited now, I headed off into the scrub although it was late afternoon and the sun was getting low. But then the sandy path completely petered out after 200 yards . . . I was almost ready to give up . . .

'Hello,' Clyde yelled, cupping his hands. Almost instantly a man stuck his head through the station door, then came out to serve us.

Clyde got out of the car with a flashlight in his hand. Every time the attendant looked toward the car, Clyde flashed the light in his eyes to blind him and to keep him from looking inside the car.

'We've been to a dance near Shamrock,' he told the fellow. The man asked about Clyde's blood-soaked shirt.

'Aw, I got drunk and into a fight,' Clyde answered.

After filling the car with gasoline and oil, he paid the man and we started out. Again I began wondering where we were going and what was to happen to us. The incidents at the two filling stations broke my morale.

. . . when a hunch told me to keep on and head towards a large stand of tamarack trees. I fought my way into this thicket . . .

. . . and imagine my delight when I got into the thick of it and suddenly saw rows of wooden pilings as far as I could see leading towards the river! No road-planks left but all the vertical pilings and several diagonal and horizontal cross-braces! And that thing was LONG! Over one hundred yards on the west — or Erick — side alone! I was so excited and I followed the remains all the way to the river, pacing off the distance. I then studied the trees to the east (the Sayre side) to memorize where I might find any remains over there although I had already been informed that absolutely nothing remained of the bridge embankment that once joined the still-remaining dirt road west of Sayre.'

We drove east for six or eight miles, then Clyde began cutting down the speed. In the distance we could see what appeared to be a bridge. When our car slowed to a stop Clyde made three short blasts with the horn. A waiting car on the far side answered with the same signal. I was sure that this little bridge, six miles west of Sayre, Oklahoma, was the point where the trio had planned their 'meet,' previously referred to by Clyde.

'Everybody out of the car,' ordered Buck.

They took Corry's handcuffs from his pocket and slipped them over our wrists to prevent our attempting to run. We were lined up along the rail of the bridge and Clyde Barrow kept us covered with a Browning automatic. Buck shook hands with the man from the other car. I could hear only part of their conversation, and that was about the wreck. After talking a few minutes with the stranger, the two walked over to where we stood. Neither Corry nor I got a good look at the stranger, because he kept his head turned to one side.

'I hustled back to the car and raced over to the other side of the river to find — in a cow pasture — that the raised dirt embankment that marked the east side of the bridge DID still survive. This was where Buck was waiting. One remaining piling was still visible and there was a horizontal foundation and other bits of bridge lumber lying about! No wonder they signalled each other by honking the car horns — the whole bridge must have been at least 200 yards long!'

'When do we get going?' Clyde asked them.

'What we gonna do with these coppers?' growled Buck. All three of the desperadoes had cursed us profanely during the ride, and in no uncertain terms had expressed their disdain for 'coppers.'

'Let's march them down the river a piece and tie them up,' suggested Clyde. I think this was one of the happiest moments of my life. For the second time during the night, I had slight assurance that I was not to die before the smoking guns of the notorious bandits.

They marched us up the river about two hundred yards. Clyde and the stranger were close behind. They kept mumbling but I could not make out what they were saying. Buck had stayed behind with Bonnie Parker. Suddenly Clyde commanded us to stop. We were marched aside to some trees.

'What would you do if we turned you loose?' Clyde asked the question.

I answered that all we could do was try to get home.

'Yeah, I know,' said Clyde. 'You'd run your legs off getting to a phone.'

'Hey you. Back up against those trees!'

Standing with your back against a tree, facing two desperate men with drawn guns, is a feeling you cannot put into words.

'What you gonna do with them?' asked the stranger. He raised his gun.

'Want 'em tended to?' he continued. I braced myself for the impact of a pistol bullet — and waited, the longest second of my life.

'Yeah, they've been pretty decent cops,' Clyde continued, 'but I've said I'd never take a cop for a ride and let him live to squeal his head off.'

The two men began tying us to the trees, punctuating every move with a curse-word.

'Tie us in a way that we can get loose later on,' I requested. 'We might die here of thirst and hunger.'

They ordered me to pipe down. About fifty paces away the stranger turned about, drew his gun and stood facing us. I will never forget that moment as long as I live. Was this merely a trick? Or was it some form of torture before death?

'Come on,' ordered Clyde. 'Let's get going.' Again, I believe he saved our lives.

So somewhere near here Marshal Hardy and Sheriff Corry were handcuffed together then tied up with barbed wire to a tree. After the lawmen freed themselves they walked to a nearby house and used the telephone to warn the sheriff at Sayre which was the nearest town. Using a file borrowed from the householder, they were able to sever the chain on the handcuffs before setting out to walk towards Sayre. After a couple of miles they came across Corry's car, bogged down and abandoned, so they decided to wait in the vehicle for the sheriff to arrive. *Below:* **Here Paul Hardy (left) and George Corry are pictured after their rescue.**

Thousands of people came to Wellington to view the wrecked Ford, which turned out to have been stolen three days previously from a Mr. R. D. Tolliferro of Madill, Oklahoma, before it was pulled out from the river bed. The car was stripped for souvenirs, sightseers even digging in the sand for ammunition which had been scattered after the crash.

Marshal Hardy had been relieved of his favourite pistol — a .44 Smith & Wesson — by Bonnie at the farmhouse but he later got it back when it was recovered from the mortally wounded Buck Barrow in Dexfield Park the following month. It was identified by the 'W' carved on the grip and returned to the marshal by the US Department of Justice.

We watched them get into Corry's car. They turned around and both cars headed back the way we came. As they disappeared into the distance, I wanted to scream at the top of my voice. I suppressed the impulse, however, and with a sheepish grin said to Corry: 'Well, how does it feel to be taken for a ride?'

'It's a relief to see that sun come up,' he answered. I believe in those few words are a perfect description of both our mental reactions. It was the first time in hours we had been able to talk with each other and not be called down.

We still faced the task of freeing ourselves. Our hands were painfully bound with barbed wire, even more securely than our feet and bodies.

After squirming and tugging for thirty minutes, Corry managed to work one of his hands free. He escaped from his bonds. As soon as he was loose he said: 'I've got a mind to just kill you.'

'Yeah, you're mighty brave now,' I replied, 'but I can remember when you had a different attitude.'

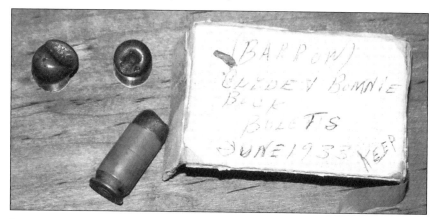

But what about these for unique souvenirs? These are the actual bullets fired by W. D. into the tyres of the Pritchard's Dodge to disable it before they left the farm.

We both started laughing heartily. It was the first time we had laughed and really meant it since we started out as the unwilling hostages of the notorious Barrows.

Marshal Paul Hardy, 1937

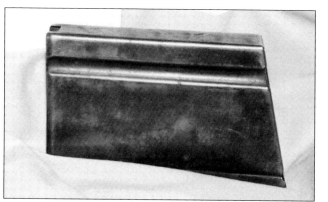

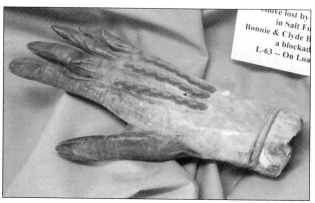

And (left) a BAR magazine still loaded with .30-06 rounds — most headstamped 1918 — and (right) one of Bonnie's gloves,

both items now on display in the Collingsworth County Museum in Wellington.

141

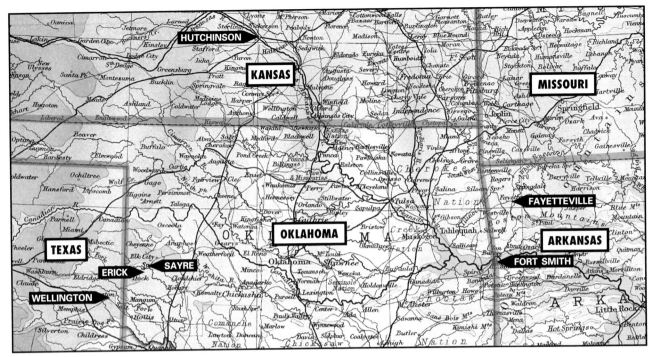

June 1933 – Foray into Arkansas

With Bonnie in great pain from the acid burns on her open wound and lapsing in and out of consciousness, Clyde drove hell for leather across the state line into Oklahoma. Although she needed urgent medical attention, it appears that Clyde put this off for as long as possible to avoid running the risk of being identified. From the early hours of Sunday, June 11, when the two lawmen were left at Sayre, the following three days are lost to history until the tired and worn-out party arrived at Fort Smith, Arkansas, early on Thursday morning. The only clue as to the gang's whereabouts during that period is that the previous day Clyde had stolen a Ford V-8 over 250 miles away in Hutchinson, Kansas. Even W. D.'s confession statement throws little light on the missing days, merely saying that 'the five of us wandered around for a while, eventually going to Fort Smith, Arkansas. We had a Ford V-8 sedan and a Ford V-8 roadster [*i.e. a convertible with a rumble seat in the turtle back*] when

we got to Fort Smith which we had stolen somewhere in Oklahoma.' The Twin Cities Tourist Camp — named after Fort Smith and Van Buren which straddle the Arkansas River — was founded by Sid and Ida Dennis in the 1920s. They established their home on three acres off the main road just south of the river and began charging 25 cents for people to camp there. 'Most of our traffic was from Texas', recalled Mrs Dennis in 1975, 'as people with a two-week vacation couldn't get much further in those days.' By 1933, the Dennis's had added cabins with hot and cold water, which cost $1 per night to rent. 'They stayed quite a while,' Ida remembered of Bonnie and Clyde, 'but we didn't know who they was, of course, till they subpoenaed us to testify in Texas later. Clyde told me they had been camping out and had an explosion and his "wife" had been burned. Bonnie was pretty bad off. She was burned all over her legs and never came out of the cabin all the time they was here.'

Left: **The cabins occupied by the Barrows are framed in the gateway. Although the Dennis's daughter Hazel, seen here posing rather shyly outside the camp office, had had some nursing training, when they called in Dr Walter Eberle, he said the patient should really go to the hospital — which of course was out of the question. So Hazel did the best she could bringing Bonnie ice cream and cold drinks to try to assuage the 100-degree heat-wave Fort Smith was experiencing, while Clyde drove into town to purchase medication and bandages. Bonnie was constantly calling out for her mother and as her condition had not improved by the weekend, Clyde set off on Sunday (June 18) to drive the 200-odd miles to Dallas. He didn't want to put Mrs Parker or his mother, who were being watched by the police, in any danger so instead he took back Bonnie's sister Billie** *(above right).*

Sid Dennis died in 1946 but Ida continued to manage the Dennis Motel into her 90s. After she died the buildings fell into disrepair being pictured here by Phillip W. Steele. Phillip did his very best to get the place preserved but . . .

. . . eventually the whole site was bulldozed. In November 2002 Jim Knight pictured the empty lot on the corner of Midland Boulevard and Waldron Road on the right. Back in 1933, as Clyde drove out of Dallas that Sunday night to return to Fort Smith, he was spotted by the local deputy sheriff, Ted Hinton. 'It was near midnight that I caught sight of a man who could only have been Clyde. I was determined to make certain — though I really couldn't have been more sure. I was confused because I did not recognize the young woman beside him as

Bonnie. But for a fleeting second, my eyes met with Clyde's as his car came in the direction I had come from. I saw that he recognised me, saw his car dig in and speed faster. My heart pounded; I spun my roadster into a U-turn and held the pedal on the floorboard. In a moment or perhaps even less, I had lost sight of him. I followed for a few lonely minutes more in the night, as fast as my car would go, perhaps eighty. But deep down I knew I was beaten. I could only return to a telephone and report another sighting.'

Clyde and Billie arrived back at the motel around daybreak on Monday. Bonnie was still running a high fever and was delirious but by mid-week she had picked up, no doubt her sister's presence helping to raise her spirits. However, with the cost of the extended stay and the constant supplies necessary to dress Bonnie's burns, funds were running low. It was decided that Buck and W. D. should carry out a robbery but some distance away so police would not connect it with the group lodging at the Dennis motel. Clyde said he would stay behind to look after the three girls but he also told his brother to look out for a nice Ford sedan to replace the convertible. The plan was for Buck and W. D. to leave quietly Friday morning but, unbeknown to the Barrows, another gang of robbers had been active in the area and a hue and cry had already been set in motion after the Commercial Bank in Alma was broken into on Wednesday night. The robbery began when Marshal Henry D. Humphrey spotted a suspicious character lurking by this alleyway *(right)* near the bank.

Alma was then a small town with a population of 800 lying some ten miles northeast of Fort Smith at the point where Route 64 joined Route 71 to Fayetteville. Humphrey, a local farmer and handyman, had only recently been appointed as part-time marshal, his primary duty being to police the town at night. It was while he was on his rounds on the night of June 22 that he followed the man into the alleyway only to be confronted by his accomplice armed with a rifle. Humphrey was relieved of his sidearm and tied up while the two men proceeded to break into the rear of the bank. The marshal was then made to lie down inside while the robbers manhandled the bank's heavy safe out through the front door. It was then winched onto the back of a truck parked outside before they drove off in a southerly direction. *Left:* Jim Knight pictured the former bank (in the centre) for us. The decorative facade was added over the original red bricks in recent years.

Left: Marshal Humphrey, seen here in earlier days with his wife Alice, son Vernon and daughters Viola and Velma, freed himself and notified the sheriff of Crawford county, Albert Maxey, at his office in Van Buren. Although no one was ever apprehended for the robbery, the safe was recovered intact and unopened on the edge of Hollis Lake, south-east of Van Buren, and returned to the bank. *Right:* At the time of the robbery, Humphrey's son Vernon ran the AHC garage which stood here where the old Highway 64 intersected the main street.

And it was while the marshal was at his son's filling station on Friday afternoon that he received a call around six o'clock from the police at Fayetteville, 50 miles to the north, that a car containing two men who had just robbed a grocery store in the town were headed his way. No doubt spurred on with the notion that these could be the bank robbers, Humphrey immediately set off, driving north (away from the camera) in a maroon Ford belonging to a Crawford county deputy sheriff, Ansel M. 'Red' Salyers, who worked close by.

Earlier that Friday afternoon, with Jones at his side, Buck had set out in the Hutchinson sedan having decided to cross the river and go north on Route 71. They were already familiar with the tortuous route — one of the most dangerous in America which wound its way over the Boston mountains — having driven this same road three months previously on their way to Joplin. They were heading for Fayetteville which was far enough away from the motel and possibly they were already familiar with the layout of the town. They targeted Brown's grocery store at No. 111 West Lafayette so, while Buck sat at the wheel of the car parked a block away, W. D. walked to the shop. Waving his pistol at Mr and Mrs Robert Brown, he relieved the till of $20 and took another 35 cents from the bag boy. Rushing outside, W. D. commandeered the store's delivery truck only to find it had a flat battery so Jones gave it a push-start down the hill. W. D. then transferred to the Ford and Buck promptly set off south at a fair rate of knots. *Right:* In 1933 Brown's was just a single storey, the upper floor being added in the 1940s. Although efforts were made to preserve it, the building was demolished in 2003.

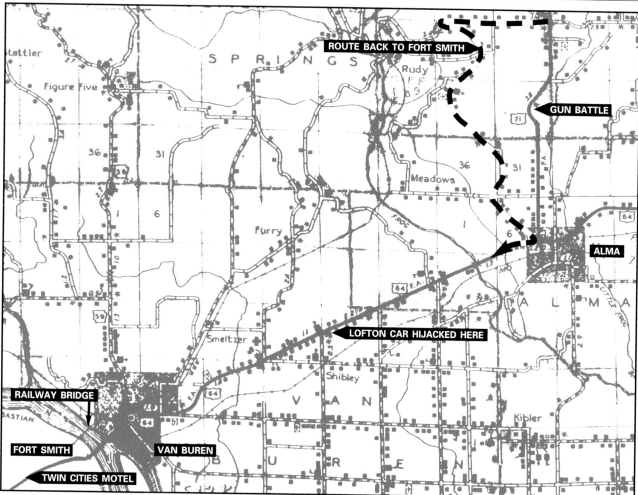

As Alma lay at the important road junction at the point where Route 71 coming south from Fayetteville met Route 64, which led to Fort Smith and east to Little Rock, it was one of the first places notified about the robbery. As Marshal Humphrey headed north with Salyers at the wheel, Buck and Jones were coming south and the two passed each other at the Kaundart Curve, a steep hill about 2½ miles north of Alma. Although the Fayetteville police had telephoned through the number of the robbers' car (225-646 on a 1933 Indiana plate), Humphrey had failed to spot it as the Ford sped past at breakneck speed but no sooner had it gone over the crest of the hill than they heard the sound of a tremendous impact. Salyers immediately turned

his car around and headed back up the hill. Travelling at speed, the Ford had run headlong into the rear of a Chevrolet but, as they approached the crash, Humphrey suddenly saw from the licence plate that this was the very car they were looking for. He also recognised the Chevrolet as it was owned by Webber Wilson who his son employed at the AHC garage. He had been on his way to Alma to take over on the night shift. Ordering Salyers to turn his car across the road to block any escape north, Marshal Humphrey, armed only with a pistol he had borrowed to replace the one stolen from him two days previously, then dismounted from the passenger door which was now nearest to the wrecked Ford.

This is where the crash occurred although in 1933 the road was much narrower, and a little further over — more or less where the white building now stands. The Chevrolet had overturned and as Wilson crawled out with every intention of remonstrating with the crazy driver who had just rear-ended him, Buck and W. D. emerged from the roadster. They had already spotted the car behind blocking the road so were in no mood to risk an argument . . . and they came out with guns blazing. Buck's first blast from his shotgun loaded with No. 4 buckshot hit Marshal Humphrey fair and square in the chest and he fell in the road-side ditch. Salyers on the far side of the car was more fortunate and he fired back with his .30-30 Winchester rifle.

H. D. Humphrey, Alma town marshal, was shot three times through the body at 6.30 p.m. Friday by two young bandits who opened fire upon him with a machine gun when he attempted to stop them near Alma after receiving a report that they had robbed a store at Fayetteville.

A posse of officers and citizens later Friday night was searching for the men near Greenwood Junction. An automobile they took from Mr and Mrs Mark Loftin of Fort Smith near Van Buren was found on Skyline Drive on Mount Vista and officers believed the men were attempting to escape afoot. The abandoned car had a flat tire.

Little hope was held for the recovery of Marshal Humphrey by surgeons at St John's Hospital here. Two bullets passed through his abdomen and the third pierced his shoulder. Witnesses estimated about 40 shots were fired by the bandits.

Webber Wilson, Alma automobile mechanic, was cut about the face and head by flying glass when the automobile he was driving was struck by the bandit car a moment before Humphrey arrived on the scene.

A. M. Salyers, Alma, escaped unhurt when the men turned the blazing machine gun upon Humphrey, who was standing on the ground beside the Salyers automobile.

The men leaped from their automobile and took Salyers' car in which they fled over a country road until they neared Van Buren, where they again proceeded on the pavement until they stopped Mr and Mrs Loftin about three miles east of Van Buren.

The shooting occurred about three miles north of Alma on Highway 71. Alma is about 18 miles north of here.

B. C. Ames, 911 South Twenty-fourth Street, drove upon the scene of the shooting just as the bandits were speeding away in Salyers automobile and the driver of the car fired at him with a revolver as the machine swept by him. The bullet went wild, however. Ames halted at the scene and brought Humphrey to near Van Buren where an Ocker ambulance picked him up and carried him to the hospital.

Ames said the bandit car passed him a short distance north of the scene of the shooting. He said the car was travelling at a terrific speed when it passed him and it was only a few moments later until he heard sounds of gun-fire and saw the men drive away from the wrecked automobile.

Although the press report (on page 148) states that no further shots were fired at Salyers, this is incorrect. Jones promptly replied with a burst from his BAR at which point Salyers realised that he was severely outgunned. Waiting for W. D. to change the magazine, Salyers ran across the road towards this house. W. D. let off another burst of automatic fire at the fleeing figure, spraying the house, barn and field beyond, but amazingly the deputy reached the safety of the massive chimney breast unscathed. With the second lawman having seemingly run away, they relieved the dying marshal of his pistol and piled into Salyers' car. W. D. took the wheel. 'Our car was wrecked,' recalled Jones years later, 'so we got in the police car and was about to take off when that law started firing. That man could shoot. All he had was a pistol (sic) and he was about 200 yards away from us, but he knocked the horn button off the steering wheel with me trying to get the car turned around and shot off the tips of two of my fingers.'

With the road south blocked by the crash, W. D. drove north back over the crest of the hill until he reached the first turning on the left. Back-tracking around country roads, he rejoined Route 64 further south near Alma and headed back towards Fort Smith. As the maroon car was easily recognisable, three miles short of Van Buren Jones pulled across the road at the intersection of Shibley Road. The building in Jim Knight's picture (above) stands on the approximate location of a combined store and filling station (below) operated by Jim Brewer whose wife witnessed the hijacking of the first car to come along which was being driven by Mark Loftin out for a peaceful drive with his wife. (The picture shows Deputy Salyers beside his own car the day after it was recovered.)

The gunman drove a short distance north from where the shooting occurred and then turned westward over a country road.

Soon after the men disappeared in their stolen automobile they appeared on the highway again and took an automobile occupied by Mr and Mrs Loftin after threatening to kill both of them. They left Salyers' car standing beside the road.

Loftin told officers he was driving toward Alma when the other car met him and drove across the road, forcing him to halt. He said one of the men leapt out of the car and ran toward him with the machine gun in his hands.

Cursing violently, Loftin said the man cried, 'I'm going to kill you right here.'

Loftin said he asked the man why he intended killing him, explaining that he was simply riding with his wife. 'I don't care; I'll kill both of you,' he said the man replied.

The robber forced both Mr and Mrs Loftin to alight, commanding them to get inside the other car. Mrs Loftin complied, but leaped through the opposite door and ran along the highway.

The gunman ran after her a short distance, threatening repeatedly to kill her, Loftin said. He finally turned about without firing and commanded Loftin to get in the car alone but the man did exactly as Mrs Loftin did and escaped.

Loftin said the man with the machine gun acted as if he was drunk and that his mouth was bleeding profusely. Officers said he probably was injured in the wreck with Wilson's car.

All available Crawford county officers were sent immediately to the scene of the shooting from where they began a systematic search of all roads radiating from the highway. Sebastian county officers were enlisted in the search.

Humphrey is the officer who was captured Wednesday night by a band of burglars who hauled the 4,000 pound safe containing $3,000 from the Commercial Bank of Alma. He was left bound with wire on the floor of the bank.

Salyers, an employee of the Mississippi Valley Power Co. at Alma accompanied Humphrey to the scene of the shooting through curiousity.

Wilson was unaware of the identity of the occupants of the car that crashed into his until after the shooting. He said the car apparently was travelling at such a high rate of speed that its driver lost control. He was beneath the wreckage of his car when the men opened fire upon Humphrey.

Salyers and Humphrey witnessed the crash as they drove toward the two cars. The robbers still were in their car when Salyers stopped his car and Humphrey stepped out to investigate.

The marshal never drew his gun. He was met by the roar of the machine gun while Salyers dived upon the ground and faced the two men.

Meanwhile, back at the crash site, a passing motorist had stopped after he was fired on by the outlaws as they pulled away, and he volunteered to take the mortally-wounded Marshal Humphrey to hospital to save waiting for the ambulance to arrive. At the same time, Deputy Salyers had raised the alarm with Sheriff Maxey's office and a road-block was quickly put on the bridge across the Arkansas. Buck and W. D. dare not risk running the gauntlet as the Dennis Motel was too close on the other side so, just short of the bridge, Jones turned off north along Route 59, climbing up towards Mount Vista overlooking the river. And it was here on Skyline Drive that the Loftin car was later found abandoned. Here Deputy Salyers displays an assortment of weaponry that he recovered from the cars. The sawn-off shotgun is a 12-bore Model 11 Remington semi-automatic and the canvas Springfield bandoliers hold .30-06 rounds in chargers, the same ammunition for loading the BAR magazines. A Government-issue Colt automatic is also visible . . . and could that be Marshal Humphrey's pistol in the holster near the stock of Salyers' own Winchester?

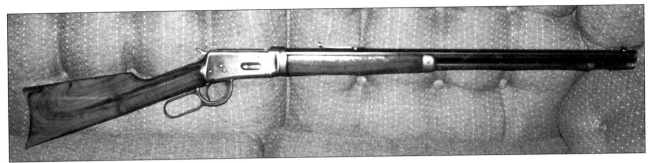

The same .30-30 Winchester Model 1894 (serial number 929294) manufactured in 1922 now in a private collection.

When Humphrey fell to the ground, Salyers said he drew his gun and fired nine times at the two men as he dived from his car to the ditch beside the pavement. The men did not turn the machine gun upon him but instead leaped from their car and entered Salyers' machine. Salyers did not fire upon them as they drove away in his car.

Salyers said the men took the machine gun and a rifle from their car as they entered his. He said they sped over a little-used road toward Rudy. He then hurried to a nearby telephone to notify officers at Van Buren.

When officers arrived they found 500 machine gun cartridges, an automatic pistol, shotgun, two coats, one bearing the name 'Mullins' printed in ink on the sleeve, and a collection of state highway license plates for Iowa, Oklahoma, New Mexico, Texas and Indiana. The car also bore two Jefferson City, Kentucky city license plates, one for 1932 and one for this year.

The two men are believed to be the same who robbed the R. L. Brown grocery at Fayetteville, 111 West Lafayette Street, Friday afternoon. They took only about $20 or $25 and drove away in Brown's delivery truck, which they abandoned about three blocks away and sped out of town in the automobile in which they were riding when they crashed into Wilson near Alma.

Mrs Brown and Ewell Trammell, delivery boy, were in the store when the men entered. They said they'd not seen a machine gun but their description of the men matched perfectly with their description given by persons who saw them near Alma.

This is the pistol taken from Marshal Humphrey as he lay dying. It is a .38 Special Smith & Wesson Military and Police Model of 1905 (serial number 335772) and had been borrowed by the marshal from his brother-in-law, Walter Patton, after his own pistol had been taken from him by the Alma bank robbers. It was left behind when the Barrow gang fought their way out of the Red Crown Tavern at Platte City the following month and is now held by the Alma Police Department.

Fayetteville officers telephoned all towns between there and Fort Smith, including Alma. Marshal Humphrey received the call at Alma and immediately went north on the highway with Salyers.

Officers said there was no connection between the men and the burglars who robbed the Commercial Bank of Alma.

Southwest American, June 24, 1933

More interesting weapons taken from Buck's wrecked roadster . . . but just look at that licence plate! Six different sets of plates were found in the car but this one is really something special — look at page 110! (Bobbie Rosborough's car had been found near Vinita, Oklahoma.) Unfortunately the shotguns are not in their original condition, the wood having been replaced, but the cut-off barrel from the 16-bore Winchester pump at the top, possibly Buck Barrow's gun which killed Marshal Humphrey, is displayed beneath the licence plate. The Colt .45 has also had new grips fitted.

As far as the police were concerned, the trail from Mount Vista was cold — the outlaws had just disappeared into thin air. Sheriff Maxey had missed the gunfight as he was away at Joplin following up a lead on the earlier bank robbery but by the time he returned on Saturday a massive manhunt was already in motion . . . but it was all too late. It was not until Maxey and Salyers had the opportunity to question Buck Barrow in Perry Hospital the following month (see page 183) that he finally learned what had

happened. Buck said that after he and his accomplice — he refused to name W. D. — had dumped the Loftin car, they waited until it was dark before crossing Arkansas along the railroad bridge *(above)* which had been left unguarded! They then walked the mile or so to the Dennis Motel to report on the day's events to Clyde. Buck confessed on his death bed that it was he who had killed Marshal Humphrey so formal legal proceedings were never set in motion for the murder.

The body of H. D. Humphrey, slain peace officer who lost his life in line of duty, was taken Tuesday afternoon from the Edwards Funeral Home in Fort Smith to his home in Alma. Mr. Humphrey died Monday morning from wounds received late Friday when he and A. M. Salyers, deputy sheriff, were targets for machine and shotgun fire from weapons believed to have been in the hands of Clyde and Melvin Barrow, alleged killers and robbers who still are at large.

Funeral service for the slain man will be conducted Wednesday morning at 10 o'clock at the First Baptist Church. Mr. Humphrey was filling his first political office. He was elected town marshal of Alma May 1.

Rev. M. C. Steward of Tecumseh, Oklahoma, former pastor of the Alma church with which Mr. Humphrey for 15 years had been identified as a leading member, will conduct the service. Burial will be in the Alma cemetery under the direction of the Edwards Funeral Home.

Fort Smith Times Record, June 28, 1933

Centre: **November 2002 and Jim Knight makes a pilgrimage to Alma City Cemetery to photograph the marshal's grave** *(left).* **In December 1986, the Alma Police Department unveiled a Roll of Honor memorial** *(right)* **outside their headquarters, Marshal** Humphrey *(centre)* **being the sole casualty listed to date. He died of his wounds in St John's Hospital in Fort Smith on Monday (June 26). (He was the fifth lawman killed by the Barrow gang not the eighth as stated on the memorial plaque.)**

When Clyde learned what had happened he could hardly have been less pleased with his brother's bungling efforts, for what should have been a simple operation to get a larger car and more cash had ended in a fiasco. Not only had they shot a lawman and stirred up a hornet's nest but they had lost their second vehicle and left a trail of abandoned cars along their escape route. And all for $20! It was now imperative that they leave immediately but there was no way that they could all cram into the remaining roadster with Bonnie still really not well enough to travel. The only option was to move out in relays so just before 11 p.m. Clyde took Blanche, Billie and Bonnie, leaving Buck and W. D. to pack up. Clyde dare not approach the river by the Fort Smith bridge so most probably made a wide detour into eastern Oklahoma. (The state line ran just west of Fort Smith.) Leaving the girls safely in the woods, he then returned to the motel to pick up the boys and by daybreak the whole party had left Arkansas.

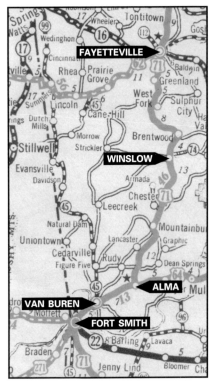

Meanwhile, Sheriff Maxey and his men were combing the area around Mount Vista where the car was found, extending the search north and east of Van Buren. Then at 11 a.m. on Saturday morning came a report that a Mrs Rogers living at Winslow, a town half-way to Fayetteville, had been stabbed and sexually assaulted in an attempt to steal her car. Inevitably the Barrows were blamed and the manhunt immediately switched to the mountainous countryside 30 miles to the north. The search was unfruitful but Sheriff Maxey, now convinced of the Barrow's guilt in the latest crime, rushed out a wanted poster, describing them as 'far worse than "Pretty Boy" Floyd because they go crazy and don't use their heads'. (A reference to the gangster Charles Floyd whose home was just a few miles to the west.) After four days the hunt was called off and when Sheriff Maxey had the opportunity to question Buck Barrow in his hospital bed, he firmly denied that they were responsible for the attack on Mrs Rogers as they were in Oklahoma at the time.

WANTED for Murder and Rape

I hold two felony warrants, each for Clyde and Melvin Barrow, who on June 23rd shot and killed Marshal Henry Humphrey while he was trying to arrest them on a robbery charge and on the next day, June 24th, they went to the home of Mrs Frank Rogers, tried to take her auto, and raped her.

Reading from left to right will describe them as follows:

No. 1: Bonnie Parker (alias Mrs. Clyde Barrow). I understand that she is burned very bad. The best that I can find out the burns are on her right thigh and right arm. Has tattoo 8 inches above right knee.

No. 2: Clyde Barrow, description as follows: Age 24 years, height 5 feet 7 inches barefoot, weigfht 125 lbs., hair dark brown wavy, complexion light, eyes hazel. He has slit in upper lip. Nose crooked, probably broken. Limps in left foot. His finger prints classification is as follows:

29 – M O 9
26 U O O 9

No. 3: Do not know his hame but can give you his description. Height 5 feet 7 inches. Age, about 28 years, weight about 130 or 135, hair, dark, medium dark complexion, square shoulders but drooped forward sharply.

No. 4: Blanch Caldwell (Mrs. Melvin Barrow). Do not know anything about her description.

No. 5: Melvin Barrow. Description as follows: Age 31 years, height, 5 feet 5 inches barefeet, weight 110 pounds, hair chestnut, eyes maroon, complexion ruddy. Finger print classification is as follows:

9 U 11 9
1 R 11 11

I will pay personally $250.00 each for the Barrow Brothers delivered to me any where in the United States. To receive the reward there does not have to be a conviction, just the delivery to me and I will pay the reward.

There were six in the party when they were here, three men and three women. Search all tourist parks as that is where they stay. And inquire of your doctors if they have been called to treat a woman that has been burned in a car wreck.

If you locate these men, arrest, wire me collect and will come for them and will pay you $250.00 each for them. Do not want you to wait for a conviction but will pay the reward for their arrest and delivery to me.

These men are very dangerous and use all precaution when you locate them. These boys home is West Dallas, Texas.

Albert Maxey, Sheriff
Van Buren, Crawford County, Arkansas

WATCH FOR THESE MAD DOGS!

BABY FACE NELSON Real name Lester M. Gillis. Wanted for killing a G-Man at Spider Lake, Wisconsin.

THESE CRIMINALS OPERATE THROUGH-OUT THE MID-WEST. Citizens—Be Alert!

JOHN DILLINGER: Wanted for Bank Robbery, Murder

PUBLIC ENEMY No. 1

CHARLES A. (PRETTY BOY) FLOYD Wanted for murder of Chief of Police of Mc-Alester, Oklahoma.

NOTIFY AUTHORITIES IF YOU HAVE ANY INFORMATION.

Dated May 15, 1934

COPYRIGHT KEY PUBLISHING CO.

CLYDE BARROW: Wanted for Armed Robbery, Murder

BONNIE PARKER: Vicious Accomplice of Clyde Barrow

$1,000 to the Person Who Causes the Capture of Any of These

Although we are jumping ahead in time, Clyde and Bonnie were linked in with 'Pretty Boy' Floyd and the worst of America's criminals less than a year later when this poster was issued. All five met their end in 1934 — Bonnie and Clyde being the first on May 23, followed by John Dillinger who was shot down by Federal agents outside the Biograph Theater on North Lincoln Avenue in Chicago on July 22. 'Pretty Boy' Floyd met his end at the hands of the FBI near East Liverpool, Ohio, on October 22, and 'Baby Face' Nelson died from wounds suffered in a gun-battle at Barrington, Illinois, on November 27 but not before he took two FBI agents with him. (See Postscript.)

But to come back to June 1933, there is one aspect of Clyde's career which we have not covered: his guns, or more specifically his acquisition and use of military firearms. Clyde is normally associated with the formidable Browning Automatic Rifle but Tom Persell is specific in his description of the weapon held by Bonnie when he was kidnapped (see page 93) being a Thompson sub-machine gun. They said that they had stolen it in Ohio but we have no further details. A Thompson does not appear to feature in any subsequent robbery or gun-battle and the possession of a machine gun by the gang does not appear in a press report until Joplin on April 13.

So where did Clyde get his BARs? Answer: by robbing the armories of National Guard units. The US National Guard approximates the Territorial Army in Britain, i.e. a reserve formation which can be mobilised in time of war or internal uprising. It was during the late 19th century that the States first felt the need for a military force to counter labour unrest in the industrialised Northeast and Midwest. The actual title 'National Guard' was first adopted by the New York State Militia in honour of the Maquis de Lafayette, the hero of the War of the American Revolution (1775-83), who commanded 'the Garde Nationale' during the French Revolution (1792-1802). *Left:* One of the most famous National Guard units was Teddy Roosevelt's 'Rough Riders' recruited from Arizona, New Mexico and Texas during the Spanish-American War of 1898. States began to build local armouries, some large and elaborate almost like medieval castles, but others, especially in the poorer towns in the South and Midwest, were simply premises adapted for the purpose. The buildings were easy targets for criminal elements to break into and the spoils were formidable. Clyde's arsenal at Joplin certainly included 'an automatic rifle' (see page 104) although this does not necessarily mean a weapon capable of fully automatic fire. In fact no BARs feature in the Joplin photographs and one would have thought that Clyde would have stood one in front of the car if he had one. The rifle that Clyde is posing with (see page 6) is the old Model 1894 Krag-Jorgensen and the other weapons appear to be mainly shotguns. And from the number of shots fired at Joplin it would not appear that an automatic weapon was used. Not until the robbery on May 19 at Okabena was a machine gun reported to have been fired (page 126), and W. D. Jones certainly used a BAR during the gun-battle on the Alma-Fayetteville road on June 23 (page 146).

This building still standing in Little Rock, Arkansas, is a good example of a 'storefront' National Guard armoury. It was built for the Little Rock Quapaw Guards during the 1880s and has been renovated within the last 10 years.

When Franklin D. Roosevelt created his 'New Deal' agencies in 1933, the Works Progress Administration instituted a programme of building new more secure armouries. This is an example of one of those, built in 1940 in Arkadelphia, Arkansas.

On his deathbed, Buck Barrow declared that they had purchased their weapons used in the Dexfield Park gun-battle (see page 164) from a soldier at Fort Sill, Oklahoma. According to firearms historian, James L. Ballou, on the black market in the 1930s a Thompson commanded a price of $2,000 and a BAR a whopping $5,000, so it is highly unlikely Clyde obtained anything for the $150 which Buck said that they paid the soldier!

The first recorded break in at a National Guard armoury which can be laid at the door of Clyde Barrow took place at Enid, Oklahoma on July 7. The town was the home of the 189th Field Artillery formed from the 2nd Field Artillery in October 1921. In this picture taken in 1928, Captain Dorsey Creason is pictured with his men outside the armoury located at Phillips University, his unit comprised mostly of volunteer students.

July 7, 1933 – Enid, Oklahoma

Sometime Friday night thieves backed a truck up to the rear entrance of the armory of First Battalion Headquarters at Phillips University; removed a pane of glass from a door to get into the building, then ransacked the quarters, taking guns, field glasses, shell magazines and other equipment.

C. A. Burns, chief of the Bureau of Identification, and C. M. Reber, state fingerprint expert, were in Enid yesterday investigating the robbery. They obtained numerous fingerprints from the glass which had been removed from the rear door, as well as from places where the guns were kept.

An incomplete check late yesterday disclosed that the thieves had taken 35 automatic pistols, all .45-calibre; three pairs of field glasses, and one pair of triple-power French observation glasses, in addition to approximately 80 magazines for the automatics, and some other equipment.

J. W. Kinton, deputy sheriff, said the place was almost a complete wreck and that a complete check had not been obtained of the loss.

Officers believe the robbery took place around midnight or shortly thereafter. The pane of glass which was removed from the rear door and carefully laid on the ground at the rear of the building, bore rain spatters from a light, early morning sprinkle. Officers believed the robbery occurred some time before the light shower.

It was on the opposite side of this glass that some of the best fingerprints were obtained.

The theft was not reported to officers until the armory was opened early yesterday, and then the report was withheld until the state operatives arrived from Oklahoma City and had obtained what evidence they could find.

Reber and Burns were to return to Oklahoma City last night after a conference with county officers in regard to the findings at the armory.

Earlier in the day the loss was broadcast to sheriffs and police officers at several points in Oklahoma.

No clues had been found last night which would lead to any early arrest, it was said.

Officers said tracks leading to the rear of the armory were believed to have been made by a small truck.

Enid Morning News, July 9, 1933

Note that the press report fails to mention the theft of any BARs. This could have been either because the National Guard were initially embarrassed to declare the loss publicly or perhaps their record keeping was not up to date. In any case, W. D. Jones stated that Clyde and Buck returned with 'so many guns that it looked like a gun factory. There were some 46 Government automatics, 45 pistols, several rifles and two or three cases of ammunition.' The old armoury has since passed away; it stood here on the campus on South University Avenue, and even Phillips University went bankrupt in recent years, its buildings now being occupied by the Northern Oklahoma College.

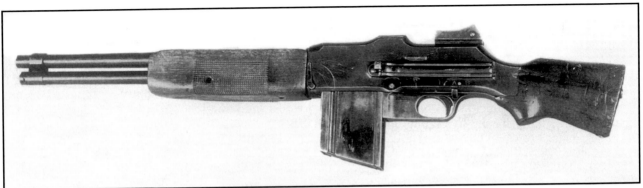

It was the incredible fire-power of the BAR which gave the Barrow gang their edge over the law. The 20-round magazine could be emptied in 2½ seconds; the .30-06 round having sufficient muzzle energy to penetrate a 3/8th in. steel plate. Clyde liked to cut the barrel back to the end of the gas cylinder and reduce the stock so it could be wielded within the confines of an automobile. This particular example, now in the FBI collection, is one of those recovered at Dexfield Park so it has to be one of those stolen from Enid — as confirmed by the later newspaper report below.

Weapons used by the 'Bloody Barrow' gang in the battles with officers in Iowa and neighboring states were stolen from a federal armory in Enid, Oklahoma, July 7. O. C. Dewey, United States Bureau of Investigation agent, said Wednesday.

Dewey went to Adel, Wednesday, to examine the guns and begin 'backtracking' the trail of fugitive gang members.

Marvin Barrow, one of the gang's leaders and his wife, both of whom were captured by officers, declared the guns were purchased from a Fort Sill, Oklahoma, soldier.

'There is no truth to the statememt the weapons were bought from a soldier,' Dewey asserted. 'They were stolen in Enid.'

The 'theft of government property' charge is one of those which brought federal Department of Justice agents into the Barrows' case, Dewey said. Also, the gang is wanted by the federal government for violation of the Dyer act, which prohibits interstate transportation of stolen automobiles.

More than 40 army automatic pistols of .45 caliber; two machine guns, and almost 2,000 rounds of ammunition were taken by the gang from the Enid armory, it was reported to Dewey.

Two of the rifles, six pistols and 70 canteens which were filled with about 1,000 rounds of .30-30 (sic) caliber cartridges, were left by the gang at Platte City, Missouri, when it escaped officers there, Dewey added.

Thirty-four other pistols, two machine guns, an automatic rifle and a quantity of ammunition were left behind by the gang when it fled from officers at Dexfield Park, Iowa. The guns will be brought to Des Moines. Dewey said.

It is believed that the three members of the gang still at large are armed only with pistols.

Des Moines Tribune, July 26, 1933

A medicine case belonging to Dr. Julian Field was missing from his automobile found abandoned west of Enid yesterday. The car had been stolen Monday afternoon. No attempt had been made to strip the car, and it was in good condition when found yesterday morning. Officers expressed an opinion that parties seeking narcotics had driven the car out of Enid and took the medicine case in hopes of finding what they wanted.

Enid Morning News, June 28, 1933

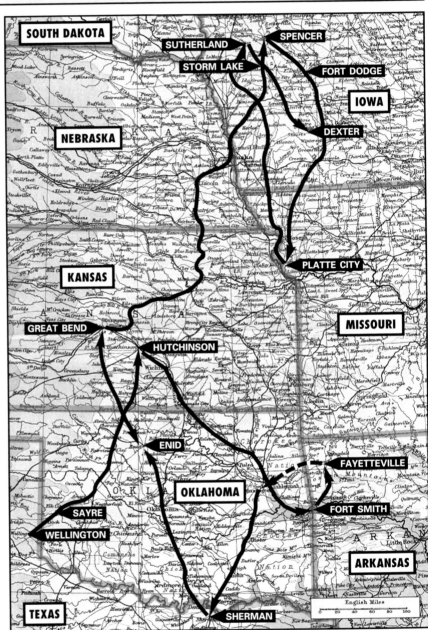

Having got successfully away from Fort Smith, Clyde, Buck, Blanche, Bonnie and W. D. set up camp somewhere in Oklahoma — the only clue being that it was a 'mountain hideout'. There were two priorities: medical supplies to treat Bonnie's injuries and to get Billie out of danger and back to Dallas. The latter journey — a 400-mile round trip — was accomplished, so we are told, on Sunday night June 25-26. Clyde drove Billie as far as Sherman, just inside Texas, from where she could catch a train home. Clyde then decided to move north into Kansas but en route he found the solution to his other problem. Passing through Enid on Monday afternoon he spotted a car parked outside the hospital in which the doctor had carelessly left his medicine bag. Either Buck or W. D. quickly started the car and followed Clyde out of town. Dr Field's car was found a couple of days later, minus his bag, but by that time Clyde's party had booked into a tourist camp at Great Bend. The map shows the known journeys of the the gang up to when Buck was captured at Dexfield.

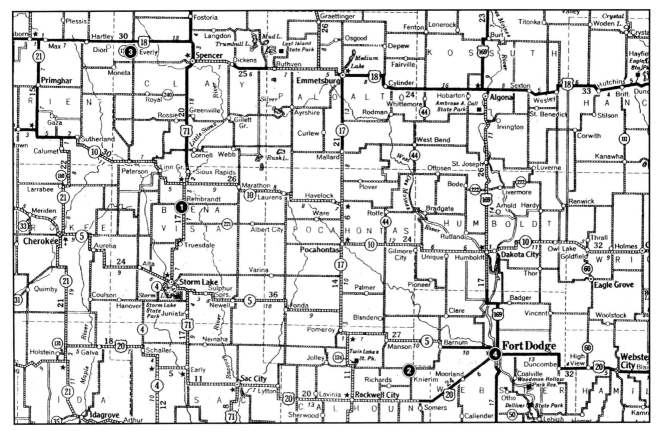

Although our tracing opposite, indicating the journeys undertaken by the gang between June 10 and July 24, follows the main roads, Clyde would undoubtedly have snaked across country using back roads. This extract from a 1932 map shows the road net in a corner of Iowa as it would have appeared in the days of Bonnie and Clyde. They would have been very familiar with this particular locality as to our knowledge they robbed three banks in the area — Rembrandt [1] (page 206), Knierim [2] (page 210) and Everly [3] (page 236) and three filling stations in Fort Dodge [4].

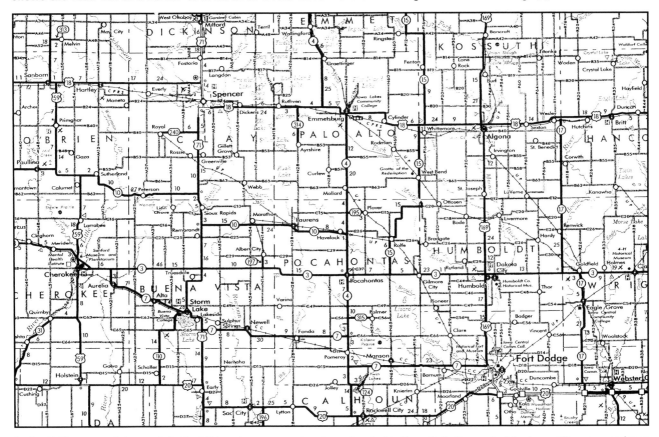

In the 1930s many of the roads in the Midwest were gravel and there were also numerous dirt roads. In 1936-37, federal highways were being constructed — for example Highway 71 which then bypassed Rembrandt on its western side was relocated half a mile to the east of the town. The new road was all concrete — then Rembrandt's only hard-surfaced street. Subsequently all the town's streets were blacktopped. This modern map covers exactly the same area.

155

July 18, 1933 – Fort Dodge, Iowa

Three unmasked and armed bandits this morning held up three filling stations within a few minutes, forced two of the attendants to accompany them while they robbed the third, and escaped with $125 to $150 in cash. The gang also robbed a customer in one of the stations.

The stations were those of the Continental Oil company at 1202 Second Avenue North, the Standard Oil company at Eighth Avenue North and Fifteenth Street and the North Side Texaco company at Ninth Avenue North and Fifteenth Street. The robberies took place shortly before 11 a.m.

The bandits drove a Chevrolet sedan with Buena Vista county license plates numbered 11-2399. The plates were stolen in Storm Lake a week ago, Chief of Police John Lochray learned after the robberies. The car can be easily identified by a damaged rear door.

The first station robbed was the Continental Oil company's at Twelfth Street and Second Avenue North. Harold M. Anderson, the attendant, was alone in the station when the gang drove in.

'I saw the car approaching from the east, first,' Anderson said. 'They turned north on Twelfth Street, then headed back and drove into the station. There were three fellows in the car. One of them jumped out of the car, flashed his gun on me. He ordered me to give him the money, and I turned over what I had in my pockets and the cash I was putting in the safe just as they drove in.

'Then he ordered me into the back seat of the car, and we drove east. I was in the back seat with one of the fellows, and the other two were in front. They didn't have much to say. One of them did say that they had a couple more jobs to do.

'We drove into the Standard station at Fifteenth and Eighth, and they held it up.'

On the morning of July 18, the two Barrow brothers and W. D. Jones drove into Fort Dodge in a 1929 Chevrolet sedan which had been stolen in Spencer, 75 miles away, the day before. It bore licence plates which had been lifted from another vehicle in Storm Lake on the 11th on their way north (see map page 164). This was the gang's first reported foray into Iowa but they would return at least twice more to carry out robberies in 1934.

Their mission on that Tuesday was to raise funds by robbing filling stations and to hit three at once. The Standard Oil garage at 721 North 15th Street is the only one of the three which has survived, the top picture showing it having undergone a face lift in 1946. *Above:* Still in business in 2000 but sadly it closed that year as a gas station to be converted into a bottle recycling centre. Roger Natte took the picture for us.

The Continental garage at 204 2nd Avenue North: pictured *(above)* **undergoing building works a year or so before the Barrow boys came on a visit, and** *(below)* **70 years later having been converted into an optometrist office.**

Harry Stark was the attendant at the Standard station. When the car drove in, he saw Anderson in the back seat and unsuspicious walked out.

One of the bandits left the car, and displayed a .45 caliber automatic pistol to give Stark his first hint of what was happening. If Stark had had any doubts of what was going on, the bandit's first words removed them.

'All right, let's have no monkey business, or I'll kill you,' the gunman said in clipped words. They went into the station and the bandit ordered Stark to open the safe.

Stark obeyed. He took the box containing the station cash from the safe and handed it and his change container to the bandit. Then he was ordered into the car, and joined Anderson.

As the bandits drove out of the station, Stark leaned over and opened the rear door of the car. The door swung wide and crashing into a metal rack, was nearly pulled from its hinges. One of the gang pulled it back, and they drove a block north to the Texaco station operated by Leon Chevalier.

When the gang drove into the Chevalier station, Leon and his brother, Justin, were talking in the drive. Two of the bandits hurried out of the car and directed the Chevaliers to get into the station building. Leon surrendered some $30 in bills and small change, and Justin, urged on by a menacing pistol, gave the gunmen two $10 bills.

The bandits then took the key from Justin's car, told Anderson and Stark to get out, and raced north. Justin asked them to throw out his car keys a few blocks north, a request that the gang politely complied with.

The bandit's car was hardly out of the station drive before Leon Chevalier had telephoned the police.

Police Captain J. J. Huebsch received the call. He reached into the gun case behind him for a riot rifle, hailed Chief of Police Lochray and in a half minute they were on their way to the Texaco station. A reporter joined them for one of the fastest rides of his life. The officers reached the station a little more than five minutes after the bandits had departed. Leon Chevalier in the meantime had telephoned Sheriff Sexe at Humboldt and requested him to be on the look-out for the bandits.

Chevalier joined the policemen and the reporter, and they raced north in the half hope of overtaking the bandits before they turned off some side road.

With Lochray at the wheel, the police car knocked off the eight miles to the Badger corner in eight minutes. There was no sign of the bandit car, however. At a filling station on the Badger corner, attendants said they hadn't seen the fugitive Chevrolet, though Lochray and Huebsch had had half a hunch that the gang might try one more hold-up before seeking cover.

The officers then explored some of the side roads along the river, and returned to town to broadcast a description of the bandits and their car. Police departments and sheriff's offices in surrounding towns were notified to watch for the car.

In the meantime, Stark had notified the sheriff's office of the robbery, and Deputy Sheriffs H. D. Crouse and Joe McMahon hurried to the Standard station.

They also decided the bandits trail lay north, and headed out on No. 169. They reached the Badger corner on the heels of the police and also explored the roads between the Des Moines river and No. 169.

According to Leon Chevalier's description, two of the bandits were youngsters, 17 to 19 years old. He said both seemed very nervous. The third bandit, 28 to 30 years old, drove the car, and directed the activities of the gang. All three were nondescriptly dressed.

The Chevrolet car driven by the gang is a 1929 four-door sedan. It was probably stolen, and Chief Lochray said he thought the gang would abandon it soon, because of its conspicuousness after the mishap in the Standard station.

The exact amount of cash obtained by the gang was not known this noon. Anderson said he thought the bandits got $50 to $60 from him. Stark did not know how much he surrendered, but thought it might be about the same amount. The Chevaliers lost $50.

Leon Chevalier was held up in his station on May 16. The Standard station at Fifteenth Street and Ninth Avenue North has been robbed many times in the past, but not recently.

The robberies were the most daring perpetrated here in several years. The brief kidnapping of Anderson and Stark prevented them from telephoning a warning to police until the bandits had completed their work, since both were alone in their stations at the time.

Fort Dodge Messenger & Chronicle,
July 18, 1933

The third garage robbed — the Texaco gas station operated by the Chevalier brothers — has seen a variety of uses since it was closed . . . from offices to a delicatessen . . . but the building was vacant when Roger pictured it in 2002. After pocketing the cash, Clyde then hightailed it out of town and disappeared — but we now know that he was planning to head south towards Kansas City 250 miles away. But, no doubt to put the police off the scent as to their true destination, the Chevy was dumped down a side road a few miles north of Fort Dodge.

It was late on Tuesday evening (July 18) that a Ford sedan pulled up at Slim's Castle, a combined service station and cafe-cum-grocery store standing at the junction of Highways 59 and 71 about six miles south of Platte City, Missouri. Clyde had driven the 250 miles from Fort Dodge in record time but was now looking for a place to hide up for a couple of days. On the opposite side of the road were two brick motel cabins with adjoining garages which looked ideal for the purpose so Clyde asked the gas station proprietor Delbert Crabtree if they were available to rent. Clyde was told they belonged to the Red Crown Tavern *(above)* across the street and that he should enquire there. The cabins can be seen on the extreme left of the picture.

July 18/19, 1933 – Platte City, Missouri

The Red Crown Tavern at the Highway Junction was the scene of an exciting gun-battle between officers and bandits, supposed to be the Barrow brothers, about 12:30 Wednesday night.

Tuesday evening two men and two women rented the two brick cottages at the Red Crown, occupying them that night and Wednesday until routed in a storm of bullets Wednesday night. Windows curtained with newspapers, continually peeping out of windows by the gang, refusing to admit any of the station employees to the cabins, hiding from view of all the members except one woman, created a suspicion on the part of Neal Houser, the manager, who consulted officers and related the actions of his guests.

Sheriff Holt Coffey, several deputies and Prosecutor Clevenger visited the place late Wednesday. Upon the advice and insistance of Clevenger, the officers were kept from taking charge and of attempting to question the strangers while an armored car was called from Kansas City, equipped to do battle.

The Red Crown Tavern was severely damaged in a fire which began in the kitchens and the building was demolished in 1967.

This is all that is left of the grove of trees which stood at the rear and can be seen in the top photo.

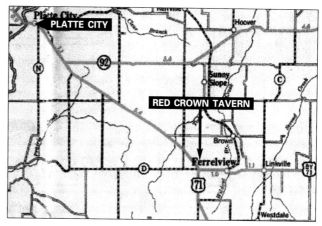

Plans for investigation and capture were well laid. The armored car was run to a vantage point between the two cabins. Sheriff Coffey, under protection of a shield, knocked on the door and informed the occupants of his mission. They answered with a request for time in which to dress, claiming to have retired. The officers were waiting, when suddenly a barrage of bullets came from the cabins and a battle was on. The first shot struck the driver of the armored car in the leg, shattering the bullet-proof glass as though it was paper, and crippling the driver's activity. This disconcerted the officers' plans somewhat, making the armored car a possible slaughter pen from the powerful guns of the bandits. Here a lull in operations occurred in favor of the bandits, who hurriedly jumped in their car, reported as bulletproof, and, in a rain of bullets, made their escape travelling towards Platte City.

Sheriff Coffey was in a precarious position throughout the combat, being between the two cabins, subject to bullets flying from each. He received a wound in his neck, one in his shoulder and the littler finger on his left hand badly shot. The bandits carried a

Left: **Red Crown Tavern had been built in 1931 by Emmett Breen, a banker and property developer from Parkville just west of Kansas City. (The city itself straddles the state line between Missouri and Kansas.)** *Right:* **It lay right on the junction of Highway 71 with the road to Ferrelview.**

good sized arsenal of firearms and ammunition, consisting of automatic rifles, machine guns, sawed-off shotguns and revolvers. In their haste they left a number of these behind.

Clarence Coffey, deputy of his father, was stationed in the kitchen, some distance away, but a bandit's bullet lodged in his arm, others grazed his cheek and forehead, leaving red scratches. He was taken to Bethany Hospital on Thursday for removal of the bullet.

The cabins presented a torn up appearance Thursday morning, bearing many evidences of the terrific battle. Bullet holes were everywhere, through doors and windows, some from outside, some fired from inside. Mirrors and other articles in the cabins were shattered. Several bullets found their way through the station proper but failed to hit any of the many visitors who had been warned of possible trouble and made to stay indoors.

The bandits left, followed by many shots. Deputies Tom Hulett and Byron Fisher are certain bullets from their guns took effect in some of the fleeing bandits. One of the women was seen to lift one of the men into the car. It is supposed the bandits stole their guns in Joplin.

The Red Crown Tavern attracted a large crowd of sightseers Thursday morning and, as news of the battle spreads, will likely attract crowds for weeks.

Sheriff Coffey is surely lucky to be alive today and as the bandits go on and read of the affair, they too will no doubt wonder how they missed him. That he and other officers are still alive, may also be attributed to the caution and insistence of attorney Clevenger, who refused to allow them to attempt an arrest until the armored car and reinforcements arrived from Kansas City.

The Landmark, July 21, 1933

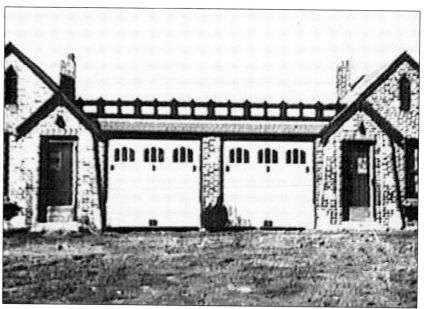

Blanche was sent in to book the accommodation, paying in advance for the two adjoining cabins with integral garages *(right)*. **Clyde, Bonnie and W. D. took the left-hand unit and Buck and Blanche the one on the right. However, the frequent comings and goings between the two cabins aroused the suspicions of the manager, Neal Houser, and he contacted the local sheriff, Holt Coffey** *(left)*. **The following day — Wednesday — the sheriff was in the restaurant when three of the party (Buck, Blanche and W. D.) came in for lunch. Later that day he received a call from Louis Bernstein of Platte City Drugs on the south side of Main Street who reported that a stranger — a 'good looking gal in a slinky riding habit' — had been in to**

purchase medical supplies: atropine sulphate (a muscle relaxant) and hypodermic syringes. The authorities already knew from Marshal Hardy that the young woman with the gang had grevious injuries to her leg, and a general warning had already been circulated to chemist shops throughout Arkansas, Oklahoma and Texas to report any attempts to purchase out-of-the-ordinary drugs. Sheriff Coffey contacted the Missouri State Highway Patrol and Captain William A. Baxter agreed with him that the strangers could well be the Barrow boys. Knowing their reputation, they decided to muster reinforcements before moving in, and wait for the arrival of a bullet-proof car from Kansas City.

Around 11.30 p.m. Sheriff Coffey gave the signal for the bullet-proof car to block the garage doors while he approached the door of the right-hand cabin behind the protection of a steel shield. According to Blanche she was washing out some clothes when he knocked on the door. 'Who is it?,' she called out, to be answered: 'I need to talk to the boys'. Then, in the pre-arranged signal, she replied in a loud voice, loud enough to be heard next door: 'Just a minute — let us get dressed.' Hearing Blanche, Clyde warned Jones: ''That's the law.' W. D. says that 'I heard Blanche Barrow tell them that the boys were over in our cabin. Clyde looked out the door and grabbed his gun out from under the edge of the bed. He told me to get out there and start the car. He started shooting out of doors and windows. I got the key off the dresser and got into the garage. Bonnie had given me the key out of Clyde's pocket to the car. I started the motor and shooting was coming from all directions. Clyde told me to open the garage door and he came and we opened it together. When we opened the door Buck and Blanche were right in front of the door. Blanche was holding Buck up, holding him under the arms.'

Stunned at the ferocity of the gun-battle, officers discuss the events of the previous night as workmen begin to repair the doors.

Echoes of the bandit battle at the Red Crown Tavern Wednesday of last week continue to percolate through the air. It has been definitely ascertained the bandits were the notorious Barrow brothers of Texas, wanted in many places for burglary, murder, etc. Escaping from the officers at the Red Crown, through the bungling of the attack by Kansas City officers, the bandits came toward Platte City, turned onto the gravel road east of town and made a cross-country exit out of Platte county. They stopped at Cleve Burrell's, (Swaney Brick), borrowed a jack and pump, and changed tires. The discarded wheel and tire were found the next day. Bloody clothes were also found in the Hoover neighborhood, left by the wounded bandits. News soon came of the bandits in Iowa, showing they had lost little time on the road.

Dexter, Iowa, became the scene of another encounter with the bandits Monday, they having been joined by another outlaw, said to be Jack Sherman, also of the Lone Star state. They were surrounded by a posse, the bandits using a fallen tree as a fortress. Ivan

Barrow and a woman, supposed to be his wife, were captured. Barrow was seriously wounded and the woman slightly. He is in a hospital, she in jail. The other three made their escape by wading a stream of water. Stealing a car from a farmer, they went toward Des Moines, holding up a filling station and taking another car as they went.

A Texas paper has commented in an uncomplimentary manner upon the Platte County officers allowing the bandits to escape. We must all confess it looks strange that four people surrounded in small cabins by 13 officers could get away, but the breaks came in favor of the bandits just at the right time and it seems to us no one is to blame for the escape, unless it be the Kansas City officers who bungled things with jamming guns and an armored car without much bullet resisting armor.

The bandit battle was a great celebration for the Red Crown and came upon its second anniversary, being just two years ago that day the tavern opened for business. The cabins, with their bullet marks and shot-up interiors have been visited by thousands.

The bandits seemed to have had plenty of guns and ammunition. They left a lot of guns at the Red Crown, some out in the country, and when routed from their fortress in Iowa left 39 pistols of different kinds and two or three machine guns.

The bandits got away from the Platte county officers all right, but there remains this to be awfully glad for all the Platte county boys in the cordon of officers are alive today. It could easily have been otherwise.

The following from the *Kansas City Star* of Tuesday is reported as the story of Ivan Barrow of the Red Crown affair, as told to Sheriff Bash of Kansas City:

'The wounded man said he was shot in the head Thursday morning in the battle at Platte City while firing from inside one of the cabins. No injuries were received by any of the others at Platte City, Barrow said, until they started out of the garage in their car. As they reached the highway, a machine gun bullet shattered the glass of their windshield, the flying glass striking Mrs. Blanche Barrow's left eye.

'Clyde went out and got him just about to the door and handed him to me. I took hold of him then and while I was putting Buck in the car Clyde was shooting. Buck had been wounded in the head. Blanche and I got in the back seat with Buck, and Bonnie and Clyde got in the front with Clyde driving. He backed out of the garage and drove off with them shooting at us. Afterwards

Clyde counted 14 or 15 bullet holes in the car but none of us was hit. They did hit both the back tires, however, and they went flat after we had gone some distance. We ran for a long while on the rim of one of them and ruined it. We put the spare on the wheel and patched one of them temporarily but it gave out later.' *Above:* It happened here . . . exactly 70 years ago!

'Two tires were shot off their car, Barrow said, but they continued driving seven or eight miles, when they stopped to dress his head wound. Later, he said, they stopped again near Mount Ayr, Iowa, to destroy blood-soaked rags, from his own wound and from Bonnie Parker, who had been injured previously in a motor accident and whose wound was reopened in the haste of escaping from the Platte City cabin camp.

'Barrow said they had gone to Platte City from Kansas.'

Mrs. Ivan Barrow was brought back to Platte County and is now in the county jail at Platte City. She is a Texas product and gives evidence of careful rearing, being refined in speech and manner. She is only 22 years old, of slight build, and a brunette. Properly attired and groomed she would be attractive, but the life she has lived the past few weeks has told upon her features and imparted the appearance of a tough character. Romance had its part in her entering the gangster field, for at first sight she fell in love with Ivan Barrow and was willing to share with him the activities of criminals. An officer describes her as a game little woman and tells how, in the face of a bullet shower, she picked up and carried her wounded husband some distance. We understand she denies having used any firearms at Red Crown Tavern, but the officers do not place much faith in this, having ascertained form a different source that everyone in the bandit gang did some shooting.

The bandits may have shot heir way out and escaped from a Platte City — Kansas City cordon of officers, but we are betting they are now thinking Platte county would have been a good place to stay away from.

Mrs Barrow was brought to Platte City by Sheriff Coffey, Attorney Clevenger and Deputy Tom Hulett from the jail at Des Moines, where she had been taken from the scene of the Iowa capture for safe keeping. She was arraigned Wednesday afternoon before Justice of the Peace Murray, charged with shooting Sheriff Coffey with intent to kill. She at once denied the charge. She is wanted by Joplin authorities for participation in the killing of two officers in Newton county. It has not been learned what disposal will be made of the woman, but we understand Mr. Clevenger is studying the matter carefully with a view of releasing her to those who can give the best assurance of conviction. Her bond was placed at $15,000 and a preliminary hearing set for August 5.

The whole bandit affair has awakened Platte county to the need of more adequate equipment for the pursuit and capture of such gangs as the Barrows, and, to this end, the sheriff has provided himself with machine guns, shields, tear gas guns, etc.

The Landmark, July 28, 1933

In July 1994, a proposal was put to the Platte County Economic Development commission's Convention and Tourism Committee that the Red Crown site was as historically important as those of Jesse James in Clay county . . .

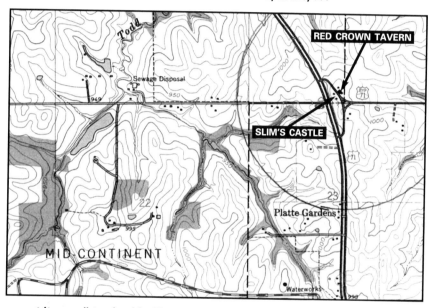

. . . yet it was all too late! In 1957 a vehicle knocked down the awning *(top)* and the fire took its toll in 1967 but it was the alterations to the road junction which sounded the death knell. New access roads from the interstate into Kansas City airport removed the last vestiges of both the Red Crown and Slim's Castle across the road. Compare the 1961 map *above* with that of 1975 *below.*

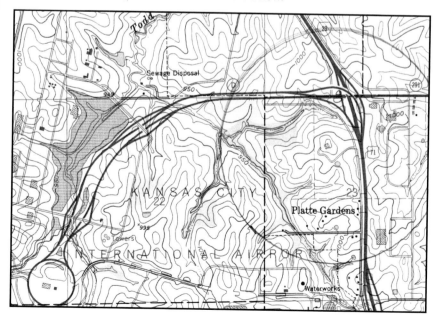

161

The Red Crown gun-battle is such an important one in the history of the gang that we felt that an aerial oblique was the best way of showing the location today. [1] Site of the Red Crown Tavern. [2] Cabins with adjoining garages occupied by the gang.

[3] Slim's Castle. [4] Course of original road in the 1930s. *Inset:* Marty Black explored the area but only odd remnants of brickwork remain, yet there is really no way of determining to which building they belonged.

July 20-24, 1933 – Dexfield Park, Iowa

The bandits who Tuesday held up three Fort Dodge oil stations were tentatively identified today as the notorious Clyde and Buck Barrow, Missouri outlaws, wanted for the slaying of two officers at Joplin in April.

Chief of Police John Lochray, Wednesday, traced the gang to a hideout near Sutherland, Iowa.

Yesterday afternoon the outlaws accompanied by a woman, shot their way out of a cordon of officers in a tourist camp at Platte City, Missouri, and escaped into Iowa. None of the officers was seriously wounded.

Last night the gang stopped on a highway near Caledonia, Iowa, and attempted to burn a bloody garment.

After the gun-battle in the Platte City tourist camp yesterday, officers found bloody bandages in the cabin occupied by the bandits and the woman.

Similar bandages were found by Chief Lochray in the gang's hideout along the Little Sioux River near Sutherland.

The outlaws, when they escaped from the Platte City camp were driving a Ford V-8 sedan. The gang that robbed the Fort Dodge oil stations used the same kind of a car in making their getaway after abandoning the stolen sedan that provided transportation for them during the hold-ups there.

Chief Lochray this afternoon outlined the chain of evidence which he believes links the Barrow brothers with the Fort Dodge robberies and the shooting at Platte City yesterday.

After the filling station robberies here Tuesday, Chief Lochray decided that the gang must have had a hideout somewhere in the vicinity of Spencer, where the car used by the bandits in the station holdups was stolen Sunday night.

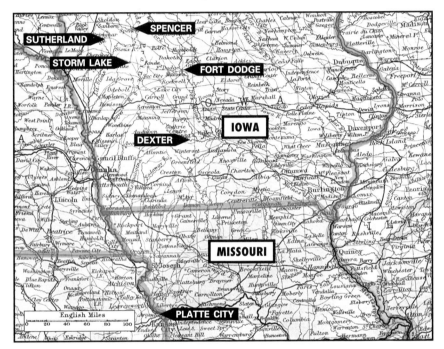

Following the gang's escape from Platte City on Wednesday (July 19), they headed back north into Iowa and made camp on Thursday just outside Dexter. Meanwhile police from Fort Dodge, one jump behind, had been following up a lead after the filling station robberies on Tuesday and had extended their investigation to Sutherland in the far north-west corner of the state near the Little Sioux River. The press report confirmed that the suspect group had left their campsite on Sunday or Monday. This would certainly have allowed them time to hit Fort Dodge on Tuesday and still book into the Red Crown on Wednesday evening — and the description fits — so it could well have been the Barrow gang.

Wednesday morning Lochray and Policeman Everett Maricle drove to Lake Okoboji, and questioned tourist camp and cabin owners in the hope of finding where the gang had been living. They learned nothing there and drove over to Spencer to talk with officers.

In Spencer they learned that a farmer near Sutherland, Iowa, had reported that a party of three men and two women, camping in a ravine on his farm, had been shooting pheasants. The Fort Dodge officers, accompanied by a Spencer man, drove over to the farm to question the owner.

The farm is located along the Little Sioux River near Sutherland in O'Brien county.

The owner of the farm told Lochray the three men and two women had spent several days in the ravine, leaving Sunday or Monday.

The farmer said he had paid the party a visit but found them anything but sociable. He saw no guns, he said, but did note that one of the men reached for his hip when the farmer walked into the hideout. There was a Ford V-8 sedan in the ravine and the farmer, suspicious, memorized the license numbers and wrote them down when he returned home.

The numbers were 11-2399, the same numbers that were later observed on the Chevrolet sedan stolen in Spencer and used by the gang in robbing the Fort Dodge oil stations.

Lochray and Maricle made a minute search of the ravine and found several interesting things.

The gang had apparently devoted considerable time to target practice, for there were many empty rifle and pistol shells on the ground. The rifle shells were of the type used in high power weapons of big game and army design. The pistol shells were .45 calibre.

The Fort Dodge officers also found bloodsoaked rags, indicating that one of the men had not long before been wounded.

Fort Dodge Messenger, July 21, 1933

However, by the time the *Fort Dodge Messenger* appeared on Friday, Bonnie and Clyde, with the injured Buck and Blanche, were hiding out with Jones in thick brush just south of Dexfield Park. This popular amusement centre with its own brook-fed swimming pool previously attracted visitors from as far away as Des Moines (pronounced d'Moyn). It had been established in 1915 and included a merry-go-round, Ferris wheel, go-carts and other rides plus a dance hall and cafés, beyond which were baseball 'diamonds'. This picture shows the park in its heyday, but by the 1930s the crowds had dropped away as new attractions were opened up like Riverview Park in Des Moines. By July 1933, the park had closed but because the surrounding area was still used for camping, the presence of the Barrows did not initially seem unusual.

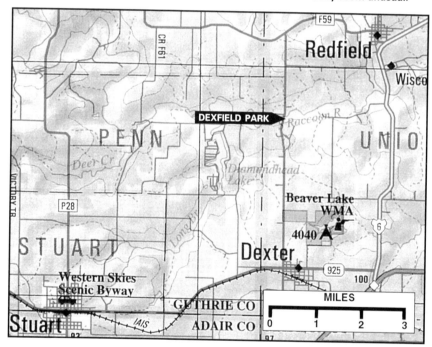

Below: Very little was left of the park by the 1960s and the vestiges were bulldozed in 1968. Today, restored to farmland, nothing remains save a pile of broken concrete from the swimming pool in the undergrowth on the right.

According to John Love, the local part-time Deputy Sheriff (also referred to as the Night Marshal) who also ran a shoe repair shop in the town, the Barrows had been in the Dexter area before because earlier that year he helped Clyde fill his radiator, not knowing at the time who he was. (Remember that pre-Joplin in April, the only photos of the gang were the early police mug-shots.) Possibly they used the same spot to pitch their camp — that we shall never know — but in any case they must have been familiar with the area because they picked a location [1] on the high ground south of the park, tucked away in scrub several hundred yards from the main road [2]. 'Iowa is an interesting place,' reported Marty Black who carried out our investigation at Dexter. 'People say "hi" to strangers on the street; motorists wave to one another while passing on the narrow dirt roads, and they'll stop to offer assistance if they see you pulled over (this happened twice while I was out of the car taking photos). Dexter lies some 25 miles west of Des Moines and I took the picture *(above left)* at the extreme western end of the town looking north up Dexfield Road. The park is — or rather was — some three miles ahead on the right, just before the road crosses the Raccoon River.' *Above right:* 'Half a mile short of the river lies the first turn-off [3] on what is now called Delta Trail. The small house on the corner marks its beginning.' *Below left:* 'The beginning of Delta Trail lies on the right. Ahead, Dexfield Road drops out of sight as it enters the river valley, about a mile wide at this point.' *Below right:* 'The bottom portion of the "D" leads to the drive to the former George Johnson farm [4]. Although the original buildings have been replaced by a beautiful brick house, the old oak trees show where the farmhouse stood as it was common practice for settlers in the Midwest to use trees to shield their homes from the bitter winter winds. It was along this part of Delta Trail that the police — and many members of the public — parked their cars during the all-night stake-out.'

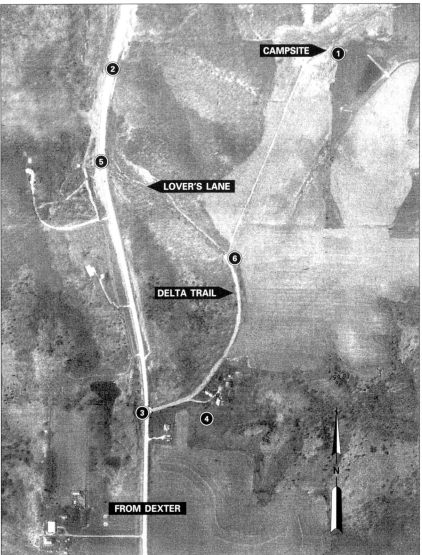

'However, not wanting to pass by the farm with a bullet-holed car and wounded aboard, instead Clyde most probably came off the Dexfield Road on the more northerly turning [5] onto Delta Trail, along what was then called Lover's Lane, a distance of about half a mile. It is a muddy track and no doubt neither it nor its reputation has changed over the past 70 years!'

Above: 'Having reached the high ground, the lane (seen emerging from the trees on the left) turned sharp left [6] and continued along what is now the driveway to Kirk Apple's farm in the right background. In 1933 this terrain was covered in thickets. Clyde then drove through the brush for another 100 yards or so before parking under the big oak tree *(below)*. Here the gang were relatively safe, hidden from prying eyes, where they could lick their wounds and take stock of their situation.'

Having driven 200 miles from Platte City with Buck grievously wounded with a .45 slug through his skull, and Blanche having shards of glass in her left eye, they were in urgent need of medical help but could hardly go to see a doctor. So Clyde had to risk driving into Dexter *(above)* having tried to disguise the bullet holes in the car with mud. Seventy years later, Marty followed in his tyre tracks: 'We were able to match-up a couple of shops in downtown Dexter which Clyde used in 1933 but most of the store fronts of the buildings have changed since then. Like many towns bypassed by the post-war Interstate highway system, Dexter has suffered from lack of business. Many buildings are vacant and in a derelict condition. Not being able to compete with the opportunities in nearby Des Moines, Dexter is really withering away. The only industry there is grain and corn. No entertainment, few conveniences, not much of anything . . . save for a dying town.'

Clyde's first stop on Friday, July 21 was to Myron Williams' clothing store *(above)* on Marshall Street. Here John Love sold him some white shirts and a new pair of shoes although Clyde made a hasty departure when he caught a glimpse of John's Deputy Sheriff's badge! *Left:* Marty: 'Now No. 709 is the Harmony chiropractic office. Although the store front has changed, the brickwork remains as it was in 1933. My wife Kathi stands in for the long-forgotten bystanders.' *Below left:* Clyde then crossed the road to Blohm's restaurant where he ordered five take-away meals and a block of ice — obviously to use on Buck's head wound. *Below right:* Also referred to as Blohm's Indian Grill, and Blohm's Meat Market, it stood here at 716-720 Marshall, the vacant lot being decorated for Halloween when Marty took his shot.

While he was waiting for his food to be prepared, Clyde walked directly across the street to Pohle's Pharmacy *(left)* as in the Depression years it was not unusual for individuals unable to afford doctors' fees to purchase their own drugs and medications. According to Lillian Pohle (seen *above* behind the counter) who served him, Clyde posed as a veterinarian in his attempt to purchase morphine.

Left: Marty found the shop under new management with the proprietor Robert Weesner on to a good thing! *Right:* Another sign in front of the original 1933 cash desk says: 'Clyde Barrow stood at this counter and cash register where he purchased peroxide and bandages. Bonnie Parker stayed in the car and left it running.' (Sadly, Bob Weesner died in February 2003.)

Clyde repeated his shopping trip to Dexter on Saturday and Sunday and although Martha Blohm and Lillian Pohle thought it odd, neither reported their suspicions to John Love. It was not until Sunday afternoon that the alarm was raised by 41-year-old Henry Nye (seen *left* in his younger days), a hired-hand working on Ed Penn's farm *(above)* on Bear Creek Road, a turning off Dexfield Road about 1½ miles from the Barrow campsite. Henry had been out in the woods looking for blueberries when he came across a bloodstained shirt. Marty followed in his footsteps north, behind the George Johnson farm on Delta Trail to the camp site area on Kirk Apple's land.

A telephone call from the Penn farm alerted John Love in Dexter who came out himself to check what had been found. *Left:* Here the Deputy Sheriff is pictured outside the small shoe shop he opened in the town some years later. *Right:* Marty found the building still standing boarded up on Polk Street.

Monday morning about six o'clock a posse composed of state agents, county officers and some local law enforcement officers from Dexter attempted to capture three men and two women, later identified as members of the famous Barrow gang from the Southwest, in their camp on the hill south of Dexfield Park.

Members of the Barrow gang are accused of four murders in Missouri and Texas, also of numerous robberies of oil stations, etc. They are desperate characters and do not hesitate to shoot to kill.

The party had been camped near Dexfield Park since last Thursday. Some member of the gang was in Dexter daily purchasing bandages etc., also five meals daily. Officers became suspicious and got in touch with state officers who thought the gang was the Barrow gang that had shot their way out of a tourist camp near Platte City, Missouri, last Wednesday, when thirteen officers attempted to arrest them. In this fight Marvin Barrow was wounded in the head.

The state men decided to try and capture the gang early Monday morning and reached the scene about midnight and made their plans.

John Love called his boss in Adel, the Dallas county seat some 18 miles away, and Sheriff Clint Knee quickly put two and two together. A call went out for reinforcements but, in true Wild West tradition, the posse which assembled in front of the Webb Lunch Stand *(above)* on State Street at the north end of downtown Dexter on Sunday evening comprised a mixed bag of lawmen and civilians. Included were two state policemen, Bill Arthur and 'Rags' Riley; a part-time National Guard officer, Dr H. W. Keller, and a small force from the Des Moines Police Department.

Webb's stood here next to a Standard Oil filling station so Casey's offering pizzas and gas is an appropriate replacement!

The gang had also been busy that Sunday with their own plans. With the shot-up Platte City car as their only form of transport, a new vehicle was essential so Clyde and W. D. set off at midday to find a replacement. They drove north to the large town of Perry where a nice Ford V-8 standing outside Ed Stoner's house on 6th Street took their fancy and within the hour it was parked back at the camp site. Marvelle Feller, the sole remaining witness of events that day, told Marty that the cars were parked on the north-east, i.e. the far side, of the oak tree in this picture. After both cars were disabled during the gun-battle, the gang retreated towards the derelict children's play house in the distance.

John Love, Dexter night marshal, Everett Place and Dallas county deputies, guarded the roads all night in case the gang attempted to leave. Omer Little of Stuart was also there from about four o'clock in the morning, helping guard the north side of the river.

Shortly after the first battle, one of the bandits, believed to have been Marvin Barrow, appeared near the bridge which was guarded by Everett Place of Dexter and a Dallas county deputy named Berger. When the bandit saw the two men, he shouted 'Don't shoot!', and ran along the side of the road just south of the bridge and went through the fence behind a large tree. Place and Berger, thinking the man was one of the posse did not shoot! After Barrow reached the tree he opened fire on the two men and a gun battle took place in which a considerable number of shots were fired, but no damage was done. Barrow, protected by the tree, disappeared into the thick weeds and brush just east of the tree. Two empty clips for a .45

revolver were found near the tree and eight or ten empty rifle shells were counted which Berger had fired from behind one of the large pillars which support the bridge, on the north side of the river. Place also took a number of shots at Barrow with a pistol.

To prevent the outlaws escaping the trap, some members of the posse *(centre)* were stationed to guard both exits on Delta Trail and on the bridge over the Raccoon overlooking the park.

Above: Today a replacement has been built about 75 yards east of the original bridge but the steel pilings from the old one still remain half-submerged in the river.

The officers walked in on the gang from the west and when within about fifty feet of them were seen by the bandits, who took refuge behind their cars and opened fire on the posse with pistols and automatic rifles. The officers returned the fire and the cars were riddled with bullets and two or three of the bandits were wounded, but they were able to elude the officers in the thick woods.

In this shot we are looking west towards the wooded ravine from where the six lawmen began their attack, moving towards the camera in their advance. Marty took the picture near Kirk Apple's large equipment shed which of course was not standing in 1933.

Marty: 'This is the reverse view of the other picture. I am now looking east towards the oak tree seen in the distance and you can see from this shot how restricted the view was as the lawmen were firing and moving uphill through brush.'

'And this is the Barrows' view looking towards the approaching lawmen', says Marty. 'I am standing just north of the oak tree.' Jim Knight gives a marvelously graphic account of what happened next in his book *Bonnie and Clyde — a 21st Century Update*: 'It was just after 5:00 a.m. and, at the campsite, everybody was awake. Blanche was getting Buck a glass of water, Bonnie and Clyde were sitting on a seat cushion they had pulled out from the Platte City car, and W. D. was roasting the last of the hot dogs from the night before. It was either Bonnie or Clyde who happened to look up and see the figures moving through the underbrush. In that instant, whatever plans Clyde may have had were changed. Surprise and extreme stress have all kinds of effects on people. Most people — even law enforcement officers — are so seldom put suddenly into truly life or death situations that it's almost impossible to prepare for them. We just react, and this was an area where Clyde Barrow had a natural advantage. When confronted with a sudden threat, some people will run; some will become hysterical; and some will simply freeze. Clyde seemed, from his earliest brushes with danger, to be the kind of person who could continue to think and function in the middle of fear and chaos. Since he also had several opportunities to experience and live through truly frightening gun-fights, he was almost always better prepared to deal with the situation than his opposition. This, along with the awesome firepower he carried, gave him a few seconds head start, and at times like these, a few seconds could mean the difference between life and death. In a second, Clyde saw it all. He yelled to everyone to run for the car, picked up the nearest BAR, and emptied a magazine over the lawmen's heads.

Nobody in his right mind stands up to military machine gun firing at him, so the six lawmen were immediately on the ground or behind cover. People up to 100 yards away were surprised to find leaves, branches and entire limbs falling around them as the .30 caliber bullets cut through the trees, and "Rags" Riley went down, stunned by a glancing blow to the head. He was the only lawman wounded. Clyde got his few seconds, but that's all. These Iowa men were shocked — as lawmen always were — at the fire-power, but they didn't run and they didn't freeze. Within a few seconds, they were all returning fire. W. D. Jones was hit with buckshot and knocked down twice before he made it to the car — small but painful flesh wounds. Bonnie limped along, helping Buck and Blanche into the back seat as Clyde covered the group as best he could. W. D. couldn't get the Ford started, so Clyde shoved him over and took his place. As soon as the engine caught, Clyde was backing the Stoner car away from the lawmen. He then turned and started out of the park but was met by gun-fire from another part of the posse. As he backed away again, he was hit in the shoulder and lost control of the car. It ran over a stump and hung up on the bumper. W. D. made a quick try to pry it loose, but they were stuck fast. Clyde got everybody out and headed back for the other car, but it was no use. The posse shot out all the windows and tires, and ruined the engine. The only thing left was to try and hide. As the Barrows headed for the woods, the posse continued to fire. W. D. was stunned again by a glancing shot, Bonnie took shot-gun pellets to the mid-section, and Buck was hit again, but they got a few minutes relief as they disappeared into the underbrush and out of sight.'

Deputy Sheriff C. C. 'Rags' Riley, the only lawman to be hit, pictured with his bloodhounds Block and Tackle.

On the run! The five members of the gang, all wounded, retreated north-east through the thickets for the protection of the woods. Their route would have been roughly along the line of the fence. When they were stopped at the woods-line by a chest-high barbed wire fence that ran north-south, they paralleled it down a fairly-steep 170-foot hill, thick with oak trees, to the river valley below, and onto the flat area of Dexfield Park.

Later Mr. and Mrs. Clyde Barrow and Jack Sherman, suspected of being Bob Brady, famous Texas bad man, crossed Coon river east of Dexfield Park and appeared at the residence of Vallie Feller which is the second house north-east of the bridge on the east side of the road. Covering Mr. Feller, his son and a hired man, they forced them to get their car ready to go, then ordered Mr. Feller to lift the woman, who was badly wounded, into the car, and then drove north. At this writing they were still at large.

In the first battle, 'Rags' Riley, a state man, was hit in the head with a bullet and knocked unconscious, but after having his wound dressed in Dexter was able to take part in the hunt.

Once they reached the woods, the ground dropped steeply away towards the river which runs behind the treeline in the background. The ploughed field was once the amusement park with the bridge on Dexfield Road on the extreme left. At this point, Clyde left the others to reconnoitre (the press report on page 171 mis-identifies him as Marvin), losing his BAR in his skirmish with the men on guard on the bridge.

Shortly after seven o'clock, police officers, state men and county deputies and vigilanties from Stuart and other towns appeared on the scene and all later took part in the hunt for the escaped bandits. An armored car from Des Moines and a plane bearing Park Findley, chief of state law enforcement body, and *Register* cameramen and reporters, followed the chase from Dexfield Park.

A search was made in the woods for Marvin Barrow, when it was learned that only three had left in the Feller's car. Officers went east to work west through the woods along the river, while men were stationed on the north and west to cut off escape in those directions.

A party of several found Barrow and his wife lying behind a log a short distance east of the Dexfield Park buildings. They were told to surrender but refused to do so, until Barrow was shot in the shoulder by one of

Retracing his footsteps to where the others were hiding, Clyde must have told them that their only escape route now lay across the river. It was obvious that Buck, now wounded again in the back, would never make it and Blanche insisted she stay behind with him. The release of the Warner Bros film in 1967 focussed a spotlight on Bonnie and Clyde and the press descended on surviving witnesses . . . particularly W. D. Jones: 'I was carrying her [Bonnie] on my back — half stumbling, half swimming — when me and her and Clyde got away from that posse. Clyde had a machine gun holding the posse off us.

He'd taken a shot in the leg and was hopping along. I'd been hit in the chest with a bullet and taken some shotgun pellets in the face and chest and was losing a lot of blood. Then Clyde caught a bullet in the head on the side. It must have bounced off a tree because it didn't go in. It just dazed him. He ran out of ammunition just as we got to a little river. We didn't have nothing to shoot with no more, but we made it across.' This is the exact spot where they crossed, climbing the embankment on the far side just to the right of the Spillers' family cemetery onto land belonging to Vallie Feller.

the posse, then Mrs. Barrow came out with her hands up and later her husband gave up. He had fired several times from behind the log. Dr H. W. Keller, a Des Moines dentist and National Guard officer, who was armed with a sub-machine gun, and several Dexter men were in the immediate vicinity of the bandits when they were found behind the log. Everett Godwin of Stuart was also present.

Barrow was suffering from wounds received in a battle with Missouri officers a week ago Wednesday. His wounds were dressed in Dexter and he was then taken to a hospital in Perry, Iowa, where it is reported that he cannot recover. Mrs. Barrow was taken to Des Moines and later to Missouri to answer charges filed there.

The chase for the three escaped bandits first led north-east of Redfield. Then a report was received that the fugitives had been seen near Panora. Sheriff Kunkle and deputies joined the chase there, which led to an abandoned cabin a mile and a half north of No. 7, north-west of Panora. No signs were discovered of the bandits, then the report came that they had held up a man near Polk City and had taken his car. Later reports had the bandits placed near Sioux City and then in Kossuth county, but so far all have been false alarms.

A little local interest was taken in the hunt early Thursday morning when Sheriff Kunkle and two deputies and seven members of the Stuart vigilanties went to a patch of timber north-west of Stuart east of Bert Davidson's and near the Richard Farrel farm, to investigate reports that fires had been noticed in the timber for the past two nights and it was thought possible that the bandits had doubled back on their trail and were in hiding there. Nothing but the remains of several brush pile fires were found.

The hunt attracted many people from this part of the country and the scene of the battle was visited by many. Trees and bushes show the effects of the bullets fired by the posse and the bandits.

The hunt for the three fugitives is being continued, but at this writing it looks as though they had escaped for a time at least.

The Stuart Herald, July 28, 1933

Another personality interviewed in 1968 was Marvelle Feller (left), Vallie's son, whose recollections were written up in his daughter's school magazine, the *Cub Gazette*: 'They approached my father and me about six o'clock Sunday morning as we were feeding the cattle,' recalled Marvelle who was 19 at the time. 'Clyde pointed a .45-caliber pistol at us and demanded a car. We had three cars, but since it was during the Depression, we could only afford tires and gasoline for one, a 1929 Plymouth. They were all exhausted and Jones was the only one who hadn't been shot (*sic*). Clyde had been wounded in the cheek and Bonnie had been shot twice. Since Bonnie was hardly conscious and bleeding badly, Clyde ordered me to carry her to the car. My mother and sister had heard news of the gun-battle on the radio and were coming out of the house to tell us. The radio announcer had warned people around Dexter and Redfield to stay in their locked houses until it was known that the three remaining members of the Barrow gang were out of the district. My father yelled at them to get back in the house but Clyde wouldn't let them. He was afraid mother might telephone someone. Clyde kept warning us not to try anything. My father explained to him that all we had was a shotgun and one shell in the house which he wasn't planning to use. Clyde also threatened to shoot our dog if he didn't stop barking. I placed Bonnie in the back seat and Jones got in with her. Unlike the episode in the movie it was Clyde, not Jones, who got in the front seat and drove away, heading west.' Also it was only when W. D. spoke to *Playboy* magazine that it was revealed that Clyde's pistol was empty . . . he had completely run out of ammunition! *Right:* The Feller farm no longer stands but this is the old entrance, from which the outlaws escaped to the north, turning toward the camera. The cornfield from where the outlaws first approached the Feller family is in the distance to the left beyond the tree-line, and inaccessible to Marty on his visit. The position of the campsite on the far side of the river is arrowed.

175

A three-hour intensive search near Panora for three suspected members of the notorious Barrow brothers gang was ended at 1 p.m. Monday by a posse of more than 50 men.

The hunt had centered near Panora when it was reported that car with a woman who had a bandaged head was seen driving that way. Later it was found that no one actually had seen the bandit car near Panora.

Earlier in the day, a man and woman identified as Mr. and Mrs. Marvin Barrow were captured in a wooded tract near Dexter, after they had been left behind by their companions, two men and a woman.

The sheriff of Kossuth county later Monday afternoon reported to the state bureau of investigation that the Barrow gang had been seen passing through LuVerne which is in the southern part of Kossuth county (north central Iowa).

The car, headed east, was driven by a woman. Three men also were in the car, the sheriff reported one of whom was lying down apparently wounded.

The car was said to be the Chevrolet coach stolen earlier, Monday, at Polk City. The license is 77-13662.

The three who escaped are believed to be Mr. and Mrs. Clyde Barrow and Jack Sherman, members of the desperados wanted for Missouri murders and hold-ups.

C. C. (Rags) Riley of Des Moines, a Polk county deputy sheriff, was wounded slightly in the head early Monday morning in an exchange of shots between all five members

When Marvelle's father reported that only three people had escaped in his car, the police realised that the other two outlaws must still be on the loose. So search parties began to comb the area. It was the National Guardsman, Dr Keller (left) and James Young of Dexter who came up against Buck and Blanche holding out behind this fallen tree.

of the bandit gang and a posse which had surrounded the woods north of Dexter.

After the three members of the gang had escaped from near Dexter, they commandeered a car from a farmer and sped to Polk City. There they held up an oil station and took the attendant's car. The abandoned machine was bloodstained and the windshield was shattered.

Park Findley, chief of the state Bureau of Criminal Investigation, flew from Des Moines in the *Register and Tribune* plane over the scene of the shooting. Pilot Charles Gatschet flew over the wooded tract in an attempt to spot the man and woman before the two members of the gang were caught and then circled over Highway 6.

In the cordon surrounding the woods were armed police and sheriffs from four counties, farmers, business men and state agents who traced the gang from Mount Ayr.

Four law department chiefs from Des Moines went to Dexter and Panora to aid in directing activities of the police officers during the manhunt Monday.

Suffering from his awful head wound, Buck was unable to struggle on any further but he still managed to raise his pistol. However, after a brief exchange of fire, in which Buck was hit three more times, Blanche stood up and surrendered. By now a photographer from the *Des Moines Register* had arrived on the scene. Herb Schwartz took a number of shots but unfortunately the negatives to most have been lost although we have been able to trace some reasonable prints. *Above:* **The original caption states that 'Arrow at the left indicates Mrs Marvin Barrow, held by officers, who screamed, "Don't die! Don't die!" as her husband (arrow at the right) lays seriously wounded in the clearing where they made their last stand.'** *Right:* **Buck lies with his knees bent up on the ground as he is tended by Virgil Musselman in the undershirt and bib overalls. Dexter café owner Harold Myers is crouching down to his left holding the towel. Dr Keller in the fedora is standing in front of the car which has been brought up to take the prisoners away.**

Above: The more well-known photo shows Blanche struggling while being held by policeman John Forbes and Ford Knapp. In the background the abandoned buildings of the amusement park. *Below:* Determined to get an accurate comparison, Marty went to Iowa four times. 'Not having anything to link the photos makes for a poor "then and now" but I'm confident that I'm close to the actual spot. We know that the buildings in the background are at the eastern end of Dexfield Park, and if we assume the hill/slope is what we see behind them and to the left, then we have the correct orientation. And the open area between the people and the buildings could be either the corral or the ball diamonds which Marvelle and other sources tell us was there. With this orientation looking west, the river is out of view to the right.'

Overview of the Dexfield Park battlefield today, looking north. [1] The outlaws' camp on a ridge overlooking an amusement park. After the lawmen open fire, and with the loss of both their vehicles, the gang retreats to position [2] at the east end of the park. [3] Clyde moves alone through the park towards Dexfield Road to reconnoitre an escape route, hoping to hijack a vehicle. [4] Clyde is turned back after a gun-fight with lawmen guarding the bridge and returns to the others via route [5].

8

SITE OF FELLER FARM

7

6 **2**

1

OUTLAWS' CAMP SITE

MODERN FARM BUILDINGS

Having spotted a suitable crossing site, Clyde rejoins the group sheltering behind a log [6]. Blanche now decides to remain behind with the mortally wounded Buck while Bonnie, Clyde and W. D. wade the river [7]. Reaching the far bank, they follow the lie of the land up a ravine, passing just east of the Spillers family cemetery on the way to the Feller farm. After commandeering the Feller's automobile they make good their escape [8] towards the highway turning north to Redfield.

The battlefield as viewed by Park Findley, the chief of the state Bureau of Criminal Investigation, as he surveyed the scene from the *Register and Tribune* aircraft in 1933. The caption when published stated: 'This photo diagram shows where the posse surrounded the hideaway of the bandits early Monday morning and engaged in a furious battle; where the bandits fled with the posse pursuing; where Marvin Barrow and his wife, unable to escape across the creek, surrendered.'

Comparison of the same area today as seen looking east with Dexfield Road in the foreground. The descriptions in the top photograph detailing the bandits' escape are approximate and may not be completely accurate.

In the shot above we are looking south with the Raccoon River in the foreground and below looking south but from a half mile further away. The escape route across the river *(above)* toward the Feller farm, and then to the highway *(below)* is illustrated. The original farmhouse — which was quite old in 1933 — was vacated several years later and has since been plowed under.

SITE OF FELLER FARM

Buck and Blanche were driven to Dexter to be treated at the Chapler-Osborn Clinic situated on the top floor of the Dexter Bank on the corner of Marshall and Dallas. The picture *(above right)* shows the building being converted into the library in 1938. Dr Keith Chapler examined their wounds: 'The main injuries that Blanche Barrow had sustained were small cuts around both eyes with small pieces of crushed glass inside the upper and lower lids of both eyes producing a traumatic conjunctivitis. Blanche was not only a highly tense nervous person, but also highly hysterical and very uncooperative at times. However, as you watched her sitting on the floor of the reception room in my office with Buck, surrounded by many of the law officers, she would become quite subdued. When she was impatient to get her eyes treated she was very cooperative, but a short time after the eye patches were removed she reverted back to the hysteria she had exhibited before. Naturally, the uppermost thought in the minds of these outlaws was to escape. Blanche stated to one of our nurses that she wanted to go to the restroom. She was stripped of everything and put into a hospital-type gown with a sheet draped around her, and the nurse escorted her from this examining room to the stairway that led to the restroom in the basement. The nurse was holding tightly to her, but when they reached the landing which had an outside door to the alley, an instant commotion was heard. She was struggling to get free of the nurse and get out the door and thus escape from the law. However, she was corralled and law enforcement officers were stationed at all exits while the nurse took her on to the restroom.

Buck Barrow had a through-and-through head wound in the front part of his skull where no vital centers are contained. This wound had occurred in the gun-fight at Platte City, Missouri, and this was the wound the gang had been treating themselves with the supplies they were getting here in Dexter. We surmised later that they were driving into town and parking their car on the north side of the building where my office was located. Then Clyde would get out leaving the motor running and Bonnie would slide under the wheel while he crossed the street to the drug store, grocery store and clothing store for supplies. I did not suspect this car because I had not been in Dexter long enough to know all of the people and they came in the evening as the stores were open until ten or eleven o'clock several evenings a week in those days. They had been pouring the peroxide into the front opening and letting it boil through three or four times each day, then wrapping the entire head in gauze and tape. Buck said it had not bothered him except for the pain in the beginning which had been alleviated with aspirin, and neither Dr Osborn nor I could believe how clean this wound was. When we saw him he was complaining of the severe pain in his back from the shoot-out that had just occurred. It was found that a bullet had entered his back and ricocheted off one of his ribs and lodged in the chest wall, posteriorly, close to the pleural cavity. We could only give him emergency care at that time, and then we told him we would come to the Perry Hospital which was the closest hospital at that time — some 20 miles north of Dexter — where the law enforcement officers were making plans to transport him.'

Marvin Barrow, believed to be Marvin Ivy Barrow, and his wife told officers their address is Route 6, Dallas, Texas. They told authorities that the other members of the gang who fled are Mr. and Mrs. Clyde Barrow and Jack Sherman, all of Dallas, Texas. Barrow said his mother, Mrs. C. B. Barrow, lives in Dallas.

Barrow was shot through the forehead with a machine gun by Keller and he is not expected to live.

Keller and Young trapped Marvin Barrow and his wife after following them down a hill three-fourths of a mile to a log, behind which the men and women hid.

This was just at the edge of Dexfield park. Keller and Young fired at Barrow and Keller, crawling towards the log, opening fire with a machine gun. Keller crawled behind a tree and shot Barrow in the head and shoulder. Then Mrs. Barrow screamed as her husband stiffened out as if dead.

Harley Thornton, Polk county deputy, carried Marvin about seven blocks into the park. Sidney Pearce, Des Moines patrolman, came into the woods and took Mrs. Barrow and her husband to Dexter.

After Barrow had been brought to Dexter, an ambulance was called from Perry to take the wounded man to the hospital there. Mrs Marvin Barrow was taken to Adel.

Riley was taken to a doctor's office at Dexter and his wound was treated. He was reported weak from loss of blood, but the doctor stated he would recover. Riley was

back on the job Monday morning after his wound had been dressed.

Additional help was speeded from Des Moines in an attempt to intercept the fleeing members of the gang.

The Barrow gang is wanted in Platte City and Joplin for slayings and holdups. According to word from Chief of Detectives Ed Portley of Joplin, a $1,000 reward has been offered for capture of all the Barrows.

Des Moines Tribune, July 24, 1933

The doctor's surgery is no more as the top floor was removed during the WPA conversion in 1938 but the Dexter Public Library, remodelled again in 1976, still sports the tell-tale window and doorway of the old bank. (The Works Progress Administration or WPA was one of President Roosevelt's measures to provide federal funding for local projects to create work for the unemployed.)

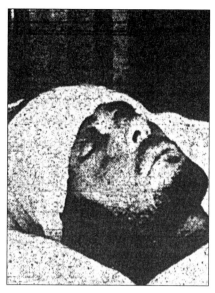

Buck was taken to the Kings Daughters Hospital in Perry (the same town where Clyde had stolen the Ford the day before) and news of his admission relayed to the Barrow family in Dallas whereupon his mother, Cumie, and brother, L. C., made immediate arrangements to drive 700-odd miles to Iowa. With them went one of Blanche's friends, May Turner, Bonnie's mother, Emma, and sister, Billie.

Marvin (Buck) Barrow, 31, alleged leader of the Barrow gang of Texas desperados, died in Perry hospital early today of wounds suffered in two gun-battles, one at Platte City, Missouri, last week, and the second at Dexter, Iowa, Monday. The cause of death was infection in a head wound. Barrow lapsed into a coma early Thursday and did not regain consciousness.

Police are seeking other members of the gang.

Press report, July 29, 1933

The hospital was located at 2323 East Willis Street. Although the old building has been replaced by the Perry Lutheran Home, nevertheless the stairway links past and present.

Buck was questioned about crimes he had committed with the gang and he admitted to police from Arkansas that he was responsible for killing Marshal Humphrey the previous month in the hold-up in Fayetteville. However he refused to name their accomplice so W. D. was still only known to the law as 'Jack Sherman'. At midday on Wednesday the family arrived at Buck's bedside having been on the road for nearly 36 hours. By then he was running a high temperature and on Thursday was hallucinating, confusing L. C. for Clyde and Billie for Blanche. He grew steadily worse, calling out for Clyde and Blanche and at 2 p.m. on Saturday, July 29, he died. The family returned his body to Dallas for burial in Western Heights Cemetery. Clyde realised that sooner or later he would join his brother so it was agreed that they would both be buried side by side with a joint headstone. Clyde chose the epitaph — one which was to ring true even in the next century — 'Gone but not forgotten'. *Right:* 'Rags' Riley visits the Barrows' grave in Dallas in 1934.

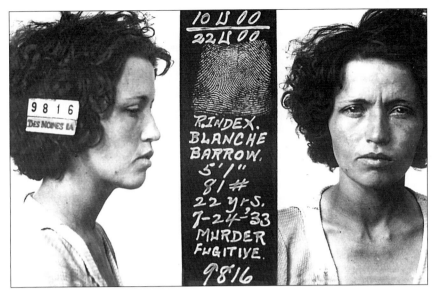

Once Blanche's eye had been treated, she was taken into custody, first to the county seat at Adel, then to Des Moines where she was photographed and fingerprinted. William Hammond watches as she washes the ink from her hands.

Mrs Blanche Barrow, held in the county jail under charge of shooting Sheriff Coffey with intent to kill, in the bandit battle at highway junction July 20, waived a preliminary hearing last Saturday. Her bond was placed at $15,000 and she is being held for the circuit court. So far Mrs. Barrow has no lawyer to represent her, and her bandit friends seem to have forsaken her.

The Landmark, August 11, 1933

Mrs. Blanche Barrow, widow of Buck Barrow, pled guilty in circuit court Monday and was sentenced by Judge R. B. Bridgeman to ten years in the penitentiary. Mrs. Barrow was in the Barrow gang of bandits that spent a day and night in the cabins at the Red Crown Tavern a couple of months ago, and when surrounded by a cordon of officers seeking their capture, shot their way out and escaped into Iowa. Buck Barrow was captured there and died of a wound received in the Platte county battle. Mrs. Barrow was captured and returned to the Platte county jail. Regardless of her assertion she never fired a gun in her life, a charge of shooting with intent to kill was preferred against her and she was held to this term of court.

Prosecuting Attorney Clevenger deserves commendation for his handling of the case, and Judge Bridgeman did the wise thing in making the sentence ten years. Mrs Barrow is a small frail, girlish woman, but evidently schooled in crime. Her hard facial features belie any innocence she might otherwise display, and it is well to separate her from better society and be rid for a time at least of her demoralizing, criminal pursuits. Little time was lost in getting rid of Mrs. Barrow, for with extra guard, Sheriff Coffey took her to Jefferson City Monday evening and she is now confined in her new home.

The old court house at Platte City and the yard around it presented a formidable appearance during the time of Mrs. Barrow's journey to the court room, her plea and sentence, and the return to jail. Located at advantageous points about the yard were officers with guns of various types ready for action. At the court-house doors, officers watched for strangers, ready to refuse admission to those unknown and armed to do battle with any one that might argue for entrance. The precaution was well taken though it proved useless and everything went along quietly, without any indication of trouble anywhere. It was feared that the gang to which the little woman belonged might make some effort to release her.

Asked by the court if she wanted a lawyer and if she knew any reason why she should not be sentenced, Mrs. Barrow in firmness and with no show of emotion answered 'No' to both questions.

While the officers used precaution to prevent any attempt to release the prisoner, and did so rightly, the writer believes all fear along this line was unnecessary. Mrs. Barrow has been in jail here two months and none of her associates have communicated with her or been to see her, no help by the characters of her crime world has been extended in her behalf. Evidently she is an outcast by her own kind for some reason no longer sharing their confidence or sympathy, and they seem to be satisfied in being rid of her. Mrs Barrow said little in praise or condemnation of her companions, but we expect she really is glad to be safely confined in the pen, safe from her own crowd, safe from further life of crime with time to lead a better, less hazardous, more profitable life.

Platte county is glad to be rid of such a character, an unwelcome sojourner, and the county and state should feel glad to get her off their hands without a long trial and great expense.

The Landmark, September 8, 1933

On Tuesday Blanche was claimed by Platte City, Missouri, to face charges of assault at the Red Crown Tavern. Later that evening, led by Deputy Sheriff Tom Hulett of Platte county and watched by J. N. McClanahan, one of the police motor mechanics, Blanche was escorted from her cell in handcuffs by the police matron, Marie Brockmeier. Found guilty, she was sentenced to ten years' imprisonment with a further year and a day added following the so-called 'Harboring Trial' held in Texas in 1935. Eventually she lost the sight in her left eye and spent her time in prison writing her memoirs. She was a model prisoner and even became friends with Sheriff Holt Coffey who had led the abortive attack at the Red Crown. Released in March 1939, she returned to Texas where she later remarried. She detested the way she was portrayed in the 1968 film, claiming that 'we were all just kids then but we were still in full control of our own lives. Clyde never held a gun to my head — I was there because I wanted to be.' Blanche died in Dallas on December 24, 1988 aged 77.

Ed Stoner's 1933 Ford Fordor Sedan pictured on Court Street in Adel, with the boiler and maintenance building for the Dallas county court-house in the background. The car had been disguised with Texas plates and, according to the reports, it had suffered 72 bullet hits

The smoke still hovered over one of Iowa's most famous battlefields as Cole Spillers, 18 years old on that day in July 1933, watched the getaway of the notorious gangsters Bonnie and Clyde.

Standing alone across the South Raccoon River in front of his family's farm, Spillers was the only person who watched as one of the gangsters dropped a Browning automatic rifle. Moments later Spillers crossed the stream, found the weapon and cradled it in his arms. But he wouldn't have it long.

If Spillers, now 72, still had the rifle, it would be worth a pretty penny. In fact, the whereabouts of dozens of guns taken from the Barrow gang's car in Iowa 55 years ago are unknown today.

The gangsters left behind dozens of .45 caliber pistols and several automatic rifles, including the one Spillers plucked from the potato patch.

Spillers was on his way to stash his souvenir when a neighbor told him, 'Nobody can take that gun away from you. That gun is yours now.' Instead of hiding his prize, Spillers boldly carried the weapon up a hill to see what all the shooting was about. He was promptly confronted by several law officers who snatched the gun from him, leaving him empty-handed.

What happened to the guns — each a potential collector's item — is an interesting question for historians and law enforcement officials. Recently, Des Moines police officials tried unsuccessfully to trace the history of a sub-machine gun they believed belonged to the Barrow gang.

As for Spillers? 'I sure wish I'd kept that gun.'

Des Moines Register, October 17, 1988

After having confirmed the location of the boiler and maintenance building, which was torn down decades ago, Marty took the comparison. The building in the background is the jail of the Dallas county sheriff's office (out of the picture to the right). This view is to the north on Court Street between 8th and 9th Streets.

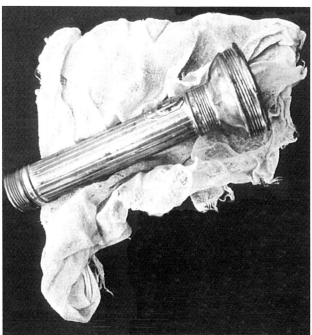

Left: **But just look what was found inside the car! There were 34 .45 Colt automatic pistols, a couple of revolvers, and either four or five 'army machine guns', i.e. Browning Automatic Rifles. The reports on the exact number of BARs recovered are confusing as one was found in bushes near the bridge where Clyde discarded it having run out of ammunition.** *Above:* **Flashlight and bloody bandages — no doubt purchased from Mr Weesner's shop!**

185

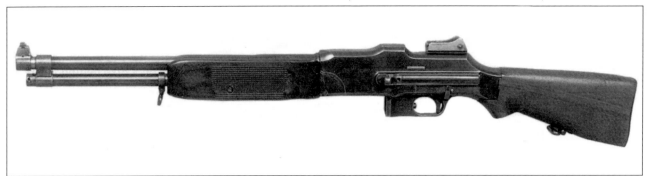

In their flight from Dexfield they had lost their entire arsenal and all Clyde had left was a .45 automatic and that was out of ammunition. *Above:* They had already lost this BAR at the Red Crown (the new front sight is a later restoration by the Missouri State Highway Patrol) and now these four at Dexfield Park *(right).* The mystery is: where did they get replacements because at the next fracas at Sowers in November, Clyde was armed to the teeth. By then, W. D. was no longer with him, having quit a month after Dexfield (see page 196). In his statement, given to police in Dallas in November, Jones tries to play down his part in the gunfights in an attempt to mitigate against his guilt, but unfortunately he gives no clue as to which National Guard armoury they robbed next. After leaving the Feller farm, he said that 'we rode some distance and wound around through side roads, and country roads for a distance of about 20 or 25 miles, and then we had a flat. In the gun-battle back in the woods, Clyde was hit several times, one through his right leg and one bullet grazed the side of his head. He had buckshot in his right shoulder. When we had this flat we took the tire off and we decided we ought to change cars, so Clyde took in after a Chevrolet and pulled up alongside and ordered the man to stop, which he did. But we were going pretty fast and Clyde couldn't stop our car very quick, running on the wheel, so the man had time to turn around and beat it before we could get back to him. We went on to where we saw a '29 Chevrolet sedan in a yard and Clyde handed me a pistol and told me to go get that car. I did and there was a man and a woman in the yard and the woman screamed but the man didn't do anything and I got in the car and backed it out and we all got in it and went on. We travelled all around in this car, through Nebraska, Minnesota and into Colorado. In Colorado, we saw a newspaper that said they were looking for us there, and we thought they were getting pretty hot on our trail, so Clyde turned back through Kansas and down into Missouri and back into Oklahoma and on across into Mississippi.'

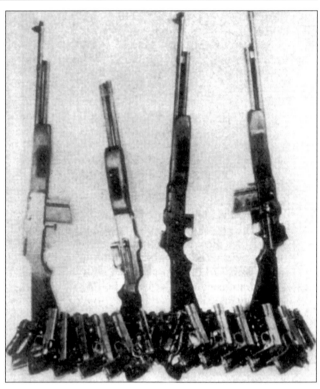

However, in Jones's later statement given at the harbouring trial, he describes them robbing an armoury in 'some small town in Illinois' and that they 'stole BARs and six .45s'. Bud Russell, the chief transfer agent for the Texas prison system, says in his memoirs that 'records show that the Plattsville (*sic*) Illinois, armory was robbed on August 20, 1933'. There is a small township spelled Plattville and it did have a National Guard armory which in 1930 was the home of Company E of the 129th Infantry Regiment. The local Veterans Hall *(above)* has now been built on the foundations of the old armoury.

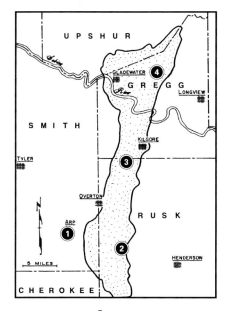

Another mystery surrounds the robbery on November 8 of the McMurrey oil refinery at Arp [1] near Overton, Texas (see map page 44). Not all historians agree that it was carried out by the Barrow gang yet Ted Hinton, one of the six lawmen who eventually put paid to Bonnie and Clyde, gives it prominence in his book *Ambush*. *Left:* The plan shows the giant East Texas oil field, the first well discovered being the Daisy Bradford [2] on October 3, 1930 followed by the Lou Della Crim [3] and the Lathrop [4]. *Above:* McMurrey still operate at the Arp Station today.

November 8, 1933 – Overton, Texas

Bonnie and Clyde reappeared in the oil fields east of Dallas in November 1933.

Though the promised 'recovery' of the sorry economic conditions was more wishful optimism of the politicians and Main Street then reality that autumn, there was money to be made in the East Texas oil fields. Since the colorful wildcatter E. M. 'Dad' Joiner had made his discovery well on Daisy Bradford's farm, a 'boom town' fever had swept a band of counties east of Dallas. Geologists who had thought Joiner crazy now were admitting there might really be an 'ocean of oil' under the cotton fields and scrub timberland around Henderson, Kilgore, and other communities. But oil production outran demand, and the price of a barrel of oil tumbled to a half-dollar or even less. Restrictions were imposed to cut production and bring prices up and curtail the shameful waste.

Even so, enterprising people like Jim McMurrey could do well enough. McMurrey set up a little refinery near the Overton community at a crossroads called Arp, not far from Kilgore, where the oil derricks already were placed so close to each other, a man could almost leap from one derrick floor to another across the town.

The first nip of fall chill had turned the leaves to a brilliant palette of color on the morning of November 8, 1933. On that morning a Ford V-8 coupe with an Oklahoma license plate appeared at McMurrey's refinery but the arrival was hardly acknowledged by the handful of truck drivers working at a loading rack outside the plant office.

Bonnie Parker, unknown to any of the drivers except as a name in the newspapers or the detective magazines, was dressed neatly as she got out of the car, looked around as any curious visitor might, and returned to the car.

In a short time, she returned with two men. The truck drivers stopped abruptly when Clyde Barrow's command rang out, 'Get your hands up!' The husky fellows complied with the order of the man wearing dark glasses; they were herded inside the refinery office.

McMurrey and his plant manager, Ray Hall, seeing the muzzles of the weapons, had no choice except to hold their hands up too. Someone apparently had tipped the bandits to the whereabouts of the 'safe' — an eight-inch pipe protruding upward from the concrete floor, a padlock securing a hinged lid on it.

'O.K.,' Clyde ordered gruffly, 'give me the key or open it up.'

McMurrey denied having a key. Barrow did not choose to argue the point at all. A pair of shots rang out. Sparks

flew as the bullet struck the lock and ricocheted — and the torn padlock fell to the floor. McMurrey and Hall and the drivers looked on, wide-eyed and scared. Clyde bent down, pulled out a wad of greenbacks from the pipe, and backed out of the refinery office. 'Make a false move and you're all dead,' he barked, and the two men retreated to the Ford coupe where Bonnie had the motor running.

As the car departed, one of the drivers took down the license number: Oklahoma 485-370. The brazen daylight robbery was immediately reported; roads were blocked routinely. And, again, there was no sign at all of the bandits. That alone would have convinced me that this was the work of Clyde and Bonnie. But I have never learned who had taken W. D. Jones's place as Clyde's sidekick on this one.

McMurrey was unaware of the bandits' identities. He wasted no time getting to his home in Dallas, and he notified Sheriff Schmid, who directed him to me. The refinery was far out in the state, more than a hundred miles from Dallas, and certainly outside our Dallas county jurisdiction. But McMurrey invited me to his house.

I listened to his story — he had lost between two and three thousand dollars to the bandits.

I heard his descriptions of the two men and the tiny 'good-looking' woman, and I showed him photographs. 'That's the woman,' he said, though he had no idea who she was.

'You'd be willling to prosecute — to go into court and swear she was one of them?' I asked. He assured me he would do his duty. Then I turned over the picture of Clyde. 'That's him! He's the one who did all the talking and shot the lock off.'

I showed him the name on the back of the picture. Though he had, apparently, never seen a photograph of Clyde Barrow before, the name sent a chill through him.

'No, Mr. Hinton,' he said, 'If it's all the same to you — forget I said that. He'd just come back and kill me. No — I'll just take my lumps and go about my business.'

The take at McMurrey's refinery was one of Clyde's largest scores up to this time. I was learning something of Clyde's habits: he never seemed to get more money than the amount of his immediate need. I'm certain that made sense to him; the longer he was a fugitive, the more likely was the chance that the bigger-money outfits had taken precautions against him. And, as one of his relatives told me, he had very little opportunity to spend money anyway.

TED HINTON, *AMBUSH*, 1979

In 1933 Bonnie's mother moved to 1214 South Lamar. Unfortunately all the houses in the 1200 block have been razed, the dereliction a stark contrast to downtown Dallas in the background. As Emma Parker explains in this extract from her book *Fugitives* published in 1934, they would often meet Bonnie and Clyde in the alleyway behind her house. She also describes how the Parker family suffered a double tragedy in October 1933 when Bonnie's sister lost her two young children from an undiagnosed stomach disorder within a week of each other. Billie Mace, their mother,

reportedly went to pieces and Bonnie was equally distressed. *Fugitives* was ghost-written by Jan Fortune very quickly in the three months following the deaths of the duo for publication in September 1934 and one has to accept that many of the incidents described are distorted or embroidered, out of sequence, or details are confused and some are even incorrect. Nevertheless, the book stands as a unique source for the dramatic events which shaped the lives of the Parker and Barrow families, and the extract reproduced here is a good example.

Texas Interlude

It was many weeks before we had any word from Bonnie and Clyde, long after we had come home and buried Buck. There were stories printed to the effect that Clyde would return for his brother's funeral; that he did return, disguised as an old woman, and wept beside the grave. In fact, by this time nothing was too wild, too fantastic and too unreal to be chalked up against Clyde Barrow. They made him a superman, gifted with super-human powers, beyond the reach of ordinary human beings. They made him a modern Frankenstein and fled in terror before the thing they had created.

Clyde and Bonnie showed up September 7, 1933. We had not seen them for four months, and what horrible and heart-breaking things had happened in those four months! Bonnie was still unable to walk without help. She was miserably thin and much older. Her leg was drawn up under her. Her body was covered with scars. Clyde also showed signs of what he had undergone. But they tried to make light of their condition. Clyde put a quilt on the ground and lifted Bonnie out of the car. I sat down beside her and held her thin hands and tried to keep the tears back. They talked of many things, but it was impossible to learn everything in one evening. It took many evenings.

They'd like some pillows, they said. They were living entirely in the car now, and they needed more pillows and some blankets, since the air was getting chilly. I suggested bringing Clyde's crutches out for Bonnie to use. We stayed late, and Clyde promised to meet us the next evening on the Eagle Ford Road. After we came home I took the pillows and blankets and crutches back to them.

They had not slept in a bed since July, or been inside a house. They had lived entirely in the car. At night they'd draw up in some side road and sleep, often being awakened by Highway Patrols and bawled out. On these occasions, Clyde would explain that they were touring and were so sleepy that they stopped for a nap. They were always believed, and sent on with a warning not to do it again, for fear somebody would run into them or hold them up.

On one occasion, Bonnie said only the fact that Clyde had become ill in the night had saved them from capture. He awakened her and after he felt better and dozed off to sleep, she heard a car coming. Something warned her that it was danger, so she stepped on the starter and swung off down the road driving. Looking in her rear vision mirror, she saw that the car was filled with policemen. She put on all speed, as they were definitely chasing her car. She called out to Clyde. Bonnie never learned to handle a car with the speed and daring that was Clyde's. Few people could.

'Its the law,' she cried. 'And they're gaining on us.'

Clyde climbed over the seat, slipped under the wheel while going fifty. He raised the speedometer to seventy, and shut off his lights. Trusting to luck, he roared along in the dark and turned up a gully. The officers, half a mile behind by now, passed by and lost him.

Bonnie said their best stunt was to drive into a town and run their car up on somebody's drive for the night. This was their safest bet, for here they could sleep in security all night long.

The following month saw the 59th birthday of Clyde's mother and the occasion was celebrated with an alfresco party near the Shannon Ranch at Paradise, some 50 miles north-west of Dallas. The meeting with Clyde and Bonnie took place on Tuesday, November 21 and, as at most birthday parties, the camera came out for a variety of family snapshots. All were set against the backdrop of a 1933 Ford V-8 coupe — the five-window model with bodywork by Murray. The Shannon Ranch is better known as a notorious criminal hideout. Robert 'Boss' Shannon was married to Ora, the mother of George 'Machine Gun' Kelly's wife, Kathryn (who bought him the gun which gave him his nickname). The ranch was used by Kelly and Albert Bates to hide the Oklahoma oilman, Charles Urschel who was kidnapped for a ransom of $200,000 in July 1933. 'Boss' Shannon served time in Alcatraz and died in 1956. When Karin Ramsay motored over to Paradise for us from Denton, she stopped to ask for directions and was told: 'The Texaco gas station *IS* Paradise!' Ora's father (Kathryn's grandfather) was Grant Bates, a descendant of the Bates family who arrived in early Texas in a wagon train with the Parker family, and this most probably accounts for Bonnie and Clyde's connection with the Shannon Ranch.

'But he was so scared he couldn't eat.' Bonnie finished the story. 'He just sat there with the sandwich in his hand, swallowing like he had a rock in his throat.'

I had moved into West Dallas now, and during the entire months of September and October, and up until Smoot Schmid tried to trap them on November 22, the kids came in to see us every single night except five. They'd either drive by the house or the filling station. Often they'd stop. Twice Clyde went in. If we didn't talk with them there they'd tell us where to meet them, and we'd drive out and be with them several hours. One evening Billie [Bonnie's sister] and I were sitting on the front porch chatting with a neighbor when Clyde and Bonnie came by. I didn't make any sign, but Billie got up and went into the house and out the back. My neighbor arose and said she'd better be getting on home. We walked down the alley and talked with Clyde and Bonnie for about thirty minutes. After they were killed my neighbor told me that she recognised them, but didn't want us to know she did, for fear something might happen and we would think she had turned them in.

It seems to me that it would have been such a simple matter to catch Clyde and Bonnie. All the law needed to do was to watch our houses, for they came in all the time, and we went out to see them. Of course, I didn't want them caught and I'm glad the officers were not smart enough to do it. For instance, there was Nell [Clyde's sister] running a beauty parlor in the Sanger Hotel, headquarters for the Texas Rangers. Nearly every night for three months Nell drove to meet Clyde; almost every time he and Bonnie visited Dallas for two years, she was with them. Yet the rangers didn't even know that she was Clyde Barrow's sister till after his death, and I believe that she told them then. Clyde called Nell over long distance through the hotel switchboard time after time, til she got frightened and made him use the shop number. If they had taken the trouble to find out that she was his sister, what would have been easier than tapping the telephone wire or checking up on Nell's long distance calls? But, who am I to tell the police how they could have captured my daughter and Clyde? They got them in the end.

EMMA PARKER, *FUGITIVES*, 1934

Above: **Bonnie is pictured with her mother and** *(below)* **Clyde with Cumie Barrow whose birthday they were celebrating.**

Cruising cops would deduce that the car belonged there and leave them alone. They used this means many times and were never caught but once. One night they had just stretched out nicely when they heard a wrathful feminine voice in the window above their heads: 'John Jones, those lousy, whiskey-drinking, poker-playing friends of yours are parked out there in the drive again, but if you think you're going to sneak out of this house tonight . . .' They never heard the rest of the dressing-down Mrs Jones gave John, because they didn't wait.

One incident which amused Clyde greatly was the story of a Texas Ranger, who with his wife, decided one night to run across the Red River bridge at Denison for a couple of bottles of beer. It was late and the ranger suggested that his wife go in her negligee. The man at the other end of the bridge sighted the ranger's guns lying in the back of the car and saw the woman in negligee. Before the ranger and his wife could get back across, the story was all over Denison that Bonnie and Clyde had just crossed Red River into Oklahoma.

Another night Clyde and Bonnie were at a sandwich shop getting their supper, when a car drove up containing four boys, who had obviously been imbibing a little too freely. One of the crew, a blustery sort of fellow, finally said: 'If you all don't stop ragging me, I'll sic Bonnie and Clyde on you.'

Hearing their names called like this, both Clyde and Bonnie leaned out, startled, and looked at the occupants of the other car. The speaker, seeing them, motioned largely with his hand and yelled: 'That looks like Clyde and Bonnie there.' Of course he was only joking, but Clyde thought he'd joke a little, too. He called: 'Come here, guy. I want to talk to you.' The man climbed from the car and swaggered over. 'What can I do for you?' he asked.

Clyde leaned close to him and spoke softly: 'You can close your face,' he said. 'And keep it closed. I AM Clyde Barrow and this IS Bonnie Parker, and if you mention our names again, we'll drill you full of holes.' The effect was startling. The man's mouth hung open, his eyes popped out, and he couldn't speak except to gurgle: 'No, sir—no, sir.' 'You go back and get in the car and finish eating your order,' Clyde told him. 'Don't make a move and don't tell anything to anybody. If you do — !'

Left: Clyde with his younger sister Marie. Right: Marie's boyfriend, Joe Bill Francis, stands on the right with Clyde, centre, and his brother, L. C. Note that the edge of the licence plate is just visible showing the figure '9'.

See how Clyde has now hidden the number plate with a hat . . . a nice pair of prints with their original Elko borders.

Finally, Clyde brings out his guns — at least a pair of Browning Automatic Rifles and a sawn-off shotgun. As they lost all their weapons following the hasty escape from Dexfield (see page 164), they must have raided another National Guard armoury. Was this at Plattville, Illinois, (see page 186)? If it was, they came away with three BARs, a number of .45 Colt autos and plenty of ammunition, although there is no press report to back this up. The birthday celebration must have been very low-key, being overshadowed by the recent deaths of Billie's children (she is notably absent in all the photos). Meanwhile, Sheriff Smoot Schmid was planning a surprise party of his own for Bonnie and Clyde! Although there has been much speculation over the years, it has never been reliably established as to who tipped him off that the two outlaws were to meet the family again the following night.

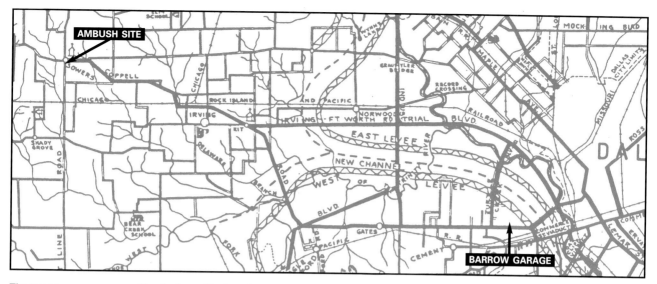

The rendezvous was near Charlie Stovall's dairy farm which lay on the Sowers road in open countryside west of Dallas. They had used the spot to meet once before so possibly this compromised Clyde's security. But it certainly was no coincidence that Sheriff Schmid and three other lawmen chose this spot to set up an ambush. This is the map of 1930.

November 22, 1933 — Sowers, Texas

On October 11, little Jackie [Billie's two-year-old daughter] *took sick very suddenly. Two days later she died. I didn't go to meet Bonnie that night, but I was with them again on the following evening. Bonnie was heartbroken over the news. Sunday evening when I went to meet them I reported that Buddy [Jackie's brother aged four] was ill with the same strange malady — a stomach disorder. Monday night I reported that he was at Bradford Memorial Hospital, some better. I missed Tuesday night. When I met them Wednesday, Bonnie, her face white and tear-swept, said: 'Don't tell me, mama. I know. Buddy's dead. I dreamed it last night. It was so real I knew it was true, and when Clyde started to buy toys to send him today, I wouldn't let him for I knew he wasn't alive any more.'*

Billie went all to pieces over this double tragedy. Our home was a bleak place indeed with the babies gone. Added to everything else, it seemed to us both that life wasn't worth the living any more.

November 21 was the birthday of Clyde's mother. We took a birthday dinner and spent the day with Clyde and Bonnie up in Wise county, close to the Shannon farm. We were to meet them the next night at the place where Sheriff Smoot Schmid was to trap them. It was the first, last, and only time that we made the same meeting place twice. Just who knew and turned us in that night is still a mystery, but I'll never believe that the police found out for themselves.

We drove to the spot just about dark. We could still see everywhere, but of course we couldn't see officers with machine guns hidden in a ditch. We were parked on the side road about seventy-five feet from the main highway. The officers were thirty feet away, concealed in the gully. In order to understand what I'm going to tell, the reader must try to get a mental vision of the lay of the land. We were parked facing away from the pike on the right side of the road. Before us this country road curved downward toward a little bridge, so that a car going down the road away from the highway would be out of range within a few seconds. It was still light enough for us to recognize Clyde and Bonnie when they drove along the pike. They started to turn in, but Clyde's sixth sense warned him.

'How do you feel about it, honey?' he asked. 'It seems phony to me tonight.'

They drove on down the pike a little way, but when we did not follow them, Clyde turned and came back, hesitated, and then cut into the lane. He had recognised us all right. He drove past us and started to turn afterwards, but we didn't know this. We thought he wanted us to follow him, so we turned on our lights making his car a direct target.

Something began popping. I said rather inanely: 'Listen to the fire-crackers.' Then we saw the flame shooting out of the guns along the ditch. There was no word of 'Halt' — no warning given — nothing. They just began firing as Clyde was preparing to turn. Clyde stepped on the gas and shot away down the hill toward the bridge. We saw Bonnie break the back glass out of the coupe with her gun, although the officers said they shot it out. But she said when she did this, she cried out to Clyde: 'I don't dare shoot. I'll kill my own mother if I do.'

'If they haven't already done it,' Clyde growled for both of us women were screaming by now and they could hear us. 'This whole road is probably lined with cops. Shoot at the ditches.'

They bumped down the road, firing on each side as they went. At the bridge Clyde said: 'You'd better pray, Bonnie. This is probably our last ride together.' They both thought there would be more officers waiting for them there. The left tire had been shot away, and two bullets had passed through the car, one puncturing the spare, and the other entering Clyde's knee and going on through Bonnie's. They said they felt the impact but had no pain, and didn't know that they were wounded till later.

Bumping along on three tires, they covered the four miles to the next highway. The officers were unable to follow them, because they had parked their cars a mile away, but Clyde couldn't know that. Meanwhile, we had been forced to sit helplessly by and witness the whole thing. There was just one good thing about our having been there. We had seen it all, and we knew that Clyde's car disappeared over that hill after the first blast from the guns.

We went down to the court-house later to look the car over after the officers had brought it in. The stories printed stated that a terrific gun battle had ensued between Clyde and Bonnie and Schmid and his men. The officers had ripped the car to bits with their guns, Clyde and Bonnie had fled, horribly wounded. Relatives were already making negotiations for funeral arrangements with local undertakers, since no person could have lived through the barrage put down on that car by officers that night.

EMMA PARKER, *FUGITIVES*, 1934

Evading, as has become a habit of his recently, a trap laid for him by Sheriff Smoot Schmid, Clyde Barrow, Dallas bandit wanted here and in many other cities for crimes ranging from murder down, fled in a machine gun bullet-riddled car Wednesday night, held up and robbed two men of their automobile as they were returning on the Jefferson road from Dallas to Fort Worth, shot at them both through their automobile window, cutting them with flying glass, then again fled toward Dallas.

With the bandit was Bonnie Parker, also of Dallas, credited by some with being Barrow's wife. When Barrow held up the Fort Worth men, Bonnie jumped from their auto by his side, flourished a pistol and assisted in the robbery.

The men who Barrow and Bonnie held up were Thomas R. James of 2515 Willing and Paul Reich, 920 Burnett, Fort Worth. They had been to Dallas for the Scottish Rite reunion. Reich is secretary of the Julian Field Masonic Lodge.

Mrs. Charles Stovall of Sowers community, where the trap for the bandit was laid and failed, was injured when a stray bullet from the guns of one of the battling parties smashed a window in her house. She was cut on the neck by a piece of glass.

Sheriff Schmid, acting on a tip received from a prisoner in the county jail, took three of his deputies — Ted Hinton, Bob Alcorn and Ed Castor — with him Wednesday evening and, armed with a machine gun, two sub-machine guns and a repeating rifle, hid by the side of the road. According to the tip they had received Barrow was coming to Dallas to visit his father and mother, who have a filling station on the West Dallas road. He has been said to have paid many visits to Dallas during the last few months but never has been caught.

The number on the car — although indistinct in this newspaper reproduction — was 565-419, confirming the link with the coupe photographed at the birthday party the previous day.

As the car approached, Schmid and his deputies recognized Barrow and Bonnie Parker and started to fire at the automobile which was moving about twenty-five miles an hour. Barrow returned the fire, Schmid said, and speeded up with a rain of bullets following him.

As quickly as the Sheriff and his men could reach a telephone they communicated with Dallas and had the alarm broadcast.

No wonder Smoot Schmid on the left looks glum, having lost his quarry yet again. With him are Ed Castor, Ted Hinton and Bob Alcorn as they pose for the press with a variety of items recovered form the Ford coupe.

The fleeing Barrows followed the Sowers road to the Jefferson road, turning to the right toward Fort Worth. Near Hersley Field the bandit overtook the car in which were James and Reich. They crowded the latter to the side of the road, fired several bullets through the car windows and ordered them to get out of the car. It was here that Bonnie aided Barrow and threatened the victims with a gun. They abandoned their own car, took that of James and again fled toward Dallas.

Ward Collier, secretary of Mosleh Shrine Temple of Fort Worth, also on his way home from Dallas, picked up James and Reich and took them to Fort Worth.

In the Barrow's car, now in the possession of the sheriff's office, are thirteen bullet holes on the driver's side and several holes in the glass, made as the slugs from machine guns passed out of the car.

Quantities of blood on the floor of the seized car, on its cushions and elsewhere indicated that the sheriff and his deputies in their brush with the fugitives near Sowers may have wounded them seriously. Bullet holes in the car doors and top were at a height that made it probable the occupants of the car were seriously wounded.

A bottle of water and a jar of white whisky were in the car, in addition a large quantity of stolen merchandise.

Among the stolen goods were two parcel post packages from Montgomery Ward, Fort Worth, to A. W. Harris, on the United States mail star route to Ivan, near Breckenridge, Stephens county.

In the back of the car were sets of automobile license plates for 1933 from Kansas, Oklahoma and Texas. There were three Texas sets.

A dirty tobacco sack containing about 100 pennies also was found in the car, and a medical kit and many articles of clothing and bedding.

Press report, November 23, 1933

Federal officers here, were chagrined Thursday morning over the manner in which Sheriff Smoot Schmid and three of his deputies allowed Clyde Barrow, notorious bandit, and his sweetheart, Bonnie Parker, to escape from an ambuscade the sheriff had laid near Sowers Wednesday night.

They went to him and offered to assist in the capture for the reason that they felt that the manner in which Barrow has been allowed to remain at liberty was a disgrace to enforcement officers in all branches of the various law enforcing agencies.

Press report, November 23, 1933

Mr James narrowly missed death when Clyde's shotgun blast ripped his hat.

An isolated country road . . . now totally transformed out of all recognition. This is the spot where the ambush was mounted — now the junction of Esters Road with Highway 183, the Airport Freeway.

Both Clyde and Bonnie had received a gunshot wound to their legs, undoubtedly caused by Bob Alcorn's gun as he was the only one who had chosen to arm himself with Clyde's favourite weapon — the BAR. Ed Castor had a .351 rifle and Schmid and Hinton .45 Thompson submachine guns but the sheriff's jammed without firing a shot. 'Alcorn, Castor, and I had fired thirty rounds from a range of about seventy-five feet and closer', wrote Hinton later, 'and the marks of at least seventeen were visible on the car, though the Ford V-8 body turned most of the fire from the Thompson I had used, except, of course, those I had fired through the windows and at the tire. Definitely, I would not go hunting Clyde and Bonnie with a tommy gun again. The BAR that Alcorn carried was the only weapon that had any telling effect — and these bullets would go through the car and pass out on the opposite side.' Bearing in mind that the lawmen had Bonnie and Clyde in their sights as sitting ducks, the ambush was a total fiasco, although Schmid claimed that 'It wasn't a total failure. At least we didn't get any of my men killed like they did up in Missouri!' The only thing that saved the sheriff was that he had a trump card up his sleeve — W. D. had been captured in Houston and had spilt the beans on the gang. Giving the newspapers something to divert their attention from his own embarrassment, he promptly released Jones's statement to the press in time for the Sunday papers.

How Clyde Barrow, West Dallas outlaw, and his gun-girl companion, Bonnie Parker, have roved the country in stolen automobiles, robbing, looting and killing with reckless abandon, was detailed here Saturday night in a confession signed by 17-year-old W. D. Jones, who has been held incommunicado in the county jail for the last ten days.

As a result of his confession, Jones was formally charged with the murder of Deputy Sheriff Malcolm Davis of Tarrant county who was killed during a gun-battle in West Dallas last January 7. Barrow and the Parker girl, whom he accuses of doing the actual killing as he sat at the wheel of their getaway-car, are still at liberty having eluded a squad of county officers who tried to ambush them on a lonely country road last Wednesday night.

Jones' account of the Barrow gang's criminal peregrinations, more fantastic than fiction and more amazing then the history of any desperado of the early West was set down in a twenty-seven-page typewritten statement obtained a week ago by a member of the district attorney's staff. At that time

the sheriff knew nothing of the confession he said.

Jones enumerated the gun-battles from which Barrow and his companion have emerged during the last year, and the countless robberies, hijackings, car thefts and petty thefts which they staged during their wanderings about the Middle West. He tells of at least five killings which he witnessed relating how Clyde and Bonnie shot down citizens and officers in cold blood, among them Deputy Davis.

During the gunfight in which Davis was slain, he said, Barrow retreated to the getaway car under cover of Bonnie Parker's pistol fire while he, Jones, sat at the wheel.

Jones detailed how he accompanied Clyde and Bonnie to Oklahoma after the Davis murder. They met Buck Barrow and his wife Blanche after Buck's release from prison early in March. They met at a town in Oklahoma, the name of which Jones could not recall.

Then, in his statement, Jones related how they forced him to accompany them to Joplin. He detailed the gun-battle with

officers at Joplin where they killed two officers, another gun-battle at Fort Smith Arkansas, where another officer was shot to death: next at Platte City where Buck received a serious scalp wound and finally the pitched gun-battle at Dexter, Iowa, on July 24 last when Buck and Blanche were captured, Buck receiving gunshot wounds which proved fatal.

Jones made it a point to explain in his statement that he was an unwilling companion with the gang explaining that Clyde threatened to kill him if he tried to get away. Jones said Clyde was afraid he 'knew too much' and would 'squeal' if he got away.

The prisoner exhibited seven bullet wounds on his body, all of which he said were suffered in gun-battles between the Barrows and officers they encountered at the various places enumerated in his statement.

The young desperado, whom the sheriff's office has held incommunicado since his arrest November 16, sat with a smile on his face as a member of the sheriff's office read his lengthy statement for the benefit of reporters.

In Dallas, W. D. Jones was paraded for the press and filmed for the newsreels before appearing in the local court-house. He had quit the gang at the beginning of September. 'I left Clyde and Bonnie near Clarksville, Mississippi, after they was healed up enough to get by without me. I'd had enough of blood and hell. But I had to pay. A boy in Houston turned me in.' No doubt he invented the story about being coerced to join the gang to try to mitigate his sentence. (See also Clyde's letter page 230.)

W. D. had been arrested by Ed Castor and Bob Alcorn at 519 Franklin Street, Houston, on November 16. He was charged with the killing of Deputy Sheriff Davis in West Dallas (see page 89) and received a sentence of 15 years with a further two years being added at a later trial in 1935 for harbouring Bonnie and Clyde. He was released in 1943 but received another six-month sentence in September 1973 for the illegal possesion of drugs. On August 20, 1974 he was involved in an altercation when he was shot dead by his assailant (see page 287).

Jones' story began with last Christmas Eve. On that occasion he said Clyde and Bonnie contacted him at a downtown dance and, with pistols, convinced him he ought to accompany them on a trip to east Texas. Jones said he protested but there was no way out.

The last time he saw Clyde was in August, when he left him in Mississippi. Jones said he remained in hiding until the newspapers stopped writing so much about the Barrow gun-battles. He said he rode a freight train back to Dallas arriving here October 15. The story ends with his arrest at Houston on November 16 by Alcorn and Castor. They had been trailing him since his return to Dallas a month before, the officers said.

What negotiations the sheriff and others had with him in jail is not known. It is known that on the night of November 18, Assistant District Attorney Winter King took the written confession from him in the county jail, which on that occasion was barred to newspaper men.

The same night the confession was made the sheriff emphatically denied that he had any prisoner in jail in connection with the Barrow investigation. He also said he had no knowledge of King being in the jail taking a statement. The same night King admitted he had been requested to take the statement by the sheriff.

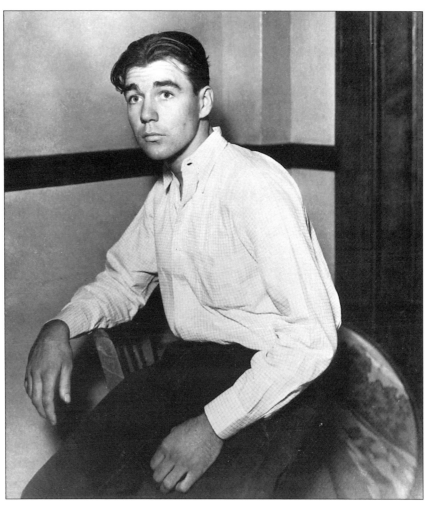

The Daily Times Herald, November 26, 1933   **Note the picture has been reproduced the wrong way round in the newspaper.**

As far as Clyde was concerned, the fact that Schmid had put members of his family in the firing line was inexcusable. 'It wouldn't have mattered if he'd jumped us alone,' Clyde is reported to have said later. 'That's legitimate. We expect that. It's coming to us sooner or later. But to stage a gun-battle with Bonnie's mother and my mother sitting there directly in range of the bullets — to start shooting when I wasn't ten feet away from their car — I'll get him for that. Why, he could have killed them both, and I'm out to get him.' On November 28, Clyde returned to Dallas to stake out Schmid's house — 5119½ Reiger Avenue — but the sheriff was either asleep in bed or not at home. Clyde was now blind with rage against lawmen in general and he also went looking for Bob Alcorn. Nell Barrow claims that she tried to talk Clyde out of deliberately targeting the law but his hatred for Schmid never abated — to Clyde he had violated his code of conduct by risking the lives of their mothers who were parked

nearby. They certainly had been in real danger for one of the rounds from Alcorn's BAR had slightly wounded Mrs Stovall in the farmhouse several hundred yards away. Clyde even thought of springing W. D. from his cell and he sat with Bonnie outside the county jail for a couple of hours to check the possibilities. To Nell, the idea was crazy. 'You'd never get inside the place', she told Clyde. 'Oh I don't know', he replied. 'Harvey Bailey got out with a toy pistol so I could get in with a machine gun.' (By a strange coincidence, Bailey was captured at the Shannon Ranch, the location of Cumie's birthday party, and sentenced to life imprisonment in Alcatraz.) *Left:* Exactly 30 years later, almost to the day, Dallas county court-house on the left bore witness to the assassination of an American president. On November 22, 1963, Kennedy's motorcade passed directly in front of the building just seconds before Oswald opened fire. *Right:* On the right is the 'Old Red Courthouse', currently undergoing restoration.

Clyde Barrow, 24, short, lean, thin-faced, his black hair slicked back, is the son of Henry B. and Mrs Cumie F. Barrow who operate the Star filling station on the Eagle Ford Road. He was born and reared in the West Dallas community, fought, fibbed and stole, and at the age of 15 had his first brush with the law.

He was arrested for automobile thievery, the beginning of every petty crook. That was on December 3, 1926. Again in 1928, he was picked up in Fort Worth, and during the month of November 1929 was arrested for

As we end Bonnie and Clyde's penultimate year of crime, perhaps we should pause to take stock of their current record. This is exactly what the press did way back at the end of 1933. It had been an incredible year for America. Deep in the Depression, a new President, Franklin D. Roosevelt, had been inaugurated in January. 'I pledge you, I pledge myself, to a new deal for the American people' was his promise and his 'New Deal', as it became known, was launched by Congress after a marathon session lasting 100 days. With lightning speed, 13 new measures were set in motion including the Emergency Banking Act, Federal Emergency Relief Act, National Industrial Recovery Act, Emergency Farm Mortgage Act and, to cheer the country up, Prohibition was ended just before Christmas. For 14 years the illicit supply of booze had led to a huge increase in organised crime which came to a head in Kansas City on June 17, 1933 when gangsters wielding machine guns killed four officers guarding an escaped convict, Frank Nash, who was also killed.

Kansas City is a bit of a misnomer as the city lies in both Kansas and Missouri and is bisected by the Missouri river. Frank 'Jelly' Nash had escaped from Leavenworth in 1930 and had been cornered by the FBI in Hot Springs, Arkansas. He was being escorted into a car outside Union Station when three gunmen opened fire. There is speculation that it was in fact a hit on Nash made to look like an escape attempt. The gunmen were never apprehended. In October 1991, the Society of Former Special Agents of the FBI placed a memorial plaque beside the entrance to their fallen officers: Raymond J. Caffrey, Otto Reed, William J. Grooms and Frank Hermanson.

The Depression had spawned its own crime wave of petty theft of motor cars, filling stations, stores and banks, and it was too easy to blame any robbery in the Midwest on Bonnie and Clyde. In this book we have only included those crimes which are believed to have been carried out by the Barrow gang — or those admitted by them — so perhaps we should be fair and illustrate some robberies that they did NOT do! A good example is the supposed robbery of the First National Bank [1] (left) on Massachusetts Street in Lawrence, Kansas. Ralph Fults, who joined

Bonnie and Clyde for a month early in 1932, claims that Clyde, Ray Hamilton and himself robbed the bank of $33,000 — a huge sum by the standards of the day. He said that the three of them stayed in the Hotel Eldridge [2] (right) on the previous night and that they apprehended the manager early next morning, forced him at gun-point to open the vault, and then made off with two large sacks of cash. Yet there is absolutely no record of any such robbery taking place in Lawrence in 1932. (*After the Battle* reader L. Martin Jones took the photos for us in March 2003.)

two safe burglaries in Dallas. One was at a Simms station. Singularly enough, he has failed since then to commit any known crimes in this city proper, except the hold-up of the Neuhoff packing plant in 1932.

Clyde's first serious acquaintance with jail came in 1930. On March 2, he was tried on seven cases of burglary and given two years in each case in Waco. The judge moved by the defendant's youth agreed to let the sentences run concurrently. But jail, even in McLennan county was not to the liking of Clyde. With several companions he broke out. Two weeks later, police of Middletown, Ohio, attempted to question him. Here, Clyde showed the first tendency of toughness, tried shooting it out with the cops. He was captured, returned to Waco, where the judge retracted his previous kindness and ordered Clyde to serve the full 14 years.

On May 21, 1930, Clyde was admitted to the state penitentiary. He was assigned to the wood-chopping squad.

Clyde's dislike for hard labor was graphically shown here. Deliberately, he chopped off the big toe of his right foot. He went to the hospital.

Mrs. Barrow is a frail, gray-haired old woman, who really inspires pity. Sobbing, she went before Governor Ross Sterling, obtained a parole for Clyde on February 2, 1932.

Clyde had no more than reached home before Dallas police arrested him for a hijacking. The next month, on April 30, J. N. Bucher, operator of a store in Hillsboro, was shot down by two youths who robbed him. Barrow and Raymond Hamilton were identified. Four months later, leaving a blazing trail of stolen cars from Corsicana, they held up and robbed the Neuhoff plant of $400. Police officers passing by gave chase but were left behind.

Clyde and Raymond proceeded from Dallas to Atoka, Oklahoma. There on the night of August 5, they went to a dance. A sheriff and his deputy approached the car. The two men opened fire without warning, killing the sheriff and wounding the deputy. Again their trail of abandoned cars led thru Dallas, where they picked up Bonnie Parker, Clyde's red-haired sweetheart. The three went ot Carlsbad, New Mexico, and when a deputy attempted to question them, they kidnapped him and drove him to San Antonio.

At Wharton and Victoria, they engaged in gun skirmishes with deputies, wounding an officer at Wharton.

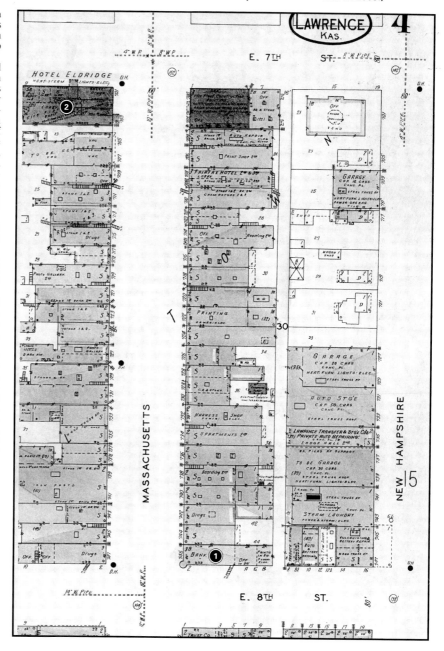

There are other robberies incorrectly attributed to Bonnie and Clyde — like that on the Texas National Bank in Coleman — and the Warner Bros. movie of 1968 only added more confusion as the production notes for *Bonnie and Clyde* claimed that 'three of the banks they raided, closed during the Depression, were re-opened for the purpose of filming'. *Above left:* All are in Texas and the first bank depicted is at Ponder, just west of Denton. It still looks very much the same today *(right)*. According to local folk-lore, Bonnie and Clyde tried to rob this bank but it had gone bankrupt three days previously — the same scenario that is played out in the film. So, have fact and fiction become blurred? The locations of the three 'movie' banks were investigated for us by Karin Ramsay of Denton. She was told that after being frustrated at the Ponder bank, Bonnie and Clyde drove a few miles up the road with the intention of robbing Krum Bank. But they found it full of customers so drove further north to rob the one at Sanger.

At this time, Clyde and Raymond split, presumably over the girl. Raymond with a companion, twice robbed the Cedar Hill bank. He was captured in Michigan returned here for trial of the bank and Neuhoff robberies and to Hillsboro for the Bucher murder. He was convicted on all of them, sentenced to serve, all told, more than 266 years.

Clyde next made a smashing appearance at Joplin, Missouri. He had been joined by his elder brother, Ivan Marvin ('Buck') Barrow, who had just been pardoned by 'Ma' Ferguson. With Buck was his wife, the former Blanche Caldwell of Dallas. Shooting their way out of a Joplin stronghold, they killed two officers. A $1,000 reward, as well as the several hundreds offered in Texas, was now on their heads.

Fleeing from Joplin, they kidnapped B. D. Darby and Miss Sophia Stone at Ruston, Louisiana, and drove them 125 miles to Waldo, Arkansas.

That was on April 27. Two months later they suffered a mishap at Wellington, Texas. Their car turned over and Bonnie was injured. They drove to a farmhouse and demanded treatment. The farmer slipped out, called the sheriff and the town marshal. The Barrows were waiting. Menacing the officers with machine guns, they loaded the sheriff and marshal in their car and drove them for hours.

'Did you know who I was?' Clyde asked the sheriff.

'No,' said the sheriff.

'It's a good thing. Seven like you did and they're pushing up daisies.' Police accuse Barrow of seven murders.

Two weeks later, Marshal Henry Humphrey, of Van Buren, Arkansas,

For the second bank we see being held up, the film company mocked up a hardware store in Red Oak, south of Dallas, to become the 'Mineola Bank'. However, Bonnie and Clyde never robbed anything in the town, and the building on the corner of Waller Street has now become a thrift store called Pennies from Heaven.

Left: The last bank robbed in the movie was once a real bank — the Farmers and Merchants Bank *(right)* in Pilot Point to the north-east of Denton.

So something just had to be done to strengthen the hand of the law as police chiefs and sheriffs were handicapped by the ability of criminals to evade their jurisdiction by simply crossing state lines. As most criminals fled on four wheels, Congress passed a new law making it a Federal crime to cross a state line in a stolen motor vehicle. The Federal Bureau of Investigation was given new powers, personnel were increased and facilities improved. And, backed by the US Attorney General, Homer S. Cummings, the FBI produced lists of criminals which they labelled as 'Public Enemies'. At the same time, a search began

to find a new maximum security prison where incorrigible offenders could be held safely. No sooner had Cummings begun to look than he heard that the War Department was about to abandon its fortress on Alcatraz Island in San Francisco Bay. It fitted perfectly with the Attorney General's plan and the island was quickly transferred to the Department of Justice. James Johnston was appointed its first Warden in October and he assumed office on January 2, 1934. The conversion was comleted by August and the first prisoners arrived in a railway carriage on the 22nd. *Above:* The exercise yard — then and now.

attempted to stop a suspicious car. He was killed by a shotgun blast. Buck Barrow admitted on his death bed to this murder. Clyde is also accused of the murder of Deputy Malcolm Davis, of Tarrant county in West Dallas, January 6, 1933, and the killing of Howard Hall, grocery clerk, in Sherman, October 11, 1932.

On July 19, a posse of 13 officers surrounded the Barrows in a tourist camp at Platte City, Missouri. The Barrows came out shooting, eluding the officers. Buck, however, was shot. Four days later another posse came upon the Barrows in a field near Dexter, Iowa. After a fierce gun-battle the officers captured Buck and his wife, but Bonnie and Clyde escaped. Buck died several days later in a Perry hospital. Blanche was given 10 years on an assault to murder charge.

During the last six weeks, Clyde and Bonnie were identified in several hold-ups near Dallas. Both police and county officers were working on information that led to the encounter Wednesday night.

Bonnie Parker, 23, is the daughter of Mrs. Emma Parker, who lives in Trinity Heights. She is the former wife of Roy Harding convicted in the death of Deputy Sheriff Fuller two years ago. Her sister is Mrs. Billie Mace, wife of Fred Mace, local criminal now in Huntsville.

Press report, November 23, 1933.

[1] Prison block. [2] Exercise yard. [3] Warden's residence. [4] Landing wharf. [5] Barracks for guards and dependants. [6] Power-plant. [7] Officers' apartments. The average number of prisoners at any one time was 260 and between 1936 and 1962 there were 14 escape attempts involving 36 prisoners. Of these, 23 were recaptured, 7 were shot and killed, one drowned, and five were never seen again. During these escape attempts, three guards were killed. Floyd Hamilton (see page 12) was sent to Alcatraz in 1940. He made an abortive escape attempt in April 1943.

By 1960 the increasing cost of maintaning Alcatraz, where all supplies, including water, had to be shipped in, had risen to a level where it cost 2½ times more to keep a prisoner on the island then in a mainland top security prison. Some of the watchtowers had already been taken out of commission to make savings which contributed to the successful escape by

three prisoners in June 1962. This was the death nell for Alcatraz and it closed in March the following year. In 1972 it became part of the Golden Gate National Recreational Area but too late to prevent several of the buildings being razed by fire, vandalism and neglect. Today it is visited by a million people each year. These are the segregation cells in D Block — then and now.

January 16, 1934 — Huntsville, Texas

Clyde Barrow, notorious Dallas desperado, today made good his boast that his pal, Raymond Hamilton, serving two life terms and 25 years additional, would not stay on a Texas prison farm.

Under cover of a dense piney woods, Barrow laid down a machine gun barrage at Eastham state prison farm near Weldon about 7:30 this morning and liberated Hamilton and four other long term convicts.

Two guards were shot. They are Major Joseph Crowson, in a critical condition at the prison hospital here, and Olin Bozeman, shot in the hip.

Simmons said that he felt certain Barrow was the man who manned the plan to liberate Hamilton from prison. Captain B. B. Monzingo of Eastham Farm said that judging by the description he got of the two men who pulled off the prison break, one was Clyde Barrow.

The spectacular break occurred as Crowson and Bozeman led a squad of 22 men from the farm headquarters toward a spot about three miles away where they were to clear away brush.

'The squad had gone only a short distance from the farm headquarters,' said Lee Simmons, general manager of the prison system, who with Warden Waid rushed to Eastham to investigate the break. Major Crowson was a few feet ahead of the squad and Bozeman was in the rear. It was a foggy morning and you could see only a few feet ahead.

'When the squad got near a big drainage ditch about six to eight feet deep and about ten feet across, there were several big piles of brush that had been cut earlier.

'Suddenly, Joe Palmer, one of the prisoners, dived into a pile of the brush and came out with a .45 automatic pistol in his hand. He let go with it right away.

'Two other convicts also dived into the brush and came out with the same kind of guns. The air was full of whistling bullets in a minute.

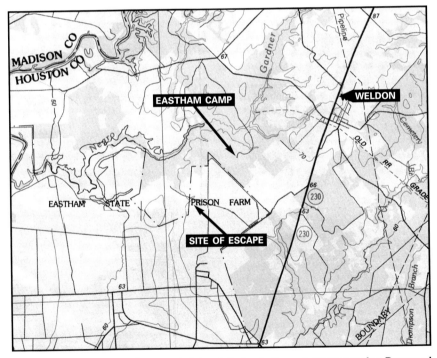

Clyde's New Year Resolution was bold and daring in the extreme: to spring Raymond Hamilton from prison. He had been given 55 years in January 1933 for armed robbery; a life sentence in May 1933 for robbing the Carmine State Bank in November the previous year with his partner, Gene O'Dare; a further life sentence in June for the Bucher murder, and still had over 200 years under appeal for other offences. Now he was at Eastham Camp. Brother Floyd was the go-between, the plan being to secrete weapons near where the convicts were working cutting wood, and have a car ready to take him to safety. It would appear that three of Clyde's old associates — Ralph Fults, behind bars since the robbery at Mabank back in April 1932, Henry Methvin and Joe Palmer — were to be freed at the same time but that Hilton Bybee had to replace Fults at the last moment as Ralph had been moved back to the 'Walls'. *Top:* This is Eastham Camp as it appears today, the site chosen to spring the prisoners being about three miles away. The small rectangle behind the building is the prison graveyard.

According to Floyd, Clyde made him plant the weapons with James Mullens, a prisoner recently released after serving 21 years for robbery although Marie Barrow was of the opinion that Clyde placed them personally. In any event, Mullens is believed to have been the second man mentioned in the press

report, and it was Bonnie who remained in the car, signalling by blowing the horn. *Left:* It is also believed that they spent the night in the car here behind this gateway on the now defunct County Road. *Right:* For the actual escape, the car was parked just off this bridge on the Calhoun Ferry Road.

'Palmer cut loose at Bozeman and dropped him with a bullet through the hip. Another shot knocked his shotgun out of his hands. Bozeman drew his gun and emptied it at Palmer. Crowson went down with a bullet in his stomach.

'About that time the weeds at the edge of the ditch moved and two men rose up. One had a machine gun in his hand and the other an automatic pistol. They opened fire, but none of their bullets seemed to take effect.

'When the first shots were fired the guards yelled at the convicts to lay down and the machine gun bullets seemed to have fired to scare them.

'Crowson and Bozeman were lying on the ground bleeding and all around them lay convicts huddled close to the earth to escape the bullets.

'Then Palmer and four others in the squad made a dash for the ditch. They dropped into it, ran toward a car parked on the road back of the farm. Someone in the car had been honking the horn all during the shooting. The car was a black Ford V-8 roadster. The men climbed onto it and the driver streaked away in the direction of Lovelady.'

When the car got away, the other convicts ran to where the guards lay on the ground. They helped them up and some ran to the farm headquarters for help.

Captain Monzingo in charge of the farm, was summoned and rushed a call to the 'Walls' at Huntsville. Simmons and Waid and other officials sped to the farm.

Crowson and Bozeman were taken to the prison hospital here. Bozeman was found not to be seriously hurt. His wound was dressed and he was taken back to Eastham.

Crowson was operated on at noon in an effort to save his life. 'He has about a 50-50 chance to live,' Simmons said.

Simmons immediately flashed word to officers over the state about the break and inside of 30 minutes roads all over this section of the state were under heavy guard.

The convicts are believed to have had more than one car for the coupe could not make much speed with seven men aboard.

Bloodhounds at the farm were called out on the theory that all of the convicts did not get into the one car and might be lurking in the woods nearby. At noon the dogs were called back in when no trail had been struck.

The convicts who escaped were Raymond Hamilton, Dallas, 9 years for robbery and burglary and from Fayette county life for robbery of the Carmine State Bank: Henry Methvin, Refugio county, 10 years for assault to murder: J. B. French, Hunt county, 12 years for assault to murder, robbery and theft of an auto: W. H. Bybee, life for murder, from Stephens county, and Joe Palmer, from Limestone county, life for robbery by firearms. Bybee originally was sentenced to death but his sentence was commuted early in 1933.

When Hamilton entered the prison system about a year or so ago he boasted to officers: 'I won't be in here long. Clyde Barrow won't let me lay around a prison farm.'

Simmons said that two farmers living near the prison farm heard the shooting and saw the fleeing convicts in the car. The farmers told Simmons the car was being driven over the dirt road at a high speed and that the front of the car was jammed with men and that two men were in the rear compartment with their heads sticking out. They said the car was heading north toward Lovelady.

The Houston Chronicle, January 16, 1934

Left: Clyde and Mullins crept down the drainage ditch in the foreground to where the prisoners would be working. *Right:* Major Joseph Crowson was the high-rider on that fateful Tuesday morning. In his dying statement he explained exactly what happened. 'I am called at the Eastham State Prison Farm "Long Arm Man" or "Backfield Man" and on the morning of January 16, 1934, Olin Bozeman was carrying No. 1 Squad. I was riding a horse and I was in front of Bozeman's squad. It was about 7:15 a.m. when Bozeman called me and said: "Raymond Hamilton has jumped my squad" and I said "Boy, that is

for something" and Bozeman said"Yes it is". Joe Palmer was in Boss Bozeman's squad and he pulled an automatic pistol. It was a .44 or .45, and Joe Palmer shot me in the stomach. He shot at me once while I was riding away. When Joe Palmer pulled his gun on me, Joe Palmer said: "Don't you boys try to do anything". I never did get my hand on my gun, and I never did shoot at Joe Palmer or any other convicts that was in the squad. After I was shot I rode to the camp and told Captain Monzingo that I was shot and shot bad. I am positive that it was Joe Palmer who shot me.'

CALHOUN FERRY ROAD

DIRECTION THAT MORTALLY
WOUNDED MAJOR CROWSON
TOOK BACK TO UNIT

'BONNIE AND CLYDE HILL
WHERE GUN-BATTLE
TOOK PLACE

BRIDGE

DITCH

OLD ROUTE OF TRINITY-WELDON ROAD WHERE CAR WAS HIDDEN OVERNIGHT AND ALSO PROBABLY THE ESCAPE ROUTE

MAJOR JOSEPH CROWSON
BORN SEPT. 14. 1900
DIED JAN. 27. 1934

Prepare to meet me in Heaven.

The major died of his wounds ten days later. Bruce Moore found his grave in Lovelady Cemetery.

TEXAS PRISON SYSTEM

W. W. WAID, WARDEN

R. H. BAUGHN
ASSISTANT WARDEN

H. E. MOORE
SECRETARY

OFFICE OF THE WARDEN
HUNTSVILLE, TEXAS
May 10, 1935

THE STATE OF TEXAS   -   IN THE DISTRICT COURT

V S   O F

JOE PALMER   GRIMES   COUNTY

WARDEN'S RETURN AFTER EXECUTION

Received, the death warrant, together with the body of the above captioned, JOE PALMER, white, from the Sheriff of Grimes County, on the 8th day of April, 1935, A. D., and the death warrant ordering the execution of the said JOE PALMER, white, on the 10th day of May, A. D., 1935.

FURTHER, that in accordance with the judgment of the District Court of Grimes County, the said JOE PALMER, white, was duly executed on the 10th day of May, 1935, A. D., at the hour of 12:07 A. M., by Warden W. W. Waid, by causing to pass through his body a current of electricity of sufficient intensity to cause his death. And the said JOE PALMER, white, was pronounced dead by W. B. Veazey, M. D., Prison Medical Supervisor, 9 minutes after the application of the electric current.

FURTHER, that by pre-arrangement with his relatives, the body of the said JOE PALMER, white, was released to Fortner and Gresham, Undertakers at Huntsville, Texas, after the electrocution and after the said JOE PALMER, white had been duly pronounced dead.

W. W. Waid, Warden

WWW:s

The man who pulled the trigger received his come-uppance at the hands of the Huntsville staff the following year, when he fulfilled his appointment with 'Old Sparky' (see page 282).

January 23, 1934 – Rembrandt, Iowa

Striking with startling suddenness, a band of four daring bandits apparently made a clean getaway after robbing the First National Bank at Rembrandt of more than $3,000 shortly after noon Tuesday. It was the first bank robbery in the state this year.

Sheriff E. A. Thompson had this entire part of the country watching for the robbers within a short time after the hold-up. The sheriff has been making investigations at Rembrandt and could not be reached today, Thursday. It is reported however, there are no tangible clues to the identity of the quartet.

Two men carried out the job while the other pair waited in the car. The two covered H. L. Haraldson, cashier, and J. F. McGrew, a customer with a gun.

Following the robbery the car drove rapidly eastward out of town. It was a tan colored Ford V-8 sedan. It is believed to have carried Kansas license plates.

The robbery occurred at 1:15. The two men, unmasked, walked into the bank and asked Haraldson to change a large bill. As the cashier turned to make the change he was astounded to hear one of the men say: "Keep quiet, and stick em up!"

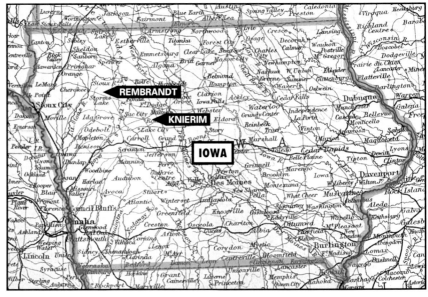

Rembrandt is a small town which was established in north-west Iowa in 1901 as a result of the expansion of the railroad in the area. In 1934 it held the dubious distinction of possessing the first bank to be robbed in the state that year! It was on Tuesday, January 23 that the Barrow gang hit town, their target being the First National Bank on the corner of Main and First.

Left: The solid construction of the bank contrasted the other timber-framed buildings along the street. The bank moved to the opposite corner of the intersection in the 1970s whereupon the original building was demolished to be replaced by the Town and Country Corner store *(right)*. This is set back from Main Street to give easy access to the pumps.

It was a large robbery by the standards of the time and netted the gang about $3,800. Lloyd Haraldson *(left)*, the owner of the bank, had just returned after lunch when two men entered and asked for change for a $5 bill. Mr Haraldson opened the vault (seen in the photo) to fetch the money tray only to be confronted by one of the men now pointing a gun who is quoted as saying: 'Keep quiet and hand over the jack if you care for your life!' The robbers then demanded that the inner safe be opened.

McGrew was also in the bank and was also ordered to raise his hands. While one man with the gun kept Haraldson and McGrew covered, the other scooped up all the cash he could locate. The time lock on the vault had been released a few minutes earlier.

In the meantime the bandit car had driven on to the end of the block and turned into an alley which passes the back door of the bank. The bandits then fled out of the back door and jumped into the car.

Despite the fact that there were passers by in the street, several of whom witnessed the robbery, the bandits worked coolly and deliberately, Haraldson and McGrew related.

Both of the men who entered the bank were about 30, they estimated. One was slim, tall and light in complexion. He wore a light coat and hat and weighed about 130 pounds. The other was heavier set about 5 feet 9 inches tall, and had sandy hair and complexion. He wore a dark coat and an aviation cap.

Pilot-Tribune, January 25, 1934

While the two men were inside — they are believed to have been Raymond Hamilton and Hilton Bybee — Clyde was behind the wheel of their car on First Avenue at the side of the bank with Henry Methvin and Joe Palmer who was lying down in the back as he felt ill. According to eyewitnesses the driver 'kept the machine moving forward and backward while the robbery was in progress' which would seem to indicate that they were not sure if their associates would leave by the front or rear exit *(above)*. The alley mentioned in the *Pilot-Tribune* report, although not very clear in this photo, runs east-west at the end of the newly-laid concrete sidewalk. The windows of the car were rolled down and a close watch was being kept in all directions. When Hamilton and Bybee emerged from the rear door of the bank, the gang then made their escape by turning right on Main Street, heading east out of the town. Before they left the bank, Mr Haraldson and a customer Frank McGrew, who had followed the robbers inside only to be immediately captured, were thrust inside the vault although this had a patent device which prevented it from being closed.

Ronald G. Haraldson, Lloyd's son, who supplied the photographs and took the comparisons for us, told us that this was not the first time that his father's bank had been robbed as it had already been hit in August 1931 . . . but that fortunately it has been trouble free since the day that the Barrow gang left town!

January 26, 1934 — Poteau, Oklahoma

The trail of five bandits who shortly before noon Thursday robbed the Central National Bank of Poteau of approximately $1,500, was lost Thursday night in the hill section of south-eastern Oklahoma.

Officers who returned here late Thursday afternoon after a foray into the mountainous area, reported they had no tangible clues upon which to continue a search for the bandit quintet. However, a number of

posses continued Thursday night to seek the robbers.

The hold-up occurred at 11.30 o'clock. Three bandits entered the bank. Two more were said by spectators to have remained on

Top: **Main Street, Poteau pictured sometime in the mid-1920s. The Central National Bank stands on the extreme right.**

Above: **From the Model T to the pick-up truck . . . Jim Knight's comparison in March 2003.**

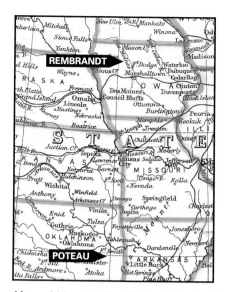

After robbing the First National Bank at Rembrandt in Iowa of more than $3,000 on the 23rd, the gang motored over 500 miles south to Poteau in Oklahoma. There, two days later, they hit the Central National Bank *(right)* and relieved it of $1,500.

Today the building is occupied by an attorney. After the robbery, Clyde and his henchmen came out of the front door and ran down the side of the building to their getaway car parked at the rear.

the outside. W. A. Campbell, cashier, and a customer, C. P. Little, were forced to lie on the floor, while Miss May Vasser, assistant cashier, was ordered to sit in a chair and warned to keep her eyes upon the floor.

During the robbery two other customers, Pat Polsom and J. M. Butler, entered and were forced inside the cashier's cage and told to lie upon the floor. Butler had entered the bank armed, having become suspicious when he saw the bandits' automobile, a Plymouth sedan, outside. One of the three robbers greeted him at the door with a revolver and disarmed him.

Accompanied by E. G. Goodnight, president of the bank, officers took the trail of the bandits about 10 minutes after the robbery. Surrounding towns were notified by telephone. It was the consensus of officers that the bandits had fled into the hills.

Miss Vasser said that she could describe but one man, the one who confronted her and who appeared to be the leader of the robbery. He was about 30 or 32 years old, weight about 135 to 150 pounds, height a little above five feet. He was wearing a dark suit, dark shoes, gray overcoat and tan kid gloves.

The bandit who confronted Miss Vasser and the other two who came into the bank were dressed 'somewhat nicely,' Miss Vasser said, but were very rough-spoken, seizing the persons slow in obeying their commands and forcing them to lie down.

Persons who saw the robbers leave, differed with others as to the number, saying only four bandits were in the party.

One bandit wearing kid gloves, came behind the counter and took all the currency and silver from the cashier's draw. They then forced one of the officials to open the safe and took all the cash from the safe. Miss Vasser said that the total loss is insured.

The robber put the cash into a sack which he was carrying, Miss Vasser said.

The Plymouth sedan is black. It headed south out of the city on highway 271, which leads into Wirter.

The bank was robbed of approximately $10,000, $6,000 in cash and $3,500 in Liberty bonds, on Dec. 26, 1931. Three men took part in this hold-up and Miss Vasser was one of the employees present at the robbery.

Two suspects later were arrested, Fred Sutton, who now is serving 15 years in the state penitentiary and Jack Kagore, who escaped several months ago from the jail at Poteau.

Southwest American, January 26, 1934

All buddies together . . . but not for long! This is the only known picture of Clyde with Methvin and Ray Hamilton who did the Poteau job. Joe Palmer may have been with them as the driver because Hilton Bybee is believed to have quit the gang after Rembrandt. The picture can be dated quite accurately as the three of them only operated together during January-March 1934. Henry Methvin in the centre is easily the most physically imposing — he being the one who would betray Clyde just a few weeks later. Hamilton on the right, although just 20, was full of his own importance and already considered himself a big-time desperado. He would leave Bonnie and Clyde in March.

February 1, 1934 – Knierim, Iowa

Two youthful, unmasked bandits held up the State Savings Bank in Knierim at 2:45 o'clock this afternoon and escaped with $300 in currency.

They also robbed Chris George, a customer of the bank, of $35.

One of the pair, a short, sallow complexioned man, carried a pistol and the other a sub-machine gun under his coat.

They entered the bank and the smaller man walked up to Albert Arenson, bank cashier, and ordered him and 'Happy' Allspaugh, of Moorland, and a friend with him to 'Stand where you are!'

While one of the bandits covered the trio, the other walked around and into the cage and scooped up the currency in the till, about $300.

During the hold-up, George, Knierim garage man, entered the bank to make a deposit. After robbing him, the bandits ordered Arenson, George, Allspaugh and his friend into the vault.

One of the gunmen asked Arenson how the vault could be locked, but Arenson said nothing.

The vault was locked open and could not be locked.

After shoving the four hold-up victims into the vault, the bandits hurried out of the bank and jumped into a car waiting at the curb and driven by an accomplice.

Arenson dashed out of the vault, picked up a .45 caliber revolver kept in the bank, and ran out the front door. He fired one shot at the bandit as he turned a corner in the street, but the bullet found no target.

The bandits fled in a light sedan and are believed to have followed a highway west from Knierim. The license plates were dusty and could not be read.

The smaller of the two gunmen was described as about 5 feet 8 inches tall, the other, at least 6 feet tall. Neither was described as more than 22 or 23 years old.

Fort Dodge Messenger & Chronicle,
February 1, 1934

And so back to Iowa! Having hit the First National Bank in Rembrandt on January 23, eight days later (on January 31) the Barrows returned to case out the State Savings Bank in Knierim (see map page 206) — as the crow flies some 45 miles to the south-east from Rembrandt (see also map on page 155). *Top:* **This is Knierim in 1900.** *Above:* **Today virtually none of the old timber-framed buildings on Center Street survive. The State Savings Bank is at the far end on the left.**

One of the bandits who last Thursday afternoon held up the State Savings Bank in Knierim has been identified as Clyde Barrow, notorious Texas outlaw, Sheriff Robert Waldburger said this afternoon.

The identification was made by Albert Arenson, cashier of the bank, and Chris George, Knierim garage man who was in the bank at the time of the hold-up and was robbed of $35 by the bandits. The robbery netted the gang $272 of the bank's funds.

Arenson and George said they were positive of their identification, which was made from photographs of the outlaw taken to Knierim by State Agent A. A. Robertson.

The man identified as Barrow was the small sallow man armed with a .45 caliber automatic pistol, Arenson and George said. The other man, a six-footer, may have been Raymond Hamilton, whom Barrow liberated from a Texas prison camp a few weeks ago.

The bandits were in Knierim the night before the robbery, according to the story told by F. W. Kahley, operator of a filling station and lunchroom in Knierim.

Kahley said a V-8 Ford sedan drove past his filling station twice early Wednesday evening, and then returned, parking in the drive. A man left the car, entered the lunchroom and ordered four steak dinners. The man said he would return for the food and drove away. He came back shortly, took the four dinners, and again drove away.

Kahley said he followed the man into the drive and looked over the car. In the automobile, waiting for the man who bought the food, were two men and a woman. The car carried Arkansas or Texas license plates he believes.

Kahley said the man who came into the lunchroom closely resembled a newspaper picture of a member of the notorious Dillinger gang, which for months created a reign of terror in Indiana and Illinois. John Dillinger, leader of the gang, and two companions were captured last week in Arizona, but several members of the gang are still at large.

Suspicious of the quartet for whom he had prepared dinner, Kahley the next day went to the State Savings Bank and warned Cashier Arenson that there were 'some bad men around town,' he said. Less than an hour later the bank was robbed.

Kahley said the man who ordered the dinners tallies in appearance with the tall man who took part in the bank robbery.

Roger Natte in Fort Dodge very kindly drove out to Knierim to picture the sites relevant to this robbery for us. He found that this house now stands on the site of Kahley's gas station where Clyde Barrow, Raymond Hamilton and Henry Methvin accompanied by Bonnie, pulled in.

Moving to the location of the cafe, Roger found that it, too, had been demolished . . .

It has been learned since the bank robbery that three men and a woman were in the bandits' car when it raced out of Knierim after the robbery.

The woman, it is believed, is 'Suicide Sal' Parker, cigar-smoking gun-woman, who is Clyde Barrow's companion.

The Fort Dodge Messenger and Chronicle,
February 6, 1934

. . . but he struck gold with the bank (on the right). No doubt because of its sturdy brick construction, it has withstood the test of time, albeit now a private residence rather than a centre of finance.

February 12, 1934 – Reeds Spring, Missouri

Clyde Barrow and his gang of outlaws, including the cigar-smoking gun-girl, Bonnie Parker, paid Stone county a visit on Monday of this week and created considerable excitement in vicinity of Reeds Spring when local officers attempted to stop the bandit car.

Barrow and his gang had stolen an automobile from the Thompson Tire Company in Springfield and headed south with it and another car. Barrow and his woman companion were riding in the new car. The cars went through Hurley and officers at Crane and Galena were notified to be on the look-out for the gang. Sheriff Seth Tuttle and other officers, including Sam Thompson, Robert Weaver, Ernest Hayes, and Robert Galloway, started to the highway north of town and just as they reached the Pine Run bridge,

Having stolen a car in Springfield, Missouri, on Monday February 12, 1934, Clyde with Bonnie beside him was high-tailing it south for the Arkansas border. Ray Hamilton and Henry Methvin were following in a Chevrolet. However the engine of the Springfield car seized near Galena so they all piled in the Chevy, little knowing that the law had already been alerted. A road-block was set up here on Highway 76. Jim Knight was shown the exact location of the resulting gun-battle by Rusty Clinkenbeard whose family once owned the property bordering the road at this point. The view is looking east from where Clyde stopped facing the officers' car some 200 yards further down the road.

I was living on lower James River, and was walking to town that day for my weekly groceries. They stopped me near Fred Tolbert's farm. They said they were lost and ordered me to get in the green Chevrolet four-door with them, and show them how to get into Arkansas.

The car was full of guns. I got in the back seat between Hamilton and the other man they called 'Gibbons'. Clyde was driving. Bonnie was beside him with an automatic rifle in her lap. They were all pretty calm. They didn't seem nervous or scared.

I had them drive to the Cape Fair road and turn toward Highway 13, south of Reeds Spring. Just before we got to the junction, in a low gap by Yocum Pond, we saw a load of armed officers blocking the road ahead. They were Galena men.

Bonnie cursed and said, "There they are! We had just as well stop and have it out with them!"

They piled out of the car and started shooting the automatic rifles at Deputy Sheriffs Ernest Hayes and Sam Thompson, who dived for cover under their car after emptying their pistols. One of their bullets came through the windshield and plunked into the car by my head. Pellets

from a shotgun rattled all over the car. There was an awful noise from the guns.

About that time Deputy Willard Kissee and Reeds Spring's Marshal (sic) Dale Davis drove their car over a hill behind us. Hamilton turned his rifle on them. They backed the car out of sight. I never saw them any more.

The outlaws then piled back into the car and gave it the gas. We ran out into the ditch going around the officers' car. Hamilton and Bonnie showered the car with bullets as we drove by. Bonnie cursed a lot. I thought they might think I had led them into the trap and would shoot me. I was scared stiff. They all looked mean and hard now.

I told Clyde to turn south on 13. We went about two miles when we saw another carload of officers parked at the side of the highway. Clyde didn't even slow down. Hamilton and Bonnie opened up with the rifles as we passed. The officers ran.

When we got almost to Berryville, Arkansas, they stopped, gave me $10 and told me to get out. They didn't harm me at all.

JOE GUNN, 1959

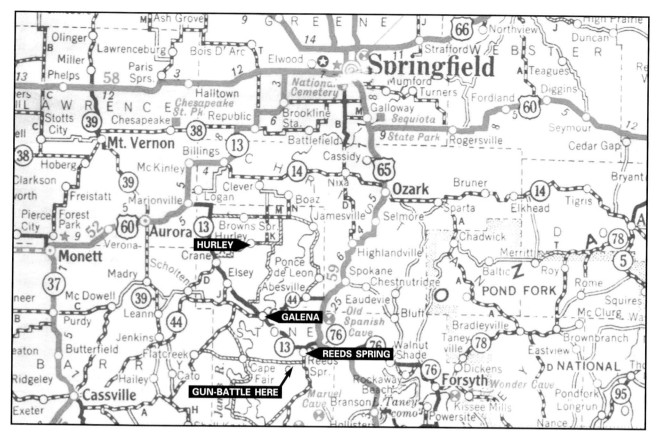

the bandit cars sped past and continued toward Reeds Spring. The officers gave chase and came upon the new car parked on the highway about two miles east of Galena where it had been abandoned. Sheriff Tuttle took possession of the stolen car and other officers continued the chase.

In the meantime Constable Dale Davis of Reeds Spring had been notified and had the highway near the underpass at Reeds Spring blocked. As the bandits approached the underpass they saw the road was blocked, turned their car around and retraced their path to the Finis White place, turned off on the Bear Den road and proceeded south. Constable Davis pursued the machine but a fusillade of bullets from the bandit car put the Davis machine in the ditch.

Other officers had gone through Reeds Spring and turned west on the farm-to-market road to Cape Fair in the hope of heading them off. About a half-mile out on the road the officers saw the car coming and stopped their car. The bandits also stopped their car about 200 yards away. Three men got out of the car with blazing guns. Two of them had machine guns and the third an automatic rifle.

The officers were driving the Chevrolet sedan of County Clerk J. A. Hall. The occupants of this car were Deputy Sheriffs Ernest Hayes and Sam Thompson and a recruit, Robert Galloway, all of Galena. One of the officers had a shotgun and the other two men pistols. They emptied their guns at the approaching bandits but soon ran out of ammunition. One of the bandit bullets went through the windshield and through the rear door of the Hall car. The rear door was open and Ernest Hayes was crouched behind the door as the bullet whizzed through the door just above his head. Another bullet went through both front and rear fenders on the left side of the car and a third hit the right front drum of the wheel putting the car out of commission.

When bandits saw that the officers had fired all their ammunition they returned to their car and drove past the officers, struck the highway and headed south. They turned

off on the Baxter farm-to-market road south of White River and near Baxter they turned south again and headed toward Berryville, Arkansas. The bandit car was trailed through North Arkansas and was lost in the Oklahoma hills.

Just as the bandits abandoned the stolen car east of Galena, Superintendent J. O. Talley of Reeds Spring came along and saw the outlaws changing the license plates to the other car and slowed down to get the license number, but was waved on by the bandits.

The stolen machine was returned to Galena and was turned over to the owner Monday night. In the car that was abandoned Sheriff Tuttle found two suede jackets presumably belonging to Barrow and his woman companion. A new hat was also found near

the scene of the gun-battle, as well as an empty machine gun clip and empty shells used in the rifle.

South of the Finis White place the bandits came upon Joe Gunn, who they kidnapped and compelled him to show them the road south to Berryville. They let him out of the car near Berryville and he returned to Reeds Spring about 11 o'clock. He said the bandits tried to kill Ernest Hayes during the gun-battle and that Hayes broke the windshield of the bandit car with a bullet but that none of the occupants of the car were injured. Evidently Hayes had saved part of his ammunition to use on the bandits as they came by his car.

The Stone County News-Oracle,
February 14, 1934

This picture shows the intersection of Highways 76 (the old farm-to-market road mentioned in the press report) and Highway 13, looking east from the top of the hill just behind the officers' car. Clyde drove past them down the hill, firing as they went, and turned right (south) towards the Arkansas state line, about 20 miles away.

We have just read from Joe Gunn's description of the latest battle in Missouri that the outlaws' car was full of guns, including 'automatic rifles', i.e. BARs. So it is somewhat of a mystery why they should now trail 500 miles to Ranger, in Texas (see map page 44), to obtain more. Mystery or not, another four Brownings plus 13 Colt automatics were removed from the National Guard armoury — the building on the right next to the Masonic Hall — and added to Clyde's arsenal.

On this operation there was a new member in the gang. Ray Hamilton brought along his new girlfriend — the wife of his former partner Gene O'Dare who was currently in prison. Even Ray's brother Floyd referred to the heavily made up Mary O'Dare as a prostitute and commented that 'My brother sure could pick 'em'. Mary fancied herself as Ray's 'Bonnie' but she was instantly disliked by Clyde, Bonnie and Henry and her presence caused much friction.

February 20, 1934 – Ranger, Texas

Sometime between 3 and 4 a.m. Tuesday morning, burglars broke into the National Guard Armory on Rusk Street, Ranger, and took four Browning sub-machine guns, 13 .45 caliber Colt automatics and between 20 and 25 clips for the machine guns.

The robbery was discovered by Patrolman Jack Roach at 4 o'clock when he made his regular rounds and discovered the front door to the armory building broken open. He notified Captain Wayne C. Hickey who made a preliminary examination of the premises and immediately wired the adjutant general of Texas, notifying him of the robbery and asking that instructions be wired him as to what he should do.

Entrance to the building was gained by prying the lock and hasp off the front door with a pinchbar.

The thieves evidently broke into the orderly room first, as the hasp was broken from the door to that room and the lock left lying where it fell just outside the door. Nothing was missing in the orderly room as

Although the Masonic lodge building still stands on South Rusk Street, unfortunately the old armoury next door, erected as the Liberty Theater in 1920, was struck by lightning in February 1990, the frontage being literally blown into the street.

far as a hurried check disclosed, though there were typewriters and other office equipment in the room.

Supply Room No. 2, where uniforms, canteens and other equipment is kept, was also broken into in the same manner and a preliminary check reveals that nothing was touched in that room.

In Supply Room No. 1, where rifles, pistols, sub-machine guns and ammunition are kept, the thieves made a pretty thorough haul.

After gaining entrance to the room by prying off the lock, which was left near the door, along with the bar used in opening the four doors on which locks were broken.

Inside Supply Room No. 1 a rack containing seven Browning automatic rifles commonly known as sub-machine guns, was broken and the four newest guns were taken. Two of these guns had seen considerable service and one was in bad order. These three guns were not molested, but the four new guns were taken.

The rack containing 13 .45 calibre Colt automatic pistols was also broken and all these guns were taken, though the ammunition bin, which was nearby, was not disturbed.

Four .22 calibre rifles, belonging to the American Legion Rifle Club, were on a table nearby, but these were not removed, nor were the Springfield rifles, with which the company was equipped.

The value of the loot of the robbery was estimated today by Captain Hickey as around $1,000 at retail prices.

Ranger officers have looked over the scene of the robbery in the hope that some clues might be found, though no report of their findings was made public.

One Texas Ranger arrived in Ranger this afternoon from Fort Worth and began aiding local officers in their search for clues, and the Department of Justice at Dallas telephoned today and indicated a federal agent might be sent to Ranger if he was requested by officers and Rangers now on the job.

The Ranger Telegram, February 20, 1934

Clyde Barrow came this way! He broke in through the front door . . . just here!

Rusk Street is still paved with original bricks as used on the famous Bankhead Highway which runs through Ranger just one block to the east. This transcontinental route from coast to coast was proposed by Senator John Bankhead who campaigned for the Federal Aid Road Act in 1916. Built between 1919 and 1923 in Texas, the road ran from Texarkana to El Paso. Known as the Bankhead Highway, it was officially Highway 1, later Highway 80, the majority of which has now been incorporated into Interstate 20. However, Ranger's main claim to fame is that it 'floated the victory [in the First World War] on a sea of oil'. During the 'Ranger Oil Boom', which began with the 1,600-barrel per day gusher on the J. H. McCleskey farm in October 1917, the population of the town grew to 45,000 but today it is barely 2,500. The oil boom was but a brief interlude for it is the nearby interstate that has left Ranger a quiet backwater but Jeane Pruett, who guided us round, is determined that the local history is preserved through her leadership of the Central Texas Historical and Genealogical Preservation Society.

Seven days later, having left Bonnie and Mary parked in a spare car outside town on Malloy Bridge Road, the three men drove up to the R. P. Henry bank in Lancaster (see map page 44). The original building *(above)*, which the bank shared with the Hammond store, stood on the corner of Henry Street and East Main but burned down in 1918. It was rebuilt on the same site but by 1934 the owner and manager, Lamon Henry was on the point of closing down — not because of the Depression but because he was sick and tired of government interference. On February 27, Mr Henry had just brought down all the money from Dallas ready to pay off their depositors when the gang struck.

February 27, 1934 – Lancaster, Texas

Two men and a woman, arrested by Sheriff Barker at Stillwell, Oklahoma, about daylight Wednesday in a Ford V-8 black sedan which was stolen in Dallas last Sunday, were being held in that town as suspects in the $4,176 robbery of the R. P. Henry & Sons private bank at Lancaster Tuesday.

The sheriff at Stillwell called Sheriff Smoot Schmid here about 9 o'clock telling of the capture. At that time he had not been able to talk to the prisoners at length. However, the sheriff gave the motor number of their car and told Schmid that the trio was heavily armed with shotguns and pistols.

Deputies Bud Walker, John Chiese and Ed Castor left within thirty minutes for the Oklahoma town. They carried warrants for their arrest which were issued after the trio had been formally charged there with theft of the car in which they were travelling.

They were charged with theft under the names the Oklahoma sheriff told Schmid they gave. These names were Ed Belt, Jack Evans and Reva Belt.

Investigation revealed the Ford V-8 1933 model sedan was stolen from in front of the home of Mrs R. L. Foster, 2402 Denley Drive, Sunday about noon. It belonged to W. E. Rogers of Malakoff. He was visiting in the Foster home and left his car parked in front of the house.

Mrs Foster told Sheriff Schmid that some of her neighbors reported witnessing the theft of Rogers' car. They said three men drew up in a green Chevrolet sedan, parked near at the curb, and one of the three men got out and stole the Ford sedan.

The car used by the bandit trio in the bank robbery was a green Chevrolet sedan. It was later found abandoned near Kleberg where

the bandit trio was seen to transfer to a black Ford sedan which a woman had parked at the side of the road. In switching cars, witnesses say they saw one of the men move a large sack from the Chevrolet to the black Ford. This was supposed to have contained the $4,176 loot.

A check on the abandoned Chevrolet revealed it was stolen in Wichita Falls Sunday night from G. Jeff Waggoner.

Investigators Wednesday had about abandoned the original belief that Clyde Barrow, Raymond Hamilton and Bonnie Parker took part in the bank robbery.

L. L. Henry, cashier, and Olin Worley, a customer, who were in the bank at the time of the robbery, viewed pictures of Barrow and Hamilton but could not identify them as the two men who came in the bank, one with a sawed-off shotgun and the other with a

The rebuilt bank was destroyed in a tornado which hit Lancaster on April 25, 1994, wiping out all the buildings on the south side of the main square. However the white tiled floor is the very same one on which the robbers trod that Tuesday in 1934. Henry Methvin remained behind the wheel of their Chevy while Clyde and Ray entered the bank by the side door.

Lamon Henry was in the process of serving a customer — Mr Olin Worley — as Bud Brooks sat nearby reading a paper. Hamilton pushed the customer out of the way while Clyde ordered Brooks to the rear of the bank at the point of his sawn-off shotgun.

Seventy years later, Jonathan Davis stands in for the six-foot tall Methvin while Jim Knight plays the part of Mr Henry. After the bank closed, it was rented out and Mary Ruth Pledger recalls still using the bank's original safe when she had her gift shop there.

pistol. They said there was a resemblance but the two men said they could not say positively the bandits were Barrow and Hamilton. However, both men say they can identify the bandits if they see them face to face.

Meantime Dallas police officers were maintaining an apparently hopeless vigil Wednesday morning for three bandits. Special squads cruised roads on the edge of the city, and all regular squads kept an unblinking vigil within the city limits until daylight Wednesday, but efforts were fruitless.

The bandits were reported to have used four cars in their getaway which led them from Lancaster towards Wilmer, thence to Kleberg, where they changed cars, and the Kaufman pike and into East Dallas where the trail was lost.

The Daily Times Herald, February 28, 1934

Right: **The vault was at the rear of the building, only the banking hall being tiled**

While Clyde kept an eye on the staff, Hamilton (who is reported to have appeared very nervous) crammed money from the cashiers' drawers into a sack fastened to his waist. He then cleaned out the safe but because bank robberies were so prevalent, Mr Henry had hidden the rest of the money — some $9,000 — in filing cabinets. Olin Worley had been relieved of $27 he had just withdrawn but before they left, Clyde asked him if it was his own money. When Olin said it was his wages for digging ditches, Clyde handed it back saying: 'We don't want your money. Just the bank's'. Although Ray had left behind $300 in coin, he got away with over $4,000. And it was the division of this loot that was the final straw in the on-going argument about Mary. Ray felt that she should get a cut but Clyde said no. When Clyde spotted Ray later giving his girlfriend some money, he hit the roof. Mary also wanted to live it up by eating in nice restaurants and staying in decent hotels — all not possible now the gang was on the wanted list all over the Midwest. Mary even caused more tension by making passes at Henry when Ray was not around. All this friction caused Clyde and Bonnie to argue which led Mary to suggest to Bonnie that they drug Clyde and steal his money. It was all too much and on March 6 Ray stole a car and made off with Mary. Once firm friends, Clyde and Ray were never to see each other again. *Left:* **Jim and Jonathan root around for any small change left behind . . . but settle for a piece of the tiled floor!**

Easter Sunday, April 1, 1934 – Grapevine, Texas

Shot before they could reach for their guns, State Highway Patrolmen E. B. Wheeler and H. D. Murphy of Fort Worth were slain by a pair of killers believed by officers to have been Clyde Barrow, Texas public enemy No. 1, and a woman companion, possibly Bonnie Parker, Sunday afternoon near Grapevine, Tarrant county, about twenty-five miles north-west of Dallas.

The woman was reported by witnesses to have shot Murphy, turning him over to pour additional bullets into him. He died in an ambulance without regaining consciousness sufficiently to identify his assailant, while Wheeler, shot by the larger of the killers, died almost instantly.

Police and county officers of both Dallas and Fort Worth expressed their conviction that the two were Clyde Barrow and Bonnie Parker. The description of the man fitted that of Barrow while discovered near where the car had stood was a cigar stump bearing the imprint of small teeth. Bonnie Parker is known for her fondness for cigars.

The theory was strengthened by a report to officers and to highway patrolmen Saturday night that Barrow and his woman companion were going to spend the night at a farmhouse near Grapevine. Search was made of several suspected places but the couple were not located.

In 1934, Easter fell at a weekend and a family meeting was long overdue. Clyde chose a rendezvous just off Highway 114 at Southlake, some 20 miles north-west of Dallas. At around 10.30 a.m. on Sunday morning, Clyde pulled off the main road some five miles north of Grapevine (see map page 44) and stopped 100 yards up an unpaved track called Dove Road. Turning the car round, Bonnie got out to exercise her pet rabbit Sonny Boy which she was going to give to her mother as a present. Joe Palmer was sent into Dallas to tell the families where they were parked while Clyde and Henry Methvin took turns to keep a look-out. By mid-afternoon no one had turned up (in fact both mothers were out and Palmer was still waiting for their return) so Clyde was whiling away the time snoozing in the back of the car with Bonnie in the front seat. Methvin was on guard armed with a BAR. At 3.30 p.m. three motorcyclists of the Texas Highway Patrol were travelling north on 114. Patrolman Polk Ivy was leading some distance ahead as his machine was fitted with a sidecar containing test equipment. *Top left:* The two patrolmen following him spotted the car parked on Dove Road and decided to turn off to investigate *(top right)*.

The two pictures are from the police re-enactment filmed at the exact location in 1934. Marty Black drove to Southlake in November 2002 to take the comparisons: 'I was disappointed at the enormous road construction taking place on Highway 114. It's now a major thoroughfare for the northern suburbs of the Dallas-Fort Worth "metroplex". Highway 114 has been modified to pass over the top of Dove Road (what we call an "overpass" and you call a "flyover"). Highway 114, seen as a two-lane road in the film is now a 6-8 lane divided highway (three-to-four lanes each direction). And, incredibly, the exit ramp for Dove Road is an additional four lanes wide! Yet the thick woods in the background remain to provide a link to the past.

The car in which the two killers were travelling had been parked in a dirt road about 5½ miles north-west of Grapevine at least since 10:30 Sunday morning, a nearby farmer reported later. The car was here with two persons both dressed in riding breeches, when he went to get a load of rocks. He had not then notified officers however.

The most tenable theory of officers was that Barrow and his woman companion had parked in what they believed to be a secluded spot to wait for Raymond Hamilton, former pal in crime of Barrow, who Saturday robbed a bank at West, abducted a woman as hostage, and fled to Houston, where the woman was released. Hamilton got away with more than $1,000 from the bank, was said to have stolen another car in Houston, and to have headed back for his old haunts in North Texas.

Unexpected approach of the highway patrolmen probably was believed by the fugitives to have resulted from a chase by officers, and brought quick and deadly resistance to imminent capture.

At 3.30 p.m. the man and woman were in their halted car, which aroused the suspicion of Patrolman Wheeler, one of the best shots in the highway service: and he and Murphy, a recent recruit, turned off the side road from Highway 114 with Wheeler in the lead. They with Patrolman Polk Ivy had previously stopped nearby and drained their crankcases and indulged in some target practice. Ivy, with a pair of highway test scales in his sidecar, had started ahead, and Wheeler and Murphy had both passed the side road when Wheeler decided to investigate the car parked there, and turned around.

Followed by Murphy, he approached with the sun glinting from the windshield of the parked automobile preventing him from seeing anyone within. As they got close two persons, apparently a man and a woman in riding breeches, got out and a few seconds later opened fire. Wheeler fell instantly with his motorcycle on him. Murphy, who was behind apparently stopped his motor and had reached into his pocket for two shotgun shells, lifting a sawed-off weapon which he no longer carried loaded due to fear of its going off accidentally from contact with the motorcycle.

The man at the car ran over, shooting as he came, apparently with a .30-06 automatic rifle, officers said. Wheeler died almost at once. Murphy, however, pitched over at the first shots and lay still. The smaller of the two persons at the car supposedly a woman,

In re-staging the murder, the police had two eyewitness accounts, one by a couple out for a Sunday drive and another from a farmer working several hundred yards away. Unfortunately for Bonnie, both police and press latched on to the latter description in which William Schieffer said a man and a woman fired on the officers as they approached them by their parked car and the woman then finished off one man as he lay on the ground. This was the version filmed and given prominence in the press reports thus irredeemably tarnishing Bonnie Parker as a callous killer.

rushed over with her gun and, turning him over, poured further shots into his breast. The two then made a dash for their machine and started away, heading toward Dallas. It was thought, however, that they turned north-east on a gravelled road after leaving Grapevine.

Ivy, seeing he was not being followed by his companions, turned round and was met by Mr and Mrs Fred A. Giggal of Dallas. He arrived at the scene of the shooting to find Wheeler dead and Murphy dying.

As soon as notified, Dallas and Tarrant county and city officers went to work on the case, sending a host of cars filled with guns at the scene. Sunday night and Monday morning the search for the slayers was being waged relentlessly over the north part of Dallas county and into Denton and Tarrant

county. Twenty-five men from Dallas police department armed with machine guns spent the night searching each by-road and main highway nearby, while ten deputies from Sheriff R. A. Smoot Schmid's office also were covering the county.

Co-operating were State highway patrolmen under Capt. S. C. Hanun of Dallas, head of this district. Joining the Dallas force were patrolmen Fred Tyler and other points who came to devote the night in search for the slayers of their fellow officers.

The killers escaped in a black Ford sedan with yellow wheels. Vigilant city officers who spied such a sedan at a local golf course gave the owner a bad fright Sunday afternoon when they went toward the car with machine guns. The owner stuck his head from behind a tree trunk to identify the machine as his.

Marty: 'The Dove "farm-track" is now a paved two-lane road but is four lanes wide at the site of the shooting which was 100 yards from the junction. It is difficult to pinpoint the exact spot where the officers were shot but the slightly-downhill aspect of the terrain seen in the film still, with the gently-sloping high ridgeline in the background, remains.

The truth was somewhat different. With Clyde asleep in the car it was the unstable trigger-happy Methvin who cut down officer Wheeler with a burst from his BAR. Clyde -- the shorter of the two – then sprang into action with his shotgun, but it was Methvin who turned officer Murphy over and shot him again as he lay dying. Methvin later admitted to a friend it was he who had killed the two highway patrolmen.

The place where the killers' car was parked near Grapevine is a favourite hang-out of Barrow and is near the place Malcolm Davis, Tarrant Deputy Sheriff was killed more than a year ago, supposedly by Barrow or his confederates.

Wheeler, 26, had been with the State highway patrol nearly four years. He was married. Murphy, 24, had been assigned to duty here last fall upon completing the training course at headquarters in Austin.

It was Murphy's first day of patrol duty since he joined the highway organization. Previously he had been assigned to weight duty, checking up on weights of trucks and had been doing race tack work at Arlington Downs.

These murders committed by Barrow, bring the total of killings charged to him and his brother, Buck who was recently killed, to nine, with one directly attributed to Bonnie Parker, Clyde Barrow's woman companion.

Sixteen Fort Worth detectives, Tarrant and Dallas county sheriffs and deputies as well as Rangers Hanna and Weems took up the hunt for the occupants of the car. The description of the machine and the occupants was sent out over the Fort Worth police radio and given officers in all parts of the state.

Authorities at first thought that the man in the automobile was Raymond Hamilton, but the fact that a farmer living near the scene said that the car had been parked there since 10:30 a.m. destroyed this theory, as Hamilton had stolen a car in Houston at 9:30 a.m. Sunday.

Highway Patrolman Ivy said he did not hear the shots that killed his two companions, the noise of his motorcycle apparently drowning out the roar of the shotgun.

Near the spot where the car had been parked were three 16-gauge shotgun shells, five .45 caliber automatic shells, three 12-gauge shells and one rifle shell, all empty.

Detective A. C. Howerton of the homicide squad of the Fort Worth police department said Sunday night there was no doubt that the killer of the two patrolmen was Clyde Barrow. He said from the description given of the man who occupied the parked car, he was convinced it was Barrow.

At an early hour this (Monday) morning officers returning from their patrolling reported that they had found what appeared to be the hideout of Barrow and Bonnie Parker in Denton county. It was an old garage with its walls resting upon a concrete base back of which men could hide and shoot if they were attacked. For 150 to 200 yards around this garage the brush, weeds and trees had been cleared away to offer attackers no cover if they attempted to storm the place. It also had been reported to officers that a woman fitting Bonnie's description had been seen in the neighborhood frequently.

The Dallas Morning News, April 2, 1934

Clyde Barrow, notorious and elusive desperado and killer, became the object of the greatest manhunt in the Southwest Monday as hundreds of county, State and Federal officers heavily armed sought him 'dead or alive' for the murder of two State highway patrolmen near Grapevine Sunday afternoon. The murder of the officers' was fixed definitely against Barrow and his companion, believed to be Bonnie Parker, by identification of fingerprints found on a bottle at the scene of the slaying.

Barney Flint, superintendent of the Bureau of Identification at Fort Worth, checked the prints and reported that they tally with those in his reports on Barrow. Murder charges against the gangster will be filed in Fort Worth before the close of the day, detectives announced.

The officers E. B. Wheeler, 26, Fort Worth, and H. D. Murphy, 24, Alto, were riddled with buckshot as they rode up on motorcycles by a car parked on a side road near Grapevine about 100 yards off the main highway. The killing occurred Sunday afternoon about 3 o'clock and within an hour highways in every direction were being scoured by officers searching for a black sedan with yellow wire wheels in which Barrow and his companion fled.

Latest reports Monday were that the car with a man and woman in it had been spotted near Alvord on the Fort Worth to Wichita Falls highway. A trap was set at Sunset, but the killer and his cigar-smoking companion failed to appear.

Earlier they were reported at Brownwood about midnight headed toward Waco. Two persons, a man and a woman answering the description of Barrow and Bonnie Parker, bought gasoline at his station about 7 o'clock Monday morning and then left without paying, a Brownwood filling station operator reported. Although the flight apparently was moving away from Dallas, every available local officer was on duty Monday morning searching for the outlaw who had long been a thorn in the side of Dallas county police and deputy sheriffs. Sixteen squad cars bearing patrolmen armed with sawed-off shotguns from the Dallas police department were circling Dallas watching for the fugitives. Sheriff Smoot Schmid called his night men back to duty and dispatched them to the hunt.

Had Clyde been alert he would most probably have taken the officers prisoner as he had done on several previous occasions when in a similar position. As it was, Methvin was never charged with the murders and the following month he double-crossed his buddies — an act which led to their deaths as we shall see. Meantime, as Texas lawmen mounted a massive manhunt for the perpetrators, the killing of the two officers was laid squarely on the shoulders of Bonnie and Clyde.

Frank J. Blake, chief of the Federal Bureau of Investigation, Department of Justice here, opened his resources of communication and identification in the hunt and assigned assistants to keep in touch with the chase.

Above: **Crowds gather at the murder site.** *Below:* **Dove Road today, looking from the overpass of Highway 114. Marty explains that 'the fenced field partially seen in the film to the right of the Ford sedan has now been built up in an embankment, and a huge complex for the Verizon mobile phone communications company was being built in that field when I was there. To the east of the Verizon complex, large brick homes are being built. Construction abounds at that site!'**

From Austin through XVP, the Dallas police radio station, state highway patrolmen were ordered to check every possible car that might hold the killers. Reinforcements will be with you immediately', the broadcast earlier stated.

The two motorcycle patrolmen never had a chance to defend themselves according to stories by eyewitnesses and other observers who had been with them a short time before.

The two, with a third patrolman, Polk Ivy, left Fort Worth about 1:30 o'clock and rode slowly in the direction of Grapevine. As they approached Grapevine, having stopped along the route several times, they passed a dirt road. Ivy rode past the road, but Wheeler and Murphy swung their motorcycles in a half circle and ventured up the road to inspect a car parked about 100 yards from the highway.

As they drew near, a man and a woman jumped from the machine and began firing. At the first charge the officers toppled from their machines into the road. The taller of the two walked over to where the men lay and fired several more charges into their bodies. Then the pair jumped into their car and fled, turning toward Dallas.

Wheeler, member of the highway patrol for four years died instantly. Murphy who had just completed his training period and was on his first patrol, died on the way to the hospital.

The Dallas Journal, April 2, 1934

'I was pleased, though', says Marty, 'to find a small section of "original" Dove farm-track a third of a mile east of the shooting site, still with the crude wooden barbed wire fence-posts that are visible in the film stills. This small section has been bypassed where it meets White Chapel Boulevard North at which point it changes from West Dove Road to East Dove Road.

Belief that the killer of the two highway patrolmen was Clyde Barrow, noted desperado, accompanied by Bonnie Parker, was expressed Sunday night by Chief Deputy Sheriff Bill Decker.

The car which Patrolmen Murphy and Wheeler approached just before they were shot by its occupants had been seen there since 11 o'clock Sunday morning. Mr Decker said if Raymond Hamilton let out his prisoner, Mrs Cam Gunter, at Houston at 9.30 o'clock Sunday morning, he couldn't have been at Grapevine two hours later, particularly by back roads. It doubtless was Clyde Barrow and Bonnie Parker.

The possibility also was suggested that Barrow had been waiting for Hamilton, whom he freed recently from the State prison farm near Huntsville.

Mr Decker also did not believe the killer had driven on to Dallas. Although the car was reported headed for this city he thought Barrow had turned north soon after passing through Grapevine.

Late descriptions of the pair seen in the car tallied more nearly with Barrow and his woman than with Hamilton. The man was said to be about five feet six inches, weighing around 140 pounds, dressed in dark tan riding pants and blue shirt. His companion also was dressed in riding pants which gave rise to reports there were two men in the car. It was a woman however, wearing brown riding pants and a brown blouse, Dallas police were informed.

The Dallas Morning News, April 2, 1934

Officer Edward Wheeler was buried in Dallas — in Grove Hill Cemetery. In later years the same burial ground would also see the interments of L. C. Barrow (1979); Blanche (1988); Billie Jean Parker, Bonnie's sister, and Ralph Fults (1993); and Clyde's sister, Marie, in 1999.

Highway Patrol officer H. D. Murphy was taken to his home town of Alto, Texas, to be buried in Old Palestine Cemetery.

MEMORIAL

Unfortunately with the road alterations, the memorial which was originally sited close to the spot where the officers were murdered has been moved to the 'wrong' side of Highway 114, albeit still on Dove Road near the traffic light (see map page 218).

Marty thought the move was probably because of the construction of the embankment on the eastern side but feels that as the inscription says 'near this site', the present location, backing onto what is locally known as 'scrub oak', is acceptable.

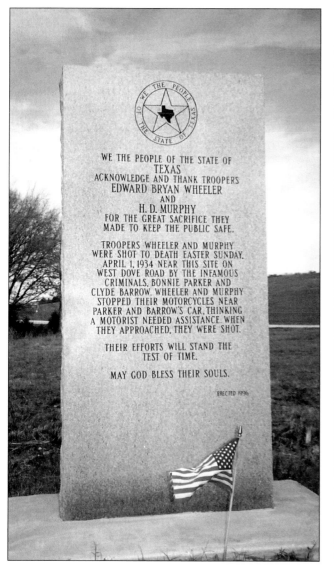

WE THE PEOPLE OF THE STATE OF
TEXAS
ACKNOWLEDGE AND THANK TROOPERS
EDWARD BRYAN WHEELER
AND
H. D. MURPHY
FOR THE GREAT SACRIFICE THEY
MADE TO KEEP THE PUBLIC SAFE.

TROOPERS WHEELER AND MURPHY
WERE SHOT TO DEATH EASTER SUNDAY,
APRIL 1, 1934 NEAR THIS SITE ON
WEST DOVE ROAD BY THE INFAMOUS
CRIMINALS, BONNIE PARKER AND
CLYDE BARROW. WHEELER AND MURPHY
STOPPED THEIR MOTORCYCLES NEAR
PARKER AND BARROW'S CAR, THINKING
A MOTORIST NEEDED ASSISTANCE. WHEN
THEY APPROACHED, THEY WERE SHOT.

THEIR EFFORTS WILL STAND THE
TEST OF TIME.

MAY GOD BLESS THEIR SOULS.

ERECTED 1996

The killer, Henry Methvin, died in mysterious circumstances when his body was found cut in half on railroad tracks at Sulphur, Louisiana, in April 1948. Although eyewitnesses saw him crawl on the track on his own, members of his family still suspect foul play, believing that his death was retribution for betraying Bonnie and Clyde. He was buried locally in Social Springs Cemetery.

223

Calvin Campbell was the local constable in Commerce, Oklahoma, a small town situated near the point where four states meet. A widower, he lived here with his daughter less than a mile from where he met his death at the hands of the Barrow gang on Friday, April 6, 1934.

April 6, 1934 – Commerce, Oklahoma

A shot blazing from the machine gun of one of two men, accompanied by a blond-headed woman, took the life of Cal Campbell, 60, Commerce constable and another shot either wounded or killed Percy Boyd, chief of police in a gun-battle that occurred about 9.30 o'clock this morning near the Lost Trail Mine, on a road west of Commerce.

The killers seized Boyd and fled in a sedan toward Chetopa, Kansas. Descriptions of the two men closely fit those of Clyde Barrow, Texas killer, his partner, Raymond Hamilton, Texas fugitive, and the woman resembles Bonnie Parker, the pair's cigar-smoking companion.

Reports from the posse at 2.30 o'clock this afternoon were that the fugitive car had been seen last about nine miles west of Chetopa, headed toward Coffeyville, Kansas.

Campbell and Boyd had gone out to the scene of the gun-battle after a motorist told them he had passed by an automobile stalled in a mud hole, the occupants of the car not wishing to have him pass. The officers had apparently started out of the car to investigate the action of the two men and woman when the fugitives opened fire.

Immediately following the killing of the two Highway Patrol officers at Grapevine, Clyde, Bonnie and Henry Methvin disappeared. Their precise whereabouts over the next five days are not known but various unconfirmed sightings were reported in Arkansas, Oklahoma and Texas. Meanwhile, the two-man team set up after the Huntsville prison break in January to track down Bonnie and Clyde was reinforced. Bob Alcorn and Frank Hamer were joined by 'Manny' Gault, an ex-Texas Ranger co-opted by the Highway Patrol, and Ted Hinton who came on behalf of the Dallas county sheriff, Smoot Schmid. Bonnie and Clyde were next spotted early Friday morning (April 6) parked on this road south-west of Commerce, Oklahoma. It must have been somewhere they thought they could safely spend the night in the car before holding up the First State Bank in the town the following morning and then beating it across the state line. (Henry Methvin was still with them although the posse of lawmen had already singled him out as the weak link.)

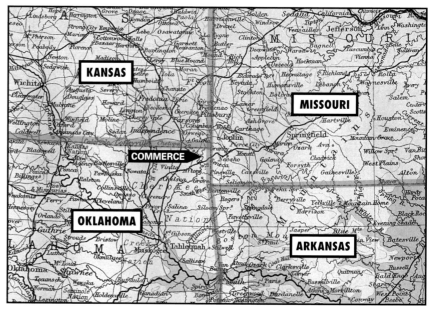

The vehicle was reported to Constable Campbell by a suspicious motorist and, taking the local police chief Percy Boyd with him, he drove out to investigate. Reaching this junction, he turned right up the hill to where Clyde was parked a couple of hundred yards away facing down the road towards them.

In 1934 this was just an unpaved country road which the recent rains had turned to mud. We are now looking back east towards the intersection from where Constable Campbell emerged. Jim Knight took the photos for us.

Three empty cartridges were found in Campbell's revolver, and Boyd's gun also was recovered, indicating both he and Boyd had engaged in an exchange of shots before the fatal missile entered the left side of the constable's body, killing him instantly.

C. M. Dodson who had heard the gun-fire jumped into his truck and drove out to the mine. When he arrived the men were starting to take a vehicle parked in the yard of Clarence Robinson nearby, but on seeing Dodson the killers forced him to pull them out of the hole. One pointed a gun at him while the chain was tied to the sedan.

Boyd was being led around the car into the seat, with blood streaming down the left side of his face and chest, Dodson said, when he started to pull the car out of the hole.

The vehicle, with the blond girl inside smoking a cigarette was facing east when pulled out, but the driver wheeled it to the west when the trio fled, Dodson stated.

About three miles further west near the Timber Hills farm, the fugitives ran across a car driven by A. N. Butterfield, farmer living near Commerce and occupied also by his brother, the auto being stranded in the middle of the road. The desperadoes climbed out of their car, one shouting: 'We've just killed two men and we're in a hurry. The law is after us'.

With that the men assisted Butterfield and his brother to move their car out of the way. They then sped on toward Chetopa. Butterfield said he could not see whether Boyd was in the car.

Dodson said one of the two men was about 23 years of age and the other about 25 to 27. He said both were blond and that one was very small, weighing around 125 pounds, and the other probably 140 to 145. One had a 'breaking out' all over his face, he stated.

Two bullet holes were noticed by Dodson in the windshield of the fugitives' car. Three holes, all on the left side of the automobile, were discovered in the car driven by Boyd.

An empty machine gun clip was found after the affray and also a shotgun shell, which would indicate the trio had at least three weapons in their possession. Boyd's and Campbell's guns were found near the shooting.

Dodson said he saw two of the outlaws' firearms when he was ordered to pull the vehicle out of the muddy spot.

A farmer living north of Commerce said he saw the blond-headed woman driving a sedan near his home, Thursday afternoon. This morning, shortly before 9 o'clock the woman and the two men were seen driving near the First State Bank of Commerce. It was believed they were awaiting the opening of the bank so they could stage a hold-up.

Shortly after the shooting, Sheriff Dee Watters and 15 officers joined in the chase for the killers. The officers traced them as far as Chetopa to U. S. Highway 73, which turns off toward Joplin. Later the fugitives were reported to have been seen stuck in another mudhole at Banner schoolhouse, about four miles north-east of Welch. The net of the law spread for miles around the Chetopa vicinity.

Miami Daily News Record, April 6, 1934

A general movement of city, county and state officers of Texas toward the Red River and Oklahoma began today as a result of the slaying of Cal Campbell, constable, at Commerce by Clyde Barrow. Capt. S. O. Hamm of the state highway patrol called Austin headquarters for reinforcements and word went out to the patrols at Wichita Falls, Gainesville and Sherman to guard bridges across the river near those points. Capt. F. A. Hamer of the Texas Rangers began rounding up his men preparatory to leaving for Oklahoma. Long distance telephone and radio orders went out for all available officers engaged in the search for Barrow and Raymond Hamilton, his desperado companion, to close in toward Oklahoma.

Press report, Dallas, Texas, April 6, 1934

In Commerce Jim met up with a local historian, Richard Crabtree, who was able to point out the salient features. The open field in the background was then the site of several lead mining operations, including the Lost Trail Mine mentioned in the press reports. The shafts are all now filled in. Even though nothing stands to mark the spot where Constable Campbell was killed, it was announced in December 2000 that $10,000 had been collected for the erection of a memorial to his memory. (At the time of writing, September 2003, it has not been erected.)

Taken for a ride: police chief Percy Boyd.

Starting out on a gangster's ride Friday morning to the accompaniment of bullets and bloodshed, and expecting the journey to end in a rendezvous with death, Percy Boyd, Commerce chief of police, was back home Saturday only slightly wounded and with a dramatic story to relate to relieved authorities and then to friends.

Boyd proceeded to tell officers of the county and Department of Justice agents his experience as a captive of the fast-traveling Clyde Barrow, quick-shooting Bonnie Parker and an unidentified man addressed as 'Boodles.'

'They let me out about 12 o'clock last night at a point nine miles south and east of Fort Scott,' Boyd related to the officers, 'and told me I could tell you everything as long as my statements were absolute truths.

'They treated me fine. The wound in the back of my head, made by a rifle bullet, was given first aid treatment by the three.

'I couldn't see out of the car much because of the mud and water splashing on the glasses, but I kept expecting Clyde to meet up with officers. He stayed off the main highways and several times retracked on the muddy side roads.

'The new Ford V-8 they were driving is a new one and has only about 3,000 miles on it. When Barrow would drive on a good road for a few minutes he would open the machine up. I saw the speedometer at 90 several times. Barrow said that the type of vehicle could go places in the mud. And did it.

'Bonnie asked me to advise the public that she was not a cigar addict. She said that all the rumors going around about her smoking cigars were the bunk. She said that the picture taken of her with a cigar in her mouth was a joke and that she took the cigar from Clyde for the photo.

'But to get back to the shooting. They fired 80 shots at Cal and me with the automatic rifles and two shots with a shotgun.

'When that bullet knocked me off my feet, I stayed down and, believe me, I almost dug into the dirt. I heard Cal groan. He was lying there beside the car.

'Barrow ran to a nearby farmhouse after the shooting stopped and the other man came toward me and told me to get up. I kidded him and he got into a good humor.

'When they couldn't pull their machine out of the ditch with a pick-up truck, they told me to help push the machine. Three

other men who appeared on the scene were forced to aid. We couldn't move the car and Barrow told us that if we didn't get the car out he was going to kill us.

'A passing truck was stopped and, by using a chain, the car was pulled from the ditch. Several persons were being held at the point of rifles by them.

'We drove west on the new state highway towards Highway 78 in the vicinity of Chetopa. Barrow got out of the car once and pushed a small truck out of the slippery ruts so that we could get past.

'They didn't seem to know the roads very well and just kept driving around, keeping off the main traveled road. Sometimes we would stop and park for a while.

'Barrow heard a plane flying overhead once and said, "There's a bug up there." He got out and looked up and then got back in the car. None of them ever showed a sign of being nervous. They had three automatic rifles, two shotguns and some pistols. Bonnie held on to a shotgun during the earlier part of the chase.

'We missed Chetopa on the south and west and drove to Bartlett, where they bought some gasoline. After that we just drove around in the vicinity of Fort Scott.

'They didn't know they had killed Campbell until they read it in a newspaper Friday afternoon late when the man unknown to me went into a Fort Scott drug store and bought one.

'We drove up and down Main Street at Fort Scott and once we passed the police station. The man who rode in the back seat with me went into a grocery store later and bought a lot of food. We drove out of town on the main highway and parked while we ate.

'I asked Clyde about the killing of the two Texas officers last week and a vigorous denial was his reply. 'He said those killings were one rap they were not guilty of and had no knowledge of the affair until they read about it in the papers.

'We also discussed the Joplin shooting during which several officers were slain. Barrow said that one of the officers had no business getting killed and that if he had acted right and drove away around the corner it wouldn't have happened.

'I don't believe there would have been any shooting if Cal hadn't fired first. I fired four shots after the battle started. I understand Cal fired three. Two of the bullets went through the windshield near Barrow. He told me later that I almost got him and that he heard it zip close.

'Barrow said that he was sorry the old man was killed but that he had to do it.

'They didn't bother to take $25 I had. They seemed to have plenty of money. My shirt was bloody and Barrow gave me a new one and a necktie. He wanted to give me a new suit, but it was too small for me.

'They never mentioned what they were doing in this vicinity. The first account we had was when someone told Cal about the suspicious looking trio parked near where the new state highway joins U. S. Highway 66.

'When we drove up Barrow shot the machine in reverse and ran it wide open back up the road. The car wobbled and went in the ditch. We got out of our car and walked toward them and when Cal saw the guns he drew his pistol and opened fire. Someone inside the car fired twice with a shotgun and then the two men jumped from the car and ran towards us with the automatic rifles, firing as they came.

'We got stuck in a ditch near Fort Scott yesterday afternoon. A group of high school students came along and tried to push us out. They were unable to do so and Barrow ordered them to go on. He then stopped a truck and made the driver pull us out. I never got out when we stopped like that and the windows were so muddy that no one could see in.'

Miami Daily News Record, April 8, 1934

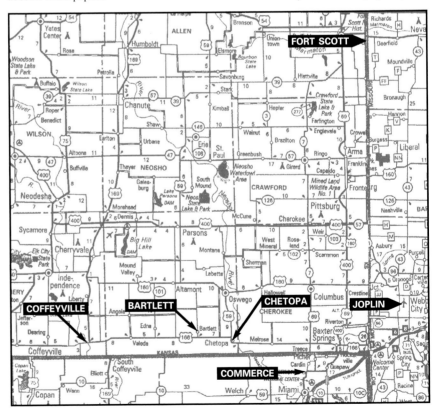

After shooting down Constable Campbell, Clyde abducted Percy Boyd who had been wounded in the head. Having spent over 12 hours in the company of the three most wanted criminals was a sobering experience and Boyd had a fascinating tale to tell when he was released unharmed south of Fort Scott. Most significant was Bonnie's plea to correct the image created by that one picture (see page 109) that she smoked cigars!

The death of Constable Campbell was the final straw. Nine lawmen had died at the hands of the gang and now all the stops were pulled out to bring them to justice. Clyde Barrow and Bonnie Parker were easily identifiable but it is interesting to see how the authorities — and the newspapers of the time — had difficulty in putting a name to the third man. As the manhunt got into top gear, the Mayor of Commerce, J. R. Grimes, asked that all local businesses close their doors between 2 and 3 p.m. on Tuesday afternoon (April 9) in tribute to the fallen officer. His body lay in state at his home before it was interred in his wife's grave in the Grand Army of the Republic Cemetery in nearby Miami.

L. G. Phares, chief of the Texas Highway Patrol, expressed the opinion that the fugitives would attempt to return to Texas, where they are more familiar with the roads.

Barrow and Bonnie Parker are accused of having killed two highway patrolmen in cold-blood near Grapevine Texas, last Sunday.

'We'll be watching for them when they come,' Phares said.

With hundreds of officers searching the highways for the killers, Captain F. A. Hamer of the Texas Rangers issued a warning to motorists to observe instantly orders or signals to stop: Any motorist who failed to obey would jeopardize his life, Hamer said.

Various unconfirmed reports were received Saturday that persons answering the description of the killers had been sighted. One came from Grapevine, Texas, another from Parsons, Kansas, said a motorist had seen a car with a bullet hole in the windshield travelling at high speed west of Dennis, Kansas.

Ed Portley, chief of detectives at Joplin, reported late Saturday that officers had been sent in pursuit of a maroon sedan answering the description of that used by Barrow and containing two men and a woman.

Miami Daily News Record, April 8, 1934

A report was received here at noon today that three persons believed those who shot and killed one officer and wounded another at Commerce, Oklahoma, were seen at Banner schoolhouse, seven miles south of here, and a posse of officers hurried in that direction. A rural mail carrier also reported seeing a car carrying two men and a woman answering the description of the killers five miles south and four miles west of Chetopa. Sheriff Bill Miller and his force were searching in the vicinity of the state line west of here for the trio.

Press report, Chetopa, Kansas, April 6, 1934

Police and sheriff's deputies in Crawford and Cherokee counties were scouting highways today in the hope of picking up the trail of two outlaws and their woman companion who killed a constable and kidnapped the Commerce, Oklahoma, chief of police this morning. Sheriff Dave Hasenplaugh at Columbus sent a posse out to search highways along the Kansas-Oklahoma border. Crawford county officers joined in the hunt.

Press report, Pittsburg, Kansas, April 6, 1934

One of the most determined manhunts in the Southwest's history — with federal and state authorities co-operating — was pushed last night for Clyde Barrow, ruthless Texas killer, who eluded capture Friday after another slaying and kidnapping.

The search for Barrow, his gun-woman sweetheart, Bonnie Parker, and a lieutenant believed to be either Raymond Hamilton or Henry Methvin, escaped Texas convicts, turned southward into Oklahoma Saturday afternoon. Police broadcast a report that a trio resembling the Barrow gang was seen headed toward Guthrie from Stillwater, Oklahoma, in a blue sedan. Heavily armed state and federal officers rushed to the Guthrie area.

Riding at breakneck speed over side roads in the Oklahoma-Kansas-Missouri border section, the outlaws successfully dodged scores of officers and national guardsmen after the shooting near Commerce.

Authorities were determined to hunt down the 24-year-old gunman, whose desperate career has been blood-splotched with the killing of nine officers. Department of Justice agents were acting upon orders from Attorney General Cummings 'to utilize every resource' to capture the outlaw and his companions.

EDNA J.
NOV. 5, 1876
JAN. 22, 1916

W. C. CALVIN
DEC. 14, 1878
APR. 6, 1934

CAMPBELL

After three Barrow gang murders within a week and with the manhunt in full swing, the next development came from a surprising quarter: Ray Hamilton. On Sunday, April 8, Sheriff Schmid received a letter addressed to Hamilton's lawyer, Albert Baskett, which he released to the press for publication the following day. Reproduced both in facsimilie and printed text, it gave the lawmen their first clue that the gang was falling apart. But, before that, we must recap to see what has happened since Ray left on March 6, so first we have to go back to March 19.

March 19, 1934 – Grand Prairie, Texas

Having quit Clyde, Mary's expensive tastes soon ran Ray short of funds so another bank robbery was imperative. For this, Ray needed his brother's help so he sent Mary to Dallas to make contact with Floyd. He was also looking after the excess guns from the Ranger armoury break-in which Ray now needed. Together with a friend of Floyd's, John Basden, he targeted the State Bank in Grand Prairie (between Dallas and Fort Worth — see map page 44) which stood on the corner of Main and Center.

Last Monday morning about 11 o'clock two gunmen entered the First State Bank in this city and made a clean get-away with all the cash in sight, which a check showed to be $1,548.76. There was very little ready cash in the bank, as the Saturday payroll check had been cashed and some of the Saturday and Sunday deposits had not been made. None of the checks were taken.

This was a very quiet and methodical affair. A high-powered car drove to the side-street and parked and two neatly-dressed men alighted and entered the bank from the front door. There was nothing startling nor unusual about that as this happens probably several times during the busy days.

On entering the bank one of the men approached the cashier's window, and it was when Acting Vice President J. F. Waggoner started to the window and he was informed that a hold-up was about to take place. Mr. Waggoner was commanded to stand still, and the command was emphasized by the waving of a pistol in the hands of a mighty nervous man. Mr. Waggoner, Cashier T. J. Yeager and Assistant Cashier and book-keeper, Miss Maud Crawford, were the only people in the bank at the time, and they were lined on the side of the bank and covered with a gun held by one of the men while the other one scooped up all the money at the cashier's window and what was in the safe in the vault, after forcing Mr. Yeager to open it.

While the hold-up was in progress, F. M. Gracey, an inspector for the Production Loan Corporation of Dallas, stepped into the bank. He was promptly lined up with the officials in the office and given positive orders to remain quiet. When informed the bank was about to be robbed, Mr. Waggoner said he raised his hands, but was immediately ordered to drop them, indicating that they were not staging a show that would attract passers-by.

As soon as the gunmen had all the cash gathered up, the employees together with Mr. Gracey were ordered to the vault and the door was closed, but it being latched did not close tight, and could not be locked in place, but the party were given orders to stay put until they heard the car on the outside move off. Exit was made through the side door, and the third party who remained in the car soon had it moving.

When the car started Mr. Waggoner left the vault and started after the bandits in his car which was parked on the side street. He trailed the bandits to Sowers and saw that they kept on the straight road to Denton. Officers who had been dispatched from Dallas were met there and they took up the trail.

Dallas and Fort Worth officers were notified and it was only a few minutes after the outlaws did their work until the city was full of laws, but at this writing there has been no developments that indicate that the bandits will be captured.

There has been all kinds of rumours floating around as to who pulled this job and it seems to be the opinion that Raymond Hamilton was one of the party, and the leading spirit. That being true, this was not his first time in Grand Prairie. Several months ago [*it was over 18 months previous — see page 58 — Ed*] he held up the interurban station, and took all the cash Agent Speer had and left town in Buddy Swadley's car which he had stolen from Mrs. Swadley, who had it parked at the school building.

The robbery had little effect on business, as it was only a few minutes after it happened until the bank was going along in its usual even tenor. The loss was fully covered by insurance.

For several weeks following the robbery of the Lancaster and Mesquite banks, deputies from the sheriff's office were sent to the smaller towns in the county, believing that would be protection. About a week before the bank robbery here this precaution was discontinued. Had the deputies been here at the time it would have been likely they would not have known what was taking place until it was all over, and the bandits travelling. This job was pulled at a most opportune time and with methodical precision. There were few people in town, and the method of entrance was not out of the ordinary in usual run of business.

The Grand Prairie Texan, March 23, 1934

Ray probably chose this particular bank as he remembered it from the day when he held up the nearby interurban office with Clyde although the press report is a little adrift on the timing — it was back in 1932, over 18 months previously (see page 58).

This was the scene outside the bank on that Monday in 1934. As far as the authorities were concerned, they had no reason to believe that Clyde was not still working with Raymond . . . that is until the papers appeared on Monday, April 9.

Anxious to clear himself of the latest murders, Ray Hamilton's letter posted from New Orleans read as follows:

'Dear Mr Baskett:
I am sending you a bill from a hotel I was staying at at the time of the killing in Commerce, Okla. I haven't been with Clyde Barrow since the Lancaster Bank robbery. I'm sending you one hundred dollars and want this put before the public and proved right away. I am sending you more money just as soon as I find out you are doing as I ask. I'm enclosing also my finger prints on this bill. I'm also leaving a letter at this hotel for you. You can call for it. My finger print will be there when you call for it. You know I try and do keep my promise. I want you to let the public and the whole world to know I am not with Clyde Barrow and don't go his speed. I'm a lone man and intend to stay that way. I wrote Mrs. M. A. Ferguson [*the Texas governor*] but I guess it was in vain. I was in Houston Wednesday night April 4, and have been here since Thursday, even April 5.
 Yours Truly,
  Raymond Hamilton.

The letter was written on stationery of the Lafayette Hotel in New Orleans and was accompanied by a $100 note and a Lafayette Hotel bill for $3.20. Hamilton had placed a fingerprint on it which was identified by the Dallas police department and by the identification bureau at the sheriff's office as that of Hamilton's right thumb. The hotel statement showed that Hamilton and a woman companion had registered at the New Orleans hotel as Mr and Mrs F. A. Murphy of Lake Charles, Louisiana. It bore the date '6-5-1934,' clearly an error with reference to the month. They had occupied Room 526, for which $3 was charged. Two telephone calls were also listed on the statement.

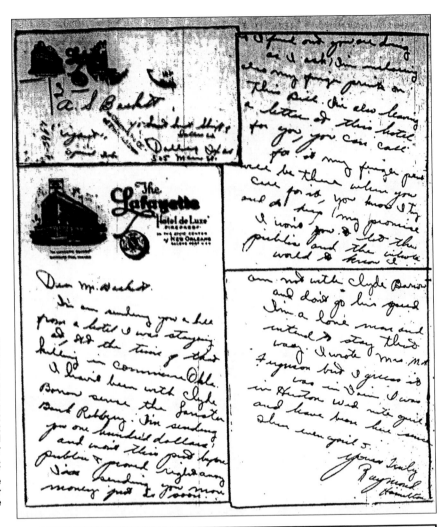

*Raymond Hamilton
c/o Dallas County Jail
505 Main Street, Dallas, Texas*

Raymond
 I'm very sorry to hear of your getting captured, but due to the fact you offered no resistance, sympathy is lacking. The most I can do is hope you miss the 'chair.' The purpose of this letter is to remind you of all the 'dirty deals' you have pulled. When I came to the farm after you I thought maybe the 'joint' had changed you from a boastful punk. However I learned too soon the mistake I had made. The first thing that aroused my suspicion was your suggestion of shooting Joe Palmer in the back while he was asleep. You soon learned about how I felt about such 'cat ideas'. Since then I have found your reasons for wanting to do this was because Joe was on the farm with you and knew what kind of a guy you were. The next impression was when we got the road 'blocked' on us in the Ozarks and you were too 'yellow' to fight [at Reeds Spring — pages 212-213 — Ed]. You cowered on the floorboard, afraid of being shot. Now that you're in the Dallas jail, you have a tested pal, W. D. Jones. You might get a few pointers from him on how to impress the people you were an innocent, or possibly, forced companion of the ruthless Barrow gang. You might be as lucky as he was in making them believe I kept you handcuffed or tied.
 When you wanted to get your Prostitute Sweetheart I thought OK. But when you were so persistent about her going to town alone that idea wasn't so 'hot.' I thought then and truly believe now that should she have gotten off without Bonnie she would have 'spotted' us all. She hails from a 'rat' family and you couldn't expect better from her.

You exposed your 'hole card' when you stole the money from us on the Lancaster 'job.' That's what I have my rear vision mirror for, to watch suspicious people. When I demanded a 'shake down' you offered such strange excuses for having the money on you I should have killed you then. I would have saved myself much bother and money looking for you. For after you writing that letter saying you didn't stoop so low as to rob filling stations I have done nothing but look for you. Should I have found you, you wouldn't have had a chance to give up. You couldn't stand the rift of the outlaw life. For one reason you were too yellow and knew you could never surrender with me and another reason you wanted to play 'Big Shot,' sleep in hotels and ride passenger trains. You weren't intelligent enough to know that you couldn't live like a king and stay out. I don't claim to be too smart. I know that some day they will get me but it won't be without resistance. You only carried your guns around to 'show off' or else kidnap women and children.
 I guess you find where your boastful long tongue has gotten you. Maybe you can talk yourself out of the 'chair.' Or maybe you can write a few more letters (try one to the governor) at least it will gain you some publicity.
 When you started the rumor about Bonnie wanting a 'cut' of the loot you sure messed yourself up. I have always taken care of Bonnie and never asked any thief to help me.
 I hope this will serve the purpose of letting you know that you can never expect the least of sympathy or assistance from me.

 So Long
  Clyde Barrow

When Clyde read Ray's letter in the newspaper, he was so incensed that he is said to have gone out to find and kill him.

But Sheriff Schmid got Ray first, so Clyde had to console himself by greeting his former partner-in-crime with his own letter.

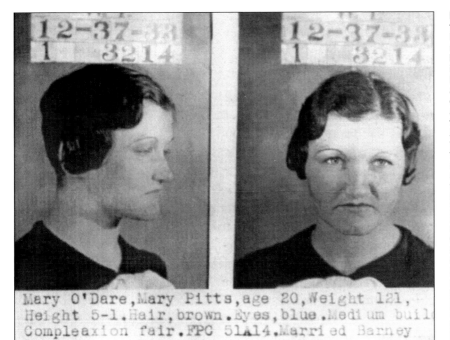

Mary O'Dare, Mary Pitts, age 20, Weight 121,
Height 5-1. Hair, brown. Eyes, blue. Medium buil
Compleaxion fair. FPC 51A14. Married Barney
Pitts.

Meanwhile, Sheriff Schmid had sought the help of the Texas Rangers to take Floyd into custody but keep him incommunicado while the search was on for Ray who Schmid thought was involved in the recent murders. The sheriff was hell-bent on bringing the gang to justice and, even if the detention was technically illegal, Floyd could easily be held on a trumped up charge. Now the lawmen tried another tack and the Dallas county Assistant District Attorney, Winter King, went to see Floyd to offer him a deal. He told him that he was being charged not only with the Grand Prairie hold-up — and any crime committed with firearms was then a capital offence in Texas — but also he would be arrested for being involved in the Eastham Farm break-out in January and so would be charged as an accessory to the murder of Major Crowson. However, if he helped in the capture of Bonnie and Clyde, all these charges would be dropped and he would be set free with a bounty of $5,000. *Below:* Although Floyd turned the deal down, Sheriff Schmid was elated when Raymond, left, joined his brother in Dallas County Jail and he even invited the press along so he could parade his prisoners 'greeting' each other for the photographers.

Mary had been arrested first on April 23 in Amarillo and she was initially placed under house arrest as bait with the hope that Raymond might show up, even though she professed that she had finished with him. She declared that when her troubles were over she was going to go back to her husband Barney Pitts. However, two days later, Ray was caught after he robbed the First National Bank in Lewisville. Following a wild chase across north Texas lasting two hours, he was finally cornered at a road-block ten miles south of Sherman. He emerged from his vehicle with the classic line: 'Don't shoot boys. I'm fresh out of guns, ammo, whiskey and women!'

The arrest of Raymond Hamilton Wednesday afternoon following the robbery of the Lewisville bank places behind bars the three hijackers alleged to have robbed the Grand Prairie State Bank on the afternoon of March 19.

John Basden was first arrested in connection with the job, and he admitted taking part in the robbery and implicated Floyd and Raymond Hamilton. Floyd Hamilton was arrested several days ago and he and Basden have been indicted.

Raymond Hamilton, who four months ago was liberated from the penitentiary and who was serving sentences totalling 263 years, was the leader in the Grand Prairie robbery and the Henry bank robbery at Lancaster.

Hamilton is now in the Dallas County Jail. His immediate indictment and trial for his part in the Lancaster and Grand Prairie bank robberies will be asked, District Attorney Robert L. Hurt said, and the jury that tries him will be urged to assess the death penalty.

'Hamilton already has 263 years of prison sentences against him,' Hurt said. 'We believe he deserves the death penalty and that a Dallas county jury will give it to him.'

'He was in the Lancaster robbery and the Grand Prairie robbery, and in either case a jury should give him death as a punishment.

'With so many years of imprisonment assessed against him, Hamilton didn't stay in prison long, and we don't think it would do any good to give him any more prison terms.

'He deserves the death penalty and if Denton county will let us try him first, we will do all in our power to see that he gets it.'

Grand Prairie Texan, April 27, 1934

By now, Mary O'Dare was also in the same Dallas Jail but she was prevented from meeting either of the brothers.

231

April 16, 1934 — Stuart, Iowa

For the second time the First National Bank was robbed Monday forenoon at 9:10 o'clock, when two robbers entered the bank. One stopped near the door, the other went to the cashier's window and asked Harold Cronkhite, assistant cashier, to change a $20 bill which he handed him. Harold gave him the bills in exchange for the $20 and as he looked up the robber covered him with a gun and said: 'This is a hold-up!'

The taller man who had stopped near the door kept the bank people covered while the other one, who was shorter, went around back of the counter and ordered the employees to sit down on the floor, telling them not to make a move and they would not be hurt.

Harold Cronkhite, Lucille Lyddon, bank employees, were in the bank and Maurece Lydon, who works at the Creamery, was there also when the robbers entered. Frank Eckardt, Vice President of the bank, went into the bank soon after the robbers entered. The one outside of the counter pointed a gun at him and told him to go around inside. Mr. Eckardt had to make a deposit and had his

bank book in his outside coat pocket. He held his arm over it and when he reached the back room he hid it in his clothes and went in and sat on the floor with the others.

The robber inside put the silver money on the counter and the bills from a drawer into a red and white striped bag. He went to the vault and demanded that the safe in the vault be opened. Harold assured him it was locked with a time lock and could not be opened. The robber finally took his word for it and told all the folk inside to go into the vault, which they did.

Both robbers then left the bank and went to a Pontiac car license No. 13-1234 Iowa, in which a young woman was sitting and drove a block south to No. 6 then went out of town east.

Mrs Mary Holmes was the first one in the bank after the robbers left and then Glenn Bufkin came in. The people in the vault called out to find out who was outside and when Mr. Bufkin told who he was, they opened the vault door and came out and gave the alarm.

Nearby towns were called by phone and notified of the robbery and word came from Dexter that the car had gone through there going east very fast.

No doubt the First National Bank in Stuart (top), some 30 miles west of Des Moines, was familiar to Bonnie and Clyde on their journeys through Iowa — remember that Dexfield Park where Buck and Blanche were captured the previous year lay not far away (see map page 165). Travelling now in one car — a Pontiac bearing Iowa plate 13-1234 — with Henry Methvin, no doubt they were short of funds since their last recorded robbery was back in February in Texas. After the killing of the Highway Patrolmen at Grapevine, the three had become separated from Joe Palmer . . . and their time was rapidly running out. Bonnie and Clyde now had less than six weeks to live. In these small backwater townships, strangers stood out and the Pontiac was spotted by several people that Monday morning. *Centre:* The bank is now occupied by the Stuart Police Department. *Above:* Here we are looking south on North Division Street with the bank on the corner of North 2nd which crosses from east to west. Bonnie parked where the mini van now stands in a small alley. The brick building on the right was then occupied by Sam Kirlin, the leader of the vigilantes who pursued the robbers. He came out of his house to go downtown while Bonnie was parked there and had to walk round her car as it blocked the sidewalk. The old timers never let Sam forget that he failed to recognise her! Facing the bank is the now-empty Kozy Korner cafe.

There are two separate vaults — this is the one closest to the door where the staff were herded and Marty Black was kindly allowed to take pictures . . . although his motives were questioned by the lady police officer!

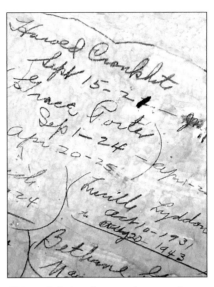

Although it has been redecorated, one area inside the vault has been left to show the names of former bank employees written on the wall, including those of Harold Cronkhite (left) and Lucille Lyddon mentioned in the press report.

Two cars of vigilantes left Stuart after the robbery trying to trace the route the robbers took. One car went to Dexter and found the car had gone east off of No. 6 at the Shaw corner east of Dexter, then turned south on the Penn Center Road. Inquiry along that road disclosed the fact that the car had travelled a considerable distance on the Penn Center Road but trace of it was lost after that.

Before the robbery both of the bandits and the woman were observed by a number of people about town. The woman was young and dressed in red. Both men were young, the taller one about 22 years old, was dressed in a gray suit and wore a shirt open at his throat; he was of sandy complexion and about average height. The other one appeared to be about 25 years old; was darker and several inches shorter than his companion and wore dark clothes. Both wore hats, one of which was green colored. Both carried automatic guns and during the robbery appeared to be rather nervous.

The car was noticed earlier in the morning by Mrs. Bert Barnett and daughter near the Lincoln Center school house.

The bandits came from the east and drove to the Standard Oil Station, conducted by the Miller brothers and had the car filled with gas by Vic Miller, who put in ten gallons of ethyl and as the tank was not quite full put in almost one gallon of ordinary gas. While the car was being serviced, Mr. Bracewell wrote down the number of the car as he thought the occupants were a hard looking lot. The car went west from the station.

About 8:30 it was standing in the street just south of Mrs Bess Gere's garage, a block north of Nassau Street. While there one of the men left it and went downtown. The car was later seen at the alley back of Ivan McGinnis' store on Division Street and moved south a short distance west of the store where one of the men went into the opening just back of the McGinnis store.

Mr. Smith, who works for Mr. McGinnis, watched the men for a while and saw them go past the bank and then go east. They went into Lovely's drug store where Verne Lovely served them with cokes. While doing so, Verne noticed that they smelled of liquor. The bandits went from the drug store to the bank.

The bank officials did not state just how much money the bandits took, but it probably wasn't over $1,500 and possibly less. The bank is protected by insurance and there will be no loss to the bank.

It was reported Tuesday that the bandits' car had tire trouble and drove into a farmer's yard near the Fred Imboden corner, three miles north of Pitzer. They were about ten minutes making the change and were reported to have gone east when they left.

The bandits worked fast and were in the bank only a few minutes. They were out and gone in several minutes before anyone knew that anything had happened. Quite a crowd gathered at the bank and in the street after the robbery.

This is the second robbery for the National Bank; the first one was pulled in March ten or eleven years ago and was a night time job. The robbers were discovered by J. K. Myers, nightwatch, and in the battle with the bandits. Mr. Myers was shot and afterwards died from the effects of the wound.

The Stuart Herald, April 20, 1934

Glenn Bufkin, pictured the year before he died in 1999. As Clyde left the bank, Glenn held the door open for him to leave and then, hearing the cries of those in the vault, released them.

Bonnie is believed to have pulled round the corner and halted where the minivan is parked, motor running ready to pick the boys up as they emerged from the bank. They then took off straight ahead, due south, to the next corner just short of the railroad-tracks where they made a left onto Route 6 (now the 925) to escape eastwards towards Dexter.

Whether Clyde was responsible for the theft of the Pontiac in Topeka on April 7 is debatable, but what is certain is that he was there three weeks later when Jesse Warren's new Ford sedan was stolen from outside his home at 2107 Gabler Street *(right and below)*. On Sunday, April 29, neighbours reported seeing a Plymouth coupe cruising the area. Mrs Warren had been out in the car that afternoon and on her return had parked and left the keys in the ignition. As she got out she remarked to a neighbour: 'It's gone 1,243 miles so now we can step it up' — a reference to the days when all new cars had to be 'run in' for the first thousand miles or so. Soon after Mrs Warren went indoors the Plymouth approached. A man and a woman were inside with a second man standing on the running board and, as the vehicle slowed outside No. 2107, the man jumped off, slipped behind the wheel of the Ford and took off.

April 29, 1934 – Topeka, Kansas

Clyde Barrow, notorious outlaw, may or may not have been in Topeka Saturday night, but reports current all over the country that he stole an automobile here created no little excitement among local officers.

The Federal Department of Justice sent notices to sheriffs in Oklahoma, Missouri and Kansas the description of a Pontiac coach stolen from C. W. Page, motor car salesman, on the theory that Barrow might have been the thief. Radio stations broadcast the report. Newspapers from all over the Middle West began calling the Topeka police station for latest bulletins concerning the visit of Barrow and his red-headed companion, Bonnie Parker.

The editors wanted to know if the outlaw and his pal shot their way out of Topeka, or if they just slipped in and stole a car to continue their mad career of crime, which has taken a heavy toll of life, and for weeks has kept every peace officer between the Mississippi river and the Rocky mountains awake

nights trying to catch the fleeing murderer who specializes in machine-gunning policemen and sheriffs.

The Department of Justice strengthened the suspicion that Barrow might have been in Topeka, and possibly stole the Page car, by announcing yesterday the finding near Ottawa of the abandoned, bullet-ridden machine in which Barrow had evaded officers since the killing of two Texas officers Sunday, April 1, and later shot to death Cal Campbell, Commerce, Oklahoma police chief, last Friday.

Page's black Pontiac coach, bearing license plates 3-3445 was stolen from 405 Douthitt, between 6:30 and 7:30 o'clock Saturday night. It belonged to the Gutting Motor Company, for which Page is a salesman. There was no indication when the bandit's car was left beside a haystack near Ottawa. It might have been Saturday.

When Page reported the loss of his car, a member of the police force jocosely

remarked that 'Dillinger is supposed to be in this part of the country, or, perhaps Barrow stole it.' Which may or may not have started the wild rumors that Barrow and Bonnie Parker paid the Capital City a visit. They usually steal another car whenever they hit a new town.

Topeka's police officers were inclined to discount the rumors and reports that the 'Scourge of the Southwest' had paid their city a visit. They had not recovered Page's car last night. They say that Barrow 'could have stolen it.' However, the Federal Department of Justice is hot on Barrow's trail and are overlooking no bets. Every clue is traced to determine the movements of the most-wanted man since Jesse James cut his historic swath, which was a narrow cowpath compared to the wide trail of murder Barrow has blazed with his machine guns during the past few months.

Topeka Daily Capital, April 9, 1934

When Mrs Warren noticed that her car was missing, she telephoned her husband (he was a roofing contractor with offices on Jackson Street) to see if, perhaps he had taken it without telling her — but he hadn't.

The American Ford Model 40 was basically just a larger version of the 1932 British Model Y *(left)* which had been designed by E. T. 'Bob' Gregorie. This had been Bob's first assignment at Dearborn under Edsel Ford, and Edsel and

Henry Ford (seen here with a company executive) so liked the slightly heart-shaped grille and the suicide doors of the European model that they just had the car scaled up for the 1933 US version *(right)* but fitted with the more powerful V-8.

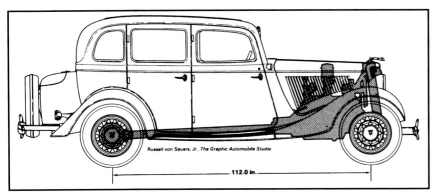

Russell von Sauers, Jr., The Graphic Automobile Studio

112.0 in.

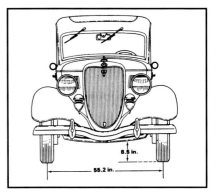

8.5 in.

55.2 in.

So why was this particular Ford so special? It is special because it was the last car Bonnie and Clyde were to steal and the one in which they were to meet their deaths just 24 days later. When Associated Press telephoned Mrs Warren on May 24 to check the serial number of their car, it matched with the one in Louisiana (649-198) although the Warren's Kansas

licence plate 3-17832 had been changed for one from Arkansas bearing the number 15-368. The Warrens had only recently taken delivery of the cordoba grey Model 40 with an olive tan mohair interior but, when they finally got the car back, an additional 7,612 miles had been put on the clock — an average of 300 miles per day.

Technical Characteristics

Type: 4-door Sedan

Make and model: Ford Model 40

Manufacturer: Ford Motor Company, Dearborn, Michigan

ENGINE
Type: L-head V-8, water-cooled, cast-iron block, detachable aluminium heads, 3 mains, full pressure lubrication
Bore & stroke: 3.0625 × 3.75 in.
Displacement: 221 cubic in.
Power output: 85 at 3,800 rpm
Torque: 150 at 2,200 rpm
Compression ratio: 6.3:1.
Induction system: 2-bbl. downdraft carb, mechanical fuel pump.
Exhaust system: Cast-iron manifolds, cross pipe, single muffler.

CLUTCH
Type: Single dry plate, woven asbestos lining.
Diameter: 9 in.
Actuation: Mechanical foot pedal.

GEARBOX
Type: 3-speed manual, floor lever, synchro 2-3.
Ratios: 1st 2.820:1
2nd 1.604:1
3rd 1.000:1
Reverse 3.383:1

TRANSMISSION
Type: Spiral bevel gears, torque tube drive.
Ratio: 4.11:1.
Drive axles: 3/4 floating

SUSPENSION
Front: I-beam axle, semi-elliptic transverse spring, hydraulic lever shocks.
Rear: Solid axle, semi-elliptic transverse spring, hydraulic lever shocks.

CHASSIS
Frame: Channel-section steel, double dropped, central X-member.

STEERING
Type: Worm & sector
Turns lock to lock: 3.5.
Ratio: 15:1
Turning circle: 40 ft.

BRAKES
Type: 4-wheel mechanical drums, internal expanding.
Drum diameter: 12 in.
Total lining area: 186 sq. in.

WHEELS AND TYRES
Tyres: Tube-type 5.50 × 17, 4-ply
Wheels: Welded spoke, drop-center rims, lug-bolted to drums.

ELECTRICAL SYSTEM:
6-volt battery/coil

BODYWORK
Body construction: Wood and steel.

DIMENSIONS
Wheelbase: 112 in.
Overall length: 182.9 in.
Overall height: 68 in.
Overall width: 68 in.
Front tread: 55.2 in.
Rear tread: 56.7 in.
Ground clearance: 8.5 in.

CAPACITIES
Crankcase: 5 qt.
Cooling system: 21 qt.
Fuel tank: 14 gal.

WEIGHT
Curb weight: 2,599 lb.

FUEL CONSUMPTION
Best: 23 mpg
Average: 16-19 mpg.

PERFORMANCE
0-50 mph: 10.6 sec.
0-60 mph: 16.8 sec.
Top speed: 81.82 mph.

OPTIONS
Clock, greyhound radiator ornament, Potter Mfg. Co. trunk, whitewalls.

PRICE (1934)
$615 f.o.b. Dearborn.

May 3, 1934 – Everly, Iowa

At about 1:00 p.m. last Thursday a Ford V-8 car bearing a Calhoun county license and containing two men and two women stopped at the South Ocheydan Street station for oil and gas. From there they drove to the first cross street north, where both men got out and proceeded north as far as the Methodist church, where they turned east on Third Street and proceeded to Main Street, where they entered the front door of the bank. Meanwhile the women drove east on Second Street and then to a point near the telephone station on Third Street, where they had a clear view of both the front and side door of the bank. After noticing that the two men had been in the bank long enough to rob it the women drove the car west on Third Street to a point near the side door of the bank.

After entering the bank one of the bandits tossed a bill to the cashier for change. The latter noted that it was a $5 bill and looked at the owner only to see a gun drawn on him while the bandit said: 'This is a stick-up.'

H. C. Clark, a local restauranteur, had just cashed checks to the amount of $20 which the robbers took with all money in the cages, as both were armed. One stayed mostly near the front door during the robbery. Mr. Clark was ordered to get in behind the counter through the east end gate but it was locked, whereupon the bandit said 'jump it,' and the order was promptly obeyed because Mr. Clark felt an automatic gun rammed against his side.

Mr. Clark was the only customer in the bank at the time and he was ordered into the vault with the cashier and Mrs. Rudolph Holst, stenographer for the First National Bank receiver, John Lawler, who had not returned from dinner.

In the vault Cashier Goodspeed was ordered to open the safe but replied that he did not know the combination, as the safe is not part of the branch bank equipment. The bandit then extracted the shells from a gun kept in the vault and threw the weapon on the floor. Upon leaving he closed the vault door upon the trio but the bolts failed to work, so the prisoners got out soon after the bandits left via the southside door, where the two women had the car ready for a rapid escape. They turned from Third Street to Ocheydan Street so rapidly that their rig

nearly capsized. The loss is about $700, but is insured.

At the outset the bandits ordered their captives to make no noise, and the whole affair worked out with clock-like precision. However, we imagine Mr. Clark made some noise when he jumped over that gate.

The cashier showed Goodspeed notifying officers of the parent bank at Spencer, while some of them and the sheriff were not slow getting over there, but the robbers are still at large, although the crime was quickly reported by daily papers and radio stations.

The robbers first appeared here at about 9:00 a.m. last Thursday when they bought a can of tire patches at Lucht's service station on North Ocheydan Street. After cruising around a few hours they evidently decided upon the time of attack and how to get away safely. Neither of them were masked and many people here say they could identify both in a showup of prisoners.

Everly News, May 10, 1934

And 300 miles of that total on the odometer of the Warren Ford was added by motoring north to Iowa for their next — and last — robbery at Everly. It was Thursday, May 3 when the car was spotted, now bearing an Iowa plate but with the easily remembered number 13-1234. (Everly lies in Clay county, the county of Calhoun mentioned in the press report lying some 50 miles away to the south-east — see map page 155.) *Top:* The bank that Clyde had his eyes on was a branch of the Farmers Trust and Savings Bank located at 301 North Main Street. *Above:* Remodelled and extended in the 1980s, it is now the State Bank which also has branches in Peterson and Spencer. Note that the local paper describes there being two men and two women in the car. In actual fact it was Clyde with Henry Methvin and Joe Palmer — and of course Bonnie. This was the last time they would see Joe. After the robbery he said that he wanted to go to see the World's Fair then taking place in Chicago, but this did not appeal to the others who were planning to go to Louisiana to visit Henry's father.

Then . . . . and now in Everly, Iowa. *Above:* Miss Bertha Holst, the bank's book-keeper, with the manager Mr O. E. Goodspeed and Mr H. C. Clark, the customer who was in the bank when the robbery took place. *Below:* Wayne Johnson, president and chief executive officer, with cashier Karla Saboe.

Clyde dropped off Joe outside Joplin as they travelled south to the Methvin home near Gibsland in northern Louisiana. This was located in Bienville parish (counties in Louisiana being referred to as parishes). Apart from the connection with the Methvins, Clyde was familiar with the area as the kidnapping of Dillard Darby and Sophia Stone (see page 115) took place not far away. They arrived within a couple of days of leaving Iowa and, after leaving Henry with his people, Clyde and Bonnie headed for Dallas to see their own families. With lawmen all over the Mid- and Southwest gunning for them, they knew that their violent career must be nearing its final showdown. There was some talk of them retiring and buying a place in Louisiana yet, as Clyde predicted in his public letter to Hamilton (page 230), 'I know that some day they will get me but it won't be without resistance'. For two years they had been on the run with Clyde being implicated in 12 murders, nine of them lawmen: Undersheriff Eugene Moore at Stringtown on August 5, 1932; Sheriff Malcolm Davis in Dallas on January 6, 1933; Detective Harry McGinnis and Constable Wes Harryman in Joplin on April 13; City Marshal Henry Humphrey near Alma on June 23; Major Joseph Crowson at Huntsville on January 16, 1934; Highway Patrolmen H. D. Murphy and Edward Wheeler at Grapevine on April 1, and Constable Cal Campbell at Commerce on April 6. Although he may not have pulled the trigger, Clyde was an accessory, before or after the fact. There had also been nine gun-battles with the law: Mabank on April 18, 1932; Wharton, August 15; Dallas, January 6, 1933; Joplin, April 13; Alma, June 23; Platte City, July 19; Dexfield Park, July 24; Sowers, November 22; Eastham Prison Farm, January 16, 1934. There had been hold-ups and armed robberies — no doubt many more than are covered in this book because positive evidence is not available — and perhaps hundreds of what is now termed 'TDA' — taking and driving away of motor vehicles. So, on the one hand, there is no disputing that the Barrows (by now Bonnie was giving her surname as Barrow) deserved all that was due to them, but somehow the nomadic outlaw life shared by these two young people in love tends to blind us as to how people viewed them at the time: as murderous criminals who had to be stopped at all costs.

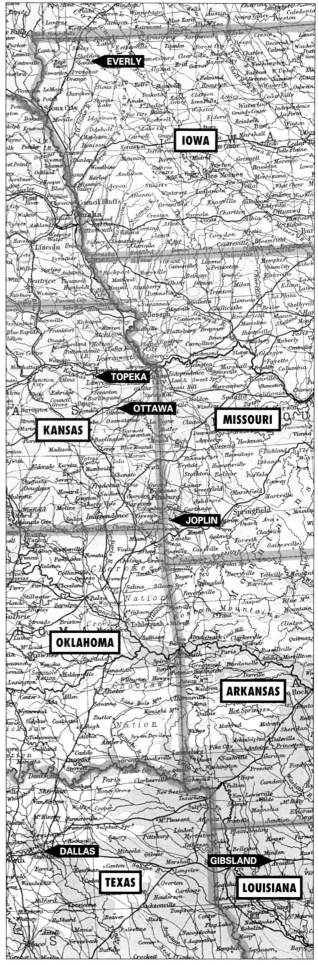

237

We saw them for the last time on Sunday evening, May 6. They drove by the filling station in West Dallas and told us where to meet them. They had chosen a spot four miles east of Dallas on a country road. We went out and were with them about two hours, I guess. I sat on the ground under the stars and talked to Bonnie for a long time that night. I remember that as she talked, she was showing me some new snapshots she and Clyde had taken.

'Mama,' she began, with that peculiar calm which she and Clyde were always in when speaking of death, 'when they kill us, don't let them take me to an undertaking parlor, will you? Bring me home.'

I reached out and seized her wrist and jerked her toward me. 'Don't, Bonnie, for God's sake!' I cried. I wanted to scream.

There she sat, so young, so lovely — only twenty-three — with the May moonlight sifting through her yellow hair and making shadows on her cheeks — there she sat and talked to me of death as calmly as if she were discussing going to the grocery store. Bonnie looked up at me and smiled. It was a funny smile — as if she were a million years older than I was; as if she knew things that I'd never learn if I lived for centuries; as if this flutter I was making about the talk of death was rather childish and so to be excused.

'Now, mama, don't get upset,' she said to me. 'Why shouldn't we talk it over? It's coming — you know it — I know it — all of Texas knows it. So don't let them keep me at the undertakers. Bring me home when I die — it's been so long since I was home. I want to lie in the front room with you and Billie and Buster sitting beside me. A long, cool, peaceful night together before I leave you. That will be nice — and restful.'

She turned one of the pictures towards me. 'I like this one,' she went on calmly. It was a picture of Clyde holding her up in his arms. They were both laughing. Bonnie's red lacquered fingers caressed the surface of the picture slowly. 'And another thing, mama,' she went on, 'when they kill us, don't ever say anything — ugly — about Clyde. Please promise me that, too.'

Bonnie gave me the poem that night, 'The Story of Bonnie and Clyde.' Clyde and Bonnie bade us all good-bye — their last goodbye — and drove away. They would be back in two weeks, they promised. But in two weeks they were dead.

EMMA PARKER, *FUGITIVES*, 1934

The Story of Bonnie and Clyde . . . by Bonnie Parker

You've read the story of Jesse James —
Of how he lived and died;
    If you're still in need
    Of something to read
Here's the story of Bonnie and Clyde.

Now Bonnie and Clyde are the Barrow gang,
I'm sure you all have read
    How they rob and steal
    And those who squeal
Are usually found dying or dead.

There's lots of untruths to those write-ups;
They're not so ruthless as that;
    Their nature is raw;
    They hate all law —
The stool pigeons, spotters, and rats.

They call them cold-blooded killers;
They say they are heartless and mean;
    But I say this with pride,
    That I once knew Clyde
When he was honest and upright and clean.

But the laws fooled around,
Kept taking him down
And locking him up in a cell,
    Till he said to me,
    "I'll never be free,
So I'll meet a few of them in hell."

The road was so dimly lighted;
There were no highway signs to guide;
    But they made up their minds
    If all roads were blind,
They wouldn't give up till they died.

The road gets dimmer and dimmer;
Sometimes you can hardly see;
    But it's fight, man to man,
    And do all you can,
For they know they can never be free.

From heart-break some people have suffered;
From weariness some people have died;
    But take it all in all,
    Our troubles are small
Till we get like Bonnie and Clyde.

If a policeman is killed in Dallas,
And they have no clue or guide;
    If they can't find a fiend,
    They just wipe the slate clean
And hang it on Bonnie and Clyde.

There's two crimes committed in America
Not accredited to the Barrow mob;
    They had no hand
    In the kidnap demand,
Nor the Kansas City Depot job.

A newsboy once said to his buddy:
"I wish old Clyde would get jumped;
    In these awful hard times
    We'd make a few dimes
If five or six cops would get bumped."

The police haven't got the report yet,
But Clyde called me up today;
    He said, "Don't start any fights —
    We aren't working nights —
We're joining the NRA."

From Irving to West Dallas viaduct
Is known as the Great Divide,
    Where the women are kin,
    And men are men,
And they won't 'stool' on Bonnie and Clyde.

If they try to act like citizens
And rent a nice little flat,
    About the third night
    They're invited to fight
By a sub-gun's rat-tat-tat.

They don't think they're too smart or desperate,
They know the law always wins;
    They've been shot at before,
    But they do not ignore
That death is the wages of sin.

Someday they'll go down together;
And they'll bury them side by side,
    To few it'll be grief —
    To the law a relief —
But it's death for Bonnie and Clyde.

BOB ALCORN, 1897-1964.

FRANK HAMER, 1884-1955

BEN GAULT, 1886-1947

Although law enforcement agencies throughout the Southwest were on the lookout for Clyde Barrow and Bonnie Parker, at the beginning of 1934 it was really only the Dallas County Sheriff's Department that had a full-time officer on the case: Bob Alcorn. When 'Smoot' Schmid became the sheriff on January 1, 1933, Alcorn had been a deputy for some eight years, and in November that year was a member of the sheriff's posse which attempted to waylay Clyde at Sowers (see pages 193-195).

Following the killing of Major Crowson (pages 202-205) the boss of the Texas Prison System, Lee Simmons, wanted revenge. His response was to establish a special post: 'Special Escape Investigator for the Texas Prison System' — a euphemistic job title for someone to 'get Clyde Barrow.' That someone was former Texas Ranger Frank Hamer who had an unrivalled reputation as a tough law-man who always got his man, albeit by doing things his own way. Hamer took up his badge again on February 10, 1934.

After the killing of the two Highway Patrolmen at Grapevine (pages 218-223) on April 1, the Texas State Police wanted one of their own men on the case. Frank Hamer insisted that he make the choice which fell on an officer who he had known and worked with for many years: Ben M. 'Manny' Gault. He had resigned from the Texas Rangers — as Hamer had done — after Miriam A. 'Ma' Ferguson became Governor of Texas in 1932 as a protest for her being too soft on criminals.

May 23, 1934 – Ambush at Gibsland, Louisiana

And so the die was cast. After the document of betrayal was signed by Governor Ferguson, it was returned to Sheriff Jordan for counter-signature. John Joyner, the Methvin intermediary, was informed the deal was on although it is not certain if he was given a copy of the agreement. (The sheriff was killed in a car accident in June 1958 and the original, presumably held by Jordan, has never been found.) After meeting with their families on May 6, Clyde, with Bonnie at his side, returned to Louisiana. There they had a bolt-hole south of Gibsland — a small cabin deep in the woods where they intended to lie up for the summer until the heat died down. One picture, reproduced in a booklet published by the *Ruston Daily Leader* in 1968, purported to show

the house — the so-called Cole farmhouse — which had been rented by Ivy Methvin in 1934 . . . but it was not the correct one! It was the private residence of Clarence Long and absolutely nothing to do with Bonnie and Clyde. The Long's were so bothered by sightseers that in the end they sued the paper for the trouble that publication of the picture had caused them. *Left:* This, on the other hand, is said to be the correct house but we are told it was intentionally burned down by owners of the land because of the continued interest showed by visitors seeking out the past. *Right:* Our sleuth, Marty Black, was determined to find the ruins and he spent ages tramping the area near Sailes where we were told the building had stood . . . but in vain!

TED HINTON, 1904-1977

Also joining in the manhunt was another Dallas county deputy, Ted Hinton. He had been appointed on January 1, 1933 when Sheriff Schmid took office and had the advantage of knowing the Barrow family and he claimed that he also knew Bonnie when she worked in the town as a waitress. As Alcorn wanted a partner to work with him on the search for Clyde, so he persuaded Schmid to release Hinton full time in April 1934. Ted Hinton's autobiography *Ambush* was published posthumously in 1979.

HENDERSON JORDAN, 1898-1958

Even while Henry Methvin was riding with Bonnie and Clyde, his parents were trying to set up a deal to get clemency for their son. A friend of the family, John Joyner, acted as a go-between to negotiate a deal through the sheriff of Bienville parish, Henderson Jordan, on the basis that Henry was willing to betray Bonnie and Clyde if he was granted a pardon from the state of Texas. At that time, Methvin had not committed the murders at Grapevine and Commerce, so Governor Ferguson agreed.

PRENTISS OAKLEY, 1905-1957

Sheriff Jordan's deputy was Prentiss Oakley. On February 19, Frank Hamer and Bob Alcorn travelled to Louisiana to meet Jordan together with a representative from the Department of Justice, Lester Kendale. The lawmen told Joyner that the arrangement had been approved and that they were prepared to draw up a formal agreement guaranteeing to wipe Henry's slate clean if he turned in Bonnie and Clyde. The document was prepared and sent to the Texas governor for signature.

Wherever the location, the lawmen knew that at some stage Bonnie and Clyde would appear in the Bienville area but their planning was rudely interrupted by the killing of the two Highway Patrolmen on Easter Sunday and Sheriff Campbell six days later. Knowing that Henry Methvin was currently with Bonnie and Clyde must have put the officers in a quandary because now it was highly possible that their 'Judas' had become a murderer. Without sight of the actual document, we cannot say if it just pardoned Henry for *past* crimes or absolved him of *all* crimes committed prior to Bonnie and Clyde being apprehended, but what we do know is that soon after the killing of the third lawman on April 6, Sheriff Jordan received a message from Henry that he was more then willing to carry out his side of the bargain. This would seem to imply that he considered the agreement absolved him from all sins. The Bienville parish sheriff may have had influence in his own sphere but certainly not up north, and the same day as

Campbell was killed the Oklahoma authorities issued a warrant for Henry's arrest, even though at that stage he was only referred to as 'John Doe'. Things were now rapidly drawing to a conclusion: the lawmen's plan being to set up an ambush on the road to the Methvin place and wait for Bonnie and Clyde to appear. But they had to be alone . . . somehow Henry had to absent himself. His chance came on Monday, May 21 when Clyde proposed driving to Shreveport, 40 miles to the west, to get something to eat. Henry told his parents that he would find an opportunity to slip away so they in turn advised Joyner who passed on the information to Sheriff Jordan. In Shreveport, Clyde pulled up outside the Majestic Cafe at 422 Milam Street and told Henry to go and buy three rounds of sandwiches. However, a police patrol car appeared and Clyde, thinking that they had been spotted, took off in a hurry leaving Henry behind. *Above:* We were lucky to find a local police vehicle parked right opposite the cafe — now Panos' Diner.

241

The four out-of-state lawmen — Alcorn, Hamer, Hinton and Gault — were currently staying at the Inn Hotel. Calling them down to his office, the local police chief told them about the incident outside the Majestic Cafe when his officers 'spooked' a car parked outside. 'The most interesting part of the story', related Ted Hinton later in his book *Ambush*, 'was what was happening inside the restaurant at that time. A young man was waiting for a stack of sandwiches and soft drinks "to go" [*i.e. a takeaway — Ed*]. When the young man noticed the car outside hurry away, he got up and left without even a fare-thee-well, without his sandwiches, and without paying for them. I glanced at Alcorn and nodded. "Henry Methvin," he said. Police Chief Bryant said he wasn't certain, but that had entered his mind. The waitress who had taken the order had told him she didn't know the man, never saw him before in her life.

But she swore she would know him the next time he came in. Next morning, we took our breakfast at the Majestic and learned from the manager the name of the lady who had waited on the fellow who had walked out. She agreed to come down to talk to us, even though she was not due to come in until the evening shift. I handed her a sheaf of photographs. "See anybody in there who looks like the man who wouldn't wait for his sandwiches?" She picked out the picture of Henry Methvin straight away. "That's him," she said. "Same eyes, same pimply face. There's no mistake."' *Above:* Following the trail of Bonnie and Clyde on the road to Gibsland in May 2003, Marty Black discusses the incident over breakfast with the current owner of the cafe, Andrew Panos, who purchased it 29 years ago, having emigrated to the States from Greece after the Second World War. The interior has since been extended.

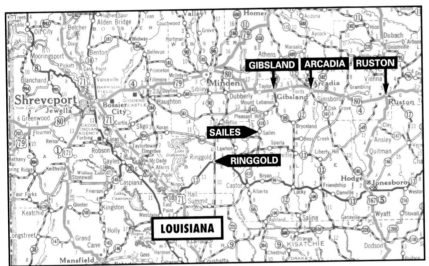

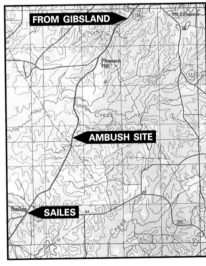

However, for reasons best known to himself, Ted Hinton (in *Ambush*) makes no mention of the pre-arranged plan to 'set up' Bonnie and Clyde even though the scheme is well attested by several principals on both sides and in later court testimony. He must have known about it but it seems that Hinton would prefer us to think it was just good police work . . . and good luck! Nevertheless, he is the only one of the six lawmen to have left a detailed account of what took place. 'Our next move was to recognise what Clyde and Bonnie would do in such a situation. With Henry afoot and out of touch, they'd make an effort to get back together again. They'd circle back to Ivy Methvin's place, near Mount Lebanon, south of Gibsland, and Old Man Methvin soon would be hearing from Henry down there. Alcorn and I had spent some miserable time down there already, avoiding direct contact with the senior Methvin but learning the region in what is called the Black Lake area over in Bienville parish. One man who would know the swampy, tree-covered Black Lake area of Louisiana best would be Sheriff Henderson Jordan of Bienville parish at the court-house in Arcadia. It was common courtesy to let him know we were coming back to his territory again, and he would do anything

we asked. Our plan to set up an ambush near Methvin's place still appeared to be sound; Methvin was not with them, we could be sure of that. We passed on through Gibsland, where we would return to make the run down to Mount Lebanon as soon as we could get with Sheriff Jordan and tell him our plan. Arcadia, the parish seat where Jordan headquartered, is a sleepy trading center of about three thousand people serving the farm and lumbering region around it. It was already late afternoon when we saw Sheriff Jordan and told him what we had heard and seen — and of our intention to stake out the most likely road leading down to Ivy Methvin's place. Jordan knew the country like the back of his hand; he could recognize Methvin on sight and knew all about him. It was settled between us where we would meet; he would get his deputy, Prentiss M. Oakley, and join us there a little later. We had a good and hurried evening meal, ordered a supply of sandwiches, filled a water can with ice water, and headed back toward Gibsland. There we turned south on what the natives call the "Big Road" through Mount Lebanon, taking the right turn at the "Y" south-west toward Sailes. This was the only graveled road that would lead out to Methvin's place.'

'We were about eight miles south-west from Gibsland when I pulled off the road and into a covering of trees. Hamer pulled up alongside in his car. There was no way we would be seen here by the passing traffic. Moss-covered trees grew so close to the road at this point that we were hidden from view — but we could see anyone approaching for almost a half mile on the road from either direction, which appeared to me to be generally east and west at this point. Our position was on the south side of the road, on a high point in underbrush that commanded a view of the road as it inclined upward at about twenty degrees on either side of us. We settled in about 9 p.m. Monday for an all-night vigil.'

This is the ambush site looking south — then and now. Although the tree-line has been cut back and the road widened since 1934, it still bears the same line giving an uninterrupted view for at least half a mile. Unfortunately two new forest tracks have recently been cut on either side of the spot occupied by the lawmen on the left.

It was a perfect spot for an ambush as the road in the opposite direction gave the lawmen a clear view for nearly three-quarters of a mile. This was the most probable way Clyde would come as he would be driving north to south to reach the Methvins. *Above:* Ted Hinton, left, armed with a BAR and Bob Alcorn at the ready.

A news photographer with the *Dallas Times Herald* had given Ted a Bell & Howell 16mm cine camera telling him that 'you need to carry it with you 'cause you're going to get 'em eventually and, when you do, you're going to need to document it'. However, this still is from a later re-enactment documentary.

'Boots' Hinton, Ted's son, kindly gave us permission to reproduce stills from his father's film. Here, he recreates the scene with the local sheriff, Ricky Hay, on the anniversary of the ambush in May 2003. 'Boots' never visited the site with his father.

Although Hinton says that they took up station on Monday evening (May 21), when Clyde, Bonnie and Henry were in Shreveport, and that he was joined soon afterwards by Sheriff Jordan and his deputy, this time is disputed by Jordan (page 252) and Hamer (page 255). The vehicles were run into the woodland so they were invisible from the road. *Above:* The lawmen were positioned in a line on the high bank on the north-east side of the road, hoping that the car would be travelling north to south which they considered the most likely directi.. to reach the Methvin place. Although Hinton writes that he was stationed first on the right as they faced the road, there is little doubt that Alcorn was at the head of the line as he was the one who could best recognise Clyde and Bonnie. Next to Hinton was Oakley, Jordan, Gault with Hamer on the far left. Should Clyde appear from the south, i.e. the right-hand side of this photo, then Alcorn would be last in line. *Right:* Marty Black scales the same bank to overlook the Ringgold Road.

Left: Alcorn was armed with a .30 Remington Model 8 semi-automatic rifle. This is another still from the re-enactment. (If Hinton had the military BAR, which one of the lawmen carried the Colt Monitor, the civilianised version produced specially for police departments, now displayed at Waco — see page 275?) Hinton: 'It became a tedious and uncomfortable time. Seldom have I ever been in such a nest of vindictive mosquitoes; they attacked the ears and neck and even the nose and mouth. They made the night pass slowly. We were dirty and unshaven; the night and day in the underbrush had left every exposed part of our face and arms crimson with smeared blood from the niggling bugs. I had a feeling, which I am certain was shared by Bob Alcorn and by Hamer and Gault, that the fugitives would appear any minute now on this road. We would take our stance, get them into our gunsights as they approached and, at the proper time, one or two of us would rise up and give them an opportunity to "Halt". In our hearts, no one had the slightest idea they would heed the command, but it would be given nonetheless.'

The second night seemed even longer than the previous one. Log truck traffic stopped at sundown; only a few cars had passed during the day. We had watched each one and were dead certain Clyde and Bonnie had not passed this way since we had taken our places in the brush and weeds with its mosquitoes, chiggers, ticks, and lice. The night with its miseries passed slowly; I glanced at my pocket watch and it was 4:17 a.m. And we settled back to wait some more.

In a short time, the silence was punctuated by the slight cough of a Model A Ford truck in the distance; as certain as the sounds of birds and animals in a swampland can be identified, the truck noise brought us to attention. We could be reasonably sure if a Model A Ford truck appeared here, it would be Ivy Methvin's.

We would stop him and see what he would tell us. Henderson Jordan said, 'Mr Methvin, we're going to have to turn that truck around, and we're going to discourage you from leaving, so you won't mind if we just kinda take you right over here easy like. We're not going to hurt you, but we'll put you right over here where you'll be safe . . . and you'll just sit quiet like.'

The truth is, Methvin protested stoutly and to no avail. He was handcuffed to a tree some distance behind our position alongside the road where we still waited, hoping to encounter Clyde and Bonnie. His arms were extended and his wrists snapped together with handcuffs so that he embraced the slender tree. The position was not quite so uncomfortable as it might appear. He could stand or he could sit. But he wasn't about to go anywhere until we allowed him to go, and that was for sure.

Even by the standards of 1934, Methvin's civil rights were violated. A case might have been made under the newly enacted Lindbergh Kidnap Law, put in by the federals, that he was 'kidnapped'. But none of the six of us who were intent on capturing or stopping Clyde and Bonnie were thinking at that moment about whether we were justified in doing what we were doing [but see page 292 — Ed].

Alcorn got into the truck and turned it around without turning on the lights. For our purpose, we wanted it facing east — but in the wrong lane of traffic at the side of the road.

Quickly we jacked up the truck's right front wheel, which would be the one in the dead center of the road, and removed the wheel. The truck would stand as bait for Clyde, who would know in an instant this was Old Man Methvin's truck. The absence of the wheel and the jacked-up right front would cause him to slow, if not to stop completely, to offer help.

Dawn broke but still there was no Clyde Barrow. It was 9 a.m. now, and a couple of log trucks already had slowed at the sight of Methvin's Model A truck, but seeing no one around it, they resumed their speed and passed on.

We began to discuss our situation. Two miserable nights and a full day had passed, and all of it had netted us nothing but another disappointment. The food we had brought was gone. We looked like the wrath of God — unshaven, eyes bloodshot, and feeling the wear of no sleep since Sunday. This was Wednesday, May 23, 1934. We agreed that we'd give it another thirty minutes, until 9:30 a.m., and then we would throw the coffee on the fire and call in the dogs, to use one of Alcorn's expressions from his hunting days.

My BAR with a full clip of twenty steel-penetrating rounds in it, my shotgun — a deadly automatic with five rounds at the ready — and two .45 caliber pistols with full clips of ammo were ready for whatever happened in the next few minutes. It was 9:15.

In the distance out of view, we heard a sound. My BAR went up to my shoulder, my sights on the top of the hill where anything coming over it would appear. Call it intuition, but somehow I knew; I felt a sensation that I won't describe as eagerness, or fear, but a sensation nonetheless when your senses tell you that a gunfight is about to begin. You will shoot at another human being, and likely, you will be shot at.

I remember the next moments so clearly, it seems I am living them right now. All of us are concealed, but the car moving toward us is in view now, at full speed, the only way Clyde ever drove. He has caught sight of the truck and appears already to be slowing. 'This is him,' I tell Alcorn. 'This is it, it's Clyde.'

TED HINTON, *AMBUSH*, 1979

Earlier that fatal Wednesday, nine miles north of the ambush set-up, Clyde pulled up outside Rosa Canfield's cafe in Gibsland. We do not know where they had spent the last 36 hours since losing Henry Methvin in Shreveport on Monday but now they stopped at one of their previous eating places for breakfast. Bonnie took two sandwiches with her when they climbed back into the Warren's automobile parked outside.

Above: Then, Gibsland was a regular watering hole on the main east-west Route 80 across northern Louisiana; now, Gibsland is dead since Interstate 20 bypassed the town to the north. No sandwiches today at Rosa's when we knocked on the shut-up cafe at 9 a. m. on May 23, 2003. From this very spot, Clyde and Bonnie set off on their last ride together . . . they now had less than 15 minutes to live.

Sixty-nine years later, another Ford Fordor sedan re-enacts the lonely ride to an appointment with death.

Centre left: **Proceeding south on Highway 154, then gravel-surfaced, out of Gibsland.** *Centre right:* **Soon they would bear right at the Mt Lebanon crossroads, and continue on 154 in the direction of Sailes.**

Above left: **Keep left at the 'Y' junction . . . before reaching the Texas Historical Commission marker** *(above)* **which now stands as a signpost indicating that the ambush location is just one mile ahead.**

At this point the car was about to come into the view of the lawmen . . . lined up, weapons at the ready, in the forest on the left-hand side of the road on the crest in the far distance. Now there is just a few hundred yards to go.

The car has descended the hill and is approaching our position at the crest of the long and slowly rising incline. I could squeeze the trigger; I could blow the man's head off. But he is slowing; his eyes are on the truck, on the jacked-up right front of the truck in the middle of the road. He will drive in front of it, or he will come into the lane nearer to me. His eyes are still on the truck. He knows this is Methvin's truck, but he sees no one.

He has pulled even with the engine part of the parked truck, twenty feet in front of me, and he is in my gunsight, though his car is still moving. Suddenly, Alcorn's deep bellow 'HALT!' arouses him. Alongside him Bonnie screams, and I fire and everyone fires, and in the awful hell and noise Clyde is reaching for a weapon and the wheels are digging into the gravel as he makes a start to get away. My BAR spits out twenty shots in an instant, and a drumbeat of shells knifes through the steel body of the car, and glass is shattering. For a fleeting instant, the car seems to melt and hang in a kind of eerie and animated suspension, trying to move forward, spitting gravel at the wheels, but unable to break through the shield of withering fire. I see a weapon go up;

Clyde's head has popped backward, his face twisted at the shock of pain as the bullets strike home.

No shots are firing from inside the car, but I do not notice. Now my shotgun is in my hand; the tan car seems to rock as it absorbs the blasts, but the car is moving forward, it is thirty feet away, thirty-five, it is getting away — the shotgun blasts seem to be urging the car onward. It is running out of control, down the hill now. My God, are they getting away again? Could they possibly survive all this?

The shotgun has used up its automatic five shots. My ears are ringing, there is a spinning and reeling in my head from the cannonade of bullets and the clank of steel-jacketed metal tearing steel. Without thinking, I am chasing after the car, firing my first pistol until it has emptied, and I am squarely between the officers who still are firing from above me and the car that is rolling absurdly to the left and heading for the bar ditch about thirty or forty yards beyond our stake-out position among the weeds and underbrush.

TEN HINTON, *AMBUSH*, 1979

The Ford slowed as Clyde spots Methvin's lorry, seemingly broken down in the nearside lane. 'This is it . . . it's Clyde'. These fatal words, whispered by Ted Hinton as he recognised the driver, sealed their fate.

'I fire again at the sickening bloody forms inside the car and rush to the driver's side to grab the door handle where Clyde is slumped forward, the back of his head a mat of blood. There is no room to open the door . . .

. . . it is wedged against the embankment where the car has come to rest. With the energy that comes from who knows where, I scramble over the hood of the car and throw open the door on Bonnie's side. The impression will linger with me from this instant — I see her falling out of the opened door, a beautiful and petite young girl who is soft and warm, with hair carefully fixed, and I smell a light perfume against the burned-cordite smell of gunpowder, the sweet and unreal smell of blood. I stand her up, full standing, a tiny frail girl she seems now, and I cannot believe that I do not really feel her breathing, but I look into her face and I see that she is dead. I carefully put her down in the car seat once more.'

'It is only an instant, a fleeting split-second, and a thousand impressions are branded into my head which is searing and ringing with shots. The shots are not coming now. I reach over Bonnie to pull a pistol from Clyde's hand, and the weapon is cold. I know it has not been fired without looking at it because it has the cold feel of gunmetal, and the hand that had clutched it is still and growing stiff and slate gray against the crimson of the blood, which is everywhere.'

'There was a sandwich that Bonnie had been eating; there was a Louisiana road map that was flecked with blood on the seat beside her. Clyde's Browning Automatic Rifle was at his knee; he had lifted it up to the window, for it was seen there. But it was not fired. Now we could see why it was not fired. One of our bullets had struck it. He had put the larger weapon aside and had reached for a pistol to fire in one last defiant act. But he never pulled the trigger.'

Sheriff Jordan inspects the contents as Hinton films the car: 'The inventory showed, in addition to the shotgun and pistol that Bonnie had in the front seat and the unfired pistol I had removed from Clyde's hand and the bullet-damaged BAR he had at his knee, three more Browning Automatic Rifles and several pistols, including one .45 caliber Colt automatic, four .45 caliber automatics, and two .38 caliber automatics. Under the back seat we found fifteen license plates, mostly from Louisiana, Arkansas, and Texas. In the rear seat were two Gladstone traveling bags of clothing, a grocery sack of canned goods and some sandwiches, and something more than a thousand rounds of ammo, including fifty clips of automatic rifle and pistol bullets. There was some camping equipment in the trunk — and Clyde's saxophone. And there were the map, Bonnie's cosmetics, Clyde's sunglasses, a detective magazine, and Bonnie's partly-eaten sandwich. Clyde had something over five hundred dollars in his wallet — we didn't bother to count it close but just noticed it.'

I am sorry I cannot divulge my source of my information and my tips, but I had made connections that proved very valuable to me. To tell the source might cause someone to get killed. I had received information that Clyde Barrow and Bonnie Parker had been visiting in the north end of Natchitoches parish. This information came from an authentic source. We studied the case and got a line on the movements of the two. At that time I contacted Agent Kendale of the Department of Justice, and the Texas officers who were with Deputy Oakley and in at the finish. The seven of us unearthed a number of facts about Barrow and Miss Parker.

Two weeks ago I called Captain Frank Hamer and the other three Texas officers and had them come in to Shreveport, where they were to await my call.

We laid a trap for them and Barrow drove his car right into it. My officers have been working on locating his hideout in Natchitoches parish for some weeks, and we had the whole thing pretty well mapped out with the information I was receiving.

On Tuesday evening at 8:30 I received the information that Barrow and Bonnie had passed throug Gibsland twice during the afternoon. We knew what kind of car they were driving, and there was no chance of us being wrong. I called

Deputy Oakley and the officers who were waiting for me in Shreveport, and we laid our trap.

We found an advantageous spot on the road we knew they were going to take, and I stationed the men so we had a clear view of the highway for some distance. I instructed them in what we were to do and cautioned them that we were dealing with a man who thought nothing of taking a life. I wanted them to take no chances.

When Bob Alcorn, a Dallas deputy, saw the car coming at shortly after nine o'clock this morning, he called to us that they were coming, and when the car came over the top of the hill we ordered them to halt. They failed to halt, and went for their guns. Barrow evidently had an automatic shotgun in his lap, for he grabbed it up.

We opened fire with automatic rifles and an automatic shotgun. It ran probably 40 feet, left the highway and hit an embankment. They were both dead when we got to them. Barrow had one of the Browning machine guns between him and the door on the left side.

We didn't take any long chances. When Barrow failed to stop, we opened fire. He was driving at a moderate speed.

SHERIFF HENDERSON JORDAN, MAY 24, 1934

The weapons were placed in Sheriff Jordan's car while he and Oakley drove to Arcadia to fetch the coroner. It was decided to leave the bodies in situ until he arrived so Alcorn and Gault were left to guard the car as sightseers were already arriving. Meanwhile, Hinton and Hamer drove to Gibsland to get a breakdown truck. There, Hinton called his chief 'Smoot' Schmid in Dallas while Hamer reported to his boss, Lee Simmons in Huntsville. Both set off immediately for Louisiana. By the time the lawmen returned, a great crowd had already gathered. 'I saw women and kids struggling along with grown men to peek inside to get a better view of the bodies in death in the car,' Hinton wrote later. 'People were on their hands and knees gathering up the spent shell casings and digging with pocket knives to retrieve bullets embedded in trees.' The coroner, Dr J. L. Wade, attested that Bonnie and Clyde had died of gunshot wounds at 9.15 a.m. whereupon the wrecker pulled the Ford out of the ditch and hitched it up for the 15-mile journey to Arcadia. Sheriff Jordan and his deputy led the procession followed by Frank Hamer and Manny Gault. Ted Hinton and Bob Alcorn brought up the rear.

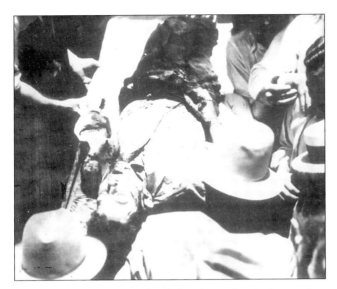

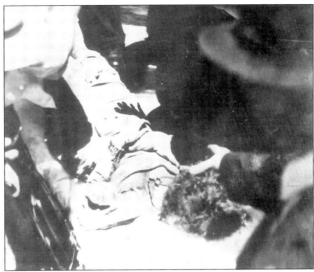

The broken bodies were unloaded at the undertaker's premises which was situated in the rear of Conger's combined furniture store and funeral parlour. The local photographer, King Murphy, was first on the scene, with his wife standing by to develop the negatives to cash in on the golden opportunity of selling the prints: $5 to the public or $50 to the press. Meanwhile Dr Wade began to examine the bodies to make out his official report on the cause of death . . . as if that was ever in doubt!

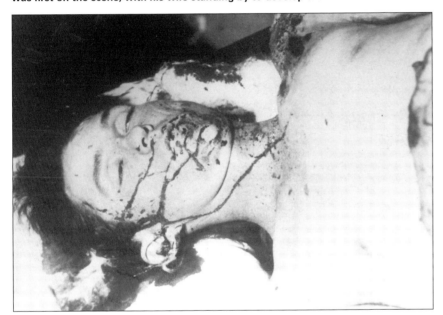

'I'm glad the trail is ended,' said Deputy Sheriff Bob Alcorn of Dallas county, Texas, who was a member of the posse and who held two warrants, one for each of the two occupants of the car, issued from a Dallas county court and charging murder.

'I have spent many hours in study of Barrow and Bonnie and their movements, and I have given most of my time for many months to bringing down these two.

'I knew Barrow on sight, having ran into him once before. His age was given at 27 but he is only 23-years-old. The Parker woman was about 26.

'But I'm glad its all over. I can rest awhile now without the worry of trying to catch this man.'

And thus history was made today in Bienville parish, when the two most famous of modern-time outlaws met death in its bounds; thus is the beginning of the last chapter in the story of Clyde Barrow, who had no regard for human life; and his sweetheart, Bonnie Parker, his lover, and alleged to be a machine-gunner of excellent record.

The Bienville Democrat, May 24, 1934

Excitement in this whole countryside ran high when word went out that Barrow and his woman companion had been killed. Officers from throughout Louisiana and Texas converged in this little city where the bodies of the two were brought by the sheriff's department. The two were removed from the site of the killing about two hours after the officers opened fire, and a procession of about 150 cars followed the remains of the notorious outlaw and his sweetheart to the Conger funeral parlors in this city. Visitors from all parts of the country came by car and plane to see the spot where the gunman and his companion met death, and to view the corpse of the man who is alleged to have slain 13 men within the past few months.

Deputy P. M. Oakley, of Sheriff Jordan's department, who was a member of the posse, drove into Arcadia to notify Coroner J. L. Wade a few minutes before ten o'clock this morning. The two were killed at 15 minutes past nine.

When the bodies of the man and woman were brought to Arcadia in the car in which they died, a procession of many hundreds of people followed, and at no time in the modern history of North Louisiana has such a crowd of interested spectators gathered in this little town of some two thousand law-abiding souls.

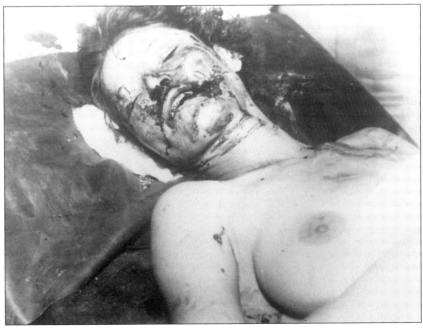

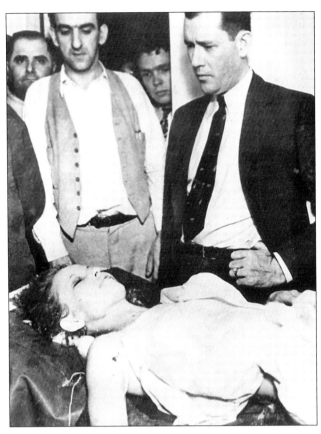

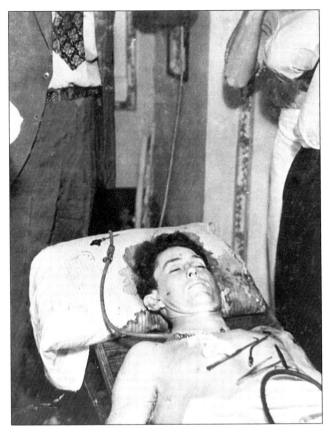

When Denny Hayes, the *Dallas Times Herald* photographer, flew in from Dallas by chartered plane, his arrival coincided with that of the law from Dallas. *Left:* Pulling up a sheet to give Bonnie some dignity, he pictured Deputy Sheriff Bill Decker, right, just as the embalming process was getting underway.

(It is standard procedure in the United States to embalm all corpses prior to burial.) One final irony was that Dillard Darby, the mortician kidnapped by Clyde the year before in Ruston, *was* called in to help (see page 117). *Right:* All we see of Sheriff Schmid is his lower half on the left!

This sleepy little town awoke Wednesday from its perennial slumber long enough to realize that it suddenly had become more than a wee dot on the map as curious visitors, frantic newspaper men and hurried photographers descended on it with a vengeance.

Two hours later it had become known that Clyde Barrow and Bonnie Parker, who boasted the notoriety of being the South-

west's No. 1 and No. 2 public enemies, had been slain by officers fifteen miles from here and their bodies brought here. Practically every resident within a radius of fifty miles was on hand standing on street corners and trying to get a glimpse of the bodies.

Earl Moore, staff photographer for *The News*, and I were assigned to make a flying trip to Arcadia for stories and pictures. We

took off from Love Field about 11 a.m. in a chartered plane piloted by Murrell Brock of Long & Harman's staff.

We landed at Shreveport because we feared the emergency field at Arcadia would not be suitable for a quick take-off. Chartering a taxicab we sped to Arcadia, Bienville parish seat, whose population is about 2,500.

In the chaotic circumstances, Dr Wade was unable to perform a full post-mortem so his report, written hastily with a pencil which soon became blunt, are almost indecipherable. Fortunately Carroll Rich made sense of the notes in his paper *The Death and Autopsy of Bonnie and Clyde* published in 1990. 'BONNIE PARKER: 2 Diam Rings — 1 wrist w [wrist watch begun here the partially deleted] gold wed ring 3rd finger left hand, Small watch on left arm, 3 acorn brooch on dress in front, 1 Catholic Cross under dress Red dress & Red shoes = Tatto on right leg 2 hearts with arrow 6 inches above R[ight] knee Roy on R[ight] Bonnie on Left side: G[un] shot wound edge of hair about 1½ in[ches] above left eye another —entered mouth on L side made no exit [deletion *sic*] Made exit at center of top skull + another about middle and Just below left Jaw bones another entering above clavicle left side ranging into neck. Another entering about 2 in below inner side left shoulder. 2 bullet wounds 1 about 2 in. below left shoulder another mid way arm fract[uring] the bone Another wound elbow left arm breaking into joint. Another shot in left breast going to chest 4 inch below Exccel [*auxilla*, the armpit] 1 shot ent[ering] left ibid 4 in[ches] below Excela breaking ribs. 6 shots entering three inches back region of left scalpula. 5 bullet wounds about middle of left thigh. Number of cut places on left leg outer side seems cut from glass, 1 cut on left ankle. 1 on top of left foot app[a]rantly from glass Bullet wound inner aspect and center of right thigh. Scar appar[en]t[l]y from burn 6 inches in length about 3½ width on outer center of right thigh appears effect of burns, another scar 6 in[ches] length 4 in[ches] width outer aspect right nee extending on across & front of knee extending 6 inches on inner side of right leg. Flesh wound inner side of right knee. Bullet wound right leg about mid way ankle and knee. Another B[ullet] wound anterior ankle, inner aspect foot about 2 in. above base of great toe. gun shot wound bone of first finger another middle finger—at bone severing the member. CLYDE BARROW: On right arm tattoode Picture of girl under which is written Grace on inner side 1 tattoo anchor and shield U.S.N. On left arm a tattoo on forearm dagger through heart and E.B.W. On left shoulder a tatoo Rose and leaves. Gun shot wound in head entering front of left ear exit about 2 inches above right ear. One entered at edge hair above left eye Several shots entering left shoulder joint. Small glass cut at joint 1st finger right hand. 7 small bullet wounds inner of right knee. A number glass cuts. Gunshot wound entering fleshy portion left thigh. 8 bullet wounds striking right side back from base of neck to angular right scapula to side back bone, one striking midway back breaking back bone.'

'The two noted desperadoes died with their guns in their hands, but without having fired a single shot.

'Bonnie's right hand, including her trigger finger, was shot off. Their bodies were literally riddled with bullets from the concentrated fire of our six rifles. They died in the car.

'Just as Clyde slumped over at the wheel the auto swerved and went into the ditch. We jumped forward and turned off the ignition.

'As inured as I am to slaughter of humans, I was sickened at the sight of Bonnie's body, nearly torn to pieces with bullets. I have always had a soft spot in my heart for women and, even though Bonnie was a despicable killer, I felt a sinking at the pit of my stomach when I opened the door and saw her.'

'We were on a graveled road near Sailes, a short distance from Gibsland. At 9:30 o'clock this morning we saw Barrow's car approaching slowly. All six of us stepped out with our automatic rifles aimed at them and I commanded them to halt. Both Clyde and Bonnie reached for their guns and had them half way up before we started shooting. Each of the five officers working with me on the detail emptied the magazines of two automatic rifles into the car.'

Word of the killing had spread like wildfire. First, Hinton's call to Dallas, made from a gas station in Gibsland, was overheard; then the telephone operator listened in to Dr. Wade's conversation with his wife before he left. As a result, people rushed hot-foot to the ambush site. The operator then informed the local paper, the *Bienville Democrat* which in turn put the news on the wire service and it reached the Dallas press by 10 a.m. During the day the crowd is estimated to have grown to over 15,000, tempers fraying as the morticians hurried to prepare the bodies for public viewing.

Five hundred persons jammed every nook and cranny of Conger's furniture store, the back of which is used as an undertaking parlor. The proprietor, when the bodies were brought in, roped off all the furniture and kept the throng milling in the aisles while back of a partition embalmers began their work.

Sheriff Henderson Jordan of Bienville parish, one of the six officers responsible for the deaths of Barrow and the Parker girl, was anxious to give the people a chance to view the bodies, but this was delayed several hours. The crowd began to grow restless and only repeated announcements that the bodies would be on view soon kept it from storming the morticians section.

The City Marshal of Arcadia admitted Moore and me to the room. We found the two outlaws literally had been shot to pieces. While the three embalmers hastened their task, made more difficult because of the scores of bullet wounds.

The undertakers estimated there were twenty-five slugs in each body. They made no effort to remove them except where necessary because of a main artery.

After an unsuccessful effort to stop the busy sheriff long enough to get details of the killing, I found Frank Hamer, former Texas Ranger captain, who had been working on the case as a special investigator. In rambling sentences interspersed with his rough humor, the old-time peace officer told how he had lain in wait by the side of the road for eight hours before the sand-colored V-8, the model with which Barrow always has been linked, wound through the sandy hills and pines into sight.

'We had definite information that they had been working in this vicinity. We laid in wait for them from 2:30 o'clock yesterday afternoon until we sighted their automobile this morning at 9:30 o'clock.

Today Conger's is no more. It was damaged in a tornado in 1992 and demolished shortly thereafter leaving a gaping hole in Railway Avenue facing the station.

Your Editor and Marty Black stand on the site of the old funeral parlour at the back of the store . . . exactly 69 years after the two outlaws were laid out on this spot.

Left: The Bienville parish court-house-cum-jail in Arcadia. The building of 1895 was demolished and the replacement built in 1953 was remodelled in 1980. Right: Recalcitrants in striped prison garb relax in the open-air exercise pen.

By this time the crowd sensing that something of more than ordinary importance was taking place at the court-house, quickly covered the half dozen blocks which separated it from the main point of interest.

The throng's choice of vantage point was well chosen. In less than five minutes the sedan that carried Clyde and Bonnie to the inglorious end of their careers was brought under its own power to the court-house yard. The windows on the left side were all shot out. More than fifty bullet holes were counted in the left front door and the windshield and the back of the car were equally well pierced.

The famous V-8 was driven into a pen surrounding the parish's jail a few yards from the court-house. The gate was locked to keep the crowd away while officers took pictures of the car and gave it another inspection.

It was here to the police compound at the jail that the death car was driven — both to secure it from souvenir hunters and to make a proper examination. Hamer (on the right with his back to the camera) believed that around 150 rounds had been fired at the car by the posse — some heavy-gauge buckshot — so altogether there are 160-plus impacts on the vehicle, some through and through from the .30-06 military ammunition. Sheriff Schmid with the floral tie is second left.

Little to match up today as the vehicle compound has now lost its chain-link fence. This is the run-in from Court House Drive.

Then . . . and now. In this reverse view of the car, the court house stands on the right. Clyde had already switched the plate once from the original Kansas 3-17832 for the Everly robbery (see pages 236-237) to Iowa 13-1234. The fact that it still bore an Arkansas tag — lifted from a car belonging to Merle Cruse of Fayetteville on April 17 — when recovered would appear to indicate a recent visit to that state. By changing plates to the state in which they were currently travelling, it helped divert suspicion which might attach to an out-of-state registration at a time when long distance road travel was a rarity.

This is the side of the car furthest from the posse and it can be seen that few rounds have penetrated both doors.

Sightseers must have been in somewhat of a dilemma in order not to miss out on the attractions: should they queue to view the victims . . . go up to the court-house on the opposite side of town to see the death car . . . or rush out to the ambush site!

Left: **Earl Moore of the** *Dallas Morning News* **took this picture of the spot where the posse had stood.** *Right:* **One of the trees — presumably on the far side of the road — hacked about by souvenir hunters for spent bullets.**

Police photo from the files of the Texas Rangers of two uniformed officers to illustrate the spot where the car came to rest.

An equally curious, though not as large, crowd was at the actual scene of the shooting. Souvenir hunters had an axe and were industriously chopping away at trees in the vicinity to dig out bullets and picking up shotgun shells. Others were interested in a little depression just off the road where Hamer and the others had laid in wait all night for the outlaws.

A few were gathered around the spot a few yards farther up the road where the bandits' machine had eased into a ditch after they had been shot down.

A bulky citizen, whom I had seen in town several times called me aside. His chest was swelling with pride.

'Look here,' he said, in the manner of one displaying a treasured possession. In his hand was an unused rifle shell. He was not reluctant to explain its deep intrinsic value.

'I got it out of the handbag,' he whispered mysteriously.

A photo for posterity taken at exactly 9.15 a.m. on May 23, 2003. Apart from the road then being gravel and narrower, this is how the shadows must have looked that fateful morning 69 years ago.

Later, the Rangers took aerial photographs of the ambush site, looking both ways along the Ringgold road.

259

Bienville officers displayed items from the cache for the press. *Left:* Deputy Prentiss Oakley with some of the 15 license plates found under the back seat. Prominent is Kansas 3-17832 — the Warren's tag — and the tell-tale Iowa 13-1234. *Right:* Deputy A. B. Rogers with some of the weaponry. Clyde's saxophone in its case is on the ground on the right.

It developed the handbag was one of the three loaded with ammunition which was found in Clyde's car. The satchels, covered with blood, had been safely locked in the rear of Sheriff Jordan's car the only time I had obtained a glimpse of them.

Other onlookers crowded around, several fishing in their pockets for the prized bullets. They plainly showed that their's was the elation that comes once in a lifetime.

And thus, with the souvenir-chasers still chopping away at the pines which lined the road, we left all physical evidence of the Barrow-Parker demise far behind for a quick return flight to Dallas.

Report by Tom J. Simmons of
The Dallas Morning News, May 24, 1934

Clyde Barrow and Bonnie Parker were killed near Gibsland, Louisiana, by Texas and Louisiana officers when the pair were shot from ambush near one of their hideouts.

Frank Hamer, a former Texas Ranger, had been on the watch for the pair for several weeks. It is said that Hamilton, a former associate of Barrow, who is now in custody charged with murder, gave information regarding the hideouts of Barrow and his companion.

The couple were shot in their car when it was travelling 85 miles an hour. The officers used machine guns and sawed-off shotguns and the outlaws were killed before they could do any shooting. An examination of the bodies revealed that each one had received fifty or sixty wounds.

Clyde Barrow and his woman companion were in the gang of outlaws that were surprised by officers near Dexfield Park last July, when Marvin Barrow was shot and captured with his wife, who is now serving a term in prison. Marvin died in a Perry hospital.

In the car in which Clyde Barrow and Bonnie Parker were killed in Louisiana last week, several number plates for cars were found among them was an Iowa number plate 13-1234, which was the number carried by the car in which the robbers who held up the bank here travelled in. A car having the same number carried the gang that robbed the bank at Everly, Iowa, not long after or before the Stuart bank was robbed.

The Stuart Herald, May 24, 1934

Left: At a press conference held in Dallas two days later, Sheriff Schmid introduced his deputies — Bob Alcorn, right, and Ted Hinton 'who over two months ago were assigned to get Clyde Barrow and Bonnie Parker, two of the South's worst killers. This was terminated in the apprehension, the day before yesterday in the state of Louisiana.' *Right:* Alcorn: 'Many other officers of several different states deserve a lot of credit that have worked and co-operated with the officers who participated in the apprehension of the two worst criminals the Southwest has ever known. In view of the fact that these criminals have been directly responsible for the killing of many of our brother officers, we felt it our duty to do our best to stop their terrorism which has extended over a period of some 26 or 27 months. Each and every officer present at the time of the capture deserves the same credit as we all did our best. I regret that we couldn't have taken them alive but that was impossible. I further regret that there was a woman that had to be killed which couldn't have been helped.'

Rather belatedly, the FBI issued this wanted poster, under the National Motor Vehicle Theft Act, two days previously.

The Bureau of Investigation [forerunner of the FBI] became interested in Barrow and his paramour late in December 1932 through a singular bit of evidence. A Ford automobile was found abandoned near Jackson, Michigan, which had been stolen in Pawhuska, Oklahoma, in September of that year. At Pawhuska, it was learned another Ford car had been abandoned there which had been stolen in Illinois. A search of this car revealed it had been occupied by a man and a woman, indicated by abandoned articles therein. In this car was found a prescription bottle, which led Special Agents to a drug store in Nacogdoches, Texas, where investigation disclosed the woman for whom the prescription had been filled was Clyde Barrow's aunt.

Further investigation revealed that the woman who obtained the prescription had been visited recently by Clyde Barrow, Bonnie Parker, and Clyde's brother, L. C. Barrow. It also learned that these three were driving a Ford car, identified as the one stolen in Illinois. It was further shown that L. C. Barrow had secured the empty prescription bottle from a son of the woman who had originally obtained it.

On May 20, 1933, the United States Commissioner at Dallas, Texas, issued a warrant against Clyde Barrow and Bonnie Parker, charging them with the interstate transportation, from Dallas to Oklahoma, of the automobile stolen in Illinois. The Bureau then started its hunt for this elusive pair.

The Bureau had jurisdiction solely on the charge of transporting a stolen automobile, although the activities of the Bureau Agents were vigorous and ceaseless. Every clue was followed. 'Wanted notices' furnishing fingerprints, photograph, description, criminal record, and other data were distributed to all officers. The Agents followed the trail through many states and into various haunts of the Barrow gang, particularly Louisiana. The association with Henry Methvin and the Methvin family of Louisiana was discovered by Bureau Agents who found that Bonnie and Clyde had been driving a car stolen in New Orleans.

On April 13, 1934, a Bureau Agent, through investigation in the vicinity of Ruston, Louisiana, obtained information which definitely placed Bonnie and Clyde in a remote section south-west of that community. The home of the Methvins was not far away and the Agent learned of visits there by Bonnie and Clyde. Special Agents in Texas had learned that Clyde and his companion had been travelling from Texas to Louisiana, sometimes accompanied by Henry Methvin.

The Bureau and local law enforcement authorities in Louisiana and Texas concentrated on apprehending Bonnie and Clyde, whom they strongly believed to be in the area. Then, it was learned that Bonnie and Clyde, with some of the Methvins, had staged a party at Black Lake, Louisiana, on the night of May 21, 1934. Bonnie and Clyde were due to return to the area two days later.

A posse composed of police officers from Louisiana and Texas, including Texas Ranger Frank Hamer, concealed themselves in bushes along the highway near Sailes, Louisiana, before dawn on May 23, 1934. Bonnie and Clyde appeared in an automobile in the early daylight. As they attempted to drive away, the officers opened fire. Bonnie and Clyde were killed instantly.

U.S. Department of Justice
Bureau of Investigation, December 14, 1934

It's a great load off my mind, and I slept soundly last night for the first time in months.

SHERIFF 'SMOOT' SCHMID, 1934

I'm glad that they were both killed; it was the easiest way out.

BLANCHE BARROW, MAY 1934

I was very close to my father [Constable Cal Campbell]. My mother died when I was only three and he devoted his life to his family, keeping the five kids together. I am sure my father didn't know who killed him. He was just going to help someone.

JIM CAMPBELL, 1968

I admit that I am relieved.

W. D. JONES, 1934

I'm glad they went out like they did. It was better than getting caught.

ROY THORNTON (Bonnie's husband), MAY 1934

They got my father [Marshal Henry Humphrey] with shot-guns — he was hit in ten places. He lived for three days and I was with him in the hospital. We sold the farm then as I couldn't work it alone. It was hard on us all.

VERNON HUMPHREY, 1968

I am glad she is dead but I am sorry she had to go the way she did, without repenting, because she surely is in Hell.

MRS E. M. STAMPS (Bonnie's aunt), 1934

There's not much to say now — it is all over. The interests of law and justice have been served.

DEPUTY BOB ALCORN, MAY 1934

We just shot the devil out of them, that's all. That's all there was to it!

FRANK HAMER, MAY 1934

I've been expecting it to end this way.

BILLIE MACE (Bonnie's sister), 1934

My father [Constable Wes Harryman] was on the porch when they shot him to pieces. We had to sell the farm and I worked where I could to support the family. It was a long haul.

CLAUDE HARRYMAN, 1968

I guess its a relief — I knew it was coming pretty soon.

HENRY BARROW, MAY 1934

I knew it was gonna happen; I just didn't know when.

RAYMOND HAMILTON, 1934

We carried out our duties as officers of the law and carried out our orders. I can truthfully say that we went through hell and came back.

TED HINTON, MAY 1934

They gunned my father [Sheriff Eugene Moore] down with shotguns and the sheriff was crippled for life. My mother was left with three children to support. She never remarried. The roughest thing for me was growing up without a father.

RUSSELL MOORE, 1968

I knew it was coming — I just felt it last night when I stayed on my knees and begged God to let me see my baby alive one more time. God, please have mercy on his soul.

MRS CUMIE BARROW, MAY 1934

Thank God!

MRS E. B. WHEELER,
(widow of Patrolman E. B. Wheeler) MAY 1934

The Funerals

Bonnie in her swansong ballad (see page 238) — virtually her last testament — saw herself buried next to her lover but Emma Parker would have none of it. 'Clyde had her for two years', her mother declared, 'and look what it did to her. She's mine now.'

Thousands of morbidly curious sensation-seekers crowded the lawn of the McKamy-Campbell funeral home on Forest Avenue Thursday afternoon to achieve the doubtful pleasure of looking at the body of a girl bandit shot down in a gun-battle with police.

Twenty police officers lined the sidewalk and held back the pressing throng while Mrs. Emma Parker, mother of the notorious Bonnie, walked sobbing up the cement strip, onto the porch and into the room where lay her slain daughter.

In another end of town, at the Sparkman-Holtz-Brand establishment on Ross Avenue, yet another crowd, but not as large, trampled over the lawn and fought for the privilege of seeing the state's No. 1 criminal as he lay mutilated in death.

The larger throng by far was at the bier of Bonnie. The gun girl, returned to Dallas at 9 a.m. Thursday, was a magnet that drew mostly women and children, a gum-chewing, loud-whispering collection. They started coming at 10 a.m. and by noon the aggregation had grown to hundreds. Funeral officials, weary of battling the curiosity-torn invaders, finally appealed to police and a squadron of officers was assigned to the home. By 3 p.m. the crowd had grown to more than a thousand.

Bonnie's brother, Buster, arrived in Arcadia to claim her remains late Wednesday evening having been misdirected to Acadia — a parish right in the south of Louisiana. Travelling through the night, the hearse finally arrived at the McKamy-Campbell Funeral Home at 1921 Forest Avenue around 9 a.m. Thursday morning. Word soon got around and crowds began to assemble to view the body. Dressed in a blue silk negligee, she lay in a steel casket with cream lining, her face having been expertly repaired and made up by Eva, wife of the funeral director, Allen D. Campbell.

263

It was at this hour the mortuary men finished their task of trying to restore a semblance of naturalness to the bullet ravaged body of Bonnie. They sent word for the mother to come.

When the big car carrying Mrs. Parker and other relatives stopped at the curb, the crowd pressed forward. For a moment it was impossible to open the car door, and then the police cut a lane thru to the steps of the funeral home. Locking arms, they held back the crowd.

Mrs. Parker stepped from the car, a handkerchief held to her face. She was sobbing audibly. Supporting her on one side was her son, Buster, and on the other, Mrs Edith Parker, Buster's wife. Together they almost carried the ageing woman up the steps. There she halted for a moment. She looked back and seemed to sigh as tho she was leaving behind every beautiful dream life had ever held for her.

The three Parkers and another aunt were closeted in a tiny room with Bonnie's body for nearly half an hour. Then the door opened. The crowd pressed forward against the door and again the police officers made their lane, cautioning the throng against speaking loudly or in any way which would further mortify the mother.

As she walked from the room, one of the funeral directors stopped her for a moment and questioned her. She hesitated and then nodded. The director waited until she had walked to her car and then announced to the crowd they would be allowed to see Bonnie's body. There was a cheer only slightly subdued.

They formed in single file and passed the body of the girl on a couch in the hall. Her body was draped with a sheet and the obvious unfairness of it all impressed even some members of the reviewing crowd.

Bonnie's sister, Billie, had been arrested the previous Saturday (as had Floyd Hamilton) and charged with the murders of the two Highway Patrolmen at Grapevine. Lawyers were still trying to get her released but it was not until Saturday morning, May 26, that forensic tests on the firearms recovered from the death car proved that they were the murder weapons. Billie was then escorted from Tarrant County Jail to Forest Avenue for the funeral which finally went ahead at 2 p.m. Here, in the dark coat holding a handkerchief, she follows her mother (in the floral dress) as the casket is carried to the waiting hearse for the six mile journey to Fishtrap Cemetery — ironically not a stone's throw from the Barrow garage on Eagle Ford Road! Clyde's brother, L. C., is the leading pallbearer on the far side of the casket.

At this time directors also announced that Bonnie would be buried Saturday, tho the time and place were not yet known. Mrs. Parker chose a silver gray casket for her daughter, a casket lined with cream against a rose background, colours for a debutante. The casket was expensively quiet.

At 7 p.m. more than 7,000 persons had seen Bonnie's body. Small boys got places and sold them to elders who did not want to stand in line. Officials of the mortuary had said the public 'reception' would continue until 9 p.m., but it appeared the line would continue until midnight at least.

Allen Campbell moved his funeral business to Oak Cliff circa 1938 while Mr McKamy continued to operate from the Forest Avenue premises until the building was demolished when the nearby freeway was cut through in the 1950s. Forest Avenue has also changed — it is now Martin Luther King Junior Boulevard.

The graveside burial service was conducted by Reverend Clifford Andrews of Oak Cliff Gospel Church. Because of the number of onlookers, members of the immediate family stayed out of sight in their curtained limousine.

Jonathan Davis and Jim Knight approach the old sealed up entrance to Fishtrap Cemetery which has now been renamed La Reunion commemorating the first settlers in the area who came from Europe in the 1850s. The last burials took place here in 1939.

A sobbing mother completed Friday an all-night vigil beside the bier of her 19-year-old daughter, who chose the crimson path of crime and paid the inevitable price.

Weeping as she left the cold, silent form in the steel gray casket, Mrs. Emma Parker fled the McKamy-Campbell funeral home as crowds of morbidly curious, which reached mob-like proportions Thursday night, began collecting early Friday for a last glimpse at the gang girl, Bonnie Parker. At 7 a.m. a long line had formed before the undertakers on Forest Avenue clamoring for admission.

The crowd will be permitted to file before the bier from 10 a.m. to 3 p.m.

Accompanied by her sister, Mrs. Plummer, and her daughter-in-law, Mrs. Edith Parker, and other close members of the family, Mrs. Parker returned to the funeral home at 7 p.m. Thursday. Since 3 p.m., when Mrs Parker had visited the parlors to select the casket for her daughter, a steady file of persons had passed before the body, resting on a couch in the parlor. Attendants estimated 14,000 persons, men, women and children, had viewed the gun girl as she rested in death.

When Mrs. Parker arrived the flow was halted, but until 1 a.m. the mob lingered with hopes the relatives would leave.

At times there were as many as 20,000 persons there, choking traffic along busy Forest Avenue. They flocked over the lawn, trampling down the grass and shrubs; they broke porch furniture, tore down a rear fence, did damage estimated at $500.

People came from all parts of South Dallas, walking and running. Others came by street car, by taxi, in family cars on bicycles and motorcycles and in wagons.

The body, still showing the violent means of death despite the best work of embalmers, was encased in the $1,000 steel casket. Bonnie was dressed in blue negligee, the body nestling in the cream and rose folds of soft satin.

The little family group sat in solitude in the parlor near the bier. Mrs. Parker cried softly into the cold hours of the dawn.

When Bonnie's father died in 1914, her mother's parents, Frank and Mary Krause who lived at 2908 Eagle Ford Road, took the children in. Thus Emma decided that her daughter should be buried in the same cemetery where the family plot was situated. Frank had been buried there in 1919 and he was later joined by his wife Mary.

Mrs Parker had wanted to honour her daughter's wish to bring her to the family home but the crowds made it impossible to move her. Instead Emma's night-long vigil was at Forest Avenue. 'Bonnie Parker Oct 1 1910 — May 23, 1934. As the flowers are all made sweeter by the sunshine and the dew, so this old world is made brighter by the lives of folks like you'.

Arrangements whereby the Sparkman-Holtz-Brand Co. were to handle Clyde's body were made nearly a year ago. The death of Buck at the hands of avenging officers convinced the family Clyde would eventually meet the same fate. It was understood a substantial part of the cost was paid at that time.

Barrow is said to have had some life insurance, a policy issued by the American National Co. when he was a child. The amount was said to be around $500. Who has been paying the premiums was not announced.

Both undertakers were forced to ask for police aid early Thursday. McKamy-Campbell organization strictly limited visitors to newspapermen working on the assignment and to police officers. Where Barrow's body lay a similar rule was made, but not enforced until nearly noon. It became evident the stream of curious were hampering the embalmers and the bodies would not be presentable to relatives in the afternoon.

Clyde had been taken to the imposing Sparkman-Holtz-Brand Funeral Home at No. 2110 Ross Avenue in downtown Dallas. The building had originally been constructed to the orders of Alfred Belo, the founder of the *Dallas Morning News* in the 1890s in the style of the family home in North Carolina. When the family moved out, for nearly 50 years it was used as an undertaker's parlour before being taken over by the Dallas Lawyers Association for their clubhouse.

Both Mrs. Parker and Mrs. Barrow viewed the bodies Wednesday before undertakers had had time to do more than wash the blood from the dead faces.

One of the most difficult tasks confronting the McKamy-Campbell embalmers was to remove the sardonic, diabolical grin from Bonnie's twisted lips. Apparently believing she and Clyde would again shoot their way out of the Louisiana trap and leave a new heap of dead officers behind them, her lips had twisted into an ironic grin when the officers appeared. She died that way and death set her lips.

Undertakers had made no effort at noon to count the wounds on either corpse. Both were completely mottled with angry black circles that showed where the plunging pellets of copper and nickel had whipped thru their yielding flesh. Bonnie's most prominent injury was her bullet-shattered right hand. Barrow had nearly all the left side of his head shot away. Undertakers cut thru the poll and left the two halves of his head hinged on the jaw sockets while they cleaned out the inside of the brain case.

The sudden bloating of death had gone from both corpses and Bonnie was the dirty, ashen gray of death with no sign of early mortification. But Barrow had blackened feet during the long ride in the heat.

Mrs Barrow had not seen the body of her son at 7 p.m. Thursday. Other relatives had visited, seen and wept over the body of the desperado who was killed in Gibsland Louisiana, with his gun girl Wednesday.

LOUISIANA STATE BOARD OF HEALTH
Bureau of Vital Statistics
CERTIFICATE OF DEATH

JUL 10 1934

1—PLACE OF DEATH

Parish BIENVILLE

Ward 3 2

District No. 7-5062

File No. 23
(1, 2, 3, etc., in the order Certificates are filed.)

7-50.61a

City

or Town GIBSLAND, LA., R.F.D.

Registered No. 6207
(To be given in Central Bureau.)

No. St. Ward
(If death occurred in a Hospital or Institution, give its Name instead of Street and Number.)

2—FULL NAME CLYDE CHESTNUT BARROW

(a) Residence. No. DALLAS TEXAS St., Ward.
(Usual place of abode) (If non-resident give city or town and State)
Length of residence in city or town where death occurred. yrs. mos. ds. How long in U. S.; of foreign birth? yrs. mos. ds.

PERSONAL AND STATISTICAL PARTICULARS

3. SEX MALE
4. COLOR OR RACE WHITE
5. SINGLE, MARRIED, WIDOWED, OR DIVORCED (write the word) SINGLE

5a. If married, widowed, or divorced
HUSBAND of
(or) WIFE of

6. DATE OF BIRTH (month, day, and year)

7. AGE Years 24 Months Days If LESS than 1 day, ____hrs. or____min.

8. Trade, profession, or particular kind of work done, as SAW-YER, BOOKKEEPER, etc. GLASS CUTTER
9. Industry or business in which work was done, as cotton mill, saw mill, bank, etc.
10. Date deceased last worked at this occupation (month and year) 1929
11. Total time (years spent in this occupation 4

11a. Veteran past wars____ (yes or no) ____ (name war) ____

12. BIRTHPLACE (city or town)
(State or Parish) ELLIS COUNTY TEXAS

13. NAME HENRY B. BARROW
14. BIRTHPLACE (city or town) PALMER
(State or Parish) ELLIS COUNTY TEXAS

15. MAIDEN NAME CUNNIE WALKER
16. BIRTHPLACE (city or town)
(State or Parish) NATCHODOCHES. CO.

17. INFORMANT E. W. BARROW
(Address) DALLAS TEXAS

18. BURIAL, CREMATION, OR REMOVAL
Place West Dallas Date 5/25/34 19
Dallas, Texas

19. UNDERTAKER S. A. CONGER.
(Address) ARCADIA LA.

20. FILED July 3 1934

MEDICAL CERTIFICATE OF DEATH

21. DATE OF DEATH (month, day, and year) 5-23, 1934

22. HEREBY CERTIFY, That I attended deceased from ____ 19 Coroner Inquest 19
I last saw h____ alive on ____ 19 death is said to have occurred on the date stated above, at 930 a.m.
The principal cause of death and related causes of importance in order of onset were as follows:

Gun Shot Wounds

(173)

Date of onset

Contributory causes of importance not related to principal cause

Name of operation none Date of
What test confirmed diagnosis? Was there an autopsy?

23. If death was due to external causes fill in also the following:
Accident, suicide, or homicide Killed by officers Date of injury 19
Where did injury occur? Bienville Par La
(Specify city or town, parish, and State)
Specify whether injury occurred in industry, in home, or in public place Public Highway

Manner of injury

Nature of injury

24. Was disease or injury in any way related to occupation of deceased? no
If so, specify

(Signed) J. L. Wade M.D.
(Address) Arcadia La.
Bienville Par. Coroner

MARGIN RESERVED FOR BINDING.

Form V.S. No. 1
N. B.—WRITE PLAINLY, WITH UNFADING INK—THIS IS A PERMANENT RECORD. Every item of information should be carefully supplied. AGE should be stated EXACTLY. PHYSICIANS should state CAUSE OF DEATH in plain terms, so that it may be properly classified. Exact statement of OCCUPATION is very important.

Clyde's funeral took place on Friday afternoon. At 5 p.m. the cortege left Ross Avenue for the three mile drive to Western Heights Cemetery on Fort Worth Avenue. The cemetery was already packed and it was only with difficulty that the coffin was brought to the grave. Even family members were prevented from reaching the family plot.

The sermon for both Clyde Barrow and the gun girl will be preached by the same man — Reverend Clifford Andrews of the Oak Cliff Full Gospel Church. Clyde's services will be at the Sparkman funeral home at 5 p.m. Friday with only the family and close friends in attendance. Mrs. Henry Barrow, the bandit's mother, wanted none of the public demonstration which was marking the passing of Bonnie. Barrow's father was quoted as saying only that he wanted Clyde to have the same kind of a funeral any other boy would have. Reverend Andrews became acquainted with L. C. Barrow in jail and wanted to preach the services for Clyde.

The Dallas Dispatch, May 25, 1934

Clyde's mother and father are pictured beside the grave heaped with floral tributes. They had lost two sons in less than nine months.

Buck's grave had never been marked as Clyde wanted them both to have a common headstone when his turn came. He chose the simple epitaph: 'Gone but not forgotten' and nothing could be more true as the gravestone has been stolen and recovered several times so that today it lies prone *(below)* encased in concrete. Clyde is on the left of Buck. Unfortunately when their parents ordered the engraving, they made a mistake in Buck's year of birth so instead of 1903 it reads 1905.

Mum and Dad now lie in the same grave, Cumie having died in August 1942 and Henry in June 1957.

POSTSCRIPT

Clyde's coat, cut to ribbons by the fusillade, is displayed on the death car at Arcadia. Souveniering the vehicle and its contents was rife on both sides of the law and even ownership of the car itself was subject to a protracted legal wrangle.

As Bonnie predicted in her 'farewell' poem, their deaths were 'to the law a relief' . . . but their demise was soon exploited by opportunist profiteers.

First in line was Sheriff Jordan. Although there was official reward money on offer totalling some $4,000 to be shared out between him and his men,

Jordan saw as the main prize, the death car. It had cost the Warrens $795.92 on March 15 but now, two months later, they were being offered up to $25,000 — at least that was the figure telephoned to the Warrens soon after the shooting by a collector in Kansas City who said that he already owned Al Capone's limo.

However, Sheriff Jordan considered that morally he had first claim on the vehicle.

'Five other men and myself risked our lives to make that car what it is today,' he declared. 'What we did to it is what makes it valuable. We deserve any profit to be made from it.'

The day after the ambush, an astute entrepreneur in Austin, Texas, contacted the state Ranger headquarters for details on the death car. Chester Schacht said he was a showman and that he wanted to purchase the car to put it on public display. But Sheriff Jordan was not going to part with it so easily. He held on to the Warren's car for two months saying he needed proof of ownership, even though the provenance of the Ford

had been reported in the press in May. Mrs Warren declared that it was 'highway robbery' that she had been forced to pay out over $3,000 merely to have her own property returned to her. *Left:* She finally got her vehicle back on August 2 and she drove the car herself to Shreveport from where it was transported by rail to Kansas. *Right:* The car had been pictured outside the railway station opposite the funeral parlour in Arcadia.

Judge Ben C. Dawkins of the Federal Court in Monroe had already ordered Jordan to appear to show just cause why he should not be held in contempt of court for refusing to surrender the Warren's car to a US Marshal on a writ of sequestration served on him. In his defence, the sheriff said he had removed the car for safekeeping and for protection against souvenir hunters, claiming that the delay in handing over the vehicle was because the serial number of the car (which was 649198) did not correspond with the number given in the suit filed by Jesse Warren. 'I am glad that Warren was able to establish his ownership of the car', Jordan is finally reported to have said. 'He has done that to my satisfaction and the car is in his hands.'

The sheriff's terms were relayed by his lawyer to the Warrens who were informed that they could get their car back on payment of $15,000. Horrified at the sheriff's mercenary stance, Mrs Warren engaged her own lawyer to file a suit against Jordan in the Federal Court in Shreveport. Even then, it cost her $3,200 in legal and court fees, plus a charge for towing and storage, before the car was released to her two months later.

The Bienville parish sheriff was also being less than helpful over the personal possessions. Initially, all Mrs Barrow had received was a gold watch and $505.32 in cash. A diamond tie pin had already disappeared when Dr Wade carried out his inspection of the body in Conger's mortuary.

Mrs. C. T. Barrow,
Route 6,
Box 112-A,
Dallas, Texas.

Monroe, Louisiana,
August 16, 1934.

Dear Madam:

Replying to your letter of August 16th will say that the only thing this court has had in its possession through the marshal was the automobile recovered at the time Clyde Barrow and Bonnie Parker were killed. I know nothing about its contents and you should communicate with Mr. Henderson Jordan, Sheriff of Bienville Parish, at Arcadia, Louisiana, to whom I am sending copy of this letter, about any personal belongings that were in the car. I take it that it will be necessary for you to furnish satisfactory proof to the state sheriff of the ownership of your son in order to recover the same. In any event, the matter is beyond the control of the officers of this court. At the same time, I am sure Mr. Jordan will be glad to turn over to you anything that can be shown to be the property of your son.

Yours very truly,

¢ Mr. Henderson Jordan,
S h e r i f f,
Arcadia, Louisiana.

HENDERSON JORDAN
SHERIFF AND EX-OFFICIO TAX COLLECTOR
BIENVILLE PARISH
ARCADIA, LOUISIANA August, 17th. 1934.

A. B. ROGERS. OFFICE DEPUTY

Hon. Ben C. Dawkins,
Monroe, La.

Dear Sir;

I am in receipt of copy of your letter written Mrs C. T. Barrow, and in order that you might understand the situation I am writing you.

Every thing in this car has already been turned over to Mrs Barrow and Mrs Parker, with the exception of the clothing that have bullet holes in them and the guns, now the guns with the exception of one have been identified by U. S. Army, I have told Mrs Barrow that just as soon as the Grand Jury meets that I will release these clothes to them.

I have refused to turn over the guns to them thinking that they were stolen property, and they have proved to be stolen with the exception of one gun and I am of the opinion that it is stolen therefore I am requesting them to prove ownership before turning same over to them.

Yours very truly,

Although it was reported in the press on August 9 that the Warrens had sold the Ford to a showman Duke Mills (Chester Schacht of Austin appears to have dropped out of the running), in actual fact they rented the car to Charles W. Stanley of Abilene, Kansas *(right)* for $150 per week. Stanley was known as the 'Crime Doctor' and he wanted to use the car as an attraction at his anti-crime lectures. He transported the vehicle all over the States on a flat-bed truck, displaying it for free but asking for a donation of 10 cents. In the end, after paying out $12,000 in rent, he purchased the car outright for $3,000 in 1938. The following year he displayed it at the Texas State Fair in Dallas but not without some trepidation as he was not sure of the reaction he would receive in the Barrow-Parker home town so, in case there was trouble, he hired Ted Hinton and Bob Alcorn to act as security guards.

The Actual DEATH CAR NOW on NATION WIDE TOUR
$10,000 REWARD To anyone who can prove that this is not the actual car in which Clyde Barrow and Bonnie Parker were killed near Arcadia, La.

See the Bullet Riddled
CLYDE BARROW
BONNIE PARKER

DEATH CAR
ON EXHIBITION - FREE

Thousands of People See This Car Each Day

The Most Talked of Car in America..
YOU READ about IT IN YOUR DETECTIVE MAGAZINE -
YOUR TRUE STORY - YOUR LIBERTY MAGAZINE - and
NOW You Can Actually See This Car on Exhibition - FREE!

Actual!   Authentic!   Unbelievable!

IT WILL MAKE YOU THINK AND THINK HARD — A RINGING WARNING TO TRUE BLOODED CITIZENS!

SIX GUNS BELCHED DEATH — OVER 160 Bullet Holes in the Car — A GRUESOME RELIC of the END of the ROAD!

FREE   **ON EXHIBITION**   FREE
Afternoon & Evening
1:00 P. M. 'til 9:00 P.M.

OCTOBER 17, 1936
JACK LANE CHEVROLET CO.
14-26 West 8th St.   Winfield

AN EDUCATIONAL and INSTRUCTIVE EXHIBITION   ★   BRING THE CHILDREN

Stanley invited Clyde's father, Henry, to come to his lecture and was complimented afterwards by Mr Barrow: 'You are the only person who ever told the real truth about how my son was set up and shot down by the law'. By now, public opinion had turned against the lawmen and their pre-emptive ambush and instead they had become the villains of the piece while Bonnie and Clyde — like so many American outlaws — were becoming folk heroes. With the coming of the Second World War, interest in the death car waned and, having earned a reported $1.5 million from it, in 1952 Stanley sold it to a movie producer, Ted Toddy, who was intending to make a film about Depression criminals and wanted to use the car to publicise the movie. However it seems it spent most of its time stored in an Atlanta garage until it found a new lease of life when the Warner Bros movie was released in 1967. But, just as Stanley had had a problem in the 1930s with the appearance of several phony death cars, so Toddy had to take an owner to court in 1969 who was displaying a fake as the real car. In July 1973, Toddy put the car up for auction in the Bay State Antique Automobile Exposition at Princeton, Massachusetts, when it was knocked down to Peter Simon *(below)* for $175,000. Peter already owned the Red Garter Casino in Las Vegas and he wanted the car to promote his Pop's Oasis Casino in Jean, 28 miles to the south, hoping to attract some of the tourists passing through on their way to Las Vegas.

In 1979, Peter sold the car to Jim Bruckner of Movieworld Cars of the Stars in Buena Park, California and although the price was not given, it is believed that Simon lost money on the deal.

It was later sold to Clyde Wade before being bought by Greg and Gary Primm for $250,000 for displaying in their casino *(above and below)* in Primm on the Nevada/California state line.

With each move, more and more pieces of the car have been stolen so today it is minus most of the front windscreen glass. The V-8 badge from the front of the radiator has gone and the seats have now been covered with plastic to protect the deteriorating upholstery, picked full of holes by souvenir hunters. Thus it was seen as prudent to shield the whole car behind glass when it was moved to its present location in Primm Valley Resort on the other side of Interstate 15. *Right:* Terry Eckert pictured it for us in its current setting. It still carries the original cordoba gray paintwork but it is rather difficult to photograph. Although the figures don't add up, according to the Texas Rangers, they fired 315 rounds of which 167 hit the car. Of these, 38 went through the front windshield; 33 in the sides and 45 in the rear.

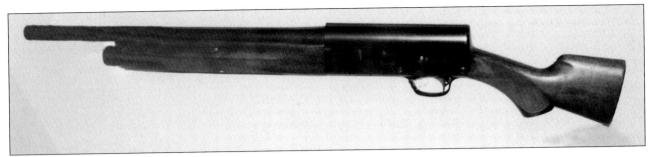

So what of the other items found in the car? Mrs Parker tried to get back the Browning Model 1911 20-gauge shotgun that her daughter had been holding when she was killed . . . but in vain. It is now on display in the Texas Rangers Hall of Fame in Waco.

The fedora that Clyde is believed to have been wearing when he was shot is now in Sandy Jones's John Dillinger Historical Society Museum, as is Bonnie's sequinned beret recovered from the death car. They were among the personal items returned to the families.

Former Ranger Capt. Frank Hamer,
Austin, Texas.

Re: Personal Property of Bonnie Parker.

Dear Sir:

From an article which appeared in the Dallas Times Herald under date line of September 27th, 1934 from Austin, I have the information that you are now in possession of and evidently laying claim to a certain shot-gun, being a 20 gauge shot-gun which bears the name of my deceased daughter; you having registered such fire-arm in your name in the Internal Revenue Collector's Office, evidently at Austin.

You are advised that as the mother of Bonnie Parker it is my desire and I at this time make claim to the right of possession of such gun as the personal property of my deceased daughter. Other officers, namely the Sheriff from Shreveport, Louisiana, has already turned over to me other personal property which belonged to my daughter.

So long as I am now planning to leave Dallas for rather an extended length of time I am turning this matter over to my attorney, Edward Meek, of the firm of Thompson and Meek, 983 Kirby Building, Dallas, Texas, and would appreciate it if you will ship the gun to Mr. Meek, charges collect for shipment, or should you care to communicate with me kindly do so through his office as I have today talked to him regarding this matter and my rights thereunder

Yours truly,

Mrs. E. Parker.
Mrs. E. Parker.

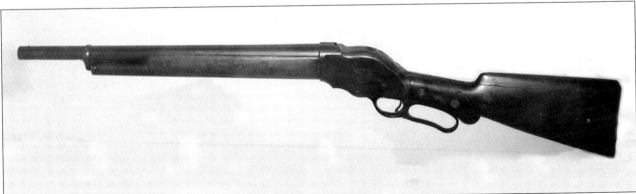

Another weapon on display in Waco is this Winchester Model 1901 10-gauge shotgun. The caption claims it was Clyde's 'wielded against the former Rangers and other officers who tried to capture him'. Walter Prescott Webb in his 1935 book *The Texas Rangers* lists two Remington Model 1911 sawn-off shotguns — a 20-gauge and a 16-gauge — which can be seen to the left of the spare tyre in the picture on page 251, the smaller 20-gauge *(top)* on the right, but none of 10-gauge. In the same film still, three BARs, minus their magazines, stand on the right but not the weapon found next to Clyde which was damaged by a bullet. Both Hinton (page 251) and Jordan in his press statement explain that it was a Browning Automatic Rifle, and J. R. Bradfield, a reporter on *The News*, goes further to say that it was one of Clyde's cut-down versions.

Right: Two more weapons displayed by the Texas Rangers are the Colt Monitor Model R80 in .30-06 calibre, top, and a .30 Remington Model 8 semi-automatic rifle — both claimed to have been used by the officers in the ambush.

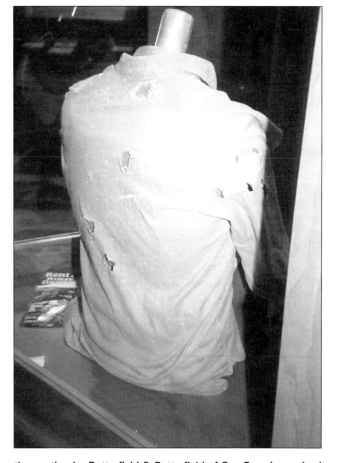

But the most macabre item of all must be the shirt bearing over 30 bullet holes, cut from Clyde's body. His bloody clothing was returned to the family in a sack and, after being washed, was put away for 60 years. The photo *(top left)* shows Clyde's elder sister Artie holding the light blue Western-style townshirt made by Wasson's of Indianapolis. In 1997, Marie Barrow decided to auction some of her brother's possessions in order, it was said, to raise money to be able to rebury Clyde and Bonnie together. 'If I can get them side-by-side resting spots, it'll be a dream come true and I'll die a happy woman', she was reported as saying, although much of this was press hype. Marie died less then two years later, her dream — real or imaginary — unfulfilled but

the auction by Butterfield & Butterfield of San Francisco raised tremendous international media coverage. With telephone bidders trying to outbid those in the auction room, the eight lots raised a total of $187,810, the shirt making $85,000 being bought by Whiskey Pete's to display alongside the car. The casino also bought 17 original snapshots from the family photo album for $12,650. The Elgin pocket watch Clyde was carrying sold for $20,700 to another bidder and a Colt semi-automatic pistol removed from the car fetched $16,100. A Winchester Model 1892 with scabbard, said to have been Clyde's but in Marie's possession at the time of his death, went for $27,600. *Above:* The shirt is now displayed at Primms Resort beside the death car.

Now it was time to eliminate the other 'Public Enemies' as Hoover called them. First was John Dillinger *(right)* who was America's bank robber extraordinaire. His raids were always meticulously planned and his party piece was to leap over the cashiers' railing. His reputation also extended to being a clever escape artiste, having got out of several prisons including Crown Point, Indiana, using a wooden pistol, in spite of the fact that specific security was in place. In charge of tracking down Dillinger was Melvin H. Purvis of the Department of Justice although J. Edgar Hoover was losing patience with the agent after several botched setbacks. In mid-July Purvis received information that Dillinger was living with Anna Sage *(far right)* a Romanian, who ran a prostitution ring in the North Side of Chicago. Mrs Sage agreed to betray Dillinger if the current deportation proceedings against her were dropped (a promise that was welshed on by the government two years later when she was deported to Europe).

The film starring William Powell, Clark Gable and Myrna Loy was playing at the Biograph at 2433 North Lincoln Avenue. Purvis stationed 16 Bureau agents around the cinema and at 8.30 p.m. Dillinger appeared with the two women, Anna wearing a red dress as she said she would. Just before 10.30 p.m. the audience began to emerge, Dillinger walking past the Goetz Country Club next door. 'He gave me a piercing look', Purvis told reporters later. 'Just after he went by and was outside the building due south, a National Tea Company store, I raised my hand and gave the pre-arranged signal. Dillinger walked on and at the mouth of the alley appeared to reach inside his coat for a gun. That was when the shots that killed him were fired.' Three of the G-men had opened fire: Clarence Burt, Herman Hollis and Charles Winstead and Dillinger was hit three times . . . took three faltering steps . . . then fell on the corner of the alleyway. *Left:* Spectators huddle round the spot. *Below:* John Binder discusses the dramatic events of yesteryear with Chuck Schauer.

On page 151 we saw Bonnie and Clyde lumped together with 'Baby Face' Nelson, 'Pretty Boy' Floyd, and John Dillinger who then bore the dubious accolade of the Bureau's 'Public Enemy No. 1'. Two months after Clyde and Bonnie were eliminated, Federal agents ended the reign of Dillinger as he emerged from the Biograph Theater in Chicago — reputedly another ambush in which the 'Lady in Red', Mrs Anna Sage, helped set him up for the kill.

On Sunday, July 22, Anna Sage tipped off Purvis that Dillinger would be taking her and his new lady love, Polly Keele, to the cinema but she did not know which one. *Manhattan Melodrama,* a movie about two slum boys growing up as friends, one becoming a district attorney the other a gangster, was currently on release, 'so,' said Purvis later, 'I felt that the clue I got early last evening that he would attend the picture show depicting the life of a man that ended in the electric chair would be a good one'.

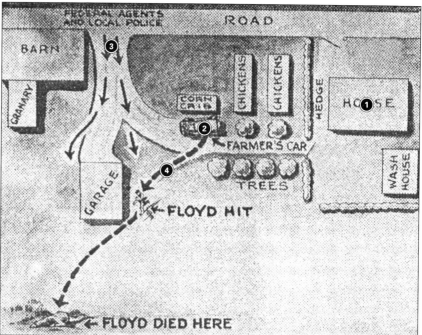

Three months after the death of Dillinger, 'Pretty Boy' Floyd met his end at the hands of the law on the Conkle Farm near East Liverpool, Ohio. Floyd had called at the farm [1] seeking a lift and he was waiting in Stewart Dyke's car [2] when two police cars were seen approaching [3]. Floyd jumped out of the car and began to run [4] for the tree line. *Below left:* The scene beside the barn was recreated a year later although the car is facing the wrong direction. *Below right:* Timothy Brookes of the East Liverpool Historical Society took the comparison for us on a foggy morning in August 2003.

Floyd made a run for it and refused to heed an order to halt. The first shot hit him in the arm but, ignoring a second warning, the next round struck his back. Floyd still tried to escape whereupon the lawmen fired a volley to bring him down.

Next in line was Charles Floyd. He despised his nickname and, according to the history books, he was neither 'pretty' nor 'a boy'! After Dillinger had been killed, Edgar Hoover passed the title of Public Enemy No. 1 to Floyd, his criminal activities then embracing some 30 major crimes, including up to ten murders.

On October 19 he was on the run in East Liverpool, Ohio. Police were combing the surrounding area and on the 22nd came to search the Conkle Farm on Sprucevale Road. Floyd had called there posing as a lost hunter and been given something to eat by Mrs Conkle but the police arrived just as her brother was about to give him a lift to the nearest bus station. Floyd took off across a cornfield and was shot down as he tried to flee, being hit, so it was said at the time, by 14 shots in the back.

Looking from the main road, past the barn; 'Pretty Boy' fell in the overgrown field in the background. The barn and the farmhouse had burned down by 1955 and the site now forms part of the Beaver Creek State Park with the area rapidly reverting to nature. Fortunately a historical marker was erected in 1994 by the Society, the unveiling being attended by several nephews and nieces of Floyd (who was buried in Akins Cemetery near Sallisaw, Oklahoma), and also the daughter of one of the police officers who was credited with Floyd's death. (The autopsy report, missing for more than 50 years, indicates only two bullet wounds were found in Floyd's body.)

This just left 'Baby Face' Nelson and he got his come-uppance the following month. A one-time member of the Dillinger gang, when the latter was killed Edgar Hoover promoted Nelson to the top spot as the Bureau's most wanted criminal. His end came in one of the most dramatic shoot-outs in American criminal history. On November 22, near Barrington, Illinois, with G-men chasing his car in which he was riding with his wife and a colleague, a running gun-battle took place at speeds of up to 75 mph, followed by a furious exchange of automatic fire as both vehicles came to a halt. Nelson was wounded yet continued to advance on the two lawmen who had taken cover behind the shelter of their car. Firing from the hip in the best tradition of a soldier advancing on an enemy pillbox, he killed both the federal agents, but Nelson's wound was mortal and he died in his wife's arms later that evening.

It was George Nelson, alias 'Baby Face' (although his real name was Lester Joseph Gillis), who had played a key role in arranging Dillinger's escape from Crown Point prison in March 1934. After his escape, Dillinger worked with Nelson on two bank hold-ups.

But it was the running gun-battle on November 22 that propelled 'Baby Face' into the pages of criminal history in a blaze of glory. *Right:* **Nelson was travelling east (away from the camera) on Highway 14 towards Chicago when Agents Bill Ryan and Tom McDade first spotted the car containing two men and a woman. Recognising Nelson behind the wheel, the agents performed a U-turn. Nelson spotted the agent's car following him and he, in turn, swung the car round. Passing the agents at high speed, Nelson performed another about turn to put him behind the agent's vehicle. As they drew alongside, Nelson's partner John Chase opened up with a burst of automatic fire from his Colt Monitor while Nelson fired his .38. Bill Ryan returned the fire with a full magazine, at which point Nelson dropped back, finally being lost to view.**

During the wild chase towards Barrington, another car containing Inspector Sam Cowley and Special Agent Herman Hollis (who, coincidentally, had helped in the killing of John Dillinger — see page 276) had passed by in the opposite direction. Hollis immediately carried out a U-turn so putting him behind Nelson. Meanwhile Ryan and McDade had raced through Barrington but lost control on a bend a half-mile out of town. However, Nelson's Ford had been hit and was losing power. Hollis was gaining on him so when Nelson reached this spot *(above)*, he swerved to a halt at the entrance to Northside Park (now renamed Langendorf Park) in the foreground on the right.

The Hudson containing agents Cowley and Hollis skidded to a stop in the middle of the road, ending up facing the way it had come. *Right:* In this reconstruction, staged on the same corner, the two cars are far too close, and the agent's car on the left should be facing in the opposite direction at least 75 to 100 feet east of the park road. All hell now broke loose. Nelson shouted to his wife Helen to take cover as he and Chase opened fire on the feds. More than 30 people witnessed the gun-battle which followed which they say lasted about three minutes. Cowley was armed with a Thompson while Hollis pulled out a shotgun. Nelson and Chase had the Monitor and a Thompson and a .351 automatic rifle. Whether it was sheer bravado, or a wish to make sure that he took the lawmen with him, is not known but having taken a slug in his belly, Nelson upped and advanced on the agent's car, firing as he went.

Left: In this present day comparison taken by Marty Black, Nelson would have moved diagonally across the road from right to left, both lawmen being cut down with bursts of automatic fire. *Right:* In 1993, a memorial to their memory was erected nearby in Langendorf Park. It includes the name of Special Agent Carter Baum who had previously been killed during an abortive assault on Nelson's hideout at Koerner's Corner in Wisconsin on April 22.

Nelson, mortally wounded, staggered to the agent's car and drove it over to the Ford. Chase picked up their weapons and threw them in the back before taking the wheel. Helen ran from where she had taken shelter and they drove off in a westerly direction. *Left:* Nelson was taken to 1627 Walnut Avenue in Wilmette, 25 miles away, but when Helen examined his wounds she found he had also been hit in the legs with buckshot. At 7.35 that evening, 'Baby Face' died. 'I didn't know what to do,' she explained later, 'so I sat there hour after hour with him'. Later the body was taken out to Niles Center (now part of Skokie). *Right:* Reaching St Paul's Cemetery, Helen decided 'that was the best place to leave Les's body and we lifted him out and laid him on the grass.' This is the spot today, at the south-west corner of Conrad Street and Long Avenue.

February 1935 — the aiders and abettors are called to account. *Left:* Clyde's mother, Mrs Cumie Barrow, is carried into Dallas County Court, located at No. 501 Main Street, alleged to have 'harboured' her son while he was on the run from the law.

Right: We saw this building from a different angle on page 197 as President Kennedy's motorcade proceeded down Main Street moments before he was shot. Part of the triple-under-pass on Dealey Plaza can be seen in the right background.

By the close of the year, five notorious criminals had been eliminated, but the law still had to get its pound of flesh from those who had helped Bonnie and Clyde stay ahead of the law for so long, and on February 22, 1935, the Federal authorities in Dallas put 20 friends and family on trial. The so-called 'Harboring trial' lasted four days with all the defendants being found guilty.

The two mothers received sentences of 30 days; Clyde's brother L.C., a year and a day and his wife Audrey 15 days imprisonment.

Marie, Clyde's younger sister who was just 16, was given one hour in custody because of her age although her husband Joe Francis, who she had married a few days before they were killed, and was four years her senior, received 60 days. Bonnie's sister, Billie, was given a year and a day.

Of those already in prison, Blanche had an additional year and a day added to her current sentence of 10 years, and W. D. Jones an extra two years on top of 15 being served for being an accessory to the murder of Sheriff Davis. Henry Methvin on the other hand, guilty of probably four murders, had a mere 15 months added to the current capital charge he faced in Oklahoma for the murder of Constable Campbell, and even that was commuted because of his co-operation in bringing Clyde and Bonnie to justice.

The main trial, which began on the 22nd, was held in the Federal Building on the corner of Bryan and North Ervay Streets. *Above:* Here the male defendents (and *(below left)* the females) are marched into the building through a small doorway beside the main entrance. *Below right:* The combined court-house and US Postal Service building was undergoing restoration in May 2003.

It really must have been an incredible spectacle — all the surviving actors in the Bonnie and Clyde story together in the same room — save for Clyde's father who was never charged with any offence. L-R: Hilton Bybee (hidden by the court official), Floyd Hamilton, 'Baldy' Whatley, L. C. Barrow, Henry Methvin, W. D. Jones, Joe Francis, James Mullins and Joe Chambliss. (Steve Davis is just out of the photo on the right.) Floyd claimed later that the apparent friendly rapport between Methvin and Clyde's brother, L. C, sitting beside each other, was because the treachery of the former was not known when this photo was taken although that is hard to believe bearing in mind Methvin's involvement had been mentioned in the press within days of the fatal ambush.

The ladies either turn their heads or hide their faces from the camera. Prominent in the leopard skin coat is Blanche with Cumie next to her on the left in the fur collared overcoat. Alice, the mother of the Hamilton boys, with the white band round her hat, sits to the left of the chair.

Other former gang members received varying sentences: Floyd Hamilton, two years, although his wife Mildred only received one hour; the Hamilton's mother Alice, 30 days; her husband Steve, 90 days; John Basden and S. J. Whatley (both friends of Floyd), and Mary O'Dare, one year and a day; Joe Chambless (Mary's father), 60 days; Hilton Bybee, 90 days, and James Mullins, four months.

The court-room on the third floor has more recently been used as a tax court.

'Well, goodbye all' were the last words spoken by Raymond Hamilton just before he was electrocuted on Friday, May 10. It was a few minutes after midnight when Joe Palmer met his death in the same electric chair to be followed by Hamilton who is seen here *(left)* with his mother on April 5 before he was transferred to death row at Huntsville. *Right:* 'Old Sparky', was retired in 1964 after the execution of 361 men; it is now on display in the Texas Prison Museum in downtown Huntsville.

Ray Hamilton and Joe Palmer escaped from death row (see page 23) in the state prison at Huntsville on July 22, 1934. Palmer was quickly recaptured but Ray stayed on the loose until Deputy Sheriff Bill Decker caught up with him in April 1935. The Texas authorities then lost no time in executing both of them on May 10.

With most of the main players eliminated, the crime wave by the 'auto-gangsters' as they were dubbed, was brought under control, and the Bureau of Investigation, renamed the FBI in 1935, with new powers and a reputation enhanced by careful manipulation of its public image by its Director, became a potent force to be reckoned with in the fight against crime.

However Hoover now had to contend with Hollywood, always looking for a good story. In his book, *The Strange History of Bonnie and Clyde*, the late Dr John Treherne included a detailed appraisal on the movies pertinent to Bonnie and Clyde, and we can do no better than to quote his words here:

Perhaps more than any other modern legend the story of Bonnie and Clyde has been manipulated by Hollywood. In many ways the film-maker's role has been analogous to that of the professional balladeers and story-tellers who developed the legend of the outlaw of Sherwood Forest or of another American psychopathic killer, Jesse James, who became Clyde Barrow's boyhood hero.

The first film to use the theme of Bonnie and Clyde followed swiftly after their deaths. Its director, newly arrived in Hollywood, was the brilliant refugee from Nazi Germany, Fritz Lang. His first American film, *Fury*, had been a box-office disaster; Lang's pessimism did not provide the escapist appeal to the cinemagoers of the Great Depression, who had enough troubles of their own.

His second film, *You Only Live Once,* was released in January 1937. It portrayed two fugitives: Eddie Taylor (played by Henry Fonda) and his young wife Jo (Sylvia Sidney). Eddie, a truck driver, is wrongly accused of murder during a bank robbery and sentenced to death. Like Clyde Barrow he mutilates himself, in this case by slitting his wrist, and arranges for Jo to smuggle him a gun into the prison hospital. He escapes just as the news of his pardon is received; he shoots the prison doctor and then the chaplain who tries to bar his way. The escape is given a nightmarish quality: the prison yard is choked with fog pierced by moving searchlight beams and blaring loudspeaker voices.

With Clyde Barrow, Buck Barrow, Raymond Hamilton, Joe Palmer and Bonnie Parker all six foot under, and Blanche Barrow, W. D. Jones and Henry Methvin out of circulation for the forseeable future, all the main characters have left the stage. Now the film-makers took over. In 1938, in a programme titled 'Crime Never Pays', the Dome Cinema in Lawton, Oklahoma, was showing a double bill: *The Execution and Funeral of Ray Hamilton* plus *The Round-up of Clyde Barrow and Bonnie Parker.*

'A crack blend of spectacular drama and romance . . . good direction, strong scripting and an arresting production,' So commented *Variety magazine* on Fritz Lang's *You Only Live Once* released in 1937.

Eddie picks up Jo (who has been contemplating suicide) and they escape by driving down endless country roads. They obtain petrol at gunpoint, but do not rob the filling station (the till is subsequently robbed by an attendant). Their flight attracts considerable publicity. They are portrayed in the newspapers as legendary figures: robbing, killing and living fast. Jo's sister, like Clyde's, complains that 'They're being blamed for every crime committed in the country.'

Although not a re-creation of the Bonnie and Clyde story, the screenplay by Gene Towne and Graham Baker incorporated a number of features from their lives and deaths. In several ways, the film is closer to Emma Parker's and Nell Barrow Cowan's improved portrait of Bonnie and Clyde [in *Fugitives*] than to the reality of their lives: Eddie Taylor is not a psychopath but an ordinary man who is harshly treated by society; he and Jo rob only for the essentials of life; Eddie murdered only because he was trapped; and above all Eddie genuinely loves Jo from the beginning.

Fritz Lang's portrayal of the two fugitives was entirely sympathetic. Jo and Eddie, the 'three-time loser', were inevitable victims. Early in the film Eddie showed Jo some frogs in a pond and told her that they mated for life and always died together.

By his brilliant artistry, Fritz Lang filled the screens and minds of 1930s cinema audiences with the powerful images of a man and a woman, both young and beautiful, ill-treated by society, fleeing from, and resisting, authority as outlaws on the country roads of America until gunned down in a police ambush.

Persons in Hiding, the next film portrayal, was very different from Fritz Lang's sympathetic interpretation. It was part of J. Edgar Hoover's campaign to strip the gangsters of the great American crime wave of their glam-orous appeal. Hoover realised that the rustic desperadoes of the Great Depression were potentially more attractive than the earlier Mafia gangsters of the Chicago era. The Hearst press and the pulp magazines had turned Bonnie and Clyde into colourful characters, but they were also seen by many people as just ordinary folk who had struck back at life and managed to share some of the wealth depicted in Hollywood films and glossy magazines.

Hoover had produced a book (actually written for him by a journalist, Courtley Riley Cooper) which purported to show criminals for what they really were and gave rather too much credit to the FBI for the destruction of the gangsters of the mid-1930s. The title of this book was also used for the film, which set out to destroy the fake glamour of Bonnie and Clyde. *Persons in Hiding* was released in early 1939, the first of a series of four films of the same name. Its story was only loosely related to that of Clyde Barrow and Bonnie Parker.

For all the film's eagerness to discredit the gangsters, the 'Bonnie Parker' role in the story was given to an extremely attractive young actress called Patricia Morison. Dorothy Bronson, as Hoover renamed her, is a thoroughly bad lot. Born on a remote farm and reared in great poverty, Dorothy is shown to be deeply attached to her mother, old Ma Bronson. At the opening of the film Dorothy is working discontentedly as a hairdresser. She pines for a more glamorous life, which includes unlimited supplies of perfume. She meets a small-time criminal, Freddie Martin (played by J. Carrol Naish), and predictably (given Miss Morison's inappropriately stunning looks) he falls in love with her.

The film was only a moderate box-office success. Contemporary critics applauded its propaganda: 'As a result of clever direction and excellent acting by J. Carrol Naish and Patricia Morison— a newcomer to pictures—the whole horrible atmosphere has been perfectly caught. These people are real, anxious, suffering human beings learning by bitter experience that "crime does not pay".'

Still the legend grew, and J. Edgar Hoover could not stop it. While he was attempting to erase the romantic image of the two young fugitives, another equally compelling version of their lives emerged.

However, on J. Edgar Hoover's 'own' film, *Persons in Hiding*, *Variety* said that its success would depend entirely on the reputation of the FBI chief to attract audiences, and it was deemed by the critic Graham Greene 'a little on the tame side . . . it's all speeding cars and montage'.

The post-war Bonnie and Clyde genre kicked off with *Gun Crazy* in 1950 which was also released with a different title *Deadly is the Female*.

In *Gun Crazy*, released in 1950, the two leading characters, Annie and Bart, share an obsession with guns. Bart Tare (played by John Dali) has grown up to be a superb marksman. He meets Annie Laurie Starr (Peggy Cummins) in a marksmanship contest at a fairground, where she is a sharpshooter in a sideshow, and is recruited to join the act. They later abandon the fairground and take to a life of crime to satisfy Annie Laurie's desires for excitement and 'things . . . lots of things, big things'. They progress from garage hold-ups to bank robberies, with Peggy Cummins's Annie Laurie wearing a Bonnie beret and taking explicitly sensual pleasure in using her gun. Bart is repelled by the thought of killing, but to Annie Laurie it is an exciting prospect and she eventually shoots two people while making her escape from a bank robbery.

The fugitives are by now nationally known criminals and are hunted by the police. They finally seek refuge in the mountains near Bart's home town, but are discovered. The posse sent out against them is led by two of Bart's childhood friends, Clyde Boston and Dave Allister. Rather than allow Annie Laurie to shoot Clyde and Dave, Bart kills her and is then himself shot down.

The portrayal of Bonnie Parker as a lusty and dominating gun moll continued in Hollywood's next variation on the legend of Bonnie and Clyde. In 1958 appeared the first film to represent explicitly the careers of Bonnie and Clyde: *The Bonnie Parker Story*.

In this film version, produced by Stanley Sheptner, Bonnie is working as a waitress in a cheap cafe in 1932. The heroine (played by Dorothy Provine) is first glimpsed behind the credit titles removing her stockings and unzipping her dress. The next scene switches to the countryside where 'Guy Darrow' (played by Jack Hogan) fondles a Thompson and shoots off the limb of a tree.

Their first criminal venture so excites Bonnie that she interferes with the get-away by moving close to him in the car, saying seductively, 'Kiss me. I said kiss me, Guy.'

Their activities soon attract considerable police and newspaper attention. They also manage to damage accidentally the car bumper of the film's version of Frank Hamer (Tom Steel) who is already in hot pursuit of the fugitives.

Guy attempts to resolve their difficulties by calling in his brother, Chuck Darrow, who, unlike his easy-going prototype, is an ambitious and resourceful criminal. Chuck is eventually shot in the film's re-creation of the ambush at Dexfield Park, Iowa. Bonnie and Guy flee, leaving Chuck in the arms of his still nameless girlfriend. Guy panics badly: 'We'll never get out of this one.' But Bonnie is now in command. She accom-

plishes their escape by the stratagem of floating Guy's jacket down the stream, thus throwing off the pursuing hounds and the posse who riddle the garment with bullets.

Bonnie (who by this time has become very bossy indeed) next organizes an operation to free her ex-husband Duke Jefferson from Clemens' Prison. She sends Guy off to hide the guns in the undergrowth near the prison and, while he is away, encounters two men (Marv and Al) with whom she quickly links arms and walks off into seclusion. Duke Jefferson is duly 'sprung' and quickly comes into conflict with poor Guy Darrow for Bonnie's favours. She does not respond to either man (perhaps because of her recent encounter with Marv and Al) and protects herself by scattering tin tacks on the floor around her bed.

Later, Bonnie meets a handsome young architect, Paul, who enters her motel room to use the telephone. Bonnie, who is alone, is much taken with Paul and his educated talk. She sighs, 'I never knew anyone like you before.'

But Bonnie has to return to work and has soon organized the ambush of an armoured truck, carrying a large quantity of money. The execution of her plan is delayed, however, by the appearance of a party of boy scouts.

Just as the delayed ambush is about to reach a successful conclusion, a posse of lawmen arrives (presumably alerted by the boy scouts). In the ensuing gun battle Duke Jefferson is shot, but Guy Darrow and Bonnie escape.

At this stage, Bonnie seeks fresh recruits and departs with Guy, for Athens, Louisiana, to pick up two likely lads. However, the elderly father of the two potential recruits is worried about his sons' descent into further crime and informs Tom Steel.

Steel comes to an arrangement with the old man and sets up an ambush for Bonnie and Guy. The two fugitives are shot down in the now traditional rain of bullets. As she dies, Bonnie's voice is heard calling: 'Paul.'

The Bonnie Parker Story in 1958 was rejected as 'a tinpot "B" gangster film.'

Things were different in the 1960s, when the legend achieved its most thorough transformation.

Arthur Penn's film version of the outlawry of Clyde Barrow and Bonnie was originally conceived three decades after their killing in the years of nostalgia for the period of Fred Astaire and Ginger Rogers. The idea belonged to two sophisticates from the staff of *Esquire* magazine, David Newman and Robert Benton. They were film enthusiasts, inspired by the works of New Wave directors like Truffaut, Godard, Antonioni, Fellini. They had also read John Toland's book, *Dillinger Days* (published in 1964), which devoted only a few scattered but evocative pages to the exploits of Bonnie and Clyde; they were enough to fire the imaginations of Newman and Benton. Working night after night to the recorded sound of Flatt and Scruggs and the Foggy Mountain Boys (to gain appropriate musical atmosphere), they eventually produced a script. Newman and Benton clearly intended to convey the powerful charm of their two main characters. In the introduction to their script they wrote:

'Bonnie Parker and Clyde Barrow headed one of the notorious gangs, and their names and deeds were well-known across the country. To many they were heroes of a kind, for they showed bravery in the face of incredible odds, daring in their free enterprise, and style in their manner. They took a delight, it seemed, in foiling the law — the small town cops, the sheriffs, the justices of the peace.'

In Newman and Benton's hands, Clyde and Bonnie were to become folk heroes — of a kind. If not downright glamorous they were to have 'style'. They would provide cinematographic fun and games until suffering the traditional fate of the Hollywood bad guys. But there was to be more to it than that: there was to be contemporary relevance.

Newman and Benton's script was rejected by a number of film companies, but Warner Brothers eventually took it. The film was to be produced by Warren Beatty, who would also take the part of Clyde Barrow. Faye Dunaway was to be Bonnie Parker. The film was shot on location during 1966 in some of the clapboard Texas towns that were then virtually unchanged since the times of Bonnie and Clyde. It was completed and ready for release by the next summer. The world premiere of *Bonnie and Clyde* took place with considerable ballyhoo at the Eighth International Folk Festival of Montreal on August 4, 1967.

Back in the 1960s there were not many actors producing films but when Warren Beatty was offered the script he purchased it for $10,000. His chosen director was Arthur Penn, right, although Faye Dunaway was not his first choice to play Bonnie. 'We'd been turned down by about ten women. I wanted Natalie Wood, Jane Fonda, Tuesday Weld, Sharon Tate, Ann-Margret — then I met Faye. I called Arthur and said I'd met an actress I knew he would like. Faye said that "I really identified with Bonnie. She was just like me, a Southern girl who was dying to get out of the South".'

Not until Arthur Penn's stylistic production, scripted by David Newman and Robert Benton *(above)* **appeared in 1967 starring Warren Beatty and Faye Dunaway did the duo really gain worldwide public interest.** *Bonnie and Clyde* **had the effect of putting the two outlaws firmly on the map.**

The fashions were deliberately adjusted to appeal to cinemagoers of the 1960s who would never have accepted Bonnie in the long dress that she invariably wore. The beret — or 'tam' as W. D. calls it on page 111 — was retained.

The murders were also played down, the only killing being the fictional shooting of a storekeeper who tries to stop their fleeing car after they rob the 'Mineola Bank' — depicted on page 200. In fact David Newman freely admitted that 'we wanted the audience to love and identify with Clyde and Bonnie from the outset, so that by the time they start doing violent things, it is too late for the audience to back away from its identification with the desperadoes'.

In *Bonnie and Clyde*, the hero and heroine are brought together even faster than in The *Bonnie Parker Story* by basically the same cinematic device. Bonnie first appears partially clothed (virtually nude), standing in her bedroom window from which she sees Clyde Barrow attempting to steal her mother's car. He also sees her, full-frontal, from where he is standing. She flings on a dress and runs down to interview the thief. They engage in some particularly banal repartee until he walks her down the street and then shows her his gun. No doubt about the symbolism here because the script

decrees that Bonnie should touch it 'in a manner almost sexual, full of repressed excitement'. Clyde almost immediately uses his gun in the robbery of a grocery store, largely to impress the watching Bonnie Parker. She is not only duly impressed, but sexually excited and, like Dorothy Provine's Bonnie, tries to make love to Clyde as he attempts to drive away from the scene of the crime.

Miss Dunaway discovers Clyde's sexual inadequacy rather sooner than Miss Provine — indeed as soon as the car stops after the getaway from the grocery robbery. She comments after he fails to come up to her expectations, 'Your

advertising is just dandy. Folk'd just never guess you don't have a thing to sell.' However Warren Beatty's Clyde persuades her to stay (despite his limitations) because, as he says: '. . . you're different, that's why. You know, you're like me. You want different things. You got something better than bein' a waitress.'

Despite his sexual inadequacy Clyde Barrow is not dominated by Faye Dunaway's Bonnie Parker as Guy Darrow was by Dorothy Provine's Bonnie. During the ambush it is he and not Bonnie who organizes their escape. He is tough and resourceful, if not particularly intelligent.

Blanche was not at all pleased with the way the screenwriters chose to let Estelle Parsons *(left)* depict her as a hysterical frightened 'Hausfrau' which was totally out of character. 'I was there because I wanted to be, plain and simple', she said in later years.

Right: The film-makers also came a cropper with the portrayal of Frank Hamer (Denver Pyle) when his widow and son sued Warner Bros-Seven Arts for $1 million damages for misrepresentation.

Probably the most memorable aspect of Arthur Penn's *Bonnie and Clyde* is the impression of verisimilitude which it conveys. The film was shot with brilliant camerawork under the huge Texas skies on the dusty plains which Bonnie and Clyde knew. Furthermore, it attempted to portray, more accurately than its predecessors, some real events from the lives of Clyde Barrow and Bonnie Parker. Even so, the film was still historically inaccurate for two reasons. First, because it was obviously impossible to portray in 111 minutes all the participants and incidents that occurred during the months of outlawry. It was, therefore, necessary to simplify the story and to eliminate characters. Thus Raymond Hamilton, W. D. Jones and Henry Methvin were combined into a single fictional person, C.W. Moss, who is casually picked up at a country petrol station. The Dallas county sheriff does not appear and Sheriff Coffey of Platte City, Missouri, becomes Sheriff Smoot of 'Platte City, Iowa'.

Historical inaccuracy resulted, secondly, from the needs of artistry; as Voltaire said, 'The secret of the arts is to correct nature.' The artistic 'corrections' in Arthur Penn's film are fascinating because the growth of the legend primarily results from the need to distort, or 're-tell the story', in terms that will be exciting and readily understandable to later audiences. He must, in the jargon of the 1960s, introduce 'contemporary relevance'. Purely fictional events are used to suggest their concern for the underprivileged victims of the Great Depression. Thus, early on in the film, Bonnie and Clyde meet a dispossessed farmer. He is about to leave his farm, where they stop for Clyde to give his newly acquired girlfriend some necessary, and no doubt sexually symbolic, target practice, in which Bonnie discharges a pistol at a suspended car tyre. At Clyde's instigation the dispirited farmer takes a loaded gun from him and shatters the windows of his former

Left: **The enigmatic face of Bonnie and Clyde's sidekick C. W. Moss (played by Michael J. Pollard) who gets Clyde's car going with the classic line: 'Dirt in the fuel line . . . just blowed it away'. Combining Hamilton, Jones** *(right)* **and Methvin in one character was necessary to avoid complicating the plot.**

home: a last gesture of defiance. An old Negro sharecropper, who is standing by, also joins in. They part with warm handshakes and much goodwill.

In another scene (after the film's version of the ambush at Dexfield Park), the wounded fugitives find themselves, at dawn, outside an Oakie camp site. Several poor families are seated around a camp fire, cooking. The exhausted C. W. Moss (now enacting his role as W. D. Jones) walks up to them and asks for drinking water. As the leader of the group hands C. W. a drinking cup, he recognises Moss's companions and says ('in really hushed and reverent tones'

according to the script), 'That's Clyde Barrow and Bonnie Parker.' The poor Oakies crowd around the car. A woman gives C. W. a bowl of hot soup. As he gets into the car the people press closer for a final look. Clyde 'nods his head in a barely perceptible gesture by way of saying "thank you" to the people.' As they drive away, a girl says, 'Is that really Bonnie Parker?'

Here then is the image of Clyde and Bonnie as friends of the poor, accepted by the dispossessed — robbing the bankers who ruin poor farmers and destroying the uniformed protectors of the wealthy.

When the real Jones was released from prison in the 1950s, he settled in obscurity in Houston. After seeing *Bonnie and Clyde,* **W. D. commented that 'they made it all look so glamourous but as I told them teenage boys sitting near me: "Take it from an old man who was there — it was hell!"'**

Left: **Jones married but the years had taken their toll and after his wife died he became a drug addict, spending several months in jail in the early 1970s.** *Right:* **While escorting a lady friend home on August 20, 1974, as he approached No. 10616 Woody Lane, Houston, he was blown away by a jealous ex-boyfriend wielding a 12-bore shotgun.**

Preparing the 1934 Ford Fordor, which Warners had acquired for the death scene, by their special effects department was one thing; making it look even more authentic for subsequent display in the Southwestern Historical Wax Museum in Grand Prairie was something else! In August 1968, Jack Turner *(above)* spent a couple of hours adding more holes — authentic bullet holes this time — to try to match the pattern of those in the Warren's car. Warner Bros had given their car to the museum on the condition that they just paid the freight from California, and it was displayed at Grand Prairie until a fire gutted the building in 1989.

Although the car had not suffered irreversible damage, it was just pulled out of the ruins and left outside to rot until it was sold for $300. It was subsequently purchased by Bob Andrews who headed a re-enactment group, and he had begun restoration when Fox Television contacted him to use it for their low-budget made-for-TV movie *Bonnie and Clyde — The True Story* featuring Tracy Needham and Dana Ashbrook *(above)*. Fox restored the car although its appearance is somewhat brief. To claim the film as being 'the true story' is a travesty as virtually every incident is portrayed incorrectly and even the characterisations, particularly Jones, are totally unbelievable.

The release of *Bonnie and Clyde* raised a storm of controversy and reopened issues that had been hotly debated three decades earlier during J. Edgar Hoover's attempt to destroy the glamour of the gangster. The furore commenced immediately after the world première in Montreal. The film critic of the *New York Times*, Bosley Crowther, was particularly vociferous in his dislike and started a controversy which another critic described as making 'the 100 Years War look like a border incident'.

The popularity of the film increased, not only in America, but in Europe, particularly in Great Britain and France. Indeed *Bonnie and Clyde* became a spectacular box-office success. yet controversy still raged, especially in the correspondence columns of some American newspapers, where Hoover's battle of thirty years before was fought again.

Other correspondents fulminated against the protrayal of 'the shoddy history of these things', and, in turn, were attacked by the defenders of Warner Brother's golden egg. An assistant professor of art history at Columbia University gave it as her opinion that 'this film just may be the greatest one produced in America since the first days of glory in the movies'. Nevertheless, by the end of 1967, *Bonnie and Clyde* was an international sensation.

When the car was put up for sale in 1998, Ken Holmes (see page 88) suggested to the Bonnie and Clyde Museum, which had been established in Gibsland in the early 1990s, that they should purchase the car but the investment proved too much for the budget of the small town. Instead Ken, now the owner of Southwestern Historical Incorporated, decided to purchase the car to use it in his travelling Bonnie and Clyde exhibition, and each May he takes it to Gibsland for the annual re-enactment of the ambush. In 1972, this monument was erected on the opposite side of the road to where the lawmen stood. (Ken has retained the original desert sand shade of the car as it appears in the movie rather then repaint it in the correct colour.)

Gibsland — 70 years on. Since the early 1990s, on the nearest weekend to the anniversary of the ambush, the events of the 1930s are restaged as part of the *Bonnie and Clyde Festival* which now incorporates Reenactments Etc of Denison, Texas, and Ken's movie car. On the Friday evening, a forum of historians, authors, local residents — even relatives of those involved — is held in the City Hall. *Right:* Ken Holmes introduces the guest speakers in May 2003: Buddy Williams, nephew of Clyde Barrow; 'Boots' Hinton, son of lawman Ted Hinton, Jim Knight launching his new book (see page 43); Bob Russell, about his uncle who was in charge of prisoner transportation in Texas, and John Neal Phillips (see also page 43) who was currently preparing a new book based on unpublished notes by Blanche Barrow. The formal title of the forum is the 'Lorraine Joyner Memorial Historians Meeting' — Lorraine being a relative of the Methvin intermediary John Joyner (Joyner shot his wife in September 1942 before turning the gun on himself.)

On Saturday the main road through Gibsland (the old Bankhead Highway) is closed off for the first of the noisy re-enactments — a staged bank robbery in which the outlaws win.

Below left: Bob Higbee, attired as a typical peace officer/Texas Ranger of the period fights back . . . but *(below right)* Bonnie wins and rounds up Jonathan Davis, left, and Ranger Bob.

289

Now it is the turn of the good guys to get their own back . . . Crouching behind the car is Keith White.

As soon as the shooting is over, a mad scramble for cartridge case souvenirs! *Right:* Re-enactors (L-R): **Steve Beavers, Bob Skelton, Javana Skelton, Josh Dilley and Lance Cryan.**

In the late afternoon, the focus of attention turns towards the ambush site on the Ringgold road . . . but before that an unusual duty for Judge Glenda Britton of Caddo parish . . .

a wedding ceremony between two Bonnie and Clyde 'fans'. Megan Guthrie and Tony Stearns are so imbued with the era that they chose this venue to seal the knot!

The ambush. In an attempt to simulate conditions in May 1934, a Model A Ford is parked as if broken down — just like the Methvin vehicle — although that was positioned on the road. Ken Holmes watches for the approach of Bonnie and Clyde.

Meanwhile, the lawmen take up position in the undergrowth facing the monument.

Above: On seeing the broken down vehicle the Ford pulls up. This picture shows one controversial aspect of the original ambush which has never been successfully resolved. Hinton (see page 246) claims that they handcuffed Mr Methvin Senior to a tree — either to keep him out of harm's way or perhaps to make it look as if he was acting under duress to try to cover up his co-operation in the betrayal. However, other sources confirm that Methvin was standing by his truck when Clyde arrived even though that would have put him right in the line of fire. *Right:* At a given signal, the lawmen open up! The re-enactors used a variety of weapons although their BAR was only capable of semi-automatic fire. *Below:* With the occupants dead or dying, the lawmen close in. The road is not closed but traffic is light. On this occasion TV cameras were present throughout the day.

It was interesting to watch the reaction of the spectators who rushed up to the car to view the blood-splattered bodies much as the crowds in 1934 had done. Javana and Bob Skelton who played Bonnie and Clyde reacted to the gun-fire with similar convulsions as in Arthur Penn's death scene, staged in this same car. Using four cameras set at different speeds — 24, 48, 72 and 96 frames per second — Penn and the film editor, Dede Allen, intercut 51 separate shots in the 54-second death sequence, creating what has been called 'one of the most powerful moments in American cinema history'.

Both the families were against a shared funeral and neither the Barrows nor the Parkers ever had any serious intentions of interring the couple together. Bonnie's mother died on September 21, 1944, so in 1945 her daughter's remains were exhumed from Fishtrap Cemetery and reburied next to her in the new Crown Hill Cemetery on Webbs Chapel Road.

With Clyde already committed to being buried beside his brother, we can only speculate if Bonnie realised that her wish declared in the last verse of her epilogue (page 238) to be buried with her lover would never happen. But your Editor, being an incurable romantic, can at least fulfil that desire on the last page of this book!

Photographs

Copyright is indicated for all original illustrations where known. Present-day photographs are the copyright of *After the Battle* unless otherwise stated.

Marty Black, left, who normally occupies a captain's seat with American Airlines, was responsible for photographing several of the important crime sites including his exemplary research at Dexfield Park. *Right:* In nearby Dexter he made contact with Bob Weesner, the local Bonnie and Clyde historian, who provided many of the photos which appear in this book from his collection. Shortly before Bob died in February 2003, Marty pictured him at his desk in his office at the rear of the pharmacy where 70 years ago Clyde purchased medication for Buck.

Atoka County Historical Society 61 top left.
Frank Ballinger 57 bottom, 111 top right, 116 centre right, 159 top left, bottome right, 160 top, 189 top, 191 top right, 192 bottom, 221 top left and right, 283 bottom.
James L. Ballou 154 top, 186 top, centre.
Baxter Springs Historical Society 96 top right, bottom left.
Bienville Parish Court-house 256 top left.
John Binder Collection 6, 108 top left, 109 bottom right, 110 bottom left, 113 bottom left, 198 top, 253 centre and bottom.
Marty Black 130 top, 131 top and bottom, 132 bottom, 133 all, 134 bottom right, 135 bottom, 136 top right and bottom, 137 top right, 138 all, 139 all, 140 top, 141 middle and bottom left and right, 158 bottom, 160 bottom, 163 inset, 164 bottom, 165 bottom, 166 top left and right, bottom left and right, 167 all, 168 top, centre left, bottom right, 169 top left, centre left and right, bottom right, 170 top right, bottom, 171 top and bottom, 172 middle and bottom, 173 top and bottom right, 174 both, 175 all, 177 bottom, 182 bottom, 183 centre, 185 centre, 218 bottom, 219 bottom, 221 middle and bottom, 223 top, 232 middle bottom, 223 top left and right, bottom right, 275 bottom left and right, 278 middle and bottom, 279 middle left and right, bottom left and right.
Timothy R. Brookes 277 middle right, bottom.
Jerry Bucher 53 top, bottom left and right.
Dr. Allen Campbell 262, 263 bottom, 297 top.
Carlsbad Current-Argus 66 bottom left and right.
Central Texas Historical & Genealogical Preservation Inc. 214 top.
Clay Platte Press Despatch 161 top left and right.
Clint Cockrill 159 bottom left.

Collingsworth Public Library 135 top.
Valerie Cranston 66 top, 67 bottom.
Robert Davis collection 41 top left and right.
Pat Delaney 70 all, 71 top and bottom, 72, 73 all, 122 top, 123 all, 124 top, middle, bottom right, 125 bottom, 126 top, 127 all, 233 top middle, bottom left.
Denton County Historical Commission 22 top right.
Des Moines Register 177 top.
John Dillinger Historical Society 24 top left, 270 bottom left, 272 top, 274 centre pair.
East Liverpool Historical Society 277 top right, middle left.
Terry Eckert 273 bottom.
Enid and Garfield Public Library 153 top.
Ford Motor Company 81 centre, 235 top left and right.
Fort Dodge Public Library 156 top, 157 top, 210 top.
David Francis, Gough Lamb Cleaners 31 top.
Gail Furrh 97 top left and right, 98 top left, 99 bottom right.
Gibsland Museum 90 top right, 222 top left, bottom left.
Ronald G. Haraldson 206 top, bottom left, 207 top left and right, centre.
Helen Hardy 287 bottom right.
Lenard Hardy 131 centre, 132 top, 134 top left and right, bottom left, 136 top left, 137 top left, 140 bottom, 141 top left and right.
Helicopters of Kansas City 162-163.
Hinton Archives 24 top right, 196 bottom left and right, 218 top left and right, 219 top, 220 top and bottom, 244 top, 245 bottom, 246 bottom, 249 bottom, 250 top and bottom, 251 top and bottom, 252 top, 260 bottom left and right, 265 top left and centre, 267 top left, 268 top left and centre.
Dorothea B. Hoover Historical Museum 105 top, 106 top left, bottom left.
Jackson County Historical Society 122 bottom, 124 bottom left, 125 top.

Martin Jones 199 top left and right.
Kaufman County Library 49 top left.
Robert S. Kerr Museum 208 top.
James R. Knight 32 bottom, 33 all, 34 all, 35 all, 36 all, 37 top and centre, 78 top, 79 both, 92 top, 93 both, 94 top right and bottom, 95 bottom left, 100 centre, bottom right, 101 all, 103 top left and right, 104 all, 105 middle and bottom, 106 top right, centre and bottom right, 118, 119 top, 120 bottom, 121 top, 143 bottom, 144 all, 145 top, 146 both, 147 all, 148 all, 149 all, 150 top and bottom, 208 bottom, 209 top right, 212, 213.
Lancaster Veterans Memorial Library 216 top, 217 top left.
Lincoln Parish Library 116 top left.
Logansport-Cass County Public Library 119 bottom left.
Missouri State Highway Patrol 11 top right, 26 top, 41 bottom, 49 bottom, 80 top, plan 102-103, 107, 108 bottom left, 109 bottom left, 110 top left and right, 111 top left, 112 top, middle right, centre right, 113 top left and right, 184 top left, 223 bottom right, 249 top, 253 top left and right, 256 centre, 260 top left.
Bruce Moore 23 bottom, 202 top, 203 all, 204-205, 282 top right.
Erik Mosbo 155.
National Guard Bureau 152 top, centre, bottom left and right.
Oklahoma Historical Society 224 top left, 226 top left.
Platte City Historical Society 158 top, 161 centre and bottom.
Charles W. Powers 58 top.
Record Newspapers, Yorkville, Illinois 186 bottom.
Chuck Schauer Collection 19 top, 20 top left and right, 40 top, 151.
Sherman Public Library 74 top, bottom right, 75 top left.
Julian Slatter 273 top left and right and centre.

As an Editor, it is always frustrating when photos arrive too late — like this one from Dr Allen Campbell whose firm buried Bonnie in Fishtrap Cemetery. But I knew I had to include it when he told me that it was taken when he played golf with none other than Robert Rosborough, the owner of the coupe Clyde used as a backdrop to their famous photo shoot! 'The picture was taken about 1990 at the Lakeside Country Club in Marshall,' says Dr Campbell. 'I was paired with Bob and rode in his golf cart for three days. I am sitting with my wife, Betty, with Bob next to me.' What an amazing picture . . . although Dr Campbell never told me who won!

Finally, a tribute to Jim Knight whose assistance has been invaluable. Jim covered many of the out-of-the-way locations as well as the Joplin and Alma gun-battles. Ex USAF, Jim currently flies for a living as a senior pilot with Federal Express.

INDEX

COMPILED BY PETER B. GUNN

Note: Page numbers in *italics* refer to illustrations. There may also be textual references on these pages.

303

BANDITS RELE

***

Unemployed ~ ~ U~ ~ster for

AN CAPTURED IN GUN BATTLE

Against Trio Sought in Crandall Burglary

WILL BE WELL REPRESENTED IN DIS'T MEET

andit Beats, Then Kills
Resisting Grocery Clerk

2 States
Bank B~

Police Seek Pair V
Customer, Took
at Okabe~

Police of two state
were seeking traces c
ing bandits who Friday
First State Bank o~
Minn., and escaped wi
mately $2,400 after mi
customer and threateni
anyone who failed to
orders.

Okabena is a commu~
inhabitants, about 185 r
west of Minneapolis
county. It is about 20
the Iowa line toward
bandits fled.

The bandits, flouris~
guns, rushed into the b~
them jumping over the
covering two ~

Funeral services were conducted from the First Methodist
church of Kemp Wednesday aft-

Complaints were filed here
Tuesday against three youths in
connection with the burglary of

Today what should
across but Tom Choate

Remark of Local Man,
"You Can't Do That,"
Leads to Death

GUN SNAPPED ON
COMPANION CLERK

Howard Hall Dies at Sani-
tarium Within Hour
After Shooting

BARROW OUTLAWS
FLEE OZARK POSS~

Mrs. Swann was the

THEFT OF FOUR
MACHINE GUNS
BEING PROBED

OFFICERS ROUTED
BY MACHINE GUN
AFTER CAR CH~

Bucher Identffies
Hamilton As Slaye

The picture of a man with a long
criminal record was identified by
Homer Glaze Wednesday afternoon
as the bandit who fatally shot Howard Hall in the robbery of Little's
grocery store Tuesday night. The
photo was mailed to Sheriff Frank
Reece by Dennis Scale, deputy sheriff of Dallas county, who heard the
description of Mr. Hall's assailant
broadcast after the shooting Tuesday night and found that this description fitted that of a man whose
picture he had. The name of the
man was not made public, although
it was announced he is wanted by
police in half a dozen cities.

Peace officers in North Texas
and Southern Oklahoma were
searching Wednesday for a young
bandit who fatally shot Howard
Hall in the robbery of Little's suburban grocery store early Tuesday
night of about $60. The bandit es-
caped with two confederates after
firing four shots at Mr. Hall, one
of them after Mr. Hall had fallen
to the sidewalk at the ~
store

Barrow

Convicte~
Luke T~

Station Att
Identify I
Leader~

Harold Anderson and Leon~
Hospital; Say He Direct~
Oil Stations Here Las~
Fugitive Outlaws Near ~

~ENCE OVER
MURDER CASE

ITASCA BANK
OPEN TODA~

BARROW FREES HIS PAL FROM

Sides Rest in the Tr~
~d Hamilton for the
~ Bucher Last April.

CLYDE BARROW~

Republican Senators Try To
~ Money Bill Action

LONG ALIBI IS
~ESENTED BY ~

Witnesses Testify~

~ the ~

"ADEQUATE"